Cooperative Security

Syracuse Studies on Peace and Conflict Resolution
Harriet Hyman Alonso, Charles Chatfield, and Louis Kriesberg
Series Editors

Cooperative Security
Reducing Third World Wars

Edited by
I. WILLIAM ZARTMAN
and
VICTOR A. KREMENYUK

SYRACUSE UNIVERSITY PRESS

First Edition 1995
95 96 97 98 99 00   6 5 4 3 2 1

The paper used in this publication meets the minimum requirements of American National
Standard for Information Sciences—Permanence of Paper for Printed Library Materials,
ANSI Z39.48-1984. ∞™

Library of Congress Cataloging-in-Publication Data
Cooperative security : reducing Third World wars / edited by
    I. William Zartman and Victor A. Kremenyuk.
        p. cm.—(Syracuse studies on peace and conflict resolution)
    Includes bibliographical references and index.
    ISBN 0-8156-2647-9 (cl).—ISBN 0-8156-0305-3 (pbk.)
    1. Security, International.   2. Developing countries—Foreign
relations.   3. World politics—1989–   4. Russia (Federation)—
Foreign relations—United States.   5. United States—Foreign
relations—Russia (Federation).   I. Zartman, I. William.
II. Kremeniuk, Viktor Aleksandrovich.   III. Series.
JX1952.C617   1995
327.1′7—dc20   94-33882

To Thomas Schelling,
strategist in conflict and its management,
our teacher

Contents

Tables   ix

Introduction   xi
   I. WILLIAM ZARTMAN

Contributors   xv

PART ONE
Causes and Resolutions

1. Systems of World Order and Regional Conflict Reduction   3
   I. WILLIAM ZARTMAN
2. Asymmetry and Strategies of Regional Conflict Reduction   25
   CHRISTOPHER R. MITCHELL

PART TWO
Sources and Interests

3. National Interests and Conflict Reduction   61
   VADIM UDALOV
4. Sources of American Conduct in Regional Conflict   78
   VICTOR A. KREMENYUK
5. Sources of Russian Conduct Toward Regional Conflict   98
   BRUCE PARROTT

PART THREE
Case Studies in Conflict Reduction

6. The Third World and Conflict Reduction   125
   GEORGI MIRSKY
7. War in the Gulf: Possibilities and Limits of the
   Russian-American Cooperation   144
   ALEXEI VASSILIEV
8. U.S.-Soviet (Russian) Conflict Resolution in the Gulf   164
   CHARLES F. DORAN
9. India and Pakistan: The Roots of Conflict   179
   THOMAS THORNTON AND MAXIM BRATERSKY
10. The Crisis in the Andes: A War at the End of the World   204
   ILYA PRIZEL
11. The Russian-American Stake in Southern Africa   224
   VITALEY VASILKOV
12. Great Powers and Conflict Reduction in the Horn of Africa   241
   TERRENCE LYONS
13. Moscow-American Interaction in the Arab-Israeli Conflict   267
   IRINA ZVIAGELSKAIA

PART FOUR
Conclusions and Implications

14. U.S.-Russian Regional Cooperation: Redefining Mutual
   Expectations   289
   EDWARD A. KOLODZIEJ
15. Mechanisms of Conflict Resolution   315
   MARK N. KATZ
16. Prospects for Cooperative Security and Conflict Reduction   331
   VICTOR A. KREMENYUK AND I. WILLIAM ZARTMAN
   Bibliography   345
   Index   363

Tables

2.1 Key Asymmetries in Protracted Regional Conflicts   28

2.2 Strategies to Maintain or Reverse Key Asymmetries   33

2.3 Types of Symmetry in Protracted Regional Conflict   41

2.4 Necessary Conditions for Regional Conflict Reduction   46

2.5 Third Parties and Regional Conflict Reduction: Principles,
Strategies, and Roles   51

2.6 Further Third-Party Principles, Strategies, and Roles   52

Introduction

I. WILLIAM ZARTMAN

The old order changes, yielding place to uncertainty. The United States, scarcely hegemonic any longer, is unquestionably at the top of the pyramid in interstate relations, but the shape of the pyramid, the structure of relations with the next layers, and the nature, force, and direction of the challenges from below are all unclear. What is clear—already from the first years of the new post-cold war world—is that local conflicts bubble up like steam and burst to the surface of the world's attention, rising from insignificant causes, pursuing an unrestrained and erratic course, and eluding any of the limitations that the earlier conflictual order used to impose on them. Third World wars in the 1990s are already as or more bloody, long lasting, and intractable than the cold war conflicts of the preceding decades. How can they be handled?

One set of analyses would focus on the western alliance, winner of the cold war conflict, and diagnose its ability to continue to cooperate versus its propensity to disintegrate. In such a situation, victorious coalitions have an unerring tendency to fall apart, in disagreement either over the leadership of the ongoing coalition or over relations with the vanquished. It takes firm and skillful leadership to hold the former partners together on an agreed course against outbursts of insecurity. Former allies may have competitive advantages to be won from different policies

This study is part of the project on Conflict Reduction in Regional Conflicts (CRIRC) supported by the Carnegie Corporation, whose assistance is gratefully acknowledged.

toward a Third World conflict, or they may simply see something to be gained from resisting the efforts of the biggest among them to lead.

Another set of analyses can focus instead on the next round of relations between the former antagonists, as they pass from conflict to potential collaboration, maintaining the same structure of relations as they had in their time of rivalry. The United States has an interest in keeping the Russian federation alive and well to avoid one potential arena of conflict and to provide a counterweight to confederating Europe; Russia has an interest in obtaining U.S. support to retain its superpower status. It takes firm and skillful leadership to hold the former enemies together in collaboration against outbursts of security. The former rivals have reputational obligations to former clients and causes to maintain, and delicate sensitivities of bipolar inequality to overcome.

This study bridges the two perspectives, with a greater emphasis on the latter set of analyses. It seeks to identify the workings of an evolving security regime, which can be called "cooperative security," with its demands on international leadership along both dimensions. Europe is necessarily a founding member of this system, both inviting Russian participation in it and playing an autonomous role within it. Indeed, one basic effect of the disappearance of the cold war is to restore a concept of Europe "from the Atlantic to the Urals" (in Charles de Gaulle's phrase) as an alternative to the Atlantic West. Neither the United States nor Russia nor cooperative security in general can be analyzed without taking European relations into account.

The study's focus, however, is on the roles and relations of the United States and Russia within this transitional regime as it moves through the challenges of uncertainty. The two stand in uniquely different relations to the security challenges from the Third World. The United States remains the leading gendarme, whether it wants to or not, too visible to use its force to control force without the sanction of the United Nations; other states, ranging from France and Belgium to India, Nigeria, and Zimbabwe, have a freer rein to involve themselves in local conflict. Russia can eventually become a member of an international security force, but its position in regard to local conflicts is shaped primarily by the fact that many of them take on their current form because of the Soviet Union's withdrawal from involvement in them. The conditions, bases, and mechanisms of cooperation between the two in Third World security issues are the subjects of this study.

The focus of this study is on conflict *reduction*, a distinction that may appear semantic but that reflects both American and Russian dissatisfaction with previously established terms. American scholarship has tended to emphasize the irreality of conflict *resolution,* arguing that conflict can be demoted from violent to political forms but is impossible to eliminate in the short run. The resulting term of conflict *management,* however, is viewed with skepticism by Russians, who see it as indicating American attempts to keep conflict alive to its own advantage. Thus, the focus on reduction of Third World wars makes slight but important corrections in the aim of the parties in line with their interests.

The workings of cooperative security are the subject of the first chapter. It analyzes the inchoate norms, behaviors, and expectations that are coming to characterize the global level security regime-in-formation. Although alternative models may be envisaged, the patterns presented in this analysis presume that future reality will be based on projections of the present, both in its conditions and its behaviors. Confronting them are the patterns of regional conflicts, analyzed by Christopher R. Mitchell in the second chapter. Their defining characteristic of asymmetry makes them exceptionally difficult to handle, and poses new challenges of escalation and intractability that overwhelm the attempts of the regions to set up their own security regimes. The global regime is required to swing into action, for the regional conflicts force themselves on its attention.

The second part of the work examines the two parties' interests, as introduced in the first chapter. Vadim Udalov, a Russian official, reevaluates interests as a basis for cooperation, and a Russian and an American academic, Victor A. Kremenyuk and Bruce Parrott, examine the sources of American and Russian conduct in regional conflict and its reduction.

In the third part, the study turns to specific regions, examining the nature of conflict and superpower roles as a comparative springboard for the analysis of future possibilities. A cooperative security regime can best be understood in its application to specific areas, and regional conflict can best be considered for reduction when it is understood in its specific manifestation. Just as the potential measures for conflict reduction depend on systemic cooperation, either global or regional, so the conflicts themselves turn out to be not merely bilateral disputes but multifaceted problems of insecurity within the entire regional system, overwhelming its meager abilities to install its own security regime. The source of conflict has its own interests and reactions, which serve as a powerful motor to the layered relations characteristics of cooperative security and regional conflict, as presented by Georgi Mirsky.

The Middle East contains the clearest possibilities for cooperative security roles for the global actors in the absence of a regional security regime, in the analysis of Irina Zviagelskaia. The Oil Gulf, contested by the Arabs and the Persians, contains challenging possibilities for cooperation in reducing conflict, as analyzed by Alexei Vassiliev and Charles Doran. The India-Pakistan region can be expected to rise in conflict and escape easy external security cooperation, as presented by Thomas Thornton and Maxim Bratersky. The Andean region poses an unusual challenge because of its position within the global economic system, yet it is beyond the reach of most external attempts at conflict reduction, as Ilya Prizel shows. African regions test the ability of the global system to reduce conflict, as Vitaley Vasilkov shows in the south and Terrence Lyons in the Horn, for they deal with state collapse rather than well-structured interstate disputes.

The concluding chapters by Edward Kolodziej, Mark Katz, Victor A. Kremenyuk, and I. William Zartman develop the mechanisms available to cooperative security in the effort to reduce regional conflict. The two efforts are complementary: Regional conflict is the major challenge to its own security that the global regime will have to face, and its reduction will be the best way for global cooperation to preserve its integrity. Global order will be defended or destroyed in its reduction of regional conflict. Cooperative security requires a new and conscious devotion to Russian-American cooperation within the framework of global states' preemptive security efforts. If these are not pursued, global security will be destroyed by balance of power mechanisms that would throw the United States and Europe into rivalry and competition for the Russian heartland or by selfish isolationism in the United States, Europe, and Russia.

Silver Spring, Maryland   I. William Zartman
May 1995

Contributors

Maxim Bratersky, a former member of the Institute for U.S.A. and Canada Studies, Russian Academy of Sciences, is director of international programs for the Russian Public Policy Center and vice president of the Russian Science Foundation.

Charles F. Doran is the Andrew W. Mellon Professor of International Relations and director of Canadian Studies at the Paul H. Nitze School of Advanced International Studies (SAIS) of Johns Hopkins University. He is the author of numerous books and articles on international politics and political economy. His most recent book is *Systems in Crisis: New Imperatives of High Politics at Century's End.*

Mark N. Katz is associate professor of government and politics and senior staff member of the International Institute at George Mason University. He has been awarded fellowships by the Brookings Institution, the Earhart Foundation, the Rockefeller Foundation, and the United States Institute of Peace. He has authored and edited books on Soviet foreign and military policy and written a number of articles on the international relations of the former Soviet Union and of the Middle East.

Edward A. Kolodziej is research professor of political science at the University of Illinois, Urbana-Champaign. He is the author of numerous articles on foreign and security policy and is currently working on a book about global security after the Cold War. He is coeditor (with Roger E. Kanet) of *The Cold War as Cooperation.*

Victor A. Kremenyuk is deputy director at the Institute for U.S.A. and Canada Studies, Academy of Sciences of Russia, and a Doctor of Sciences (history). He has published widely in Russian and other languages, including articles in *Processes of International Negotiations, Windows of Opportunity,* and *The Cold War as Cooperation.* Dr. Kremenyuk is also the author of *Conflicts in and Around Russia: Nation-Building in Difficult Times.* Since 1988 he has been an International Institute for Applied Systems Analysis research associate in the Processes of International Negotiations Project.

Terrence Lyons is a senior research analyst in the Foreign Policy Studies program of the Brookings Institution, where he currently coordinates the conflict resolution in Africa project. Among his most recent publications is "Crises on Multiple Levels: Somalia and the Horn of Africa," in *The Somali Challenge: From Catastrophe to Renewal.* He has participated in U.S. observer missions in Ethiopia and Eritrea.

Georgi Mirsky is professor and senior research fellow at the Institute of World Economics and International Relations (IMEMO), Russian Academy of Sciences. In 1992–93 received a grant from The John D. and Catherine J. MacArthur Foundation. In 1991–93 he was a visiting fellow at the U.S. Institute of Peace and assistant professor at the School of International Service at the American University, Washington, D.C. He is the author of *The Military in Third World Politics* and *Asia and Africa: Continents in Movement,* among other works in Russian and English.

Christopher R. Mitchell is the Drucie French Cumbie Professor of International Conflict Analysis at George Mason University and director of the university's Institute for Conflict Analysis and Resolution. His major works include *The Structure of International Conflict, Peacemaking and the Consultants' Role,* and *New Approaches to International Mediation,* and his works in progress are *Gestures of Conciliation* and *A Handbook of Problem Solving Approaches to Protracted Conflicts.*

Bruce Parrott is professor and director of the Russian Area and East European Studies program at the Paul H. Nitze School of Advanced International Studies, Johns Hopkins University. He is the author of *Politics and Technology in the Soviet Union* and *The Soviet Union and Ballistic Missile Defense.* His most recent book (coauthored with Karen

Dawisha) is *Russia and the New States of Eurasia: The Politics of Upheaval.*

Ilya Prizel is associate professor in the Russian Area and East European Studies program and coordinator of East European studies at the Paul H. Nitze School of Advanced International Studies, Johns Hopkins University. He is the editor of *Post-Communist Eastern Europe: Crisis and Reorientation* and author of *Latin America Through Soviet Eyes.* He is currently writing on national identity and foreign policy formation in Russia, Poland, and the Ukraine and is editing a book on post-1989 Poland.

Thomas P. Thornton is adjunct professor at Georgetown and Johns Hopkins universities. He has written extensively on South Asia and the former Soviet Union. From 1977 to 1981 he was a senior member of the National Security Council Staff and has served on the Policy Planning Staff of the Department of State. From 1982 to 1993 he was a member of the Asian Studies faculty of the Paul H. Nitze School of Advanced International Studies, Johns Hopkins University.

Vadim Udalov is a career diplomat of the Russian Ministry of Foreign Affairs. Since 1987 he has been a staff member of the Research Coordination Center of this ministry and in 1991 he was a visiting fellow at the United States Institute of Peace. He is published in the Russian journal *Mezhdunarodnaya Zhizn'* and the *Annals of the American Academy of Political and Social Science.*

Vitaley Vasilkov, formerly of the Institute of U.S.A. and Canada Studies of the Russian Academy of Sciences, is currently deputy director of the Museum on Revolution and Reform in Russia, Moscow. He has published a number of edited works and articles on the former Soviet Union's and the United States' involvement and policies on the continent of Africa.

Alexei Vassiliev is the director of the Institute of African Studies of the Russian Academy of Sciences. He was a *Tass* correspondent in the Middle East, and is the author of a book on Saudi Arabia and a number of other works on the Arab world.

I. William Zartman is Jacob Blaustein Professor of Conflict Resolution and International Organization at the Paul H. Nitze School of Advanced

International Studies of Johns Hopkins University. He is the author of *The Practical Negotiator* (with M. Berman) and *Ripe for Resolution*, and editor and coauthor of *The 50% Solution, The Negotiation Process*, and *Positive Sum*, among other works. He directs the Conflict Reduction in Regional Conflicts (CRIRC) project between SAIS and the Institute for U.S.A. and Canada Studies of the Russian Academy of Sciences.

Irina Zviagelskaia is a graduate of the Leningrad University and received a doctorate in history from the Institute of World Economy and International Relations. Since 1982 she has been a senior researcher at the Institute of Oriental Studies, where she specializes in the international relations of the Middle East. She is the author of *The Role of the Israeli Military in State Policy Formation* and *American Policy toward Conflicts in the Middle East, Mid 1970s to 1980s*.

PART ONE

Causes and Resolutions

1

Systems of World Order and Regional Conflict Reduction

I. WILLIAM ZARTMAN

The threat of a superpower World War III has vanished, yet the peace of the world lies shattered by bloody endless wars in the Third World. As with each successive disappearance of a global security system, there comes a transition in international relations, dominated by problems of liquidating the old order before a new world order can be established. After the collapse of the cold war, as after the end of colonialism, conflicts explode where they were formerly contained by the previous system of world order, and the world is left without any firm sense of expectations and restraints in security matters. In the Third World, as in Eastern Europe and central Asia, the major challenge is the absence of regional security regimes, at a time when the inchoate nature of new states makes conflict likely, tempting, and even functional. Current regional security regimes are tentative and unreliable, their members unwilling and unable to enforce local security norms. On the global level, the United States, clearly primus inter pares among autonomous supporting or restraining partners, is torn between its isolationist and interventionist proclivities. In pursuing an active policy, it faces competing demands for cooperation with Russia and the European Union (EU), both conglomerates preoccupied with their own internal consolidation and unable either to block or to broker regional conflict. All are torn over the choice of an appropriate role to play and over the nature and dictates of their interests in regard to regional conflict.[1]

These uncertainties are contrasted and confronted by the inevitability of continuing regional conflict in the Third World (including the Balkans and Central Asia), stemming from the unstable, developing nature of Third World states and their relations. Third World conflicts begin at home, with intranational conflicts of self-determination and ideological conflicts for central government control, for which external support has been easy to attract and the cold war order, like the colonial order before it, kept the conflicts alive but within bounds. International conflicts also flow from the developing relations among neighboring states, where adjacent territory is easily coveted and claimed and where uncertain rank and relations in the region cause conflicts of order. Both types of conflicts, however, also arise in the post-cold war era because of the withdrawal of one of the superpower patrons, removing a balancer and a source of order that kept local conflicts under control. Because national and regional orders are only settling in, stability is found not in rigid defense of the status quo but in provision for just and orderly change. Methods and mechanisms for management of such conflicts operate under a handicap when they are characterized by as much uncertainty as the relations they are supposed to regulate. Yet a current world order—whether new or transitional—requires structures and practices that can handle the conflicting energies released by the collapse of the cold war order and can channel change toward political processes and solutions and away from violence.

It is tempting to assume that international relations of conflict and cooperation have been so globalized that they can be conceived of as occurring within a single collectivity of different-sized actors. The contrary reality is that the actors are numerous enough, geography irregular enough, cultural identities strong enough, and interests parochial enough to break up the globe into systemic levels and regions. It is as if, instead of a General Assembly, the United Nations did its business through an interacting constellation containing the Security Council and a number of regional commissions. To understand conflict and its reduction, one must analyze both the systems of interaction at the regional levels and then their relation to a system of selected actors with greater power and responsibilities termed global. Both levels have their own dynamics, and the structures and practices, methods and mechanisms, need to reflect that segmented reality.

Systems and Roles

Like Fashoda (1889) and Korea (1950–54), the Gulf wars (1979–91) marked a major turning point in the place of regional conflict in the current system of world order.[2] Fashoda showed that the Third World was covered by a European colonial grid within whose spaces conflict would be repressed by the dominant colonial power but between whose spaces the European powers would delimit their holdings by war if necessary. Similarly, the Korean War showed that bipolar zones of influence would flow into unclaimed spaces under the cover of regional conflicts, with boundaries between the zones being delimited by force if necessary. Each clash globalized a regional conflict and marked the consolidation of a world order system. In each of the previous systems, regional conflict was to be kept within bounds by the hegemonic power when occurring within its zone of influence or control, and by the superpowers and their clients through either conventions of crisis or carefully calibrated military confrontations when occurring between zones of influence.[3]

The Gulf wars marked the reverse effect, the end of a previously restraining system of world order. The two wars were a series of adventures undertaken by a regional power, Iraq, in the belief that it could get away with aggression because the target could no longer call in superpower reinforcements. In the first case, the target, Iran, was beyond cold war assistance because it was geographically too close to the Soviet Union for the United States to help but politically too far from the Soviet Union for Moscow to support. The war still took place within the context of the cold war but it was not bipolarized, and the parties were not acting as agents of the cold war contenders. Nonetheless, it was the workings of the bipolar system that made only a lengthy and ambiguous response possible.

In the second case, the opposite obtained. The end of the bipolar system led Saddam Hussein to believe that no one would have the interest to take practical steps to oppose his local venture against Kuwait (although he also seems to have hoped for Soviet support thinking that Iraq was on an interbloc boundary and the cold war was still on). Among the bundle of motives of the Bush administration for responding with force was the need to affirm that the end of the cold war did not open the door to unrestrained aggression in regional conflicts. Extraordinary cooperation between the United States and the then-USSR, as analyzed below by Doran and Vassiliev, opened up possibilities for a new era.

The response adopted, however, was vintage interbloc cold war, the reemployment of the old measures out of context. The United States rounded up an international posse and acted as sheriff. The status quo was reimposed, aggression was repelled, the world organization was mobilized, force overwhelmed force, and no underlying grievance was resolved. Ironically, although international change was refused in the region of conflict, repelling the aggression released roiling forces of internal upheaval within the states involved, especially Iraq and Kuwait, and increased the pressure for change elsewhere in the region, most notably in Palestine.

There were other ways in which the conflict could have been handled, other than through a sheriff's response. The U.S.-led coalition could have tried preventive diplomacy before the crisis, seeking to deal with the outstanding grievances within the context of a structural balance among the three leading powers—Iraq, Iran, Saudi Arabia—of the Gulf region, in a mender's role. Or it could have earlier acted to halt all arms supplies and other measures of support for Iraq, and proclaimed the sanctity of all states and boundaries, dampening the conflict. Or it could have let the conflict come to a head and then relied on long-range economic and military sanctions and supports during the crisis, trying to curb the aggressor by nonviolent means as a sign of a new era in international relations, in an umpire's role. Or it could have embarked on a full military conquest to set things fully aright and impose a government in its image at the end of the crisis, in a crusader's role. Or it could have allowed events to unfold toward a new equilibrium of power and then headed a move to legitimize it as part of the new order, as a midwife.[4] Or it could have been split by states pursuing their separate interests and seeking to undermine a collective response and collective cohesion, in a spoiler's role. In addition, the coalition could have sat out the crisis, leaving the regional conflict to regional auspices. These eight roles—sheriff, mender, dampener, umpire, crusader, midwife, spoiler, bystander—differ along two dimensions, the degree of involvement and the degree of partisanship, and correspond to the principal options open to the predominant power. Around them the roles of other states can vary along a crosscutting dimension from pluralist independent to centralized coordinated action.

Although there may be other roles conceivable,[5] these eight constitute the major strategies available to great powers in or out of coalition before a regional conflict. Crusader refers to military intervention and occupation not simply to end the conflict but to eliminate the problem by installing a government in the intervenor's image that is designed to eliminate the problem. Sheriff refers to military intervention in the conflict on the side of "right," meaning generally on the side of one of the parties and usually on the side of an established government. Umpire refers to indirect intervention on the side of right through economic measures, financing fourth-party intervenors, providing military supplies, and supporting regional efforts and organizations. Mender refers to diplomatic intervention to seek a solution among conflicting claims all of which are judged more or less legitimate. Dampener refers to indirect intervention by withholding the means by which the parties could pursue the conflict and by reinforcing the legitimacy of the status quo. Bystander refers to a hands-off nonintervention of any sort, leaving the conflicting parties to work out their problems, and even interdicting other regional intervention. Spoiler refers to individual singleshooting, by whatever means, to break up collective action.

What are the criteria for choice among these options? A primary element is effectiveness and efficiency: the ability of the strategy to accomplish the task of conflict reduction at an acceptable and comparably advantageous cost. That criterion, however, does not stand alone, for it is unrealistic to assume that conflict reduction is the only policy determinant. The prior determination hangs on the interests of the potential intervenors. This question will be addressed in the subsequent section of this chapter. Even further back in the sequence of criteria lies the conflict itself and the international system in which the conflict and strategy is located. It is assumed, in the following discussion, that whatever the system of order and conflict, it is composed of regional states and constellations in the Third World and an expanded global system of the First and Second worlds, referred to here as external states.

The sheriff's role used by the United States in the second Gulf war and by the United States and the USSR in cold war confrontations was quite different from the usual role adopted previously in Third World conflicts. The crusader's role was the one practiced in the 1980s by the United States in Grenada and Panama, countries within its zone of influence, and by the USSR in Afghanistan, similarly within its zone. In most other areas, superpower policy showed much less involvement. In a broad sense, American policy in Third World conflicts has been to maintain a structural balance among the parties in order to allow the conflicts of principle to be resolved by the parties themselves—a mixture of an umpire's and a mender's role. This broad role took many forms in many conflicts, from mediating conflict reduction or a partial settlement often partially favorable to one side (as in Zimbabwe, Namibia, Sinai, Eritrea, or Lebanon) to reinforcing a party to keep it in the contest and move the confrontation toward stalemate (as in Pakistan, Chad, or the Western Sahara). In all these cases, it was the parties themselves who eventually came to an agreement on the principles governing the dispute and their application to it. Not all of these and other attempts worked to the same degree and not all were performed with consummate skill, but they did indicate a lesser degree of involvement than the sheriff's role, with a partisanship that varied.

The choice of roles is determined by the perceived nature of the challenge. Sheriffs, as noted, solve no problems; they assume that regional conflict is a clash of good and evil, that one-sided aggression is obvious, and that the only grievance is against the aggressor. If the problem is seen as a criminal deviation from the status quo, the solution is to return to the status quo and the role choice is between a sheriff and an umpire. Unfortunately, although there occasionally are cases of clear aggression, many regional conflicts, such as the first Gulf war between Iran and Iraq, the Arab-Israeli conflict, and the Kashmir dispute between India and Pakistan, not to speak of internally derived regional conflicts in Ethiopia, Sudan, Angola, Lebanon, Sri Lanka, Philippines, Colombia, Peru, El Salvador, and Chad, had no obvious aggressor and arose more from shifting populations and regime successions than from state law breaking.[6] More frequently than ever before, regional conflict in the coming decades is likely to arise from the need to manage change and provide transitions to more stable states and relations, rather than from the need to oppose aggression and prevent change. In a world where territorial conquest is ruled illegitimate but where violent conflict is permitted for the exercise of self-determination, an order limited to blocking aggression will be largely static and irrelevant.

However, facilitating change and judging grievances constitute an approach to regional conflict far more difficult to coordinate than are marching orders to combat aggression. If change is to be channeled in a particular direction, there has to be agreement on the outcome or at least the process, lest different parties work for different changes, or, more likely, one party work for change and the other for the status quo, returning the world to a cold war. A sheriff's role can be declared on the spot and an ad hoc coalition assembled for the occasion, but a coalition to adjudicate and legislate on permissible processes and directions of change needs greater continuity and institutionalization. All the available models require a quantum leap rather than an evolution to fill the role, and the available mechanisms are ineffective as constituted and difficult to reform. The UN General Assembly is unwieldy, the UN Security Council is elitist, and the Organization on Security and Cooperation in Europe (OSCE) is restricted in its scope. These will all be discussed; the point here is that dealing with regional conflict as change rather than as aggression requires more complex and probably ongoing criteria and coordination for roles and order than are now available.

Classical models for world order systems include the balance of power, with shifting alliances against a threatening power; collective defense, with fixed alliances; and collective security, with a preexisting commitment to oppose any aggressor within the system.[7] Whereas the cold war moved from a balance of power to a collective defense system, the second Gulf war was the closest thing to collective security that the world has seen in a long while, with a double-tiered structure on the global and regional levels linked by a common principle. Not all the details were exactly in place, but the members of both the UN and the Arab League were committed to oppose aggression by any one of their members, and did so in close coordination. Some people, but few states, sided with the aggressor, as Mirsky describes below. The largest divergence was in the tactical positions within the coalition, in what could be viewed as a healthy and even helpful pluralism had not both the predominant power and the aggressor been obdurate against any use of diplomacy to allay their confrontation.

The major divergence of the Gulf operation from the collective security model—and the difference between any of the three classical models and the contemporary situation—is that contemporary relations play on two levels with marked power differences. In reality, the Gulf war was a response of the global powers to a regional conflict, in cooperation with regional powers, and not a response of one system level to a conflict within its midst (as a response of the Arab League alone would have been). These differences from collective security on the contractual, systemic, and tactical levels suggest a variant better understood as *cooperative security*.

The lateral diversity of tactical roles and positions that is so important to cooperative security can be best illustrated by examining the activities not only of coalition partners in the Gulf War but also of "allies" on the western side in such crises as Chad and Shaba. In Chad, the United States and the French coordinated their response to the Libyan invasion in July 1983, but only after an elaborate Alphonse-and-Gaston routine in which neither side wanted to appear to be doing the other's bidding. The most mixed picture of coordination in a multilateral action occurred in the two Shaba invasions (1977, 1978), where France and the United States established rapid collaboration and allocated responsibilities and three African countries (Morocco, Senegal, Togo) joined in the operation, but where deficient coordination and bitter rivalry characterized the French and Belgian military operations.

Membership in the Gulf war coalition in 1990–91 did not prevent France, the European Community (EC), and the USSR from attempting diplomatic initiatives to seek compliance with the UN Security Council resolutions without war; these moves were not encouraged by the United States and may not even have obtained much access to U.S. officials. The

European (9 January), French (14 January), and Soviet (19–23 February) initiatives failed to preempt military action; but the continuing Soviet initiative (after 23 February) succeeded in the limited sense that it helped prepare the eventual Iraqi withdrawal and cease-fire. It would have been appropriate for the United States to give greater encouragement and appreciation to these initiatives, even if they were to fail because of Iraqi obduracy. On the other hand, the military collaboration within the coalition was a remarkable achievement of combined command and operations.

In sum, in military operations, close coordination and cooperation is necessary; in diplomatic operations, a degree of autonomy is useful but it should be complemented by full access and encouragement along diverse paths to an agreed-upon goal. Such tolerance and coordination does not come naturally, and the combination of diplomatic autonomy and cooperation contains enough contradictions to invite mixed signals and bad feelings. Still more practice is needed in the exercise of coordinated pluralism. Indeed, the dynamic of the system itself is provided by competing centrifugal and centripetal efforts—centralizing coordination by the primus, against self-assertive autonomy by the pares. Whereas the dynamic of balance of power lay in the balancing and of collective defense lay in the competition between alliances, cooperative security hangs on a tension between centralizing and disintegrating pressures. Beyond the problems of signals and feelings is the fear of a worse danger, a multipolar evolution of the current system.

Although there may be several alternatives to a unipolar cooperative system, whether its role focus be on the sheriff, the ombudsman, or the umpire, the most prominent one is gradual multipolar disaggregation. This would involve the further weakening of the United States or at least rising isolationism that would turn its attention inward, and the reorientation of other states' interests into competitive policies toward regional conflict. For new reasons of ideopolitical or geopolitical interest, Europe or European states, Russia, and possibly even Japan and China could develop and support different clients in regional conflicts or different contenders for government leadership in internal disputes, and play a spoiler's role. The post–cold war era is not old enough to provide examples (except possibly for Cambodia), but an Iraq of Saddam Hussein that would have accepted the February 1991 mediation of the Soviet Union could have been enough of a step in the direction to cause concern. Instead, a monopolar cooperative security or concert system has a good likelihood of remaining in place, if the United States will wake up to play its role, and the real choice is between different notions of conflict and consequently different roles, both for the system and within the system.

The question is rather, within that system, what can be the patterns of cooperation with the U.S.? The heritage of World War II and the cold war suggest a continued close coordination with Europe in an alliance based on Atlantic values among the free world winners. Another heritage of World War II and the aftermath of the cold war, however, suggests cooperation with Russia, to maintain the post–cold war reversal, to keep Russia from being a loose cannon on the world deck, and to respond to competition and restiveness from the European Union. Optimally, and with a skillful diplomacy, the United States will not have to pick its allies and will be able to lead multilateral cooperation to deal with regional conflict. Realistically, even that exercise is more likely to involve shifts from one partner to another, with even periods of cooperation with one against the other.

Conflict and Interests

Writers about interests in international politics have always found it hard to make statements that are both significant and generalizable.[8] The best that can be produced is a typology or checklist, rather than a guide to content or judgment. In considering the interests of outside great powers and superpowers of the global system, it may help to break down the topic into interests in conflict itself, interests in the parties to the conflict, and interests in the management of conflict. A further categorization into coincident, nonintersecting, and conflicting interests is introduced by Udalov in a subsequent chapter to facilitate analysis. Regional conflicts fall into three categories: (1) intrastate separatist or internal subnational conflicts for self-determination with external support (Sudan, Eritrea, Cyprus, Sri Lankan Tamils); (2) intrastate replacement or internal ideological conflicts for central government control with external support (Lebanon, Afghanistan, Mozambique, Angola, Chad, Cambodia, Rwanda, Ethiopia, El Salvador, Iraq, Nicaragua, and Peru and Colombia without external support); and (3) interstate claims on neighboring territories (Ogaden, Kashmir, Kuwait, Sahara, Chad, Israel). In almost all cases, these conflicts come to the fore now either because they involve states emerging from Communist control (Ethiopia, Angola, Mozambique, Afghanistan, Cambodia) or because they involve parties supplied and restrained closely or distantly by cold war competitors (El Salvador, Somalia, Palestine, Peru, Colombia, Chad). The sources of the conflict are all homegrown, but the current form and outbreak is generally released by the end of the cold war.

Interests in conflicts of self-determination are determined by the strategic value of the integral state and the breakaway state, and by the precedent value of the exercise of self-determination. In general, external states favor an internal settlement of subnational conflicts, using solutions such as government authority, democratic pluralism, power sharing, and federalism, rather than secession; exceptions are provided by egregious cases, such as Bangladesh and possibly Eritrea, where secession is the price of saving the country. In the other cases cited, there is no great power support for any of the secessionist movements but instead general support (without much risky involvement) for peaceful settlement.

Interests in conflicts of government control dictate a more varied response, along ideological lines. When not ideologically determined, external states' interests have tended to favor the incumbent government. Yet it is the egregious if frequent cases which pose the real challenge. Despite variations, ideology has been only secondary to the problems of Idi Amin, Jean Bedel Bokassa, Goukouni Weddei, Mobutu Sese Seko, Hissene Habre, Siad Barre, Mengistu Haile Meriam, Pol Pot, Saddam Hussein, Leopoldo Galtieri, Dimitrios Ioannides, and many others. Their offense was a repressive regime, whose aggressiveness was an extension of its domestic policy. External states' interests in such cases are on soft ground: interests of opportunity, commitment, sunk costs, and avoiding the unknown and its danger of an even worse alternative. These are the hardest cases for conflict management, for containment of external aggressiveness only preserves the domestic problem and sets the stage for conflict against the repressive regime, with the danger of external involvement. However, for Galtieri and Ioannides, and, it is hoped, Saddam Hussein, resolute opposition to the external adventures started a chain of events that toppled the dictator, without a need for external states to do it directly.

Interests in territorial conflicts, like those in self-determination, are governed by the precedent value and by the source of the rival claims; the means of effectuating the claim determines its legitimacy, for any claim enacted by peaceful agreement of the two parties, including a referendum, would receive outside support. In none of the cases cited has any outside state taken a position other than in favor of the established border until changed by peaceful settlement and referendum.

In sum, except for ideological affinities, external powers' interests in all three types of regional conflict tend to favor peaceful settlement, above all for reasons of precedent. Except for reasons of a local balance of power (Iran-Iraq), external powers do not have much interest in conflict per se, and would benefit more from seeing it resolved than from seeing it continue. Conflict strains their relations with the region and the states in it, forcing them to take sides when it is not in their interest to do so. Only when the conflict is in a rival power's backyard, is it in a great power's interest to see it continue, and that type of situation is characteristic of a bipolar confrontation more than of the current system. The United States has never had any interest, for example, in seeing conflict among French-speaking African states or within Latin America, and both the Soviet Union and the United States (as well as all other external powers) have concluded that the end of conflict in Angola, Mozambique, Ethiopia, and Cyprus is more important than a particular winner or loser.

There is, however, a fourth source of regional conflict at a broader level than the preceding three: the conflict over regional structures themselves, over rank and relation of states within the region, and the regional order that these elements produce.[9] The conflict over Kuwait was a conflict over territory but also over the predominance of Iraq versus Saudi Arabia, Iran, Syria, and Egypt in the overlapping eastern Arab and Gulf regions. The conflict over Kashmir is a conflict over territory but also over the structure of the subcontinent; the conflict over Cambodia is an ideological conflict over state governance but also a struggle over the structure of Southeast Asia; the conflict over the Western Sahara determines the structure of the Maghrib and its stability; and so on. This is probably the most difficult aspect of change to handle in regional conflict, for there are no principles to apply, no procedures to honor, and no guidelines for external state interest. Outside states' interest is shaped by such elements as a stable distribution of power and expectations, a structure than can itself deal with change and challenge, and a limitation on temptations to adventures and escalating rivalries.

Probably the strongest *interests* associated with regional conflicts concern relations *with the parties*. Outside states have ideological, strategic, or friendship ties with individual regional states, besides their interests in maintaining a stable distribution of power within the region. Although conflict itself may disturb both these interests, conflict may also be necessary to preserve a stable distribution of power and may also force the outside state to reassess its friendships and to act accordingly. A tilt toward one state rather than another in a regional conflict may be predictable, but it generally occurs only at the cost of some other bilateral relationships that the outside state would like not to disturb.

The basis of these bilateral relationships comes in many forms: expatriate populations, markets, raw materials, investments, strategic locations, ideological supports, historical relationships, among others, usually termed "interests" (in the plural). A voluminous analysis could be (and some have been) made of each of these, but two characteristics are necessary to note here. First, interests, the sources of interest, never come in singles, and so never give a clear indication for strategies. Some major dependencies, such as oil, may be dominant but they are always part of a bundle that carries contradictory indications. The most that interests can indicate clearly is intensity, for they tend to be positive and therefore additive. Second, interests determine interest but rarely roles. There are different ways to protect interests, ranging from crusading to bystanding, and the choice among them is the product of other considerations under discussion here.

Interest in conflict management is dependent above all on the relations that outside party has with the conflicting parties and on the degree of hurt and opportunity caused it by the conflict; humanitarian interests (the degree of hurt caused by the conflict to the conflicting parties themselves) run a far distant second. The greatest impulsion for outside states to take some part in regional conflicts is provided by the pain and strain the conflict brings to their relations with the conflicting parties. This participation can take a range of forms. France came to the aid of its client, Chad, in 1983 after being vigorously pressed to do so by a number of French-speaking African states, and the United States and the other members of the Contact Group began mediating the Namibian disputes when the African Group in the UN threatened to embarrass them with a call for sanctions against South Africa. The Soviets could not support Syria and Egypt to Egypt's satisfaction in the 1970s and 1980s, despite efforts to do so, and they tried to mediate the Ethiopian-Eritrean conflict in the early 1980s when both clients, parties to the conflict, demanded their exclusive support. Sometimes, this response to negative pressure becomes an opportunity; wars create the possibility for creative diplomacy and a chance for a new settlement of regional grievances, but again, only if the perceived opportunity outweighs the likelihood of recent pain.

As noted, it is hard to total all these considerations into a generalization not riddled with exceptions, but some conclusions are evident. There is usually a broad interest by external states in a peaceful resolution of a conflict, or at least in using a violent conflict as an occasion for facilitating regional restructuring and conflict resolution. External states enter into regional conflicts to create a more stable outcome because of the strains the conflict poses to their bilateral and regional relationships. If those strains are of low intensity and part of the normal cost of operating in the region, they may provoke no involvement at all by the external state. As they increase, however, they make interference more compelling. Intervenors may be impelled to save their friends from disaster or assure their friends a prominent role in the region, but they have the greatest interest in facilitating a stable regional distribution of power that will lower the chances of further regional conflict. In the postwar period, the greatest interest by external states in supporting or exacerbating regional conflict came from their fear that the other side of the cold war would do it if they did not; such preemptive interest has presumably passed with the cold war, and even if a multipolar system evolves, it is much reduced. If there is a lesson from the Gulf War that transcends its many unique features, it is that a bystander role does not stand up against the exigencies of external states' interest in the Third World, as unsuccessful American attempts to play that role in the mid-1990s have shown.

These considerations of interest form a general background to the discussion in the following chapters on interest, identity, and behavior by the United States, Russia, and the regional participants in Third World conflicts. The three elements are separate and interacting. States do not act on interest alone (any more than do supposedly rational persons). Even acting rationally, their notions of interest depend on the ways in which they perceive their own identities, and then these rational calculations are mediated by behavioral traditions and other sources of conduct. Previous discussions of interest are helpful not only in highlighting the rational bases of behavior for prescriptive analysis but also in separating interests from other sources of policy as an aid to understanding reality.

Order and Management

Systems of world order in particular and of international relations in general are conceived and conceived of to handle challenges to their stability. Hitherto, little effort has gone into equipping them to handle conflict preemptively, to consider grievances, or to deal with change.[10] Indeed, if these challenges were taken on as tasks of the system, they would certainly conflict with its prior goal of self-maintenance or equilibrium, at least in the short run. This potential contradiction is inherent in any entity; purpose and existence as goals often clash in firms, movements, states, parties, and even individuals. An international relations system is such a low-level organism that the two goals are identical and the contradictions are slight. Taking on a wider goal, such as preventing conflict or facilitating change, would make the contradictions greater.

Furthermore, in an enthusiasm for a more intrusive calling that seems to be indicated by both system and interests, it is important not to rush up the ladder of unattainable institutionalization. A search for more effective means of handling change and conflict within the evolving world order has often led idealists into a reckless embrace of world government and the scornful disdain of realists and practitioners. The challenge is to be constructively realistic, handling slightly expanded frontiers of change and conflict within a realizable system of cooperative security.

The following discussion in this and subsequent chapters is based on assumptions about current and future conditions throughout the rest of the decade (or millennium). The first, as already indicated and elaborated below by Mitchell, is that Third World wars and other conflicts are likely to continue in frequency and to rise in relative importance as the cold war slips into history. Protracted conflicts and sporadic outbreaks of war are endemic conditions of the developing countries.

The second, explored in Part 2, is that the United States remains primus inter pares but timid in its leadership, venturing into conflict on occasion with its sleeves rolled up to set things straight, and then re- turning home. A facilitating role that helps an evolution already in course, as Lyons discusses below in regard to Ethiopia, is likely to be more typical of American responses to Third World conflicts than the highly visible role in the Gulf war. The role of European allies, as that of Portugal in Angola, discussed by Vasilkov, or of regional powers, as that of India in Sri Lanka, as discussed by Bratersky and Thornton, is typical of the coming era and likely to receive American—and other powers— encouragement.

The third, also the basis of Part 2, is that, whatever its name or form, there is certain to be a major power centered in Russia and involving some type of union relations and a common foreign policy with other autonomous republics. This restructured "Soviet" entity will certainly be preoccupied with its internal problems and weakened by a lack of dispos- able resources; its foreign policy will be collective, but may well involve more direct interests from some of the component republics than has hitherto been the case. It will not be "the other superpower," but it will be an important player if only because of the audience that it can appeal to throughout the Third World and because of its atomic weaponry.

By the same token, Europe is unlikely to have overcome its problems of incoherence and polycephalism by the end of the decade. Both the countries and the Union will be major players, too, but hampered by the competition among themselves as they learn to move together. Moving together, after all, poses the prior question, "To whose tune?" On the other hand, Japan and China, for their own reasons, are not likely to have grown into an important conflict management role before the next century.

Finally, it is assumed that the range of relations among the superpowers and other global powers in the aftermath of the cold war confrontation can take forms summarized as C5-I: condominium, consultation, collaboration, communication, concert, and isolation.[11] Although the first, of shared bilateral domination, is unlikely and, indeed, to be avoided, and the last is unfortunately possible and also to be avoided, the middle range contains subtle differences that can be crucial. Consultation is the tightest, implying periodic harmonization of policy, and collaboration is used to refer to a looser coordination with compatible differences; communication means simply notification to avoid surprises, and concert suggests a loosely institutionalized forum for joint action.

Without firm institutions, regional conflict reduction under cooperative security means process. Examining various mechanisms and spelling out detailed procedures in depth will be done in subsequent chapters of this work. As a beginning here, components of a conflict reduction process within the current pluralistic, hierarchical, monopolar system will be laid out as criteria for the later discussion. It would be neater if a conceptual construct existed from which such components could be deduced, but none does. Instead, it will be necessary to establish a logical set of parameters or necessary and sufficient components of the basic notion of cooperative security from which guidelines can be derived. Ingredients of such a system would be regular informal meetings of global powers for establishing an agenda, a set of principles or norms as a policy referent, an articulated relationship between the global concert and the regional structures, a relation between UN forums and the concert systems, and a coordinated diversification of roles. Within these components, a cooperative system for preventive and crisis management can be operated; absent any of them, functional equivalents will have to be invented or the system will lamely hop from crisis to crisis.

Cooperative security depends on agenda setting and *executive coordination,* through regular informal meetings of top representatives of the major or core states. The model is the annual western economic summit, where current issues are discussed to create a general basis of understanding even if not a formal consensus. The extraordinary enlargement of the summit's attendance and agenda to include Mikhail Gorbachev and a discussion of some political topics in May 1991 was a major step toward making this proposal a reality. The meeting is one of executive coordination, far from the false legislative analogy of parliamentary diplomacy as practiced in the UN General Assembly, or from the formal decisions produced by the UN Security Council. Yet it is a helpful predecessor to such formal activities. Although the agenda would cover primarily the relations among the participants, it would also include regional conflicts as they merited attention. Attendance would involve the leading western states, Russia, and Japan, the successor great powers to the Big Five of the postwar era. Although this is clearly an oligarchic exercise, it corresponds to the responsibility of power better than does the mixed formula of the Security Council. Functional equivalents can also be found on the North-South dimension in such executive forums as the annual French-African summit or the biannual commonwealth meeting.

Executive coordination is needed to give focus and harmony to the *role diversity* that the oligarchy demands and that cooperative security requires. Sheriffs may be needed in time of crisis, but crises can be both managed and avoided by the use of other roles. To keep them supporting rather than undercutting each other requires tolerance, trust, and communication, but it provides greater possibilities for saving face and allowing a way out than does a solid phalanx of developed countries dictating conduct to the Third World. The Good Cop–Bad Cop routine is as old as Abraham, effective as long as the cops work for the same police force. The Contact Group in Namibia as an alternative to Organization of African Unity (OAU) sanctions, the Contadora Group's Arias Plan as an alternative to the Reagan administration's contras, and the various mediation attempts in the Falklands war, the Iran hostage conflict, and the Afghan war all show the possibilities of constructive pluralism, even if all were not successful. Pluralism is the mark of the multipower constellation after the cold war; what cooperative security adds is the element of communication and coordination.

Despite some institutional covers, this diversity is still the pluralism of states, not of regional structures. It was India, not the South Asian Association for Regional Cooperation (SAARC), which mediated the Sri Lankan conflict, to its rue and regret; if Nigeria intervened in Liberia along with other states and under the cover of the Economic Community of West African States' Military Observation Group (ECOMOG), and Syria intervened in Lebanon with the blessings of the Arab League, the prime agent was the regional power, not the organization; and the European Community's effort in Yugoslavia was stalled as much by dissension among its members as by the South Slavic conflict itself. Organizations are not yet coherent actors, but they do have a legitimizing role to play that needs developing.

Coordination, besides being procedural, also requires substantive standards, or *principles,* that are used to govern various situations of conflict. The principles associated with OSCE serve as an example.[12] Standards and codes of conduct are important when the aim is to consolidate and legitimize the status quo, but they become crucial when the purpose is to stabilize and channel change into legitimate and predictable directions. In a new era where the enemy is not predetermined, it must be clear what one is for in order to be clear whom one is against. Whether such principles are substantive, such as state sanctity, or procedural, such as self-determination, they need to be carefully considered and their implications seriously studied, and they need clear enunciation.

Principles matter. If Somalia was obliged to develop peaceful relations with its northern and southern neighbors, it was in large measure because of the OAU members' firm insistence on its norm on boundaries, and if Morocco is obliged to pass its military control over the Western Sahara through a referendum, it is because Morocco's opponents have been able to mobilize UN and OAU norms on self-determination. Some types of conflict are more susceptible to standards and codes of conduct; it is easier to enunciate such principles covering self-determination, boundaries, or territorial integrity than it is to regulate ideological contests over government control or contests of rank and rivalry. Even so, principles can be useful where they are applicable, limiting the scope of conflict and channeling the formulas for its solution.

Two types of principles are needed, one relating to procedures, notably of the intervening powers of the cooperative security system, and the other to outcomes, notably of conflict situations. In each case, the legitimacy and the limits of the parties' actions are addressed so that others know what is intended, what to expect, and what is permissible.[13] Procedural principles can cover such matters as the criteria for military intervention, the criteria for diplomatic recognition, the criteria for self-determination, the level of responsibility for handling the conflict, and the distinction between humanitarian and security responses. As an example, all these items were addressed in unilateral declarations and joint statements in regard to the Yugoslav crisis as it evolved throughout the first half of the 1990s. Outcome principles current throughout the decade centered in the "4 Ds": demilitarization, deideologization, democratization, and development.[14] All four refer to ways to reduce conflict by banning its most harmful means and substituting political and economic mechanisms for handling its sources.

Because the organs of the United Nations provide collective decisions for action and principles for legitimization relevant to regional conflict, *relations with the UN system* need to be assured. The UN, however, is not the cooperative security system. The Gulf war and the Somali affair left a curiously dichotomous impression of the United Nations; to the coalition it was a striking example of the revival and constructive use of the world organization, but to many in the Third World it was a case of the UN bullied and hijacked. Although political decisions will not satisfy everyone, care should be taken to minimize this sort of division as much as possible, by securing support from both "houses" of the body. The next issue in the use of the UN concerns the extension of the collective cover from simply the use of the blue flag to the operational command itself.

The UN is a powerful resource and a major improvement on the concert system of the post-Napoleonic period. Yet it plays its role differently, as an ombudsman or umpire rather than as a sheriff's strategy. As a sheriff, it becomes a formal source of authority and standards, binding the secretary-general; as ombudsman or umpire, the two plenary bodies are used to the same end but the secretary-general is left much creative leeway, as seen to a limited extent in Namibia, Western Sahara, Somalia, Afghanistan, and the first Gulf (Iran-Iraq) war, where he provided both technical services and creative mediation. In this role, satisfaction is more nearly universal. But the secretary-general cannot be expected to supplant the role of leading states, only to complement it. In all the above cases, the UN agent was a facilitator and technical assistant, following or preceding the crucial role of regional or global powers. They were the parties whose relationships with the conflicting states brought the states to consider management of their conflict. The secretary-general does not have that kind of weight or leverage, and demanding it of him would burden the office with overexpectations. However, neither can cooperative security supplant the three major UN organs. The coordinating meetings act as a caucusing group outside the UN's formal framework, using it in a way that reinforces its authority and acceptance.

Finally, the global concert needs to maintain *relations with regional structures*. The absence of regional security regimes has been identified at the beginning of this chapter as the fundamental problem of current Third World relations, although as Mitchell's following chapter shows, often pieces are in place that can be used to build regional regimes. The answer currently given to the problem is the widespread implantation of Conferences on Security and Cooperation to overcome regional conflict.[15] The proposal is helpful as a goal toward which regional relations can evolve but not as a short-run solution. The Conference on Security and Cooperation in Europe grew out of evolving inter-European and intra-European relations under the umbrella of a change in global rivalry, conditions not present in any other region of the world except southern Africa, and, in the foreseeable future, the Middle East. A Conference on

Cooperation and Security in Southern Africa (CCSSA) has been mooted and a Conference on Security and Cooperation in the Middle East (CSCME) discussed.[16] In many other regions, however, the evolution has been away from, not toward, increased responsibility in conflict management, as seen in changes over the lives of the OAU and the Arab League.

Yet, as subsequent chapters and particularly the case studies show, Third World conflicts occur in clearly identifiable regional contexts and are contained by regional limits. Ostensibly intrastate conflicts of secession or replacement rapidly become transnational and then interstate conflicts of rank and relation according to the dynamics of the regional system, and then flow no further, bounded by regional interactional identity. Africa, acting through the OAU, turned the southern African conflicts over to the Front Line States, the Western Sahara conflict to the Maghrib, and the Liberian conflict to ECOWAS. The India-Pakistan conflict led to its logical extreme in the breakup of Pakistan within the structure of the south Asian region and pulled global neighbors—Russia, China—and other superpowers—the United States—into its maelstrom, but not Third World neighbors in other regions. The Arab-Israeli conflict has multiple dynamics defined by its region, but even Muslim neighboring states, such as Turkey and Iran, remained outside direct involvement in it. Third World conflicts are part of regional system dynamics (dynamics that include regional cooperation, hierarchy, and leadership as well) and can be handled and understood only within that context. Even the testing exception of the Andes has its intraregional similarities, but the conflicts jump from their intranational incidence to causes within the global system.

At the same time, the closest relations between global states and Third World regions have been bilateral ties of friendship and support, operating particularly in regional conflict. The push and pull dimensions of these relations complement each other well. Third World states appeal to external states to borrow power unavailable at home or in the region in the conduct of their conflicts, and external states respond to consolidate relations in the region and often to keep an arms market open. The cold war impetus of the push dimension is presumably gone, but the commercial attractions remain, for secondary as well as primary external states. If other political as well as commercial interests persist, the way is open for a ready spoiler's role within regional structures. Such attentions undermine the coherence of regional regimes, and call for a high level of global consensus on regional arms control, higher than that achievable for example in 1950 in the arms embargo on the Middle East or in 1977–79 in the Conventional Arms Transfer (CAT) talks.[17]

Furthermore, it would seem that there is little in the way of formal assistance that external states, operating alone or in concert, can offer to help regional organizations. Because the strength and legitimacy of regional institutions in dealing with regional conflict lies in their autonomy, external assistance could undermine their major asset.[18] The only legitimate source of external assistance would be regional organizations' "senior model," the UN, and there the potential assistance is limited. The UN Security Council could have authorized requested assistance from itself or the secretariat to the OAU peacekeeping operations in Chad, as it did in the Western Sahara, but there was little the UN—or external states—could have done to reinforce the conflict management capabilities of the Organization of American States (OAS) in the Beagle Channel dispute or of the Arab League in the Kuwaiti or Lebanese disputes. Indeed, given the structure of regional relations, a firmer role in these conflicts would merely have provided a heightened occasion for internal divisions.

Yet encouragement toward greater regional responsibility in handling regional conflicts can be a major contribution of the pluralistic, coordinated global security cooperation. Coordination of external states' efforts removes the potentiality for regional states to run to external sources of support for their divisions. If such escalation is blocked, regional states can be turned back to their own conflicts with a charge to manage them, lest the cooperating external states have to take regional affairs in their hands. Such pressure can lead Third World regions on the longer road to their own institutionalized cooperation, in a CSC of their choice. This is the reason why it was such a sound policy for the United States *not* to intervene in the Liberian conflict, despite heavy criticism, but instead to let Africa learn to handle its own conflicts.

It may be objected that cooperative security, as so described, is an unreal delicate exercise, demanding coordination among prickly partners, collective but self-restrained hegemony over young and sensitive Third World states, and agreement on principles that specific interests may challenge. That is true. It is also true that the system is no more delicate than the ideal of collective security, often debated but never attained, but no more delicate either than the careful calculations necessary to a balance of power system or the abstract commitments required in collective defense. These systems have existed and have even worked. Their imperfections lead to a hope for something better but no more difficult to achieve.

Notes

1. For another Soviet-American effort to take stock of relations after the cold war, written while there still was a Soviet Union, see Richard Smoke and Andrei Kortunov, eds. *Mutual Security: A New Approach to Soviet-American Relations* (New York: St. Martin's, 1991). See also Zaki Laidi, ed. *Power and Purpose after the Cold War* (Providence, R.I.: Berg, 1995).

2. See Glenn Snyder and Paul Diesing, *Conflict among Nations: Bargaining, Decision Making, and System Structure in International Crises* (Princeton, N.J.: Princeton Univ. Press, 1977), and also Paul Pillar, *Negotiating Peace* (Princeton, N.J.: Princeton Univ. Press, 1983).

3. See Cora Bell, *Conventions of Crisis* (New York: Council on Foreign Relations, 1974) and Roger E. Kanet and Edward A. Kolodziej, eds. *The Cold War as Cooperation: Superpower Cooperation in Regional Conflict Management* (Baltimore: Johns Hopkins Univ. Press, 1992).

4. The term was used by Assistant Secretary of State Herman Cohen in regard to his role in Ethiopia, discussed in detail below by Terrence Lyons; see *New York Times*, 26 May 1991. See also Lynn Wagner, "Processes for Impasse Resolution," International Institute for Applied Systems Analysis, Luxemburg, WP-91-43.

5. Edward Kolodziej has proposed additional possibilities, including humanitarian, and revolutionary. Humanitarian refers to a different purpose, and revolutionary may be included under crusader. Spoiler, noted here, is a very different role, often played by the two superpowers in the other's zone of influence during the cold war, and unlike the others is an individual, rather than a collective, response.

6. See Joseph Montville, ed. *Conflict and Peacekeeping in Multiethnic Societies* (Lexington, Mass.: Heath, 1990); I. William Zartman, ed. *Elusive Peace: Negotiating an End to Civil Wars* (Washington, D.C.: Brookings Institution, 1995).

7. See Inis Claude, *Power and International Relations* (New York: Random House, 1962); Morton Kaplan, *System and Process in International Politics* (New York: Wiley, 1957).

8. Hans J. Morgenthau, *In Defense of the National Interest* (Lanham, Md.: Univ. Press of America, 1983); John Burton, *Conflict: Resolution and Prevention* (New York: St. Martin's, 1990).

9. See Kenneth Boulding, *Stable Peace* (Austin: Univ. of Texas Press, 1976), 58f; Howard Wriggins, ed. *The Dynamics of Regional Politics* (New York: Columbia Univ. Press, 1992); I. William Zartman, *Ripe for Resolution: Conflict and Intervention in Africa*, 2d ed. (New York: Oxford Univ. Press, 1989).

10. See Michael Lund, *Preventive Diplomacy and American Foreign Policy* (Washington, D.C.: U.S. Institute of Peace, 1994).

11. Craig Nation, *Conflict Reduction in Regional Conflicts: Restructuring Soviet-American Relations in the Third World* (Bologna: The Johns Hopkins University School of Advanced International Studies, Bologna Center, 1990), esp. 27–29.

12. See Victor-Yves Ghebali, *La diplomatie de la détente: la CSCE 1973–1989* (Brussels: Bruylant, 1989); and Janie Leatherman, *Principles and Paradoxes of Peaceful Change* (New York: Cambridge Univ. Press, 1995).

13. See Stephen Krasner, ed. *International Regimes* (Ithaca, N.Y.: Cornell Univ. Press, 1983), esp. pt. 3.

14. Nation, *Conflict Reduction in Regional Conflicts,* 16–19.

15. Alice Rivlin, David Jones, and Edward Meyer, *Beyond Alliances: Global Security Through Focused Partnerships* (Washington, D.C.: Brookings Institution, 1990). See also Ashton Carter, William Perry, and John Steibruner, *A New Concept of Cooperative Security* (Washington, D.C.: Brookings Institution, 1992) and Janne Nolan, ed. *Global Engagement: Cooperation and Security in the Twenty-First Century* (Washington, D.C.: Brookings Institution, 1994).

16. Resolutions, Conference on Peace and Security in Southern Africa, Center for Foreign Relations, Dar es-Salaam, 28 Feb. 1991; Hearings on Africa and Middle East, Commission on Security and Cooperation in Europe, U.S. Congress, 4–19 Aug. 1991, 14 Oct. 1993; Olusegun Obasanjo, ed. *The Kampala Document: Towards a Conference on Security, Stability, Development and Cooperation in Africa* (New York: African Leadership Forum, 1991).

17. Barry Blechman and Janne Nolan, *The U.S.-Soviet Conventional Arms Transfer Negotiations,* Foreign Policy Institute Case Study no. 3 (Washington, D.C.: School of Advanced International Studies, 1987).

18. Note, however, the direct financial assistance offered by the United States to the OAU to support its conflict management capabilities, in bills prepared in 1993 and 1994 by the House Subcommittee on Africa of the Committee on Foreign Affairs.

2

Asymmetry and Strategies of Regional Conflict Reduction

CHRISTOPHER R. MITCHELL

The new world order will have to cope with four distinct types of regional conflict: classical international, intranational replacement, and intranational separatist, plus a transnational overflow of any one of these into another. Moreover, the most salient types of conflict that present problems for reduction or resolution are likely to be intranational or transnational for two reasons. It is generally agreed that intranational regional conflicts are the most difficult to reduce, settle, or resolve, and their tendency to attract other parties as patrons or interveners rapidly "transnationalizes" them. However, it should never be assumed that we have seen the last of classical international conflicts. The two Gulf wars, the Anglo-Argentine war over the Falklands/Malvinas Islands, and the continuing Russo-Japanese dispute over the Kurile Islands all indicate the need to include this fourth category of regional conflicts in any consideration of conflict reduction strategies.

Whatever the differences, however, there are common principles for reducing or resolving all types of regional conflicts, leading to the development of practical, useful, and general strategies of conflict reduction or resolution. Two such principles stand out. First, all are concerned with change and are fundamentally structured as being between pro-change and pro-status quo parties. Second, the "conflict system" in regional disputes is frequently highly asymmetric, and this factor has a major influence upon both the strategies of the adversaries in pursuing

25

their conflict and on the opportunities for, and obstacles to, achieving a reduction of that conflict, whether this outcome is attempted bilaterally or with the assistance of some third party.

The Nature and Variety of Asymmetry

The concept of asymmetry embraces far more than the customary conception of a "power imbalance" between parties in a conflict.[1] Commonsensically, the cases of David and Goliath, the United States and Grenada in 1983, and Finland and the Soviet Union in 1939–40 involved imbalances and were clear examples of asymmetric conflict, as are the conflicts between the Ethiopian government and the Oromo Liberation Front or the Iraqi government and its dissident Kurdish community. The last two cases are more directly relevant examples of asymmetry for a discussion of future intranational conflicts, and also show that asymmetries can change as a conflict develops over time. Asymmetry is a dynamic as well as a multidimensional phenomenon, consisting of a differential distribution of relevant resources and salient characteristics between adversaries in a conflict system.

This definition immediately raises questions about the meaning of "relevant" and "salient." Relevant to what? Salient for whom? The answer depends on the conflict under analysis and on the circumstances of the conflict at the time. A "relevant" resource for one conflict may, indeed, be the degree of coercive potential possessed by each of the adversaries, but it may also be the relative amount of external sympathy and diplomatic support enjoyed by the parties. At another stage of a conflict, it may be the parties' relative degree of popular commitment to prosecuting that conflict. At a still later stage such commitment may be replaced by another characteristic, such as the parties' relative internal elite cohesiveness. At a stage of direct negotiation the "relevant" resource may be one party's possession of a bearable alternative to agreement should negotiations fail compared with the other party's lack of such a bearable alternative.[2]

The definition also points to asymmetry as an emergent property of a conflict system,[3] coming in many shapes and sizes (see table 2.1). An important one is legal, or status, asymmetry, while others include resource or capability asymmetries[4] (containing but not confined to the asymmetry of coercive potential usually known as a "power imbalance"), and behavioral asymmetries of tactics. However, there are many other attributes on which a substantial asymmetry will clearly affect the course of a conflict and its probable outcome, such as moral and structural asymmetries and asymmetries of interdependence and commitment.

Moral asymmetries involve the manner in which the parties view their dispute as concerning issues of right and wrong, justice and injustice. While there are conflicts in which a moral dimension is absent, this is rarely the case in protracted regional conflicts, where "rights" to existence as a political entity, "rights" to lost territory (opposed by "rights" to existing boundary preservation) or "rights" to secede or self-determine (opposed by "rights" to maintain an existing polity) are all prime questions. Moreover, protracted regional conflicts are usually perceived psychologically, and defined tactically, as moral crusades. Frequently the moral asymmetry, as perceived by the parties, takes the form of a mirror image, with moral right wholly on the perceiver's side and moral turpitude characteristic of its adversary. The conflict is then "fought out" partly in moral terms, success going to the party that seizes the "moral high ground" in the eyes of external third parties.

Structural asymmetries, on the other hand, involve differences in the nature and conditions of the conflicting adversaries' distinguishing characteristics, some of which can alter rapidly over time while others remain relatively static. Salience of goals, often stable, can change quite suddenly when a trigger event takes place or a key threshold is crossed. Similarly, levels of cohesion within the rival parties can remain high or low over long periods. However, they can alter rapidly when conditions in the parties' environments change—when, for example, a key patron becomes less supportive of a strategy espoused by one intraparty faction but opposed by another. In contrast, leadership security often appears highly volatile for parties in protracted regional conflicts, and threats to decision-making elites arise from a variety of sources and create situations in which one party might well have a relatively secure leadership yet face an adversary whose leadership remains in power only by the narrowest margin.

However, if it is the case that conflict systems can be characterized by multiple asymmetries or symmetries, it seems likely that clusters of asymmetric attributes will typify certain subtypes of regional conflict—indeed, such "clusters of asymmetry" may be usable to categorize types of conflict, rather than more conventional classification schemes.

Asymmetry and the Dynamics of Intrastate Conflicts

It is a truism that conflicts between unequals are conducted differently from conflicts between equals. This is conventional wisdom, but not wisdom in systematic form. If protracted regional conflicts are asymmetric in many ways, how is this likely to affect the detailed strategies pursued by the parties, and can one assist analysis through useful gener-

Table 2.1

Key Asymmetries in Protracted Regional Conflicts

Nature of Asymmetry Between Party 1 and Party 2	Definition
Capability	
Coercive Ability	Degree to which P1 can coerce P2, and not vice versa
External Support	Level of help afforded P1 by outside 3Ps
Access	Ability of P1 to have self/goals recognized as part of political agenda in relevant decision-making processes
Visibility	Ability of P1 to be noticed in general public arenas
Cost Experience	Level of loss experienced by P1 from conflict
Survivability	Ability of P1 to survive major setback of defeat
Bargaining Ability	Ability of P1 to conduct skillful negotiations
Structure	
Intraparty Cohesion	Number of significant cleavages within P1
Leadership Legitimacy	Extent to which leaders in P1 can claim to be rightfully in power
Leadership Insecurity	Degree of challenge to leaders' incumbency within P1
Constituent Mobilization	Degree to which rank and file in P1 are involved in conflict
Elite Entrapment	Extent to which P1 leaders have committed their political futures to success in conflict
Commitment	
Goal Salience	Importance of issues in conflict to P1
Constituent Commitment	Level of rank and file support for P1 goals
External Dependency	Degree to which P1 continuing conflict depends on support from external patrons
Commitment to Change	Degree to which P1 goals involve change in status quo
Expectation of Success	Level of perception of probable success in conflict through current P1 strategies
Interdependence	
Isolation/Interdependence	Link of P1 to other salient conflicts
Parallelism	Degree to which conflict sets/follows precedents in other salient conflicts
Historical Justification	Degree to which conflict can be linked to historical precedents or exemplars

Legality/Status	
Representativeness	Degree to which P1 leaders' right/ability to represent P1 is generally accepted
Existence	Degree to which P1 right to exist as a party is generally recognized and accepted
Legitimacy	Legal standing of P1
Morality	
Existential Acceptance	Degree to which P1 accepts P2 right to exist and contest
Issue Acceptance	Degree to which P1 recognizes that P2 may have a case · to be dealt with
Goal Acceptance	Degree to which P1 accepts the legitimacy of P2's goals
Behavior	
Violence	Level of violence used by P1 against P2
Coercion	Level of coercion used by P1 against P2
Persuasion	Degree of persuasion used by P1 against P2
Conciliation	Degree of conciliation used by P1 with respect to P2
Avoidance	P1 efforts to avoid dealing with the dispute or with P2

alizations about the dynamics of such conflicts? An initial suggestion might be that the broad strategies open to adversaries in asymmetric intrastate conflicts attempt to either maintain or increase favorable asymmetries for exploitation when these exist, or reduce or reverse unfavorable asymmetries that work to the detriment of one's own fortunes in the struggle. In many historical examples of regional conflicts, a key to understanding why parties act as they do often seems to be that strategies are primarily aimed at first equalizing (and later reversing) an advantage enjoyed by the adversary or at maintaining (or even increasing) some inequality that confers advantage on one's own side.

The most obvious example of this in protracted regional conflicts that pass the threshold of organized violence is the effort by a weaker party to acquire coercive resources with which to offset those available to their opponents. Arms to defend themselves against government troops and security forces are clear examples of the results of this strategy, as are training facilities and instructors for fighters, safe areas for training, and secure infiltration routes. Equally, however, a stronger party will bend every effort to keep its adversary from acquiring such resources and to build up its own means of coercion, thus maintaining its advantage on what, inevitably, comes to be defined as one of the key asymmetries for prevailing in the conflict. Many protracted intranational conflicts thus become miniature arms races, the key factor being the gap between the coercive potential of incumbents and insurgents.

Similarly, in protracted regional conflicts between states, the search for arms and other resources to supply a coercive advantage, however temporary, becomes one of the dominant features of the interactions between the core parties and their patrons and allies. A classic arms race thus takes place within a regional arena. The underlying dynamics of all such processes, however, involve parties' efforts to maintain or alter an asymmetric balance in coercive resources, which include capacities to resist others' coercion.

While efforts to reduce or maintain asymmetry in coercive capability constitute a familiar and accepted strategy in both international and intranational conflicts, other types of "asymmetry change" strategies are less obvious but equally important and there are many of them. For example, parties in legally asymmetric conflicts devote much time and effort to either reducing or maintaining the "legal distance" between them. In regional intranational or transnational conflicts, incumbents often emphasize their recognized legal status as a member of the international community and the lack of such status on the part of the adversary. Central to this strategy is the incumbents' insistence (1) on the status of insurgents as rebellious "subjects" or "citizens"; (2) on their own right (and capacity) for dealing with events within their own territorial boundaries to the exclusion of all other legal entities, whether international organizations or other governments; (3) on their right to represent and speak for all their citizens (including "the rebels") in international forums; and (4) on their right to control the activities of all outside bodies (relief and development organizations, for example) on their national territory.

In contrast, insurgents and their patrons frequently attempt to reduce such asymmetry by undermining the basis of the incumbents' legal status, negatively and positively. Negative attempts involve insurgent efforts to cast doubt upon the legality of both the incumbents themselves and upon the legal standing of the political regime and, in separation conflicts, the entire political system. Thus Eritrean organizations argued that the incorporation of Eritrea in the Ethiopian empire in 1962 was an illegal act, contrary to the agreement for a federal system concluded under UN auspices (although many Eritreans also argued that this agreement itself had no real legal standing in that they were not fully consulted about its conclusion or implementation, quite apart from its ignoring the lack of any historical connection between Ethiopia and

Eritrea). Given this "illegality," no Ethiopian government had any right to make decisions on behalf of Eritreans or to claim to represent them in the international community. Ethiopian incumbents, in this view, had no better legal standing than representative Eritrean organizations, even though these were regarded generally as "insurgent."

The positive method of reducing legal asymmetry attempts to establish or to increase the legal status of the insurgent organizations themselves. Typically this might well be entitled the "candidate government or state strategy," for it consists of a series of interlocking moves designed to replicate the international "presence" and contacts of a formal state or government structure. Among such moves are: (1) Establishing "quasi-embassies"—information offices, official representatives—in key locations throughout the world—in the capitals of patrons or friendly countries, then in capitals of regional and global powers and centers for international organizations. (2) Attempting to obtain some form of affiliation with relevant international organizations, such as the UN, the World Health Organization (WHO), or the Arab League. At the very least, an office is opened near the organization's headquarters; at most, observer status or some equivalent is sought and, if gained, used to reinforce arguments about legal status and recognition. (3) Setting up contacts with key opinion leaders in key countries, often including those involved in the media and local politics. Part of this increasingly involves the employment of paid local lobbyists and—at least in the United States —public-relations firms to make a case for the insurgents and to ensure that their case is constantly and positively put before key groups and individuals. (4) Finally, a key part of this strategy involves insurgent leaders' making regional or world tours to meet—and be seen meeting —as many of the world's prestigious political leaders as can be arranged. The ultimate end of this candidate government or state strategy is either the declaration and general recognition of separate statehood in separatist intranational conflicts, as in the efforts to establish a Palestinian state by the Palestinian Liberation Organization (PLO) in 1988 or those to establish a Turkish Federal Republic on Cyprus in 1984, or the recognition of insurgent leaders and institutions as legal incumbents in the case of replacement conflicts, as in the recognition of a new state of Bangladesh following the successful, Indian-assisted secession of 1972.

In a parallel fashion, many actions and strategies by adversaries in classical international regional conflicts can be understood as efforts to redress or preserve an imbalance in legal status by the rival parties. In many such cases, however, the important imbalance concerns the issue not of formal, legal status but of the legal rights underpinning the parties' claims to, or possession of, the resource in dispute. Many protracted regional conflicts typically involve this kind of legal imbalance over territory. One side possesses or controls a territory, and bolsters that possession through some legal right based upon inheritance or uninterrupted and unchallenged enjoyment. The other party challenges that legality by reference to some past enjoyed but presently denied rights (historical allegiance as in the Moroccan claim to the Western Sahara) or to some other, allegedly overriding legal principle (rights to self-determination as in the case of the Åland Islanders or the Ogaden Somalis). Strategies in such conflicts revolve around efforts to have one's own version of favorable legal imbalance accepted in an international court or, if this is too risky, by almost all other powerful governments so that possession of the resources in dispute can either be confirmed (and justifiably defended) or denied (and justifiably altered).

On the other hand, some international regional conflicts exhibit aspects of legal imbalance that involve the existential status of one or other of the immediate adversaries. Claims to Kuwait in the second Gulf war, for example, were couched in terms of the illegal establishment of that state by the British colonialist regime that separated it from its previous "unity" as part of the Ottoman Empire to deny Iraq secure access to the sea, claims countered by arguments regarding the established and accepted existence of Kuwait as a "recognized member of the international community" since 1961.

While every example of a protracted regional conflict is unique, there will likely be a fairly typical "profile" of asymmetries confronting many regional adversaries. For protracted intranational conflicts, it seems probable that many insurgents are likely to find themselves facing very similar negative asymmetries, just as many incumbents are likely to enjoy many similar positive ones. Thus incumbent and insurgent strategies for defending or reversing key asymmetries are likely to be similar from case to case. See table 2.2.

Asymmetry and the Principles of Conflict Reduction

Parties in conflict seldom consider strategies of altering asymmetry as a means of reducing or even resolving conflict. Gaining a better position, for example, is not seen as a move from which to bargain for a cease-fire, negotiate a compromise settlement, or achieve a satisfactory resolution of the conflict. Undermining an adversary's legal positions is a means of winning, not compromising. For this reason alone such continuing efforts—and particularly those that appear imminently successful—will pose problems for third parties seeking to initiate any con-

Table 2.2
Strategies to Maintain or Reverse Key Asymmetries

Dimension		Direction of Asymmetry*	
		Positive (Maintain/Exploit)	Negative (Reduce/Reverse)
Capability			
Coercive Capacity	INC	Keep resource advantage	—
	INS	—	Increase resource base for struggle
External Support	INC	Exclude other parties from further roles	—
	INS	—	Involve other Ps as patrons or as supporters
Access	INC	Maintain own access to key processes; deny INS access	—
	INS	—	Increase own access to relevant political processes
Visibility	INC	Insulate as domestic issue and insist on noninterference	—
	INS	—	Publicize conflict and case; encourage discussion in all public arenas
Cost Experience	INC	Isolate effects of INS costs	—
	INS	—	Increase level of costs suffered by INC and knowledge of these
Survivability	INC	Minimize effects of INS strategy on political legitimacy	—
	INS	—	Insure key leaders and symbols against misfortune/failure
Bargaining Ability	INC	Maintain own negotiating skills/structure; deny to INS	—
	INS	—	Develop negotiating skills/system to offset those of INC
Structure			
Intraparty Cohesion	INC	Maintain own unity but divide and rule INS by cooptation	—
	INS	—	Increase own unity while dividing INC supporters

Dimension		Direction of Asymmetry*	
		Positive (Maintain/Exploit)	*Negative* (Reduce/Reverse)
Leadership Legitimacy	INC	Maintain legitimacy by minimizing disruption	—
	INS	—	Increase own legitimacy by success in the field and undermine that of INC
Leadership (In)-Security	INC	Maintain against threat from within party re strategy against INS	—
	INS	—	Increase by success of efforts and by dealing with intraparty critics
Constituent Mobilization	INC	—	Keep appropriate, nonalarmist level in own followers, and undermine INS
	INS	Maintain high level through success	—
Elite Entrapment	INC	Follow strategies that fulfill public commitments	—
	INS	—	Equalize level of adherence to claims and goals
Commitment			
Goal Salience	INC	—	Keep issues in dispute peripheral
	INS	Increase salience of issues to INC	—
Constituent Commitment	INC	—	Undermine INS morale and commitment; increase own
	INS	Maintain high level of own morale; undermine that of INC	—
External Dependency	INC	—	Maintain own low level of dependency and deal with INS on own terms
	INS	Reduce own dependency on external support	—
Commitment to Change	INC	—	Increase commitment to level needed to undermine INS support

	INS	Maintain own commitment at level needed to optimize support	—
Expectation of Success Through Coercion	INC	Maintain anticipation levels	—
	INS	—	Undermine INC's expectations of early success
Interdependence			
Isolation/ Interdependence	INC	Insulate conflict from others in which INC is engaged	—
	INS	—	Increase interdependence of own conflict with others offering promising models
Parallelism	INC	—	Maintain uniqueness of conflict being pursued
	INS	Emphasize parallels with many "similar" conflicts	—
Historical Justification	INC	—	As above
	INS	As above	—
Legality			
Representativeness	INC	Ensure that recognition of INS leaders is generally denied	—
	INS	—	Obtain general recognition of own leaders
Existence	INC	Ensure existence of INS as legitimate party is in doubt	—
	INC	—	Gain general acceptance of legitimate right of existence
Legitimacy	INC	Maintain own superior legal standing	—
	INS	—	Undermine INC legal standing
Morality			
Existential Accceptance	INC	Ensure that INC denial of INS right to exist continues	—
	INS	—	Obtain recognition of own existence, from INC
Issue Acceptance	INC	Maintain denial of INS case	—

Dimension		Direction of Asymmetry*	
		Positive *(Maintain/Exploit)*	*Negative* *(Reduce/Reverse)*
	INS	—	Obtain acceptance of there being a case to be dealt with from INC
Goal	INC	Maintain denial of legitimacy of INS goals and objectives	—
	INS	—	Gain acceptance of legitimacy own goals and objects
Activity Levels			
Coercion	INC	Maintain or reduce to low levels; deter and control	—
	INS	—	Escalate to new levels

*Typical asymmetries in the early stages of a regional intranational replacement or separatist conflict.

flict reduction or resolution process. These problems may arise from both the structure of asymmetries between the adversaries and from adversaries' efforts to reduce or maintain what are perceived to be key asymmetries.

Adversaries attempt to maintain or increase asymmetries that will increase their chances of winning the conflict and to reverse disadvantageous ones that will prevent this outcome. They are certainly not trying to reduce asymmetries to some point of equality. In contrast, third parties tend to follow strategies to reduce asymmetries to the point where the equality of the adversaries will, it is hoped, lead them to consider the reducing or resolving their conflict. Any third-party strategy based upon a fundamental effort to reduce asymmetry must presuppose that such a reduction will affect the parties' readiness to disengage, to establish some form of "cease-fire," to search for alternative means and options, to talk or negotiate, or to accept third-party help in resolving the conflict. The strategy is based on a simple argument: Equals make peace more readily and more easily than unequals.

In the light of previous arguments about the conflict-generating and maintaining propensities of asymmetries, this assertion should not be surprising. For example, as previously noted, parties in regional conflicts seek to maintain or reverse asymmetries in coercive potential as a means of winning the conflict. On the one hand, an equalization of coercive potential should contribute to the adversaries' realizing that neither is likely to "win" and to their considering ways to reduce and perhaps resolve their conflict. This argument would certainly be congruent with two hypotheses. The first of these is that regional conflict reduction is facilitated by a mutual hurting stalemate and an equalization of both the balance of coercion and the balance of advantage (for example, the situation at the end of the 1973 Middle East war). The second hypothesis is that empowerment of a weaker party (increasing that party's ability to harm its adversary and to withstand the latter's ability to impose harm) is necessary before any genuine search for a settlement proves possible, on the grounds that the stronger party will seldom contemplate the need for anything other than a coerced or imposed "solution" until the weaker poses a realistic threat of countercoercion.

On the other hand, there are counterarguments to the thesis that equality favors conflict reduction. Conflicts are essentially dynamic phenomena. Hence, a previously weaker party's catching up in coercive capacity with its previously stronger rival may lead the former to redouble its efforts to change that balance of capability still further, so that it becomes the stronger and can dictate a settlement; the latter may redouble its efforts to maintain its marginal advantage to avoid being dictated to. In these cases, imminent coercive symmetry may lead to increased rather than reduced conflict, somewhat as outlined by Organski in his theory of "rear-end collision."[5]

Furthermore, there may be no straightforward, linear relationship between relative coercive capacity and the probability of conflict reduction. Very high coercive inequality between parties may lead to avoiding or reducing conflict, on the grounds that the weaker may be more ready to end its efforts at protest and coercion, while the stronger may be willing to consider making a more generous offer to avoid the possibility of trouble later, as in the arrangements worked out in the late 1980s between the Indian government and the Gurkhas and the Mizos. In contrast, very low coercive asymmetry may just as certainly lead to a willingness to consider alternative solutions, as anticipated costs of coercion escalate, levels of violence increase, probabilities of success through coercion recede, and stalemate looms.

These alternative scenarios suggest that, if both great coercive inequality and near equality are likely to produce a frame of mind favorable to conflict reduction by antagonists, a lesser degree of coercive equality is likely to contribute to intractability, as one antagonist strives to maintain or increase a favorable but marginal asymmetry, and the other strives to reduce and reverse it.

An equally complex relationship exists between the likelihood of conflict reduction and other forms of asymmetric structure in a conflict system. For example, high levels of legal asymmetry, where one party's legal status is solid and the other's completely uncertain, may lead to peaceful settlement. An ethnic minority putting forward demands for autonomy, or "home rule," to a set of legally unchallenged and unthreatened political incumbents—such as the German-language community in Italy's South Tirol—is one example. In contrast, high levels of legal symmetry, the parties having no alternative other than to regard each other as equals in status and recognition, might also lead toward conflict reduction and a resolution of the dispute. An example might be the attaching of a Palestinian team to the Jordanian delegation to the November 1991 Madrid talks.

On the other hand, consider the dimension of intraparty cohesion and how different patterns of asymmetry might affect the probability of conflict reduction. Clearly, a common strategy of parties in regional conflicts is to reduce the other side's internal cohesion ("divide and rule," or split off the "moderates" from the "intransigents"), while maintaining its own internal cohesion, thus denying similar opportunities to the adversary ("from unity comes strength"). However, it also clearly seems that, for any conflict reduction or "resolution" not based solely on the probably temporary disintegration of one side, both sides need to be relatively cohesive to agree separately about common goals, some joint terms for a settlement, and then on efforts to begin building new relationship. A major problem for conflict reduction in Mozambique has been the lack of cohesion of Renamo, and a similar problem faced successive Sudanese governments in 1969–72, toward the end of the first Sudanese civil war. This argument suggests that, as far as asymmetry in intraparty cohesion is concerned, both sides have to be cohesive for any conflict reduction to occur. If both are riven with internal factionalism such that agreed-upon demands and a negotiating platform cannot be constructed, the conflict is likely to continue. It is equally likely to continue even if only one side is structurally incoherent. Only when both sides can agree within themselves and organize coherently will any reduction of the conflict be likely, although such a situation can, alternatively, lead to redoubled efforts to achieve a "victory."

A different argument might be put forward about symmetry in commitment to the goals in conflict. If both parties have a similarly low level of commitment to their own goals or if one party is highly committed to a goal which remains a matter of some indifference to the other side, some simple compromise should be available. If both are thoroughly committed to achieving their conflicting goals, however, the chances of conflict reduction and resolution are at their lowest. It appears to be the type and level of asymmetry rather than simply whether the parties are symmetrically or asymmetrically committed to their goals and interests that affects the likelihood that a conflict can be reduced or resolved.

That some equalizations may improve the chances for conflict reduction while others may make it less likely (thus arguing for sometimes increasing rather than reducing asymmetry) leads to a dilemma. In which direction might third parties try to alter the relevant asymmetries between adversaries to improve the likelihood of conflict reduction or resolution? Both the practical and the theoretical dilemma can be illustrated by considering a regional conflict system in which one party is highly cohesive while the other is as incoherently organized as, for example, the internal opposition to President Saddam Hussein within Iraq after the 1991 Gulf War. For a third party facing such an inequality, the theoretical question is whether conflict reduction or resolution can best be aided through greater symmetry by making either the one party more cohesive or the other less cohesive. A priori, it seems unlikely that the conflict reduction will be much advanced by reducing the level of intraparty cohesion for one of the adversaries toward the level of incoherence in the other. Why make it as difficult for one side as for the other to formulate an agreed-upon and coherent set of goals or to ensure that any temporary truce or more permanent settlement is equally difficult to enforce on rival intraparty factions? In this case, clearly, the chances of conflict reduction are likely to be increased by equalizing the internal cohesion of the adversaries at a high level, although, paradoxically, such a strategy will also make it easier for both to throw their organized strength and resources into a quest for victory.

The point of this example is that it is theoretically possible to talk about reducing asymmetry between the adversaries in two quite dissimilar ways, only one of which appears likely to lead toward conflict reduction. Theoretically, at least, symmetry can be achieved either by increasing the internal cohesion of one party until it matches the level of internal cohesion of its rival or by reducing the level of intraparty cohesion of the more integrated adversary until it matches the low level of the first party. In this example, then, it seems reasonable to argue that asymmetry in intraparty cohesion will diminish the likelihood of conflict reduction, but this diminishment will also be a result of a high level of symmetry in which both parties are internally fragmented. Only in the second, symmetric situation, where both are internally cohesive, will conflict reduction be likely. One needs, therefore, to be clear that, as far as the characteristic of intraparty cohesion is concerned, there are two possible types of symmetry, only one of which is likely to lead toward any reduction of the conflict, all other things being equal. Hence whether third parties should try to move an asymmetric relationship to one of greater symmetry to enhance the likelihood of conflict reduction needs to be preceded by asking what type of symmetry is envisaged and whether any move in this direction will lead to conflict reduction rather than exacerbation. See table 2.3.

Third Parties and Conflict Reduction Strategies

Any third party planning to intervene in a protracted regional conflict will need to base a conflict reduction strategy on creating or enhancing either (1) "positive" symmetries, that is, equalities in the conflict system that lead toward reduction and settlement rather than an escalation or exacerbation of the conflict; or (2) "positive" asymmetries, or inequalities that have the same effect.

Both strategies should be founded upon a principle and a similar underlying purpose: to produce a diminished sense of imminent success through existing (usually coercive) tactics by demonstrating (1) a greater willingness to consider alternative courses of action to reduce or resolve the conflict, (2) an increased consciousness of alternative options that might fruitfully be pursued to achieve the parties' basic values and needs, and (3) a sense of there being diminished constraints or obstacles in the pursuit of conflict reduction or resolution for both adversaries.

In many ways this may seem an unusual approach to conflict reduction or resolution. Normally one analyzes differences between such processes by asking questions about third-party aims. Does a particular approach aim at facilitating long-term change, at achieving a temporary cessation of coercion and violence, at controlling or suppressing the behavior of adversaries, at negotiating and then supporting a compromise settlement, or at finding a solution to the issues in conflict? Alternatively, one asks about the methods themselves. Do different approaches involve various forms of diplomatic leverage? The overt or covert threat of third-party coercion? The insistence that adversaries conform to and use existing norms, rules, principles, or legal systems? The provision of additional resources that make the construction of compromise settlements palatable to adversaries? The careful and difficult analysis of interests and alternatives? The creation of new options or alternatives that might lead to a durable solution?

These are all legitimate ways of understanding conflict reduction

Table 2.3

Types of Symmetry in Protracted Regional Conflict

Dimension	Asymmetric	Symmetric/Low	Symmetric/High
Coercive Capacity	P1 greater than P2	Both low capacity	Both high capacity
External Support	P1 has high and general support; P2 has none	Both have no external support	Both have substantial external support
Access	P1 has open and continuous access to key decision-making processes	Neither has easy access to key decision-making processes	Both have open and continuous access
Visibility	P1 has high visibility in internal and international arenas	Neither has any significant visibility	Both highly visible in domestic and international arenas
Cost Experience	P1 suffering no/low costs. P2 suffering high costs	Neither party suffering high or salient costs	Both parties suffering high costs
Survivability	P1 faces no threat to its existence; P2 seriously threatened	Neither party vulnerable to current threats	Both are vulnerable to current threats
Bargaining Ability	P1 has full range of skills and institutions to negotiate	Neither party has requisite range of skills or institutions	Both parties possess range of skills and institutions
Intraparty Cohesion	P1 united; P2 contains many salient splits and divisions	Both parties contain many salient splits and divisions	Neither party contains significant cleavages
Leadership Legitimacy	No doubts about legitimacy of P1 leaders; P2 elites have no accepted or legitimate base	Neither elite is generally accepted as legitimate	Both elites' legitimacy is widely accepted
Leadership Security	No challenge to leaders in P1; significant challenge in P2	Both leaderships under serious internal threat	Neither set of leaders under significant challenge
Constituent Mobilization	P1 has major involvement of followers; P2 has only limited involvement	Neither party has significant involvement of followers	Both have high involvement of rank and file followers

Dimension	Asymmetric	Symmetric/Low	Symmetric/High
Elite Entrapment	P1 leaders are solidly trapped in present aims and strategies; P2 leaders have flexibility	Both parties have significant freedom of action and flexibility	Both sets of leaders are trapped in current aims and strategies
Goal Salience	P1's goals are of key salience; P2's are only peripheral	Neither parties' goals are highly salient	Both parties' goals are of high salience
Constituent Commitment	P1 has high rank and file support; P2 has little such support	Neither party has high level of rank and file support for its goals	Both parties have high support for its goals among followers
External Dependency	P1 is highly reliant on external aid; P2 is self-supporting	Both parties have low dependency on external aid and support	Both parties are highly dependent on external aid and support
Commitment to Change	P1 is highly committed to status quo; P2 is committed to major change	Neither party seeks significant change to status quo	Both parties seek major change to the status quo.
Expectation of Success	P1 has high expectation of success through present policy; P2 has low expectations	Neither party has high level of expectation of success through present policies	Both parties have high expectations of success through its policies
Isolation/ Interdependence	P1 is involved in sole dispute; P2 in many	Neither party is involved in other disputes	Both involved in many other disputes
Parallelism	Conflict involves many precedents for P1; none for P2	No precedents clearly involved for either party	Many salient precedents are involved for both parties
Historical Justification	Significant historical precedents for P1; none for P2	No historical precedents are involved for either party	Both parties have salient historical precedents involved
Representativeness	P1 leaders are widely accepted and recognized; P2's are not	Neither set of leaders accepted generally	Both sets of leaders are widely recognized

Existence	P1 widely recognized as a legitimate party; P2 is not	Neither party generally recognized or accepted	Both parties given general and wide recognition and acceptance
Legitimacy	P1 right to its case generally recognized; P2's is not	Neither parties' right to make case or claims widely recognized	Both parties' right to make case/claims is widely recognized
Existential Acceptance	P1 accepts P2's right of existence, but not vice versa	Neither party accepts other's right of existence	Both parties recognize the other's right of existence
Issue Acceptance	P1 recognizes P2's right to have and make a case, but not vice versa	Neither party recognizes the other's right to have/make its case	Both parties recognize the other's right to have/make its case
Goal Acceptance	P1 accepts P2's goals as legitimate	Neither party accepts other's goals as legitimate	Both parties accept the other's goals as legitimate
Coercion	P1 using high levels of coercion; P2 low levels	Neither party using high levels of coercion	Both parties using high levels of coercion

strategies that indicate how third-party intervention might most productively affect relevant asymmetries and symmetries within the conflict system, to produce a greater probability of conflict reduction and resolution. However, examining some of them in more detail does raise questions about a previous central, if tentative, assumption that, because adversaries' strategies in protracted regional conflicts involve the maintenance or reversal of asymmetries, it is axiomatically the case that conflict reduction strategies should also aim at achieving symmetry on key dimensions. Already it appears clear that although some forms of equalization strategy are likely to lead toward conflict reduction, others are likely to lead toward conflict escalation. Each dimension needs to be treated individually and on its merits.

For example, high symmetric internal cohesion appears to be favorable to third-party efforts at mediation, while high, equal legal status seems propitious for adjudication, arbitration, or negotiation. Similarly, equalization through a general recognition of one party's claims might push a previously legally advantaged party toward recognizing the desirability of an attempt to treat with a previously ignored or discounted rival. Hence, a third-party strategy of affording some recognition to one party to a regional intrastate conflict (perhaps merely as "insurgents" or "co-belligerents") might enable the two sides to treat with each other more easily. Again, in the case of coercive capacity, it might prove that the best conflict reduction strategy should aim at reducing the level of superior coercive capability of the dominant party to somewhere near the level of its weaker rival, positing that the achievement of symmetry of coercive capability, but at a much lower level, might confront both parties with the prospect of costly stalemate and thus the inducement to consider alternative ways of coping with their conflict and with each other.

Similarly, should both parties be highly committed to their goals, one third-party strategy might be to reduce the commitment of both to a lower but still symmetric level. In contrast, in a situation involving commitment asymmetry, efforts might well be made to lower the commitment level of the more committed party, thus equalizing commitment of both at a lower level and paving the way for a negotiated settlement. In another example, conflict reduction strategies might be an attempt to influence the extent to which the leaders of the adversaries have entrapped themselves in the pursuit of goals through limited means. If both sets of leaders have, by reiterated public statements, by the commitment of substantial resources, and by tying their prestige and survival to success and "victory" thoroughly entrapped themselves into the continuation of coercive, win-lose policies, it might be possible to lower the level of entrapment for both sets of leaders simultaneously to the stage where both have a greater degree of freedom to change existing policies. Theory suggests that symmetry at a low level of entrapment may offer the best chance of conflict reduction.

In complete contrast, it might be easier and just as productive to reduce the commitment level of only one side, perhaps by providing that party with alternatives, thus increasing the asymmetry of commitment and enabling the now less-committed party to make now less-valued concessions to the more committed. Should such asymmetry of commitment be achieved, at least one side will be enabled to consider conflict reduction moves and this, in itself, may reduce the level of entrapment of its rivals. All examples presented so far suggest that there may be no simple relationship between symmetric conflict structure and probable conflict reduction, but a multiplicity of strategies for third parties seeking to reduce any of the four types of regional conflicts.

Modalities of Regional Conflict Reduction and Resolution

If protracted regional conflicts are to be reduced or resolved, a wide variety of potential tasks, roles, or functions for third parties (and, whenever possible, for the parties themselves) exists, aimed at bringing about appropriate conditions of both symmetry and asymmetry in the conflict system such that they move the conflicting parties toward deescalation and termination. These functions go well beyond those of mediation, conciliation, and good offices, which have, conventionally, been the main tasks for third parties trying to ameliorate conflicts in their or other regions.[6]

Note that this argument does not say that the bringing about of one or other "optimum" patterns of symmetric or asymmetric relationships between adversaries is sufficient to ensure the major reduction of a protracted regional conflict but merely that there are likely to be key dimensions where the "right" level of symmetry or asymmetry has to be achieved before any conflict reduction is likely. These dimensions might be regarded as providing both the necessary conditions for conflict reduction and, by implication, an outline of required third-party strategies if such necessary conditions are to be achieved or even approximated.

Conventional thinking holds that one such key dimension would be that of coercive capability, on the grounds that only after parties have achieved a "hurting stalemate," or equivalent capacity for imposing costs on each other, will their leaders be ready to contemplate a reduction of conflict and some search for an alternative relationship or a resolution. The key condition conducive to conflict reduction thus appears to be cost symmetry. A second attribute dimension of a regional conflict system on which symmetry seems to be a necessary condition for major conflict reduction is that of intraparty cohesion at a high level. Third, for major conflict reduction to take place it seems necessary for both parties to be in a situation where there is no major threat to either leadership such that both are thoroughly inhibited from even contemplating conflict reduction initiatives. Leadership security has to be as high in one party as in the other and, if it is not, then one function for a third party is to diminish the level of leadership insecurity in the party scoring high on this attribute. Whether this is done by building up domestic support for the leadership or undermining and replacing it is an interesting theoretical conundrum as well as a practical nightmare for third-party strategists.

Beyond these three aspects of conflict system structure, other dimensions also seem important in determining whether parties move toward conflict reduction or escalation. See table 2.4.

Table 2.4
Necessary Conditions for Regional Conflict Reduction

Dimension	Third-Party Dilemmas: Exacerbating Structures and Relationships	Third-Party Objectives: Conditions Conducive to Conflict Reduction
Coercive Ability	One party has a major advantage in coercive ability	→ Both parties have an equal ability to harm and coerce each other
Intraparty Cohesion	Both parties face major internal divisions	→ Both parties are internally unified
Leadership Insecurity Unchallenged	Both parties are experiencing major challenges to the existing leaders	→ Both parties have a secure leadership
External Dependency	Both parties are highly dependent on external patrons who pursue their own interests in a proxy conflict	→ Neither party is significantly dependent on external patrons or allies
Goal Salience	Both regard goals in conflict as essential and nonnegotiable	→ At least one party regards goals as nonessential, implying alternatives and thus as compromisable
Elite Entrapment	Both sets of leaders have been trapped for some time in current goal commitments and strategies	→ Neither set of leaders is entrapped in issues or strategies by their past
Acceptance	Neither party accepts other's right to exist nor leadership's right to represent	→ Both parties accept other's right to exist and the leadership's right to represent

Two groups of questions now arise about the seven key dimensions outlined in table 2.4. For example, in the case of parties' coercive capability, (1) should a third party's objective be to reduce both sides' coercive capability to a low level of equality that unambiguously indicates equal impotence to coerce the other side into surrender? Or should it be to equalize the adversaries at a level from which both can impose major harm on each other without prospect of final success? Is the important factor the level of hurt from some stalemate or the remoteness of any prospective success? (2) How might outside third parties practically equalize coercive capability of adversaries at the desired level? It is seldom that parties outside protracted regional conflict are in the position of the U.S. government at the end of the 1973 October War in the Middle East, and can follow the strategy of equalizing by halting a conflict in a virtually unbearable stalemate in which both sides have equal ability to continue to harm the other. More likely, opportunities will exist for third parties to equalize adversaries' coercive capacities at low or, at least, lower, levels, by affecting arms supplies, credits for military purchases, training facilities, replacements, and all the other items used by parties in conflict to coerce each other into a more reasonable frame of mind.

An alternative strategy for reducing adversaries' capacity to harm each other to an equality of impotence is to emplace a peacekeeping force between them to act as an insulator. Although this might do little, in and of itself, to reduce adversaries' relative capacity to inflict future harm, it can nullify a major imbalance for a time, at least temporarily producing a balanced, symmetric incapacity to do further material harm to each other. Not unnaturally, such a strategy is likely to be fiercely resisted by the party enjoying the advantages of any existing asymmetry.

The argument for reducing coercive capacity provides a flavor of how difficult a reduction strategy for regional conflict is likely to be in practical terms. The principle of trying to achieve an equally low level of capability of harming each other conducive to conflict reduction is easy to enunciate. However, the practical difficulties of reducing both adversaries to even a rough low level of equality in coercive capacity are likely to be profound, given a new world order where the instruments of coercion will still not be easy to obtain, where regional and global patrons and supporters are likely to remain easily available even with the ending of cold war rivalries, and where arms quarantines are still likely to be difficult to organize and sustain. For example, it seems clear that even the Soviet withdrawal of itself and its armed support for the government of Afghanistan in Kabul and the lowering of official U.S. government support for the coercive capabilities of the various mujahid insurgent groups did not reduce the adversaries' coercive capability, which was kept up from other sources and which was certainly not equalized to a level that moved that system toward conflict reduction and resolution (save in the simplest sense of relatively reduced violence).

Similar theoretical and practical problems attend conflict reduction strategies that address symmetries and asymmetries of other key conflict system attributes, although some appear theoretically less ambiguous than others. For example, for the second key dimension in table 2.4, intraparty cohesion, it would clearly seem to be conflict exacerbating if both parties suffered from major internal divisions or if one party was united and the other was highly divided. In this case, an initial theoretical proposition would argue that both parties would need to have a high degree of internal cohesion for conflict reduction to be initiated with much hope of success. However, the practical problems for third parties seeking to bring about this conducive condition remain significant. Tactically, how might outsiders go about unifying divided (or even incoherently articulated) parties as a step toward creating conditions that encourage conflict reduction? Aid to only one faction, thus encouraging others to merge with it? Undermining of support for other factions from other external patrons? Intraparty conflict resolution efforts, bearing in mind the possibility that newfound unity might be channeled into renewed coercive efforts and the conflict thus exacerbated? With this and other dimensions, the tactical dilemma is real. Efforts to reduce and resolve the conflict in Afghanistan have broken down on the inability of outside third parties to resolve differences between the various factions in the anti-Kabul alliance and attain even the minimal level of cohesion exhibited by the Kabul government.

Similar arguments can be advanced for the other dimensions that influence the likely success of conflict reduction. If third parties are attempting to produce conditions conducive to conflict reduction, one of their functions will surely necessitate a review of the relative levels of leadership insecurity within the parties involved. Where one or both leaderships are facing a major internal challenge, it is unlikely that either will be in any position to run the undeniable risk of seeking an arrangement with their external adversary, secure leaderships being necessary for any successful peacemaking. Should third parties therefore follow tactics of shoring up existing leaderships by helping them undermine internal challenges, thus fulfilling the function of freeing them from constraints in choosing a course of action leading toward reducing their primary, external conflict? Or is the function of a third party to wait until the intraparty conflicts have resolved themselves and a new and secure leadership is in place in both adversaries? Or should a third party assist in removing insecure leaderships and their replacement by more popular and unthreatened leaders, in the belief that these leaders are more likely to contemplate peace? All such tactics involve an effort to increase the likelihood of conflict reduction and resolution through achieving a symmetrical relationship of high leadership security, but the implications for third-party tactics are profoundly different.

The same sort of dilemma arises in the case of external dependency. One obvious third-party strategy in cases of high external dependence of adversaries is to reduce that dependence by disentangling the interests and activities of the external patron from those of the primarily regional adversaries. This was successfully accomplished in the case of the civil war in Afghanistan, where both parties were highly dependent on external support, and in Ethiopia-Eritrea, where only one party was so dependent. However, there are equally plausible arguments to the effect that third parties seeking to construct conditions conducive to conflict reduction could use the leverage of the adversaries' patrons to bring about a readiness to contemplate deescalation and a settlement. Hence the focus of activity shifts from the parties themselves to the interests of their patrons and their patrons' willingness to seek alternative means of fulfilling these and then to put pressure on their clients to contemplate some conflict termination. An example of using patrons' leverage to pressure parties toward formal negotiation can be found in the role of the Front Line States in the 1979 Zimbabwe settlement, when the interests of all the supporters of the Patriotic Front (Mozambique, Tanzania, and Zambia) had become focused on reducing their own continuing material and political costs through a negotiated settlement.

Goal salience seems slightly less ambiguous, given that it is the very importance and nonnegotiability of the issues in conflict that underpins parties' unwillingness to consider conflict reduction. Hence the equally high salience of goals and objectives is usually a major conflict-maintaining factor. Theoretically, one function of third parties is to reduce the salience of goals to the parties, by suggesting viable alternatives or substitutes or by suggesting alternative means of attaining underlying interests, values, and needs.[7] Practically, as usual, this is easier said than done. Attempting to achieve such an objective for both adversaries appears overly ambitious, even if not impossible. Tactically, then, the task for third parties would seem to be to try to create an asymmetry of issue salience in the conflict system, which could then result in a willingness of one party to seek a settlement by compromising on goals no longer perceived to be as salient as they once were. U.S. guarantees of oil supplies to Israel in the 1970s may have made the goal of retaining the Red Sea oil fields at Abu Rudays much less salient to the Israeli government simply by fulfilling the need for energy security through alternative sources. Other situations are unlikely to be so simply transformed by offering alternative sources of material goods, however, and the problem of how to reduce a party's goal salience when those very goals are important enough to fight over in the first place requires much more theoretical analysis and subsequent subtlety in third-party practice. The unfolding settlement of the conflict between the Spanish government and the Basque community in northern Spain, through a gradual but increasing transfer of real autonomy to the Basques and their discovery that underlying interests can be met by means other than total secession, indicates that such changes in goal salience are not completely beyond the bounds of possibility.

Our two final key dimensions appear to offer similar tactical challenges to third parties seeking conflict reduction. Clearly, a situation in which both sets of leaders are the victims of entrapment, brought about by the very costs suffered throughout the conflict and the level of public commitment to success through coercion is unlikely to lead toward conflict reduction unless third parties can arrange to move that situation toward a symmetric relationship of low entrapment for both parties. The need here is for third-party strategies that permit and assist decommitment by parties and their leaders, that offer new situations in which old commitments can be abandoned, and that permit leaders to scramble out of the political nets in which they are jointly enmeshed. A symmetrical low level of elite entrapment must somehow be sought as a prelude to conflict reduction. Similarly, a situation where one party fails to accept either the existence of its adversary or the legitimacy of the others' leaders in any representative role is unlikely to lead toward the reduction of any conflict. Third-party functions here might involve the equalization of acceptance by the adversaries as a prelude to the introduction of conflict reduction that can take place between (roughly) equivalent entities, and that avoid the use of such processes themselves to undermine the position of the other side. Once again, the third party is confronted with the task of devising tactics that lead toward a symmetrically high level of acceptance as a necessary precondition for conflict reduction.

Tables 2.5 and 2.6 invite further discussion about the seven key attribute dimensions of regional conflict systems.

Two final points need to be made about table 2.6 and its predecessors, and about the general argument that third parties have a wide variety of roles and functions to perform in creating conditions conducive to the reducing or ultimately resolving protracted regional conflicts. First, the hypothesis of symmetry rather than asymmetry appears to be generally supported. There might well be validity in the first argument considered in this chapter that, although adversaries tend to follow strategies of maintaining or reversing asymmetries to impose a settlement, third parties might well attempt to move relationships toward symmetry to create conditions conducive to conflict reduction and, ultimately, resolution. There are exceptions to this, as in the case of issue salience for reasons of practicality or constituent commitment for reasons of principle. Nonetheless, the general pattern that emerges does suggest that, as far as most dimensions are concerned, equalizing adversaries

Table 2.5

Third Parties and Regional Conflict Reduction
Principles, Strategies, and Roles

Dimension	Principle	Conflict Reducing Strategies	Role or Function
Coercive Capacity	High Symmetry (Equal ability to harm)	Control availability and use of coercive instruments	EQUALIZER INSULATOR
OR	Low Symmetry (Equally low prospect of victory through coercion)	Control availability and use of coercive instruments	INSULATOR
Intraparty Cohesion	High Symmetry (Equal ability to agree goals and de-escalation strategies)	Assist disunited parties toward great coherence in organization and on issues in conflict	UNIFIER
Leadership Insecurity	Low Symmetry (Equal sense of security and freedom of action)	Assist in reducing leaders' sense of internal threat in both parties, especially that resulting from moves toward conflict reduction	REASSURER
External Dependency	Low Symmetry (Equal lack of support and interference from outside)	Disengage external patrons from conflict or use patron's influence to move toward conflict reduction	DECOUPLER
Goal Salience	Asymmetry (Differential ability to make/ exchange concessions and sacrifices)	Explore new and innovative solutions; provide parties with opportunity to exchange differently valued concessions; provide side payments to offset loss through concessions	REFRAMER INFORMER UNDERWRITER
Elite Entrapment	Low Symmetry (Equal lack of unbreakable commitments to victory through coercion)	Develop de-committing formulas; provide leaders with means of escaping hampering commitments; provide leaders with chance to consider mutually supporting "releases"	REFRAMER RELEASER FACILITATOR
Acceptance	High Symmetry (Equal recognition of other party and leadership)	Provide channels and forums for discussions that avoid issues of formal recognition; recognize parties in ways that do not undermine one another's public status	FACILITATOR LEGITIMIZER

Table 2.6
Further Third-Party Principles, Strategies, and Roles

Dimension	Principle	Conflict-Reducing Strategies	Third-Party Role or Function
Isolation	High Symmetry (Equally low connection of parties to other disputes)	Increase the level of isolation of conflict from others and distinguish between issues and principles involved	DECOUPLER INSULATOR
Constituent Commitment	Asymmetry (Differential value placed on issues in dispute)	Alter relative levels of followers' goal commitment and issue salience	REFRAMER INFORMER
Expectation of Success	Low Symmetry (Equal lack of belief in victory by current strategies)	Decrease level by providing leaders with opportunities to "reality check" on other's abilities, determination, etc.	REFRAMER FACILITATOR
Cost Experience	High Symmetry (Equal and widely shared knowledge of material and other costs)	Increase awareness of present and likely future level of costs concomitant on policy of seeking goals through strategy of coercion	REFRAMER
Visibility	High Symmetry (Both parties' cause and case well understood by key outside parties)	Increase outside awareness/ understanding of less-visible party's aims, support base, etc.	REFRAMER PUBLICIZER
Survivability	High Symmetry (Equally low existential threat to both parties)	Help to decrease level of vulnerability to final destruction of parties and convey durability to other	PUBLICIZER
Bargaining Ability	High Symmetry (Equal level of confidence in ability to negotiate with any adversary)	Increase range of skills available to party with weaker ability thus ending fear of engaging in noncoercive strategy	TECHNICIAN

is more likely to lead toward reducing conflict than escalating it. Equal parties are more likely to engage in terminating conflict than are unequal parties.

Second, a query arises from the sheer number and variety of tasks that this "conflict system structure" approach implies: Is there any single institution that might be able to carry out all (or indeed many) of the third-party functions deemed important (or even desirable) to reduce protracted regional conflicts? The list of third-party functions implied by the approach is long and varied. Accepting that it will need a variety of third parties even to begin to fulfill crucial roles and to carry out important functions, what types of institution and organization (local, regional, or global) might be available to undertake any of the functions discussed above, and thus contribute to creating conditions conducive to regional conflict reduction and then to conflict resolution?

Conclusion

The argument up to now has been that it is more fruitful to use overall conflict reduction as a focus rather than more traditional approaches focusing either on those organizations that act as third parties, usually as peacekeepers, fact finders, or mediators, or on initiatives or episodes of peacemaking. There are many intellectual advantages in taking conflict reduction as the analytical focus of attempts to understand how some regional conflicts end while others protract and endure. Using such an analytical starting point enables analysis to encompass all the varied tasks, strategies, and functions that might contribute to reducing and eventually resolving the various types of regional conflicts. This is particularly so with those strategies not normally associated with traditional "peacemaking," such as uncoupling, insulating, or reframing, and those, such as underwriting or endorsing, which are usually neglected in traditional studies of mediation practice and involve helping build a new relationship between previous adversaries in the aftermath of any negotiated, mediated, or facilitated agreement.[8]

Given this broad conception of conflict reduction involving many tasks, functions, and roles, the idea of a "third party" becomes much broader than in traditional analyses. Many agencies or institutions are able to contribute to complex reduction and resolution processes. Therefore, the range and variety of "appropriate" resources becomes greater and within reach of institutions and agencies quite unable to fulfill the requirements for the narrow band of traditionally conceived "peacemakers." A regional research center or a conference could, in this framework, contribute new ideas and alternatives to the process, thus undertaking a strategy of reframing. A regionally respected but globally organized religious organization could perform a strategy of endorsing either the start-up of some negotiation between adversaries, or of any conflict-reduction agreement. A business consortium could perform the strategy of inducing by providing the possibility of resources at some appropriate stage of termination. A regional intergovernmental organization could follow a legitimizing strategy by recognizing—at some level short of "full" diplomatic recognition—the right of insurgent leaders to represent their people on limited occasions or in political arenas. In a more familiar manner, a coalition of regional governments could organize and enforce an arms embargo on adversaries, thus acting as an equalizer, preliminary to others enacting the role of intermediary.

Viewed within this broad framework, it is not the case that many regions of the world lack institutions or organizations able to undertake one or other key role as third-party conflict reducers or resolvers. It is true that, if one takes a conventional view that successful third-party conflict reduction essentially involves powerful peacekeeping forces, mediators with leverage and vast resources, and solutions kept in place by sanctions, the paucity of potential conflict reducers in certain regions of the world—sub-Saharan Africa, south or Southeast Asia, the Middle East—leads inevitably to the idea that only "global" powers in a new world order have any potential as successful conflict reducers or resolvers. In contrast, a conflict-termination process model suggests that, while a limited range of roles may be beyond local or regional actors, there remains a vast range of necessary and useful tasks that can be undertaken by a variety of agencies that are not necessarily global in scope nor resource-rich, and also that local or regional bodies can become effectively involved in termination, even enacting some of the central roles discussed above. (For example, endorsing, contributing to, or manning a peacekeeping force; brokering development schemes that provide alternative ways of fulfilling the interests and needs of one party to a conflict; or participating in global efforts to control the flow of arms to adversaries and thus equalizing their capacity to inflict mutual harm.)

Thus for any protracted regional conflict there are likely to be many potential conflict reducers or resolvers who can contribute to the forwarding of conflict reduction by pursuing important strategies that contribute to producing necessary conditions for acceptable and self-sustaining solutions. Such third parties can operate on all levels, depending upon their appropriateness for fulfilling a role and the availability of other potential third parties possessing similar resources. An effective system of regional conflict reduction can involve third parties from a variety of levels who work together to produce appropriate conditions for conflict resolution to begin. These levels are:

1. Global, involving international organizations, such as the United Nations secretariat and the International Court of Justice; governments with global interests and reach which operate in concert and within the United Nations and the Organization on Security and Cooperation in Europe (OSCE); and also the International Committee of the Red Cross (ICRC), the World Council of Churches, Oxfam, the International Negotiation Network, and even the International Society for Political Psychology.

2. Regional organizations such as the Organization of African Unity (OAU), the Arab League, or the Association of South East Asian Nations (ASEAN); governments with a mediating vocation, such as Algeria, Togo, or Uruguay; regional nongovernmental organizations, such as the All-Africa Council of Churches; and subregional cooperative organizations of contiguous countries, such as the Economic Community of West African States (ECOWAS), the Southern African Development Community (SADC), the Front Line States, the Contadora Group; and bilateral trading and business organizations, such as Cooperation North in Ireland or the joint Chambers of Commerce on Cyprus.

3. Internal organizations, which can follow a surprisingly wide range of conflict reduction strategies in helping bring about the necessary conditions for the start of a conflict reduction process. The activity of some local government bodies in Northern Ireland in creating violence-free zones or of church leaders within El Salvador in assisting the local peace process are examples.

With all these sources potentially available to contribute toward conflict termination, a first theoretical task is that of suggesting some match between available institutions on the three levels and the conflict-reducing strategies they might successfully pursue. Which, for example, of the seven necessary strategies and functions might particular types of third parties from the various levels best undertake? Evidence for suggesting relations between potential actors and particular roles, functions, and strategies is anecdotal at best and speculative at worst. A start might be made simply by listing organizations that have, in the past, made some useful contribution to regional conflict reduction processes and then by analyzing the nature of that contribution.

A word of warning is necessary at this stage, however. Although in theory the range of third parties potentially available to forward conflict reduction in any regional conflict might be large, in practice regional conflict reducers might prove to be rather thin on the ground in some regions of the world. This adds some force to familiar arguments about the paucity of local or regional peacemakers and the need for global action. However, although it might be that some regions lack a conflict-reduction ability over the whole range of possible conflict-reducing strategies, it is equally so that (1) all regions possess much ability for fulfilling many of the key roles that contribute to successful conflict termination; (2) where important regional abilities are lacking, they can be developed, particularly for the roles and tasks that do not require massive material resources; and (3) even when lacking regionally, abilities could be "borrowed" from outside the region and combined into some overall regional process for reducing or resolving protracted conflicts.

For all these reasons, one should never assume that there exists little or no conflict-reducing potential in regions or localities where protracted intranational, transnational, or international conflicts take place. Nor is it the case that the only solution to the undeniable plethora of such conflicts currently occurring is some globally based new world order, in which the responsibility for "maintaining the peace" and reducing regional conflicts lies with a few governments with the leverage and resources that enable them to enact a narrow range of traditional conflict-reducing roles, too often amounting to suppressing the overt manifestations of the conflict, enforcing settlements with leverage or undertaking mediation with muscle, or with bankbook.

In the broader conflict termination framework suggested here, the tasks of creating the necessary conditions for conflict reduction by working on the conflict-exacerbating asymmetries that typify protracted regional conflicts are undoubtedly complex and difficult. However, I would argue that the framework discussed in this chapter, by acknowledging the major complexities of protracted regional conflicts and by emphasizing the customary asymmetric structure of such conflict systems, usefully underlines the need to deal with all aspects of these complex structures in any successful effort to reduce and ultimately resolve them. With such complicated structures and complex termination processes, moreover, it is clear that there are a large number of essential roles to be enacted. A central task for any theoretical analysis is to develop a clear understanding of how, at what stage of the conflict, in what sequence, and by whom such roles can be enacted in order to create the conditions for more than a temporary reduction of the conflict.

Notes

1. "Power imbalance" is a concept that becomes difficult to operationalize in any unidimensional form when analysed in detail.

2. Those familiar with the writings of Roger Fisher and Bill Ury will note that this idea derives from their conception of a negotiator's strength being enhanced by (or largely deriving from) having an acceptable BATNA (Best Alternative To No Agreement). As Jeffrey Davidow points out in his study of the triangular negotiations to end the Rhodesia-Zimbabwe conflict held at Lancaster House in 1980, both the British conveners and Bishop Muzorewa's delegation had a great advantage denied the Patriotic Front delegation, in that the former would both have been relatively content with a "second class solution" (the recognition of the existing Muzorewa Government even at the risk of a continuing guerrilla war), an "alternative to no agreement" that would have been highly unsatisfactory to the PF delegation. This form of asymmetry among the parties had a significant effect upon the course and outcome of the negotiations and the eventual termination of the conflict. See Jeffrey Davidow, *A Peace In Southern Africa* (Boulder, Colo., Westview, 1984).

3. Treating various forms of asymmetry as *emergent properties* of the conflict system itself, rather than as properties of the subsystems (the parties) whose interactions make up that system, becomes a useful device for categorizing and comparing conflict systems in a variety of ways.

Conflict systems can be asymmetric in a wide variety of fashions, depending upon the attribute of the system which is under analysis. It is undoubtedly the case that we are unlikely ever to discover a perfectly symmetric conflict system, given the virtually infinite number of ways in which parties in conflict might differ from one another. The important analytical task is to elucidate those attributes that are highly influential in shaping the course of a conflict and its outcome, and to determine the differences resulting from symmetric or asymmetric distribution of such attributes and their impact on the likely course and outcome of the conflict.

4. I discussed this dimension as *relational* asymmetry in a previous paper on types of asymmetry. See C. R. Mitchell, "Classifying Conflicts: Asymmetry and Resolution," *Annals of the American Association of Political and Social Science* 518 (Nov. 1991): 23–38.

5. See A. F. K. Organski, *World Politics* (New York, Alfred Knopf, 1958).

6. See my essay "Motives for Mediation" for another view of the range of roles open to third parties confronted with a violent regional conflict or a volatile and unstable situation involving regional adversaries. In C. R. Mitchell and K. Webb, eds. *New Approaches to International Mediation* (Westport, Conn.; Greenwood, 1989).

7. The central purpose of many of the formal and unofficial interventions using "problem solving workshops" is to provide conflicting parties with an opportunity to examine (and possibly modify) their range of objectives by analysing their underlying interests, the available means to achieve these, and alternative, creative options that might increase the latter.

8. As Mark Katz suggests elsewhere in this volume, an important third party role may frequently involve arranging elections or plebiscites to endorse a compromise solution, or to signify that the original conflict will henceforth be conducted within institutionalized rules and procedures.

PART TWO

Sources and Interests

3

National Interests and Conflict Reduction

VADIM UDALOV

Interest usually appears at the forefront of politics during periods of major turbulence in foreign policy. Such was the case, for example, in the United States in the post-Vietnam–pre-détente period. It is happening in the Russian confederation as the leadership and members of the academic community call for the pursuit of the "true," not imaginary, interests of new sovereign units. Curiously, the discussion about the essence of, and criteria for, determining foreign policy interests has again spread to the United States. The problems confronting Washington because of the changes in the Soviet Union, Eastern and Western Europe, and the Middle East have aroused a renewed concern for some reliable foreign policy landmarks, and again the search turns to the appropriate meanings of *interest*.[1]

A general feature of all these discussions is the failure to agree on the formulations of foreign policy interests. Underneath this argument lies the absence of common criteria, and still deeper lies a lack of agreement about the very nature of interest as a category.

This chapter attempts to clarify some theoretical parameters of interest in foreign policy, and then to apply these conceptualizations to the problems of conflict reduction.

Much of this research was done at the United States Institute of Peace, where the author spent March through August 1991 as a Visiting Fellow. He would like to express his gratitude to the institute for providing this opportunity.

Interest in Policy-making

There is a striking terminological confusion surrounding the idea of interest. "Needs," "requirements," "ends," "goals," "objectives," "aspirations," "preferences," "aims," "values"—all these terms are often used interchangeably with "interests." Even in such a comparatively "honed" document as President Bush's report on the national security strategy of the United States are several cases when one and the same element of the strategy is called "interest" in one place, "goal" in another, and "objective" in still a third.[2] On the other hand, President Clinton's foreign policy statement to the U.N. General Assembly on 27 September 1994 contained no reference to "interests" at all, but referred to different types of new world values.

All this confusion occurs, so to speak, within one language—English. If one takes into account that other languages—Russian, for instance—would have a different system of terms with different sets of connotations, there is no wonder that any international discussion about "interests" would resemble a conversation among the deaf. As diplomatic intercourse between the two countries, both in official and especially semiofficial, track-two setting, becomes increasingly focused on deep-rooted motivations—usually referred to as interests—this ambiguity can seriously hamper mutual understanding.

American scholars have put forward quite a few arrangements of this variety of terms into some logical order. One of the recent approaches is structured upon *needs,* which are claimed to be fundamental, objectively determined, and nonnegotiable reasons for human behavior on all levels, from individual to international.[3] Picking out a limited assortment of basic human needs, such as survival, security, and identity, this approach reduces all of decision making to satisfying these needs but in no way explains the dynamics of this process. Some independent role is allotted to values, though without specifying the relationship of values to needs. As for interests as part of determining a course of action, they hardly receive any attention.

Another branch of research, on the contrary, considers interest a basic element of motivation. In the opinion of most specialists in psychology and the theory of negotiations, interests "tend to be central to people's thinking and action, forming the core of many other attitudes, goals and intentions."[4] Both needs and values are viewed as simply different labels for interests. The main distinction is seen to be between what people "care about or want" (i.e., interests), on the one hand, and what "they *say* they want" (positions), on the other.[5]

In the Soviet tradition that Russia has inherited, interest has been treated as a key element in the formation of foreign policy, but not a singular one. It constitutes only one of the many links in the chain of political decisions. This chain includes what can be expressed in English as *requirements, interests, objectives, and actions*. Requirements (akin to needs) are the starting point in forming a policy, their satisfaction being the driving force behind it. They are directly rooted in the objective realities constituting the state's environment. Interests are defined as derivatives of requirements, a result of their recognition.[6] Requirements, as part of objective reality, participate in policy making only by being converted into interests, that is, in a subjectivized form. Thus, interest as an element of policy making is on the boundary between objective reality and its subjective reflection in the consciousness of decision makers. As for objectives and actions, their choice is based on interests on the consecutive stages in this process.

However, on closer inspection, this system, though seemingly flawless from the epistemological point of view, turns out to be not very helpful in practical terms. According to it, to determine an interest, it is necessary first to formulate the underlying requirement, but what one gets when such a formulation is given is not just a requirement but a recognized requirement, which means an interest. Whatever formulation would be proposed, it begins to exist and activate the policy already as an interest.

As one of the leading Soviet theorists of international relations, E. A. Pozdnyakov, noted, "The recognition may be either true or false, correct or mistaken. . . . history knows of many instances when states often become participants of such events, which, as becomes evident later, contradict their true interests. But this can be determined with sufficient clarity only post factum. At the moment when the events are actually taking place, the foreign policy of the state is guided by the interests, reflecting the requirements, as they are comprehended at this given moment."[7] Perhaps more than that. Even post factum it is impossible to definitively say what exactly the "true" interests consisted of; any such judgment will bear an imprint of a subjectivity—different from the one that was involved at the moment, maybe a more enlightened one, but still subjectivity.

To explain this ambiguity, it is necessary to turn to *values*, or, more precisely, the *system* of values that guides decision makers. Being a prism through which they look at the world, this system subjectivizes the requirements. The content of the emerging interests thus depends on the design of this device.

The concept of values occupies an important place in any conceptual framework developed in the English-speaking world, though this place is seldom specified. Instead, values are "scattered" all over the conceptual "space" of those who think and write about these issues. Though the concept was not alien to Soviet thinking, it usually did not become an integral part of it either, the main emphasis being laid on requirements as objective determinants. It is clear, however, that the concept is indispensable in examining interests. As James Rosenau has pointed out, "Interest is rooted in values ("what is best")."[8]

Values are not, however, simply one more link in the chain of choices in policy-making. They remain an independent factor that affects each of the choices. The whole process can be visualized in the following scheme:

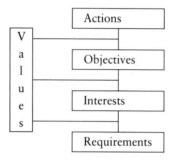

This system, however, still does not explain fully what is interest. Beyond the requirements-interests difficulties is the interests-objectives connection. Between interest as a point of departure in the consciousness of the decision maker and a concrete action, which he decides to undertake, it is always possible to detect not just one level—objectives—but many more.

If one turns to a classical example from the history of the Cuban missile crisis in October 1962,[9] the immediate Soviet objective—to place the missiles on the island—flowed out of several underlying objectives: to create a deterrent against a U.S. invasion of Cuba; to improve the Soviet Union's military-strategic position vis-à-vis the United States; to secure the recognition of the status of the Soviet Union as a world power, equal to the United States and free to choose its friends and allies wherever it saw fit.

Each of these underlying objectives can be regarded as an interest in relation to the ultimate objective of stationing the missiles, but in turn, each interest can be reduced to a succession of more general multiple ends. For instance, the deterrent was necessary to defend the Communist regime in Cuba; it was important to maintain the momentum of the world revolutionary process and to protect the geopolitical ally of the Soviet Union; the expansion of the world revolutionary process was sought to bring about an eventual victory of communism on a global scale; the ally was necessary to change the balance of power between the USSR and the United States and between the socialist and capitalist camps; and so forth.

In other words, between the level denoted in the above scheme as interests and the level of objectives, there are a number of intermediate motivation steps, all of which can be considered both objectives and interests. The more specific the definition of the motives, the more they acquire the character of objectives; the more general they sound, the closer they are to what is understood as interests in the traditional sense. There is a continuum of interests turning into objectives during policy-making and objectives being reduced to interests as a route for policy analysis. It is probably the comprehension of this continuum that caused many scholars writing in English to implicitly blend interests and objectives together under the term "goals." There should be no objections to such a unification of essentially interconnected concepts, except maybe on the grounds that it would be difficult to find a specific equivalent for this term in other languages, Russian among them.

In the light of this, it seems appropriate to support the view that "[the national] interest is what the nation, i.e., the decision-maker, decides it is"[10] even though during subsequent discussions this approach was usually criticized as of little analytic and practical use. It merely begs the question, on what basis did the decision maker decide what his interests were? A further clarification can probably be suggested. Interests are whatever decision makers, having some idea of what the requirements of the situation and their ultimate objectives could be and given their system of values, decide they are. This clarification, however, only reinforces the contention that interest is essentially an "empty" category that can be filled with almost any substance that would make sense to decision makers. As for the utility of this notion, it can be best revealed by examining how interests, as given variables, "behave" during policy-making.

Hierarchy of Interests

As I. William Zartman pointed out in the first chapter, interests come in a bundle. Policy-making—if a coherent and intelligent policy is expected to result from it—should ideally amount, first, to untangling this bundle by separating its elements, and, second, to arranging and knitting them to produce some kind of fabric with its peculiar properties. How can theory help?

First of all, it should be stressed that, as follows from the above, it is hardly correct to try to single out kinds of motives with certain degrees of generality and label them as interests as opposed to objectives. Such a distinction can be justified, however, to simplify the picture, and for this purpose it will be adhered to in the rest of this chapter.

Next, the relationship between interests and objectives is the same as between ends and means. Objectives would serve as means for satisfying interests, which in this conjunction will appear as ends.[11] As each means can serve more than one end, each objective can be related to several interests at the same time. To use again the example of the Cuban missile crisis, Nikita Khrushchev was interested in the survival of the Communist regime in Cuba both as an important asset for the Socialist camp and as an addition to the military-political capabilities of the Soviet Union itself. Toward this end one could probably also add his domestic political interests.

From this follows an important point: the decision tree—the image often used to visualize policy making—does not have the shape of an actual tree. True, the choice of objectives based on an interest does involve a few alternatives. Each of these choices, however, tends to incorporate other interests considered relevant by the decision makers, the aim being to "kill many birds with one stone"—that is, to satisfy several interests by setting one objective.[12] For example, John F. Kennedy's decision to impose the naval blockade of Cuba stemmed from a combination of, and a compromise among, a number of interests, such as preventing the shift in the balance of power sought by Moscow, appearing sufficiently tough in the eyes of the domestic public and establishment, and avoiding a dangerous escalation that could have led to an uncontrollable collision.

Within this framework it is possible to address the problem of the role of power, which, certainly, cannot be avoided when examining different factors affecting foreign policy making. The school of political realism is known to claim that power considerations are *the* factor predetermining the outcomes of this process, all the rest being subordinated to the quest for power.[13] The point that interests should be and are defined in power, in essence, means that the whole array of interests is boiled down to this common denominator.

The line of argument pursued here would support the opposing view —that power is only one of many goals in foreign policy, considered by decision makers along with other goals (in our terminology, interests and objectives),[14] such as the pursuit of peace, good relations with neighbors, or maintenance of communication lines. An important addition is needed, however. Although most other interests would come and go, the interest in power, specified in any possible fashion, would still permanently remain relevant for any state within a competitive international system. In this sense there should be no disagreement with Hans Morgenthau's contention that "whatever the ultimate aims of international politics, power is always the immediate aim"[15] (except, again, the puristic objection to the use of the term "aim").

The interests taken into account by decision makers while determining objectives are divergent not only in their substance but also in their perceived importance. Depending on the issue area and specific situation, some of them are ranked higher than others. A decision maker would always have an interest in peace, but at the same time he would be interested in achieving some particular end, such as the withdrawal of the Soviet missiles from Cuba. It is still a historical puzzle what would have been Kennedy's preference had Khrushchev refused to bargain. However, the outcome of that crisis did reveal one of Khrushchev's preferences: to ensure that the Americans would not invade Cuba, even at the price of giving up the military advantages the missiles could have created.

In other words, as long as all the interests considered relevant can be reconciled, decision makers will try to do so, but at the same time keep in mind some order of priority. For instance, Cyrus Vance was described as being convinced that "anything that involved the risk of force was a mistake,"[16] in stark contrast to Alexander Haig's infamous statement in the early 1980s that "there are things more important than peace."

This leads to *hierarchy of interests*,[17] as a result of untangling the bundle in which they come. Even within a more or less structured hierarchy, however, interests retain a considerable freedom—to interact with one another in different ways. Three types of such interaction of interests can be discerned: *coincident, nonintersecting, and conflicting*.

Coincident interaction occurs when what can be called resulting interests, that is, interests of more specific character derived from divergent underlying motives, turn out to be identical. For instance, there were not one but at least two Soviet interests in preserving the Communist regime in Cuba, one ideological and the other military-political. Naturally, coinciding interests produce an overlapping impact, causing the policy to give a tilt in a direction prompted by these interests.

Nonintersecting interaction of interests, as parts of a single hierarchy, coexist with amplifying the outcome, but also without hampering one another, their advancement being limited only by the power resources available to a given state. For instance, such were Soviet interests in creating a foothold in Cuba and in resolving the problem of West Berlin on favorable terms. Nonintersecting interests often get linked with one another in the consciousness of decision makers, and still more often they become parts of complicated diplomatic packages, but strictly speaking, they are related to different issues and can be satisfied separately.

When there is conflicting interaction, interests constantly "fight" for predominate position to influence the political process. They can mutually offset one another, but often one of them gains priority, predetermining the choice between different, and also, as a rule, mutually exclusive, political courses of action. Khrushchev's interest in shifting the balance of power and at the same time avoiding a major military confrontation is an example. It should be pointed out that an inherent incompatibility of interests is rarely the case. Usually what appears as mutually exclusive interests results from decision makers' inability to find solutions—that is, to formulate objectives—that would be satisfactory to both interests. This does not, however, make the tension between such interests less pronounced.

To sum up, the development of policy-making depends not only on the composition of the hierarchy of interests but also on the interaction between its elements. These two factors constitute the chief aggregate determinant in framing policy. The roles and strategies states are willing and able to perform in relation to situations, as proposed in chapters 1 and 2, also take shape according to what interests are seen by policy makers in these states as involved in the situations in question, how they rank these interests, and how they manage to play them against one another.

Whose Interests?

Most of the literature devoted to the interests pursued by states in their foreign policy tends to focus on *national* interests. This approach, however, misses the fact that states and nations are quite different entities. This distinction may be not especially salient for the English-speaking world, accustomed to the usage of the word *nation* in the meaning of state in its relation to other states,[18] but for the Russian ear the difference is more noticeable.

The ideas of nation and state and, consequently, their interests were glued together during the formation of nation-states.[19] These states have largely proven to be cohesive, and there is a trend to their further consolidation. At the same time, however, quite a different tendency has developed—toward forming international, or, better, *transnational,* entities. To be sure, such entities are also not new in this world. Religious and racial groups are two most evident examples. What was added to them after nation-states had come into existence was a transnational social class, "proletarians of all countries," then evolving into the international Communist and workers' movement. After World War II, yet another collective entity began to be perceived as significant—mankind as a whole.[20]

Forming new communities had an objective basis, but in regard to interests it is important to emphasize that these processes unfolded in the social consciousness of people. Under the influence of these transformations, new identities emerged,[21] joining the already existing national and, in most cases, some other collective identities. Just as any person privately thinks and acts simultaneously as an individual, as a member of his family, as a supporter of a political party, as a citizen of his state, as a representative of humanity, and so forth, decision makers acting on the state level cannot help serving also as agents of the transnational communities with which they identify and whose interests they therefore recognize and try to help satisfy.

How the interests of these collectives will be defined is a separate matter that will be pursued in later chapters. Decisions would be made by those in charge of conducting foreign policy based on their personal and historical experience, an estimation of the capabilities of the given state, and many other considerations. In any case, they would strive to satisfy the whole multitude of interests, evoked because of their *multiple identity.* All these interests would become elements of a single hierarchy of interests.

A single hierarchy means, first, that the interests should be ranged in a specific way; their place in the hierarchy will depend mostly on the degree of a state's self-affiliation with the entities under consideration. From this perspective, Soviet foreign policy, for instance, could be interpreted as combining the interests of what was broadly defined as progressive forces (the modified version of class interests reflecting the new realities), the self-regarding interests of the Soviet Union (the term *national interests* is not exactly appropriate here, because the Soviet Union was not a nation-state), and the collective interests of the international community at large. The ranking of these three groups of interests, however, has not been the same. Until 1985, the Soviet Union considered itself primarily part of the global revolutionary movement and a vehicle to pursue its interests. After 1985, a dramatic shift in Soviet political thinking in favor of the universal human interests took place. This thinking gives higher priority to the "national" interests, as the Soviet Union becomes Russia, Ukraine, and other nation-related states.

Second, all these multifaceted interests, being parts of a single hierarchy, can interact with one another in the three ways described earlier as conflicting, nonintersecting, or coincident; they can mutually deny one another, they can avoid interference with one another, or they can turn out to be identical. Class interests as pursued by the Soviet Union and its "national" interests for a long time exemplified the third way that interests interact. Class interests and national interests although different in their origins, usually interacted with each other in a coinciding or, at least, nonintersecting pattern: whatever was beneficial for the Soviet Union was seen as equally advantageous, or at least not detrimental, for the world revolutionary process.

This coincidence largely accounts for the difficulties that confront researchers who attempt, based on Moscow's foreign-policy behavior, to explain whether it was seeking world revolution or only the maximization of its traditional great power posture. When there is such a coincidence, or even nonintersection, of interests, the outcome of policy making—actions—does not provide enough evidence about which motives prevail.

Only for contradiction between interests does the correlation of motives become more or less salient. If both interests are relatively close in their priority, but mutually incompatible, the problem of a trade-off would loom large, and the tension would be the greater the higher position such interests occupy in the hierarchy.

The Soviet behavior in regard to the Iraqi invasion of Kuwait furnishes a good example of this effect. Originally the Soviet leadership tried to pursue in this situation primarily universal human interests, as they were conceived of .in the "new political thinking." Prompted by these interests, the Soviet leaders not only condemned Iraq's aggression and supported sanctions but also agreed to the use of force. For some time, they were even prepared to contribute Soviet troops to the coalition for the liberation of Kuwait. However, this idea was strongly rejected by those who favored a more self-centered policy. In their opinion, in that situation the Soviet Union could not afford risking its political-military resources by participating in military adventures, especially against a country that, until then, had been an aly, and in a region extremely close to its borders. Furthermore, at the last moment a flurry of diplomatic activity attempted to avert the military strike.

An explanation for this shift can be found in the contradiction that arose between the universal human interests and the interests of the USSR, as applied to this concrete situation. Had it not been for this perceived contradiction, the trend toward more reliance on self-regarding interests, which was developing independently of the Gulf crisis in the Soviet foreign policy, would not have produced such an effect. It is possible to surmise that if the residual class interests had interfered in this internal conflict between the universal human and the "national" ones—and in this situation they would have very nicely coincided with the "national" interests—the Soviet position regarding the war might have changed in a fundamental way. Fortunately, this did not occur. That it did not, even under such tense circumstances, suggests that this group of interests in the now-Russian hierarchy had been sufficiently downscaled.

One more important point should be made about the interests pursued by states in their foreign policy. It has been noted that it is not states as such that work out and conduct foreign policies, but people—concrete personalities—who lead these states. On the one hand, they are supposed to integrate and pursue the interests widely shared by their fellow citizens in relation to other countries, including both national and transnational interests. At the same time, however, decision makers cannot entirely strip themselves of their own interests, which mostly lie in the domestic sphere.[22] Their vested interests in, for instance, winning more public support than potential political rivals, pushing through a nomination, or even helping their relatives in their private endeavors can, and usually do, also become more or less important factors affecting their choices. Whether these factors are "more or less" important than others will again depend on how the decision makers prioritize their many identities. To put it simply, the question would be whose interests they would prefer to pursue if these interests were incompatible.

If we now try to fit these observations into what was said earlier about policy making in general, the conclusion is that the structure of multiple identity of the decision makers constitutes the core of the system of values and therefore predetermines the composition of the hierarchy of interests.

Interests and Modalities of Conflict Reduction

Interest has long been employed for the study of conflicts and ways of coping with them. Drawing on the most successful attempts,[23] let us try to formulate some propositions about conflict reduction.

First of all, it should be noted that the three types of interaction between interests—coincidence, nonintersection, and mutual exclusion —are relevant not only to their interplay within one hierarchy but also to the interaction of interests expressed by different states. Coinciding interests predetermine cooperation between these states, nonintersecting interests allow for neutrality, and mutually exclusive interests generate conflict.[24] Given the diversity of any state's interests, in most cases a hierarchy would include all three types and therefore would in principle provide for a mixed relationship of elements of both cooperation and conflict. What makes conflict prevail over cooperation is mutually exclusive interests rising in their respective hierarchies and gaining a predominant position.

An especially interactive process is known as the security dilemma. It starts when one of the sides, believing that some favorable opportunities are opening up to satisfy its interests, tries to promote them. The opposite side perceives these attempts as threatening some of its own interests and comes out to defend them. These actions, in turn, are seen as a threat by the first side, and so on, along an action-reaction-counteraction course, until on both sides the interests dominate the hierarchies. Conflict, then, can be viewed as escalatory interaction between such interests resulting in their willing the highest priority for the parties involved.

With this in hand, the following framework for comprehensive conflict reduction, as Mitchell discussed it in the preceding chapter, can be suggested.[25] It should comprise three basic patterns: (1) interrupting escalatory interaction between supposedly mutual exclusive interests (which would correspond to crisis prevention) *(conflict containment);* (2) reducing the heightened priority of the interests *(conflict settlement);* or (3) seeking their disappearance *(conflict resolution).*

Starting with the third mode, conflict resolution, which is often considered the most desirable outcome, it must be admitted that it is also the most difficult one to achieve. On the one hand, the disappearance of conflicting interests can be effected if the parties simply redefine the interests involved in nonmutually exclusive terms. To do so, they must reexamine the underlying motives that caused them to formulate their resulting interests and try to realign these motives or rerank them or both. The alternative formulations of resulting interests can conceivably produce a nonintersecting or even coinciding type of interaction with the interests of the former antagonist.

Under sufficient pressure such a redefinition can certainly be effected. The outcome of the Cuban missile crisis provides an example of how an "either-or"(missiles–no missiles) dispute was reconsidered in somewhat different terms ultimately by both sides: no invasion–no missiles. The problem, however, is that such a pressure, instead of catharsis, can produce more rigidity, ultimately leading to an uncontrollable escalation— a gamble, which at some point can violate the limits implied by the wish to reduce the conflict.

The disappearance of particularly intransigent conflicting interests can in principle be accomplished by eliminating the identity underlying these interests. This was evidently what happened to class identity in the post-1985 Soviet foreign policy making. For such dramatic changes in the hierarchy of interests to take place, however, a drastic restructuring of the whole system of values is required. This is rarely the case; usually some residual elements of the old mentality persist, causing the corresponding interest to slide down the hierarchy rather than vanish altogether, which would mean not resolution but settlement.

One more way of getting rid of the incompatibility of interests is to try to eliminate one of the conflicting political units and its interests. Regretfully, this is still an often practiced approach. It long underlay the deadlock between Palestinians and Israelis, as Zviagelskaia discusses below. In most cases it does not yield the desired outcome. The interests involved in international disputes, though defined subjectively, that is, by individuals, usually transcend personalities and acquire an existence of their own. Apart from that, this approach has nothing to do with what is implied in conflict reduction, because it involves violence as a means of resolution and because the approach tends to create more conflict, such as the complications with the Kurds after Operation Desert Storm.

Settlement, as distinct from resolution, is based on downgrading the mutually exclusive interests that resist the attempts to redefine them. Under this pattern, the interests continue to exist but at a lower priority in their respective hierarchies.

In principle, the interests can slide down by themselves, under the impact of factors irrelevant to the conflict in which they are involved. More than that, such a slide does not necessarily have to be symmetrical to produce a settlement. For instance, Iraq's interests vis-à-vis Iran, which for a long time prevented reaching a final settlement between them, lost their significance for Baghdad immediately after 2 August 1990, leading to major unilateral concessions.

Another version of settlement is based on counterbalancing the conflicting interests with additional coinciding ones. Here, again, such a shift can occur without direct connection to the conflict. Environmental and other global problems hardly were a result of Soviet-American confrontation, but their aggravation provided additional incentives for ending this confrontation.

Paradoxically, countervailing interests can also be amplified by the conflict itself, or, to be more precise, by its side effects. The hierarchies of interests of the parties would always include interests jeopardized by the escalating conflict or might be better satisfied without it. The chief problem to be solved here would be to locate in the respective hierarchies the coinciding interests discriminated against that would encourage the sides to end the conflict. In other words, to settle a conflict between two parties, it would be useful to reveal some internal conflict within the hierarchies of each of them, that is, to see whether there is any explicit or implicit trade off between equally relevant, but mutually exclusive, interests, and to what degree a reverse trade-off is feasible.

To this end, one could first try to find out what are the entities, mutually recognized by the conflicting parties as viable, whose interests are infringed upon because of the conflict, such as national interests in civil war, class interests in interethnic or international conflicts between proponents of the same class affiliation, race interests in international or intertribal or interclass conflicts, and so on. Whatever common identities and corresponding crosslinking loyalties can be distinguished should be appealed to. Ultimately, the last resort would be appealing to universal human interests and recognizing their highest priority.

On the other hand, there can be coincidence in conflict-breaking thrust of entirely divergent interests: national or human or both on one side, religious or class or both on the other, or any other combination. Their common feature in this respect is that they would be increasingly threatened by the conflict. In short, one could look for what is perceived by the parties as primary threats, and by accentuating them try to galvanize the respective interests and mobilize them to oppose the mutually exclusive ones.

Then, however, the question is how one can accentuate threats. *Deterrence* seems to be addressing this question. In a broader conceptual context, using threats constitutes one of the chief elements of the theory of conflict management. Note, however, that conflict management implies not only de-escalatory techniques, but also the possibility of taking an escalatory approach to the conflict, that is, deliberately exacerbate it to the proportions that would begin to inflict intolerable hurt on the parties.[26]

Theoretically, this approach can look attractive, especially having in mind that by building such a pressure, one can induce policy makers not only to downplay but also to reconsider the mutually exclusive interests, thus bringing about conflict resolution, not just settlement. Practically, however, especially under the current international circumstances, such a risky approach seems to be unacceptable, even if the technique is additionally outfitted with institutionalized crisis-control mechanisms.

Hence an explicitly conflict-reductionist type of conflict management is required. It should employ an alternative method of galvanizing potentially countervailing interests, by creating enticing opportunities rather than hurting stalemates, for their satisfaction.[27] This type of management should still be trying to induce in the adversaries the sense of hurt—not so much to their present posture ("This conflict is growing too painful and dangerous, I cannot stand it"), but to their potential future status ("This conflict makes me lose favorable opportunities, I must seize them"). Further, this version of conflict management should be applied with special vigor and creativity for conflict containment at the early stages of escalation, where it can be expected to bring most valuable, though not necessarily spectacular, results.

It can be argued from this vantage point that despite the limitations imposed on the utility of interest by the inherent role of subjectivity in the definition and prioritization of interests, the idea of interest should still be viewed as a necessary conceptual tool. As for the subjectivity per se, accumulated in the systems of values of decision makers, the analysis presented here shows that these systems are accessible for management and even allow some adjustment. A primary way to reorient them would be to address threat and opportunity perceptions and manipulate them to effect favorable shifts in respective hierarchies of interests, which, in turn, the systems of values would, in the longer run, somehow accommodate.

To consolidate such adjustments and to perpetualize the conflict-reductionist mode of building the hierarchies of interests, such indirect impact achieved through manipulating perceptions should be supplemented by a direct penetration into these systems of values by the ideas underpinning conflict reduction. One such idea, in our view, is that conflict reduction can best be attained by consciously avoiding the definition of interacting interests in mutually exclusive terms.

Notes

1. One example of such a discussion being reanimated in the United States is a set of three thoughtful and provocative articles by Alan Tonelson ("What Is the National Interest?"), Joseph S. Nye, Jr. ("Why the Gulf War Served the National Interest"), and Christofer Layne ("Why the Gulf War Was Not in the National Interest"). See *Atlantic Monthly* 268, no. 1 (1991): 35–81.

2. *National Security Strategy of the United States* (Washington, D.C.: The White House, 1990).

3. See Burton, *Conflict: Resolution and Prevention;* John Burton and Frank Dukes, eds. *Conflict: Human Needs Theory* (New York: St. Martin's , 1990).

4. Dean G. Pruitt and Jeffrey Z. Rubin, *Social Conflict: Escalation, Stalemate, and Settlement* (New York: Random House, 1986), 10.

5. William L. Ury, Jeanne M. Brett, and Stephen B. Goldberg, *Getting Disputes Resolved: Designing Systems to Cut the Costs of Conflict* (San Francisco: Jossey-Bass, 1988), 5.

6. See, for example, R. N. Dolnykova, *Metodologiya i metodika prognozirovaniya vneshney politiki nesotsialisticheskikh gosudarstv: opyt sistemnoy organizatsii ponyatiy* (Methodology and methods of predicting the foreign policy of nonsocialist states: an attemp at a systematic organization of notions) (Moscow: Nauka, 1986), 59–100; M. A. Khrustalev, *Sistemnoye modelirovaniye mezhdunarodnykh otnosheniy: uchebnoye posobiye* (Systemic modeling of international relations: an educational textbook) (Moscow: MGIMO MID SSSR, 1987), 54–55, 62–63.

7. E. A. Pozdnyakov, *Sistemnyy podkhod i mezhdunarodniye otnosheniya* (The systemic approach and international relations) (Moskow: Nauka, 1976), 122.

8. James N. Rosenau, "National Interest," in David L. Sills, ed. *International Encyclopedia of the Social Sciences,* vol. 11 (New York: Macmillan/Free Press, 1968), 34.

9. There is a heavy reliance in this chapter on that experience especially because it has been extensively described in the memoirs of the participants and examined in the scholarly literature from different perspectives, including that of interests and decision making in general.

10. Edgar S. Furniss and Richard C. Snyder, *An Introduction to American Foreign Policy* (New York: Rinehard, 1955), 17.

11. Ralph L. Keeney and Howard Raiffa, *Decisions with Multiple Objectives: Preferences and Tradeoffs* (New York: John Wiley and Sons, 1976), 41.

12. The interaction between objectives, or interests, in decision making has been thoroughly explored and described in Snyder and Diesing, *Conflict among Nations,* and Martin Patchen, *Resolving Disputes Between Nations: Coercion or Conciliation* (Durham, N.C.: Duke Univ. Press, 1988).

13. Hans J. Morgenthau, *Politics among Nations* (New York: Knopf, 1957); Kenneth Waltz, *Man, the State, and War* (New York: Columbia Univ. Press, 1954).

14. Alexander L. George and Robert O. Keohane, "The Concepts of National Interests: Uses and Limitations," in Alexander L. George, *Presidential Decisionmaking in Foreign Policy: The Effective Use of Information and Advice* (Boulder, Colo.: Westview, 1980), 224.

15. Morgenthau, *Politics among Nations,* 25.

16. Zbigniew Brzezinski, *Power and Principle* (New York: Farrar, Straus, Giroux, 1983), 44.

17. The notion of hierarchy of interests, or objectives, has been mentioned by a number of authors, but rarely elaborated upon. See, for instance, Fred A. Sondermann, "The Concept of the National Interest," *Orbis* 21, no. 1 (spring 1977): 129; K. J. Holsti, *International Politics: A Framework for Analysis,* 5th ed. (Englewood Cliffs, N.J.: Prentice Hall, 1988), 122.

18. Joseph Frankel, *National Interest* (London: Pall Mall, 1970), 15.

19. See Charles A. Beard, *The Idea of the National Interest: An Anlytical Study in American Foreign Policy* (New York: Macmillan, 1934).

20. See Robert C. Johansen, *The National Interests and the Human Interest: An Analysis of U.S. Foreign Policy* (Princeton, N.J.: Princeton Univ. Press, 1980).

21. The role of identity in social and political processes has been largely overlooked in the literature on international relations, or at least not explicitly addressed. For some exceptions, see: Morton Deutsch, *The Resolution of Conflict: Constructive and Destructive Processes* (New Haven, Conn.: Yale Univ. Press, 1973), chap. 4, "Group Formation"; Terrel A. Northrup, "The Dynamic of Identity in Personal and Social Conflict," in *Intractable Conflicts and Their Transformation,* ed. Louis Kriesberg, Terrel A. Northrup, and Stuart J. Thorson (Syracuse, N.Y.: Syracuse Univ. Press, 1989), 55–82.

22. See Richard Neustadt, *Presidential Power: The Politics of Leadership from FDR to Carter* (New York: Macmillan, 1980); Morton H. Halperin, *Bureaucratic Politics and Foreign Policy* (Washington, D.C.: Brookings Institution, 1974).

23. Among them, especially noteworthy, are: David A. Lax and James K. Sebenius, *The Manager as Negotiator: Bargaining for Cooperation and Competitive Gain* (New York: Free Press, 1986); Roger Fisher and William Ury, *Getting to Yes: Negotiating an Agreement Without Giving In* (New York: Penguin, 1981); Ury, Brett, and Goldberg, *Getting Disputes Resolved;* Pruitt and Rubin, *Social Conflict.*

24. For more detailed examination of these topics, see V. Udalov, "Balans sil i balans interesov" (Balance of power and the balance of interests), *Mezhdunarodnaya zhizn',* 1990, no. 5: 16–25; Vadim V. Udalov, "The Concept of Balance of Interests and U.S.-Soviet Interaction," *Annals of the American Academy of Political and Social Science* 518 (Nov. 1991).

25. A somewhat different, though particularly stimulating, framework used for addressing the problem of conflict reduction was used by William Collison in *Conflict Reduction: Turning Conflict to Cooperation* (Dubuque, Ia.: Kendall/Hunt, 1988), 16–52, 123–30.

26. See I. William Zartman, "Explaining Disengagement," in *Dynamics of Third Party Intervention: Kissinger in the Middle East,* ed. Jeffrey Rubin (New York: Praeger, 1981); Idem., *Ripe for Resolution.*

27. See I. William Zartman, "Beyond the Hurting Stalemate," paper presented to the International Studies Association, Atlanta, 1992.

4

Sources of American Conduct
in Regional Conflict

VICTOR A. KREMENYUK

The sources of American conduct in regional conflict are many. Among them are sources of both material and spiritual origins, as well as sources born of specific American traditions and sources prompted by the need to respond to developments in the external environment. It is evident that the U.S. policy in regional conflict is not in essence an array of ad hoc decisions (though sometimes they appear so) but, on the contrary, is something deeply entrenched in the American policy tradition. This distinction is important to emphasize in order to assess properly how far the United States government and public are ready to go in their moral and physical involvement in foreign conflicts.

It is also important for Russian policymakers because to an overwhelming extent, at least until recently, Moscow's policy in regional conflict was a mirror of American actions. Without the same historical background of involvement in regional conflict as U.S. foreign policy possesses, the Soviet policy of involvement was born in the mid-1950s as a response to the American policy of "encirclement" of the Soviet territory, starting with NATO in Europe (1949) and on through the Middle East (the Baghdad Pact of 1954), Southeast Asia (SEATO of 1954) up to U.S.-Japanese and U.S.-South Korean security arrangements (early 1950s), regarded in Moscow as an intolerable repetition of the "cordon sanitaire" policy of the 1920s and early 1930s. As a reciprocal response, the policy of "assistance to the national-liberation movements" was developed in Moscow and transformed into a huge global network of obligations and military presence.

From the assessment of American involvement in regional conflict as an attempt to create an "arc of encirclement" came the Soviet decision in the mid-1950s to engage in Arab-Israeli conflict through military assistance to Egypt. Then, military and economic assistance went to Soekarno's Indonesia, Nehru's India, and Nkrumah's Ghana. With the further U.S. involvement in Vietnam, Congo, Laos, and some other "hot spots" in the 1960s, the Soviet policy of involvement was worked out until it unfolded into a global Soviet-U.S. rivalry in almost all regional conflicts. In the political and military setting of the early and mid-1950s when the crucial decisions were taken in Moscow on involvement in the Middle East, Indochina, Indian subcontinent, Indonesia, Africa, and, further, in the Caribbean, there was simply no place for a proper understanding of the nature and history of the U.S. involvement in regional conflict. Now, much later, when a reappraisal of the sources of the U.S.-Soviet confrontation is conducted, it is highly appropriate to try to understand the motives of U.S. policy to assess the possibilities of the U.S.-Russian cooperation in regional conflict reduction.

Traditional Sources of U.S. Involvement

The origins and sources of U.S. involvement in regional conflict are well studied both in the United States and Russia. In the United States, this topic was several times addressed by serious scholars from different angles. The first wave of interest followed the political situation of the late 1950s when it became evident that the U.S.-Soviet rivalry was gradually shifting from Europe to the Third World. In strategic thinking this shift was conceptualized by Thomas Schelling in his *Strategy of Conflict*[1] (1960): the upcoming impossibility of a strategic conflict required the spread of the U.S.-Soviet confrontation to much lower levels of conflict, specifically regional conflict.

As a rationalization of this conclusion, which was promptly incorporated by the official policy (the doctrine of "flexible response" proclaimed by President Kennedy in early 1961), a host of research both on American tradition and the current situation in the Third World appeared in the American academic and nonacademic press. Among them were the works by Morton Halperin, Robert Tucker, Henry Kissinger, Robert Osgood, M. Taylor, and some others who were studying the problem of the regional conflicts from the point of view of the strategic theory, as well as George Liska, Jerome Slater, Myron Weiner, A. Campbell, Nathan Leites, C. Wolf, and many others who studied the regional conflict within the framework of both American traditions and the U.S. interests in the Third World. Besides, there was also a group of researchers (Samuel Huntington, James Coleman, Joseph LaPalombara, and others) who were interested in the same subject from the point of view of political science.[2]

Soviet literature on the subject, at least until the mid-1970s, was mainly concentrated on the historical analysis of the U.S. involvement in regional conflict. These were works by A. Guber, L. Zubok, G. Sevostianov, and some other Soviet historians who were studying the U.S. involvement in the Third World as a part of a larger framework of the history of the U.S. interventions in local conflicts starting from the late 1800s.[3] By the mid-1970s, works by V. Gantman, Evgeny Primakov, and V. Zhurkin appeared where the U.S. involvement in regional conflicts was studied mainly as a part of the U.S.-Soviet rivalry and as a foreground of the evolution of the global conflict.[4] The U.S. involvement in regional conflicts as part of U.S. foreign policy in separate areas of the world was studied by Gyorgy Chufrin, Georgi Mirsky, Vitaly Naumkin, Andrei Shumikhin, and some other researchers of the younger generation. My works of the late 1970s–early 1980s fall into this category.[5]

To summarize what was written by both Soviet and American scholars, the following conclusions may be drawn on the sources of American conduct in regional conflict. First, involvement in regional conflict, as it is identified now (and previously very often called "local war"), is not something alien to the U.S. foreign policy tradition. As a continuation of the conquest of the American continent, it became one of the cornerstones of the military build-up and foreign policy foci for the United States almost immediately after the Revolution. In this regard, the war with the Barbary pirates off the North African coast in the early 1800s is very often mentioned to support the conclusion that, for the American Founding Fathers, the idea of using force in remote areas to defend what was regarded as legitimate U.S. interests was quite appropriate. This idea is important to emphasize as a counterweight to the other U.S. foreign policy tradition, isolationism. Although the United States was not inclined to be drawn into the conflicts of the Old World and the great power rivalry until World War I, it was leaning in a quite opposite direction in relation to local wars and conflicts. There, the United States was ready to seek as active a policy as possible, as was evident in the Pacific, Caribbean, and Central America for almost all of the nineteenth and twentieth centuries.

Second, most U.S. involvement in regional conflict was highly ideologized. This may be explained as a result of the American democratic process, which required both public and congressional support of the administration's decisions on involvement in a conflict and its continuation, especially if it had budgetary implications. Maybe this was also a result of the desire to present American involvement as something totally different from the colonial wars waged by the European powers. The net result, however, was that each case of American engagement was explained as "fighting tyranny" or "supporting freedom and democracy" or "defending legitimate American interest" or, at least, "saving American lives." This conclusion indicates not simply the wrappings of the policy of involvement but the type of rationalization used and hence the goal setting, diplomatic backing, search for allies, and many other things that can explain the contents traditionally inserted by the U.S. policymakers in their effort in seeking a victory in regional conflict.

Third, among the main motives and interests of U.S. involvement in regional conflicts, economic and business considerations played a highly visible role. They were mainly connected to trade, investment, freedom of navigation, and other important aspects of the U.S. policies, and were transferred into a strong pressure on the administration to use force or diplomacy to back the U.S. business and defend its interest. To regard this aspect from the angle of the U.S. conduct in regional conflict, however, the preponderance of business considerations gave great flexibility to U.S. actions and enabled them not only to pursue military victory whenever possible but also to find diplomatic solutions, a compromise based on mutual benefit, rather than to insist on rigid policy that very often leads other nations to a political impasse. As contrasting evidence, when the U.S. involvement was prompted by other than business considerations (such as Vietnam), its policy was fruitless and self-damaging and ended with a political debacle.

Fourth, with the advent of the superpower status of the United States and development of anti-communism as the focus of U.S. foreign policy, the whole structure of motives, rationales, and patterns of U.S. involvement in regional conflict greatly changed. The obsession about fighting communism, as Hans Morgenthau has observed, has changed not only the traditional U.S. foreign policy but also the understanding of the reality that formed it.[6] Involvement in regional conflict was regarded since then as a part of the "global rivalry" and that it brought into play such considerations as strategic planning, force deployment, alliance building, foreign assistance programs, and many other aspects that, in the end, have elevated the priorities of the regional conflict to U.S.-Soviet confrontation. In this respect, the U.S. policy in regional conflict has become a part of its global strategy, which bore an imprint of ideology, thus transforming the traditional U.S. approach into a moral crusade.

It would be wrong, however, to understand this change as a total rejection of the traditional U.S. approach to regional conflict. In the approach that developed in U.S. foreign policy after 1947 (the Truman Doctrine) and especially after 1949 (point four of Truman's address to the Congress), a specific blend of both traditional and messianic policies emerged that dictated U.S. conduct in regional conflict up to the unsuccessful war in Vietnam. This approach consisted mainly of rigid, ideologically biased, military-oriented policies that projected the U.S. global strategy into volatile areas of the Third World without any due respect both to the objects of this policy and to the final aims. The idea of fighting the pro-Soviet (or pro-Chinese) forces in the Third World could not be regarded as a serious basis for the policy, for it simply disregarded the real volume of U.S. resources and the real objectives because of gross oversimplification of what was happening in the Third World and of the nature of its conflicts.

Critical Reappraisal of the Sources of U.S. Policy

The devastating criticism of U.S. policy in the Third World conflicts that followed the Vietnam debacle drew a distinctive line between two periods in the evolution of this policy in the post-World War II era. The focus of this criticism was directed against the so-called policy of the "global interventionism," which developed out of President Kennedy's "flexible response" doctrine (which emphasized the necessity to counter the Communist "subversion" at the appropriate level of conflict) and of President Johnson's doctrine announced in 1965–66 after the Dominican crisis and the escalation of war in Vietnam. Both doctrines prescribed a direct U.S. military involvement in regional conflict as a part of the "global strategy" and as a constituent part of the U.S. policy directed at "drawing a line" to the Communist offensive in different areas of the Third World.

The anti-Communist and other ideological overtones and the overestimated strategic connections between the U.S. policy in regional conflict and its global confrontation with the Soviet Union had made this policy grossly counterproductive. First, the rationale for involvement had been distorted from defending what could be described as American interests properly to some loose ideological goals that turned the United States into a world "fire brigade" squeezing the U.S. resources without bringing any visible result. This rationale could be identified as an imperial burden without an empire and respective dividends. Second, the policy made the United States a party to any conflict on the side of those who could be regarded as anti-Communist allies without any possibility of making the U.S. position flexible enough to play an intermediary role in the conflicts where there was absolutely no need for a direct U.S. involvement. Third, this policy created an unnecessary dependence between U.S. strategic interest in confronting the Soviet Union and the volatile, highly unpredictable Third World setting.

All these considerations have provoked a mixed response among the U.S. policymakers and academic experts. Most of those involved in the debates favored a great reduction in the American presence in regional conflict: military withdrawal, cuts in assistance programs, distancing from the most ambiguous conflicts and most compromised friends (which later developed into the human rights policy). This conclusion took into consideration both the criticism of the previous policy and domestic consequences of Vietnam, which produced widespread grassroots protests and a cleavage between presidential power and the Congress, which eventually led to President Nixon's resignation in 1974 because of the Watergate scandal.[7]

Alongside these debates, however, were alarming voices both from the conservative and liberal sides of the American political spectrum. These views reflected the understanding that irrespective of the decisions taken in Washington, the whole situation in the Third World will continue to be highly explosive. So, Zbigniew Brzezinski warned that if the United States went too far in its withdrawal from the Third World, it might provoke a whole series of new crises.[8] Senator J. William Fulbright advocated a policy of a "new internationalism," which meant refocusing the American policy in regional conflict, making it more conciliatory, oriented toward conflict resolution, and healing the most painful wounds of the Third World.[9]

To understand these voices properly it is necessary to remember that, among the traditional American sources of involvement in regional conflict were two very general but nevertheless important features. One was closely connected to the traditional American adherence to change. This feature has been developed as a continuation of the traditional American thrust toward progress, be it technological, social, or moral, and has grown with the years into a philosophy based upon the veneration of the basic human values, such as freedom, democracy, prosperity. Once the United States was involved overseas, in some distant country, it was forcing change—maybe not always in a consistent way—but it was pouring money and effort into backward societies hoping within some time to bring them stability and prosperity. Indeed, the record of the American effort proved to be fruitful in Japan, South Korea, Taiwan, and Thailand, among others. This adherence provided a specific network of mutual interests. Many of the Americans personally involved in such effort insisted on continuing involvement, while the recipient nations were interested in continuation of political, military, and economic ties with the United States.

The other feature of this relationship was that historically the United States proved to be a "poor colonialist." The typical American inclination to solve issues instantaneously, with one shot, very often acted as a constraint for a long sustained effort in those cases where the type of regional conflict demanded such an approach. As it became clear that a long history of involvement in the Third World gave rise to a certain interdependence between the U.S. national interest and the interests of progressive change in the dependent countries, although those interests demanded both a sustained effort on the part of the United States and a decisiveness to carry out its obligations, it was difficult to expect that a simple revision of the previous policy would change the American interest.

What was needed was to find ways to merge the objective necessity for continued American involvement in regional conflict with the need to make it less counterproductive for U.S. interest and more constructive for the recipient nations. As a possible solution to the anxieties about continuing and self-damaging U.S. overengagement in regional conflict and about a possibility that U.S. withdrawal may be followed by a sequence of regional and global crises (which later was supported by the evolution of the Yom Kippur War in 1973 into the oil crisis of 1973–74), various new proposals appeared. Among them were quite interesting and attractive ideas about the U.S. attitude toward regional conflict, which was less oriented toward military force, stressing the importance of multilateralism instead of unilateral actions, and the importance of preventing escalation of regional conflict.

At the end of the 1960s, this idea was embodied in the concept of "controlling conflict." Two important works were published in 1969 in the United States. One was a brochure of the United Nations Association of the USA;[10] the other was a book by Lincoln Bloomfield and Amelia Leiss, a result of a research project sponsored by the Arms Control and Disarmament Agency (ACDA).[11] Both works probed the ideas of "controlling conflicts" and tried to summarize the U.S. experience in regional conflict in such a way as to give it a totally new focus. They argued that the unhappy result of the war in Vietnam has emphasized the need to reject the unilateral, military-oriented policy of direct engagement in regional conflict, that the visible perspective for the United States in the 1970s would be a row of sharp conflicts in the Third World, and, besides, that the best policy, which would both guarantee U.S. interests in those regions of the world and avoid any further "Vietnams," would be to control the conflict through nonmilitary, noncoercive means using the capabilities both of the United States and of the United Nations, which could not exclude even possibly coordinating with the Soviet Union.

In another work on the same issue, a computer-aided system for handling the information on local conflicts, also a result of the ACDA-sponsored research, Bloomfield even worked out a series of proposals that enriched the assortment of the U.S. policy means with the measures of controlling the evolution of conflicts through a tight control over arms supplies and military and economic assistance, thus achieving the goal of keeping these conflicts under U.S. control.[12]

In late 1960s–early 1970s, when the ideas of conflict control were born, they did not attract the scope of attention by both the public and policymakers that they deserved. The obsession was with taking the U.S. troops out of Vietnam and to demonstrate properly to the public that there will be "no Vietnams." This was the essence of the Nixon Doctrine (1970–73) and this was what finally has become the contents of the U.S. foreign policy. Though among experts the ideas of the conflict control have acquired some importance, they were largely ignored at the policy-making level. At least some of these ideas, including the idea of conflict reduction through abstention from direct U.S. military involvement and through control over arms supplies including attempts to find acceptable agreements with the Soviet Union, were incorporated into the U.S. foreign policy under the Carter administration (1977–80).

The importance of the Carter administration's legacy for the ideas of conflict control and reduction is even greater because of the decision to incorporate the principles of human rights observation into the official policy. These principles were prompted by quite different considerations, not directly connected to the problems of conflict control, but once introduced into the U.S. foreign policy through the respective legislation, they have also become a tool of conflict reduction, for they have additionally refocused the U.S. policy toward a support of U.S. allies and dependent regimes that refrained from open abuse of human rights, thus reducing the aggressiveness of the military in the Third World.

However, in giving a broad view of the evolution of the U.S. policy in regional conflicts in the 1970s, it should be stressed that during that decade policymakers were much more concerned with the "linkage" of this policy with the U.S.-Soviet relations than with the issues of conflict control per se. As a direct evidence, the famous "Brzezinski-Vance controversy" may be cited, when two leading foreign policymakers of the Carter administration were at odds on the issues of focusing the U.S. policy in regional conflict. There were two visions of this policy: one expressed by Brzezinski, was addressing the necessity of direct linkage of this policy with the U.S.-Soviet rivalry;[13] the other, supported by Cyrus Vance and Andrew Young, concentrated on the ideas of conflict control through indirect means, including control of the arms transfers, increasing aid for development, and emphasis on human rights.

In the final result, though President Carter shared the views of Secretary Vance and Ambassador Young, Brzezinski's vision triumphed because of the revolutions in Iran and Nicaragua and the Soviet invasion of Afghanistan. The Reagan administration, which came to power in 1981, completely incorporated the approach shared by Brzezinski in the previous administration (without necessarily paying tribute to its author) and for most of the 1980s, at least until 1986, the rigid, militaristic approach, which concentrated on the U.S. direct involvement in regional conflicts, prevailed. It was not a replica of President Johnson's policy in the late 1960s, but many of the same ideas and sources of the American policy became visible in the U.S. actions. At least, this was what some foreign observers, including some in the Soviet Union, noticed.[14]

Conflict Reduction and Conflict Resolution: A Revival of Ideas

Since the days of the Geneva conferences of 1953 and 1954 when the great powers found solutions to regional conflict in the Korean and Indochinese armistices, ideas of conflict resolution in the Third World sponsored by the Big Five have been floating around. Though they have never been implemented since then (with one exception—the Geneva Conference on neutrality of Laos in 1962), still their attractiveness could explain the interest of many researchers both in the United States and the Soviet Union. In the United States it even gave impetus to conflict resolution research mainly based in Ann Arbor and described in the *Journal of Conflict Resolution,* as well as in many other centers: George Mason University, Harvard Law School, Paul Nitze School of Advanced International Studies, and some others. Some aspects of the conflict resolution were studied in the USSR under the auspices of the Association of Political Science headed by G. Shakhnazarov.

For most policymakers and observers, conflict resolution appeared highly idealistic and irrelevant. For all its attractiveness, the ideas could not be regarded as a basis for a sound policy, because, besides an appropriate international setting unthinkable in the years of the cold war, they also demanded a thorough and detailed technology for handling and solving conflicts. Although the charter of the United Nations and the statutes of the International Court of Justice held some general clauses on how to solve dispute in a peaceful manner, in the day-to-day practice of the great powers, as well as of the nations directly involved in conflicts, there was absolutely no knowledge, or practice, or even desire to put these clauses into service. As it seemed, the ideas of conflict resolution were doomed to play the role of some idealistic principles with little or no hope of ever being used as a practical tool.

With the first signs of thaw in the cold war between the United States and Soviet Union, the situation in regard to regional conflicts changed. The first attempts to find durable solutions for conflicts in and around Afghanistan, Nicaragua, Namibia, and Cambodia were undertaken with mixed results. In some cases these efforts proved effective: an agreement on Afghanistan, on Namibia, elections in Nicaragua, but, as has become evident, these efforts were insufficient either in bringing durable peace to Afghanistan or in providing a secure setting for the Persian Gulf region. So, alongside efforts to bring peace to areas that long were conflict-ridden, the need to think in wider terms about reducing the whole conflict potential in different regions of the Third World has become urgent.

The goal of conflict reduction in this respect cannot be regarded as something separate or independent from the whole conflict resolution effort. Although the proclaimed task of the superpowers, as well as that of the world community, continues to be comprehensive conflict resolution, reduction of conflict, of violence, and of the possibilities of escalation becomes much more practical and realistic if it is remembered that the current conflicts and crises are very resistant to any effort to find peaceful and noncoercive means of resolution and have already acquired a kind of immunity against pressures from the superpowers. So, without rejecting the ultimate goal of resolution, conflict reduction can be regarded as an attempt to bring more stability into the state of the current conflicts, as well as into the situation in the Third World. This would involve the introduction of substantive standards and principles, or a "code of conduct."

The idea of a "code of conduct" was born as an offspring of the general attempt to introduce some stability into unlimited U.S.-Soviet rivalry both in strategic areas and in regional conflict. After the Cuban missile crisis in 1962, a joint effort to codify U.S.-Soviet strategic relationship was considered necessary. Starting from the 1963 "hot line" agreement, both nations went a long way through 1971–72 agreements on the perfection of the "hot line," avoidance of escalation of accidents on and over high seas, avoidance of accidental launches of nuclear missiles, and other measures to avoid nuclear war, including the agreement of 1973 on prevention of nuclear war. There was no parallel or similar action in their relations concerning regional conflict, aside from abortive attempts to hold talks on the Indian Ocean, the Middle East, and conventional arms transfers in 1977–78, although the intensity of conflicts in the Third World, as well as the growing prospects of U.S.-Soviet confrontation over these issues, demanded some stabilizing effort. Hopes to find approaches to handle this problem through some general standards of conduct, such as the U.S.-Soviet Basic Principles Agreement (BPA) signed in 1972, proved futile.[15] The confidence and trust necessary to compensate for the inadequacy of some of the general clauses in the document was lacking, as were understandings that could, at least in some cases, prescribe the conduct of both powers, individually as well as bilaterally, in regional conflict.

The idea of a "code" is quite close to typical American thinking based upon the philosophy of a compromise, of a legally binding agreement, but was alien to Soviet thinking, which either disregarded formal agreements because inside the Soviet Union a written law was never a source of a binding rule or turned them to its own advantage. To make this idea realistic several points should be stressed that have made their way into the American foreign policy. It is especially important to do so if new possibilities of cooperative security are to be combined with the traditional sources of the American conduct and their evolution in the course of overcoming the consequences of the cold war.

First is the dominance of the long existing tendencies toward "conspiracy theory." Such thinking appeared in the late 1940s as a rationale for U.S. involvement in regional conflict and since then has continued as a part of the U.S. foreign policy attitudes. For some time after Vietnam it might have seemed that this theory was definitely dead, but events of the 1970s and the active Soviet role in the Third World in that period soon contributed to its revitalization. One of the last evidences of its importance for the American political process was President Reagan's speech in the United Nations on 25 October 1985 where his escapades against "foreign subversion" were evidently prompted by the "Communist conspiracy" theory.[16] It is appropriate to recognize that the typical Soviet rationalization for the policy of unilateral involvement was also based on the premises of the "imperialistic intervention" theory. In this sense both sides mirrored each other in looking for the explanations behind their policies.

As long as both sides were trying to explain the roots of Third World instability and the basis of their policies through the theory of "foreign subversion," there could be no hope for an introduction of the conflict-reduction approach. This approach has a chance of survival only if there are at least several points of consensus including, importantly, a shared vision of the causes of tensions and conflicts in the Third World. If, instead of seeing each other's role as a primary cause of conflict, both sides could come to a joint understanding that the primary causes of these conflicts are far away from their reach and that their interference in the political situation in the regions leads to continuation of the conflicts, then maybe they could come to a common conclusion on the actions they could take that would significantly reduce the scope of these conflicts.

Second is the attitude toward the idea of Russian-American cooperation in conflict reduction. Unthinkable in the traditional American approach, this idea deserves serious attention and analysis now. The main problem is the striking difference in the U.S. and Russian approaches to "conflict" and "resolution," which are typical in the thinking of both sides. The American approach to regional conflict is basically described by the "general theory of conflict," which postulates that conflict is a "pathology" that can be remedied through a concerted action.[17] For Soviet thinking, based upon the Marxist-Leninist theory, conflict is the continuation of the "objective contradictions," which can be dealt with only through coercive means, like revolution, war of liberation, and civil war. It is only in recent years that this view has been radically changed for a more conciliatory approach that cherishes peaceful solution through national reconciliation rather than a militant one.

In this matter, analysis of the sources of the American conduct is a key to answering the question whether the two powers can work out a compatible approach that would facilitate their dialogue as well as a joint search for conflict reduction. Given all the existing differences in political cultures and political systems, it seems that the challenge of cooperative security is not insurmountable, for among the traditional elements of American conduct flexibility and focus on mutual benefit occupy quite a visible place and, now that ideological differences with the former Soviet Union are behind with the end of the cold war, it is possible to think realistically of cooperation in this field. The place of the ideological component of the rivalry might even be filled with an attachment to international law long abandoned and forgotten in the years of the ideological crusade.

Possibilities of U.S.-Russian Cooperation
in Regional Conflict Reduction

As the analysis of the sources of the American conduct in regional conflict and of its recent evolution shows, cooperation in this field between the United States and Russia should be considered. The testing ground for this hypothesis has been the actions of both powers in the second Gulf war, a better test of cooperation than any subsequent conflicts such as Bosnia or Cambodia. Although this case has demonstrated both reserves and still-existing constraints for both powers cooperating reducing regional crises, it would be useful for this study to try to identify three general issues: (1) what are the results of the Gulf crisis that should be taken into account in the Russian-American cooperation in regional conflict reduction: (2) what type of cooperation would be needed for future conflict reduction that can be regarded as both desirable and realistic; and (3) what are the indispensable prerequisites for such a cooperation?

Results of the Gulf Crisis

The fact that both superpowers did not act in exactly the same manner during the crisis was an important irritant. Many people on both sides had an illusion that if Russia (then the Soviet Union) and United States agreed to act together against the Iraqi aggression in Kuwait, the most logical outcome would be that they should behave symmetrically: issue the same warnings to Saddam, dispatch equal amounts of troops, allocate the same amount of resources, and so fourth. Perhaps this is an exaggeration, but essentially it is the main explanation for the widespread feeling of bitterness about the results of U.S.-Soviet cooperation during the crisis, both among the public and among the policymakers. The idea of role diversity has not yet taken hold.

One may agree that possibly it would be much better for international security as well as for U.S.-Russian cooperation if both superpowers could act together in a very primitive but psychologically reassuring way: not only issue joint statements but also share exactly the same burdens in dealing with any threat to the international security, including in regional crises. Here, however, is the first and maybe the most important lesson for the Gulf crisis: that, even with the best intentions of both powers to act together in meeting the challenges to their security and that of the other members of the international community, they exist in different geopolitical, strategic, economic, and other conditions and must act correspondingly. This constraint is usually called "asymmetry" and it would be not simply wrong but also damaging for their cooperation to disregard it. The obligation to act together should never become suicidal for any of the partners, otherwise their partnership, instead of acting as promoter and facilitator of their desire to help each other, may very easily turn into an unwanted burden and a source of mutual irritation. There are grounds to believe that in the second Gulf war the U.S. administration, contrary to the feeling of the U.S. public and legislators, was acting according to this rule, and the asymmetry of actions undertaken by Washington and Moscow did not leave any scars on the tissue of their imminent partnership.

The second important lesson of the crisis is that, with all the differences in the positions of the superpowers, both domestically (economic and ethnic crises in the Russian Federation) and internationally (the former Soviet connection to Saddam), there still was enough space for identification of their common interest and that interest prevailed throughout the months of the crisis. The importance of this conclusion is evident; after decades of cold war, doubts about the durability of the Russian-American partnership in fighting local aggression and in keeping the existing world order intact have a solid ground. It would be simply naïve to brush off all the sediment deposited by years of mutual suspicion and mistrust (sometimes grounded, sometimes imaginary) and hope that the relationship could be started one day from a clean page. Inevitably, if we compare the previous and existing psychopathies, including the dominant modes of thinking, the existing strategic postures, and the mountains of weapons directed against each other, with the first fragile seedlings of cooperation and partnership, one could expect that in a crisis suspicion would outweigh cooperation. A reading of the conservative press in Russia makes this quite evident.[18] But, as became clear in the crisis, the attractiveness of the ideas of cooperation has become so powerful that it permitted the leaders of both owners to continue to adhere to the principles of the Joint Statement of 3 August 1990 and to resist both the attacks of the conservatives and the temptation to start polemics that could inevitably ruin the partnership.

The third lesson of the crisis is that, beyond the goodwill of the leaders of the powers, there still are simply no rules and procedures that would place their desire for cooperative security on the basis of an established practice. The years of the cold war have left a striking vacuum in the structure and contents of new security cooperation, and this vacuum is still to be filled. Although the Soviet Union and the United States had already worked out and established some understandings and mechanisms for mutual cooperation in avoiding nuclear war (the hot line agreements of 1963, 1971, and 1985, for example), in checking and verifying each other's military activity in accordance with the intermediate Nuclear Forces (INF) treaty and later agreements through space observation and sometimes ground control, and in some other areas, their attempts to cooperate in dealing with regional crises are still not accompanied by the effective mechanisms. This may explain their initial controversies over the role of the United Nations, the extent of powers of the multinational effort, and some other things.

Type of Cooperation

One of the issues that deserves immediate discussion in the aftermath of the crisis is the type of cooperation that could be both realistic and desirable for Russia and the United States in order to approach seriously the existing differences in their positions as well as in the sources of their conduct. From the very beginning, in trying to address these issues, some combination of UN capacities with bilateral superpower cooperation should be analyzed as a basis for action. Although it would be wrong to brush off the possibilities that still exist within the UN mechanism (it is important to remember that the UN mechanism is a result of great power cooperation during World War II) and that practically were never used,[19] it is evident that there are cases and conditions when direct U.S.-Russian cooperation is indispensable.

One aspect to reexamine is the two powers attitude toward the idea of the revival of some of the mechanisms of the United Nations for which there already are provisions in the charter, notably the Military Committee, and an expansion of the scope of powers of the secretary-general. Russia already several times had addressed the issue, most recently in President Yeltsin's statements.[20] There was an adequate response from President Clinton. In both countries there are both enthusiasts who think that the UN may become the prime element in fighting international aggression and skeptics who quite justifiably direct their attention to the weaknesses of this organization. It is evident, however, that without a thorough and detailed discussion of the part of the burden in reducing regional conflict that should be carried on by the UN, the whole idea of cooperative security may become inoperative.

Principles of Cooperation

It is evident that without some basic principles—negotiated explicitly or tacitly—it will be difficult to count on reliable cooperation between Russia and the United States. Part of that cooperation is the codified understanding of the purpose of their collaboration in reducing regional conflict, or a return to the notion of standards and principles. So far, there are some elements of such understanding—discussions of arms transfers, of the "ground rules" to be followed by the superpowers and other powers in different areas of the world,[21] and of the international rules and procedures for peaceful dispute settlement. So far, however, all these discussions are subordinated to vague and unspecified goals of conflict resolution. Without rejecting the importance of this concept, one should understand that conflict resolution can become a practical political goal only in the broadest context of changing the whole international environment including overcoming the legacy of the cold war, developing mechanisms for dispute settlement in U.S.-European (EU)-Japanese relations, and on the regional level. In the nearest future, the goal of reduction of regional conflict may become not only an object for discussions but also a practical goal for the superpowers.

In a way, this sounds like a revival of the Basic Principles Agreement of 1972 after it had been successfully forgotten in a squall of criticism by skeptically minded observers, but the world is coming again to the point when some political issues cannot be solved without such basic principles, even if they are not discussed in public or negotiated on the governmental level. There is a need for some general policy guidelines along which both sides can act unilaterally, bilaterally, or multilaterally without undue suspicion or concern about the other's intentions. In the new conditions of bilateral relations, the idea of a "code of conduct" could be revived to introduce some elements of restraint and cooperation in the conduct of the United States and Russia. Such a "code" could contain some agreed-upon norms, such as rules of war, provisions for arms supplies, observation of the rights and immunity of civilian populations, and others, and could introduce some stabilizing momentum even into the military actions and especially into the normal, nonmilitary course of events in a conflict. Such an approach would increase the chances for peaceful settlement of conflicts and promote such conflict-reduction measures as national reconciliation and democratic elections.

Among such guidelines, several items should be singled out. First, the use of military force to defend one's own interests or the interests of a larger community of nations. Both the experience of Vietnam and that of Afghanistan prompt the conclusion that the big powers should abstain from using their armed forces directly against their opponents in regional conflict. Opposite to that conclusion, however, the experience of the Gulf crisis shows that a superpower's military force may become a major instrument in fighting aggression if it is accompanied by a consensus among the permanent members of the UN Security Council and the support of the majority of the members of that organization. So, using a superpowers' military capabilities to defend international peace and security ceases to be a taboo if it has a blessing of the other powers and is undertaken under the umbrella of the UN Security Council. This approach leaves some ground for discussing the conditions under which a superpower may use force—unilaterally or multilaterally—but establishes the principle of a "world policeman" for the big powers along the lines Franklin D. Roosevelt was thinking in his idea of the United Nations.

Second, the attitude toward the use of force by regional or local powers. With the completion of the cold war rationalization of the use of force by these states (right of self-defense, right of revolutionary change, and so forth), a strong and grounded doubt appears whether it would be wise on the part of the nations-exporters of the modern weaponry to continue the previous policies unchanged. This concerns the Russian Federation, as the largest supplier of arms in 1988–90, but also the United States, Great Britain, France, Germany, Italy, and other arms exporters. Though the issue was approached several time (and the most advanced case was the Soviet-American discussions of the arms transfers in 1977–78), there is still a large misunderstanding around the problem of regulation of arms trade mainly centered on the issues of legitimate self-defense, freedom of trade, clandestine operations, and many other matters. It is evident that a search for solution here will not be easy but there is no way to avoid it.[22]

Third, principles about peaceful, nonviolent means of conflict reduction, including intermediary role of the powers or of international organizations, good offices in starting the reconciliation of antagonists, supervision of free elections, and many other matters directly connected to resolution of conflicts. This is especially important in the light of the experience when both the United States and the then-Soviet Union agreed to cochair the Middle East peace process and decided to play the key mediating role in bringing all the participants of the conflict to negotiations. Thus the problem of working out acceptable procedures and mechanisms for both powers and for their relations with the antagonists in the conflict becomes not simply desirable but absolutely necessary.

.   .   .

The rationale of studying the sources and history of the American conduct in regional conflict can best be explained by the goals of this book. Will it be possible to count on American participation in regional conflict reduction and for effective Russian-American cooperation in this area? Will the traditional sources and patterns of American conduct in foreign affairs permit it or will they generally exclude any realistic possibility? These and other related questions deserve a thorough examination and discussion both on official and nonofficial levels.

It is agreed generally in Russian-American documents that the time and need for a comprehensive resolution of regional conflicts has become extremely urgent. There is, however, both an academic and a practical problem over the way to start the process and to avoid misjudgments in this important area, for otherwise the Russian-American relations may hit the reefs of the regional conflict as happened in the 1970s. In this respect the idea of cooperative security for conflict reduction, insofar as it does not contradict or replace the task of conflict resolution, may be regarded as a sound policy basis for creating a much more stable world order in the interest of all.

At the same time, a realistic appraisal of the possibilities of cooperation in regional conflict reduction needs to incorporate an assessment of a future Russian role because of the events happening in this country. The following chapter will give judgment on this matter but here it is necessary to emphasize that current developments in the Russian Federation may even help in finding ways for regional conflict reduction. The former Soviet Union has experienced its own "regional conflicts" and become a commonwealth of independent states. It has run into the need to find nonmilitary political means to deal with those conflicts and it has contributed to a rapid accumulation of unique experiences in this field, which should be and, it is hoped, would be shared with other nations. If this experience is helpful in working out reliable models of conflict reduction and resolution, Russian participation in the whole task of conflict reduction in the Third World would become a valuable contribution.

Notes

1. Thomas Schelling, *The Strategy of Conflict* (Cambridge, Mass.: Harvard Univ. Press, 1960), 253.
2. To avoid long lists of American publications on this matter, I could direct an interested reader to an overview of this literature in one of my earliest works, *Politika*

SSHA v razvivayuschikhsia stranakh. Problemy konfliktnykh situatsiy 1945–1976 (U.S. policy in the developing countries: problems of conflict situations, 1945–76) (Moscow: Mezhdunarodniye Otnosheniya, 1977).

3. A. Guber, *Filippinskaya respublika 1898 goda i amerikanskiy imperialism.* (The Philippines Republic of 1898 and American imperialism) (Moscow: Nauka, 1961); L. Zubok, *Ekspansionistskaya politica SSHA v nachale XX veka* (U.S. expansionist pollcy in the beginning of the 20th century) (Moscow: Nauka, 1969).

4. V. Zhurkin and Ye. Primakov, eds. *Mezhdunarodnye Konflikty* (international conflicts) (Moscow: Mezhdunarodnye Otnoshenya, 1972): V. Gantman, ed. *Mezhdunarodnye Konflikty Sovremennosti* (Contemporary international conflicts) (Moscow: Nauka, 1983).

5. Besides the work already mentioned in n. 2, they include (all in Russian); *U.S.A. and Conflicts in Asia* (Moscow: Nauka, 1979); *The Crisis Strategy of Imperialism* (Kiev; Politizdat, 1979); *USA: Struggle Against National Liberation Movements* (Moscow: Mysl, 1983); *Washington Against Revolution in Iran* (Moscow: Mezhdunarodnye Otnoshenia, 1984); as well as a good number of publications in collective works.

6. Hans Morgenthau in the introduction to Jerome Slater's *Intervention and Negotiation: The U.S. and Dominican Revolution* (New York: Harper, 1970), x.

7. A thorough analysis of the lessons of Vietnm for American society was published later: Anthony Lake, ed. *The Legacy of Vietnam: The War, American Society, and the Future of American Foreign Policy* (New York: New York Univ. Press, 1976). In the Soviet literature this debate was analyzed in my book, *U.S.A.: Struggle Against National-Liberation Movements*.

8. *Newsweek* 1 Feb. 1971, 52. .

9. *War/Peace Report,* May 1971, 3–7.

10. *Controlling Conflicts in the 1970s. A Report of a National Policy Panel Established by the UN Association of the U.S.A.* (New York: UNS/USA, 1969).

11. L. Bloomfield and A. Leiss, *Controlling Small Wars: A Strategy for the 1970s* (New York: Alfred A. Knopf, 1969).

12. R. Beattie and L. Bloomfield, *CASCON: Computer-Aided System for Handling Information on Local Conflicts,* ACDA/WEC = 141, Dec. 1969.

13. Z. Brzezinski, *Game Plan: Geostrategic Framework for the Context of the U.S.-Soviet Contest* (Boston: Atlantic Monthly Press, 1986).

14. Victor Kremenyuk, "Po, staromu, scenariyu interventsionisma" (By the standards of the old interventionist scenario), *SSHA: ekonomika, politika, ideologiya,* 1981, no. 5, 52–58.

15. Alexander George, ed. *Managing U.S.-Soviet Rivalry* (Boulder, Colo.: Westview, 1983).

16. *Department of State Bulletin,* Dec. 1985.

17. Schelling, *The Strategy of Conflict,* 3.

18. See, for example, articles in *Sovetskaya Rossiya* (Soviet Russia), *Krasnaya Zvezda* (Red Star), and other conservative publications in the Soviet Union during the months of the crisis.

19. However, it would be well to remember that the UN mechanism was used by the superpowers even in the years of the cold war in dealing with some aspects of the reduction and control of some regional conflicts: Congo, Cyprus, Sinai, Golan Heights, Lebanon, Namibia. In other cases, when the UN could not be used directly, derivative mechanisms were used, for example, observation teams in Indochina and Korea.

20. Such views were first presented in M. Gorbachev's undelivered speech in the UN, published in *Pravda* on 16 Sept. 1987, and in his address to the UN General Assembly on

7 Dec. 1988. President B. Yeltsin reiterated these ideas in his speech at the United Nations in September 1994.

21. See, for example, J. Gowa and Nils H. Wessel, *Ground Rules: Soviet and American Involvement in Regional Conflicts* (Philadelphia: Foreign Policy Research Institute, 1982).

22. Some of these issues were already discussed in the Soviet press after the analysis of the lessons of Afghanistan: V. Kremenyuk, "Gorky opyt—seryeznye vyvody" (Bitter experience—serious conclusions), *SSHA: ekonomika, politika, ideologiya,* 1989, no. 7, 49–53.

5

Sources of Russian Conduct
Toward Regional Conflict

BRUCE PARROTT

This chapter analyzes the Third World policies of the USSR and ex-
plores the policies likely to be pursued by the loosely affiliated successor
states that have emerged from the collapse of the Soviet regime. To put
these issues in context, the chapter first sketches the long-term determinants of Soviet Third World policy and delineates the causes of the
reappraisal of Soviet international strategy that began in the early 1980s.
Next it examines the political forces and calculations that produced a
fundamental reconceptualization of Third World policy after Mikhail
Gorbachev became general secretary of the Soviet Communist party in
1985. The chapter concludes with some thoughts on the alternative
Third World approaches that post-Soviet governments, particularly Russia, may follow in the future.

In this discussion, Soviet- and post-Soviet Third World policies are
taken to be the product of the state's international circumstances and
international strategy, the ruling elite's conception of the state's interests
in the Third World, and the state's domestic ability to pursue those
interests. The analysis assumes that objective international conditions

Some of the ideas developed in this chapter are drawn from my "The Soviet System,
Military Power, and Diplomacy: From Brezhnev to Gorbachev," in *The Dynamics of Soviet
Defense Policy,* ed. Bruce Parrott (Washington, D.C.: The Woodrow Wilson Center Press,
1990).

exert a powerful influence on any state's commitment and pattern of behavior in regional conflicts. The analysis also assumes, however, that most sets of external circumstances can be dealt with through different foreign-policy strategies, and that a state's choice of strategy will be shaped by its ideology and domestic institutional structure, as well as by its military and economic capabilities. In other words, the chapter examines both the international and the domestic determinants of Soviet and post-Soviet behavior in the Third World.

The chapter seeks to show how the long-term interplay of international and domestic determinants gradually gave rise to a global, competitive Soviet Third World policy and how recent changes in these determinants have precipitated a drastic shift emphasizing reduced Third World involvement and peaceful resolution of regional conflicts. During the early decades of Soviet power, the USSR's Third World policy was strongly influenced by major security threats from Europe and East Asia and by the foreign-policy tradition of Tsarist Russia. Although the Russian Revolution and the Bolshevik political outlook created a strong ideological disposition to exploit conflicts in the diverse regions that later came to be known as the Third World, in practice Soviet decision makers were generally quite cautious about becoming directly involved in such conflicts. Instead they devoted most of their attention and limited resources to the sorts of contiguous threats and opportunities that had preoccupied Tsarist policymakers.

Between the 1950s and 1980s, shifting international and domestic conditions led Soviet policymakers to alter their international strategy and to assign heightened importance to exploiting conflicts in the Third World. This gradual policy change was caused by the USSR's improved security situation vis-à-vis continental military threats, by the country's enhanced ability to conduct a global geopolitical competition with the West, and by the adventitious opportunities resulting from the West's withdrawal from colonial possessions in Asia, Africa, and the Middle East. Expanded Soviet capabilities and a greater sense of security thus allowed the regime to give freer reign to its ideological inclination to exploit Third World conflicts.

As shown below, this strategy of global competition with the West ultimately collided with the increasing weaknesses of the Soviet system. By the mid-1980s, thanks to the poor stewardship of Leonid Brezhnev and other Communist party oligarchs, the Soviet state had become seriously overextended internationally and domestically. The overextension of the Soviet system was one major reason that Mikhail Gorbachev and the new generation of party leaders who came to power in mid-decade undertook a far-reaching reevaluation of Soviet international strategy and domestic goals. The reevaluation yielded a decision to scale back Soviet Third World commitments and a heightened desire to promote the political resolution of Third World conflicts. To a large extent, the domestic transformation that occurred under Gorbachev destroyed the ideological and institutional underpinnings of the highly competitive Third World policies pursued by the USSR in previous years.

Looking toward the next decade or two, the chapter suggests that protracted internal crises and political upheavals will push Russia and the USSR's other successor regimes to reduce their Third World involvements and initiatives even further. In the short run, Russia will probably have to cope with some violent conflicts in and between former Soviet republics, particularly in the Caucasus and also possibly in Central Asia. Together with its grave internal difficulties, these nearby conflicts are likely to make Russian policymakers wary of playing an independent role in Third World conflicts farther from home. In the longer run, as Russia recovers economically, it is likely to experience a strong revival of interest in the portions of the Third World lying along the perimeter of the former Soviet Union. Whether this policy will entail cooperation with the western powers to reduce regional conflicts will hinge primarily on the political and economic order that finally emerges inside Russia. In any case, Russia seems unlikely to return to the levels of far-flung Third World involvement and competition with the West that the USSR pursued at the height of its international power.

Soviet Policy: From Socialism Under Siege to Global Superpower

International Strategy and Ideology

Thanks to their Marxist-Leninist ideology and historical experience, the leaders of the USSR customarily viewed relations with the outside world through a perceptual lens that highlighted the pervasiveness and unavoidability of international conflict rather than the possibility of co-operation. Soviet leaders and analysts interpreted international events as elements of an unfolding international struggle between the forces of "socialism" and "capitalism"—a struggle that they claimed was destined, sooner or later, to result in a worldwide victory of political forces favorable to the USSR. Although Soviet leaders generally applied this outlook with much tactical flexibility, they did not treat the reduction of Third World conflict as inherently desirable. Instead they viewed the exacerbation and manipulation of regional conflicts as a useful means of promoting Soviet interests vis-à-vis other great powers, and they treated the reduction of such conflicts as a tactical adjustment justified only in situations that might otherwise endanger the Soviet Union and Soviet interests.

During its early decades the Soviet regime, although ideologically sympathetic to antiwestern groups in the western-dominated colonial territories, did not usually attempt to exploit regional conflicts far from Soviet borders. Because imperial Russia had been a continental power rather than a maritime or trading state such as Britain or Holland, its chief efforts to colonize the precursors of modern "third world" regions had centered on contiguous areas, such as the Caucasus, Turkmenistan in Central Asia, and Mongolia and Manchuria in the Far East.[1] Together with the new Soviet state's relative weakness, this traditional Russian continental orientation influenced the Soviet leadership's international strategy. Soviet policymakers worked to establish their hold over former Tsarist territories. Faced with the rise of aggressive Fascist states in Germany and Japan, they concentrated on protecting the USSR from direct assault, giving little more than rhetorical support to revolutionaries and nationalists in western-dominated colonies.[2] This continental orientation persisted in the years immediately after World War II, as Stalin struggled to rebuild the ravaged domestic economy and to consolidate Soviet control over Eastern Europe. Although he did underwrite the North Korean attack on South Korea, mostly he behaved extremely cautiously when opportunities arose to exploit regional conflicts far from the USSR's borders.

The salience of the Third World as an arena of competition against the USSR's great-power rivals gradually increased in the decades after Stalin's death. Under Khrushchev, in the 1950s and early 1960s, Europe remained the principal arena of East-West struggle, as the Soviet leaders sought to solidify their hold over Eastern Europe and to force western diplomatic recognition of a separate East German state. However, the rising wave of anticolonial movements offered a new bridgehead in the struggle to undermine western influence. The postwar anticolonial movements sweeping across Asia, Africa, and the Middle East were fueled—logically enough—by powerful antiwestern sentiments, and Moscow, which had historically expanded into adjacent regions rather than overseas territories, was able to present itself as the champion of the colonial victims of western exploitation. In practice, many inhabitants of the emerging Third World implicitly accepted the Leninist idea that imperialistic behavior was characteristic of the highly developed western countries, but not of Soviet Russia.[3] These circumstances allowed the

USSR to score Third World gains while investing relatively few economic resources and still less for military assistance or direct military commitments.[4]

After removing Khrushchev from power in 1964, the Brezhnev leadership made further modifications in Soviet international strategy. Convinced that Khrushchev had engaged in dangerous international posturing toward the United States during the Cuban missile crisis and the face-offs over Berlin, Khrushchev's successors adopted a steadier foreign-policy style that eschewed East-West confrontations in Europe. Thanks partly to changes in the complexion of the West German government and the Soviet shift toward limited détente with the West, Brezhnev and his cohorts were able to win western diplomatic recognition of the German Democratic Republic and expanded western economic inputs for the rest of Eastern Europe, as well as for the USSR itself.[5] These diplomatic and economic results appeared to consolidate the USSR's domination of Eastern Europe and to make its position on the European continent more secure than at any time since 1917.

With the Soviet position in Europe apparently stabilized, the Soviet leaders put heightened emphasis on the East-West struggle for influence in the Third World as an integral dimension of their concept of East-West détente. As they argued in polemics against the Communist Chinese, the expansion of Soviet military power and the improvement in U.S.-Soviet relations would create a more favorable environment for "national liberation struggles" in the Third World. At the 1971 Party Congress, Brezhnev declared that the USSR would pursue a policy of peace but would also give a "firm rebuff" to probes from aggressors and "undeviatingly support the peoples' struggle for democracy, national liberation, and socialism."[6] Speaking more broadly, Foreign Minister Gromyko also underscored the limited character of détente with the West: "Peaceful coexistence is a specific form of socialism's class struggle against capitalism. This struggle . . . will continue in the field of economics, politics, and . . . ideology, because the world outlook and the class goals of the two social systems are opposite and irreconcilable."[7]

In the Third World the main curb on Soviet exacerbation of conflicts remained the Soviet desire to avoid general war and to promote the central interests of the Soviet state. In some cases geopolitical calculations led Brezhnev and his fellow oligarchs to try to mediate Third World conflicts; their rivalry with China, for example, led them to resort to mediation to prevent an all-out war between India and Pakistan in 1965. The Soviets also strove to dampen regional conflicts that they feared might put them on a collision course with the United States or otherwise injure key Soviet interests. Their behavior in the Middle East in the early

1970s demonstrated an inclination to restrain Third World clients and slow the pace of regional conflict when Soviet state interests required.[8] Similarly, their refusal between 1973 and 1975 to supply North Vietnam with the additional military resources needed to conquer South Vietnam suggests that they attached more weight to the possible political and economic benefits of U.S.-Soviet détente than to an early Communist victory in Vietnam.[9]

Nonetheless, these were cases of expediential moderation, not signs of a serious interest in conflict reduction. From 1975 onward, the Brezhnev regime, convinced that the United States lacked the political will to resist deepened Soviet involvement in Africa and Asia, frequently worked to exploit preexisting regional conflicts or decide them through military means rather than to reduce such conflicts through political accommodations. Shortly after Soviet hopes for an infusion of American economic resources were dashed by congressional passage of the Jackson-Vanik and Stevenson amendments, the Soviets provided North Vietnam with the military means to launch a victorious assault against South Vietnam. In the second half of the decade, the USSR became more actively involved in providing military supplies and advisors to the anticolonial rebels in Angola and to Soviet clients in the Horn of Africa. The invasion of Afghanistan in 1979 marked the high point of Soviet efforts to use military means to determine the outcome of Third World conflicts and the apogee of Soviet willingness to ignore the possible consequences of such behavior for Soviet relations with the West.

The International Correlation of Forces and the Soviet Domestic System

This approach to the Third World was closely linked with the Brezhnev regime's ambition and instinctive optimism. Brezhnev and his cohorts had been steeped in an ideology compounded of Russian nationalisms and Marxist-Leninism and that appeared to be vindicated by the historical experiences of their generation. As adults, Brezhnev and his associates had witnessed the USSR's transformation from a largely peasant society into a major industrial state, had participated in the titanic struggle against Nazi Germany, and had seen the USSR move from international isolation to become leader of a far-flung coalition of Socialist and pro-Socialist regimes. They also had been affected by the euphoric Soviet expectations and western self-doubts that flowered after the launching of Sputnik in 1957.

It is not surprising, then, that the Soviet leaders voiced optimism about long-term trends in the international "correlation of forces." For most of their time in power, they remained confident that history was on the side of the Soviet Union and its allies, and they believed that through carefully calculated policies they could make the USSR America's geopolitical equal and take a long step toward the ultimate goal of socialism's world triumph. As Brezhnev told a party audience in 1970, the West remained strong, and "determined action by all the revolutionary forces is needed to overthrow it." Despite the West's strength, he assured his listeners, "the struggle between the two world systems will ultimately end with the triumph of communism on a global scale." [10] Official optimism peaked in the mid-1970s. Adopting a tone of triumphalism, Brezhnev declared that the USSR had never before been so strong internationally, and he and Defense Minister Ustinov proudly pointed to Soviet achievements in promoting the victory of Third World clients as evidence of Soviet gains in the long-term global competition against the West. The list included Vietnam, Cuba, Angola, and Israel's Arab opponents in the 1973 Mideast war. [11]

Influenced by these attitudes, Soviet foreign policy was designed to minimize change in the Soviet domestic system. Near the end of the 1960s, a few leaders, such as Kosygin and later Brezhnev himself, began to express veiled doubts about the system's economic dynamism, and these doubts contributed to the decision to pursue a limited détente and strategic arms agreements with the United States. [12] The doubts did not, however, shake the leadership's instinctive belief that political authoritarianism and state direction of the economy provided a capability for long-term military growth at least equal to that of the United States. In the leaders' view, carefully crafted policies, including selective reliance on western technology and grain to compensate for the shortcomings of central economic planning, would still permit the USSR to compete successfully against the United States in the international arena.

Thus, although the USSR cautiously sought during the 1970s to decrease its isolation from the world capitalist economy, its dominant impulse was to remain separate from the West politically and even economically. [13] By proclaiming that unremitting ideological struggle was integral to détente with the West, the party leadership justified attempts to wall off Soviet society from foreign political and cultural influences and to suppress heterodox thinking at home. The effort to insulate society from such influences was a key feature of the party's traditional drive to legitimate the domestic political order by contrasting it with the alleged defects of liberal political systems abroad. Although growing commercial contact with the outside world prevented an all-out campaign against "bourgeois ideology" at home, the policy of cultural insulation did help stifle the reformist impulses that had surfaced in the late 1950s under Khrushchev.

The USSR's involvement in the Third World tied in with the Soviet leadership's desire for a sense of political legitimacy. Supporting left-wing regimes and insurgent movements in the Third World helped buttress the party leadership's claim that it headed an international movement ultimately destined to reach into every corner of the globe. As Foreign Minister Gromyko proudly remarked, it had become unreasonable to expect that any important issue anywhere in the world could be resolved without Soviet participation. Whether Soviet involvement in Third World conflicts legitimized the regime in the eyes of ordinary Soviet citizens is quite doubtful,[14] but it did play a big part in legitimizing the Soviet domestic order in the political elite's own eyes. In an authoritarian system with strong institutions of coercion, political stability depends far more on the self-legitimation of the elite than on acceptance of the elite's legitimacy by the citizenry at large.

Although the authority to decide about involvement in regional conflicts undoubtedly rested with the top party leadership, several bureaucratic actors probably influenced decisions in cases when the leadership was ambivalent. One of these was the central Committee's International Department, which enjoyed much independence from the Ministry of Foreign Affairs. The International Department and Ministry of Foreign Affairs operated under separate politburo "curators"—Mikhail Suslov and Boris Ponomarev in the case of the International Department, Andrei Gromyko in the case of the ministry—and the International Department appears to have played a lead role in exploiting Third World conflicts. Although solid evidence is difficult to come by, the institutional division of labor between the organizations may have reflected a lack of close coordination between Soviet policy toward the United States and Soviet policy toward the Third World.[15]

The expanding Soviet involvement in the Third World also enjoyed some support within the military establishment. By the end of the 1960s, authoritative Soviet pronouncements on military doctrine and statements by some senior military officials were putting new emphasis on Soviet military support of Third World clients against "imperialist aggression" from the West.[16] Although rather sparse, the evidence suggests that in the mid-1970s Minister of Defense Grechko may have embraced a broader conception of armed forces' mission—a conception including support for national-liberation movements against western attempts to "export counterrevolution" in the Third World—as a desirable step.[17] Among the military services, the navy was the leading proponent of greater Third World involvement, which provided a useful supplementary justification for the campaign waged by Admiral Gorshkov, navy commander in chief, to built a large blue-water fleet.[18] The other military branches, especially the Ground Forces, remained far more concerned about Soviet military missions and commitments in the European and Asian continental theaters, but the favorable shifts in the East-West geopolitical balance and the steady growth of the total defense budget during Brezhnev's first decade as general secretary minimized resistance from these components of the military.[19] Arms exports to the Third World probably appealed to military planners as a means of reducing the unit costs of producing weapons and maintaining a cost-free surge ability to equip new Soviet military forces in case of a major international crisis or war. The use of Soviet weapons in Third World conflicts also provided a valuable testing ground in which to evaluate the combat performance of Soviet weapons.[20]

In addition, the prospect of large hard-currency earnings from expanded arms sales to Third World clients probably exercised a strong attraction for Soviet leaders and economic planners seeking to expand trade with the West. Although the USSR at first offered concessionary terms to Third World arms recipients and allowed them to pay in local currencies, during the 1970s, as the scale of these transfers increased, the Soviets began to press for hard-currency payments, particularly from clients in the oil-rich Middle East. Partly in response to new sales opportunities in the Middle East after 1973, the Brezhnev leadership began to supply top-of-the-line weapons to the USSR's closest Third World clients, on occasion even before supplying such weapons to Warsaw Pact allies. According to one source, by the early 1980s almost 80 percent of Soviet military shipments to the Third World were paid for in hard currency. Between the early 1970s and early 1980s, the share of arms transfers in Soviet hard-currency earnings rose from an estimated 3 percent to between 25 and 30 percent.[21] During the 1970s, as the USSR began to seek wider access to western economic inputs, growing Soviet arms exports may have upset the United States, but they also provided hard currency earnings with which to finance imports and technology transfers from the West.

Finally, the KGB may have had an interest in exploiting certain kinds of Third World conflicts. Along with the GRU, the armed forces' intelligence directorate, the KGB's foreign-intelligence department under Brezhnev helped train and equip Third World groups that were committed to revolutionary change and that sometimes engaged in terrorism (meaning the use of violence against nonmilitary targets). Depending on the circumstances, the Soviet government sometimes counseled these groups to eschew terrorism or military means in favor of political struggle, and in many instances it remains unclear whether the USSR favored specific military or terrorist acts that occurred. Nevertheless, Soviet publications did not suggest that resort to violence or even to terror necessarily excluded the Third World client from Soviet assistance; rather they frequently showed a high degree of ex post facto flexibility, which suggested toleration of such methods. Often the Soviet media redefined the behavior of specific Third World clients as nonterrorist at the moment when the USSR began to extend assistance to those clients; likewise the media redefined the same behavior as terrorist in cases when Soviet assistance to the clients was ended. The KGB and its East European counterparts also provided assistance to some Third World client regimes in setting up their security services.[22] It therefore seems a reasonable surmise that the KGB embraced the use of violence or terrorism or both in a number of Third World conflicts.[23] This conclusion is all the more plausible because the USSR's internal political regimentation and isolation from foreign societal contacts made the Soviet state relatively invulnerable to terrorist attacks and therefore removed an important domestic motive for opposing international terrorism.

Global Overextension: Caution Without Conflict Reduction

Ideology and Global Strategy

In the late 1970s and the early 1980s, a series of new developments raised painful questions about Soviet global strategy, including policy toward the Third World. After the Soviet invasion of Afghanistan, growing American skepticism about arms control led the United States to shelve the unratified SALT II treaty, and the Reagan administration came into office with the avowed intention of reestablishing U.S. military superiority. Meanwhile NATO confirmed a plan to deploy new U.S. intermediate-range nuclear forces (INF) in Western Europe if the Soviets refused to dismantle their SS-20 missiles. No less important, the rise of Solidarity and the ensuing crisis in Poland unexpectedly threatened Soviet dominance of Eastern Europe and raised doubts about the stability of the USSR's own domestic political order. All these clouds appeared on the horizon at a time when a sudden and worrying drop in Soviet economic growth was exacerbating the tensions among the various claimants on the national budget, and when U.S.-led sanctions against the Afghanistan invasion had reduced access to western grain and technology. Although uneven and sometimes self-contradictory, the western response to the invasion of Afghanistan represented a serious challenge to the Soviet effort to segregate East-West relations from the Soviet pursuit of international influence through Third World conflicts. Together these developments provoked an acrimonious internal controversy over the effectiveness of Brezhnev's policy of limited détente. Although some members of the elite apparently favored adopting a more conciliatory stance toward the West, the main public challenge to Brezhnev's approach came from party and military hard-liners. The advocates of the hard-line view contend that the danger of war between the superpowers had increased dramatically, and they warned against underestimating it. They also charged that the Soviet Union had recently lost the geopolitical initiative to the United States and could recapture it only through more vigorous action. So far as one can tell, their complaints focused principally on the strategic military balance and the political-military situation in Europe, not on the Third World.

Brezhnev and his short-lived successors, Iuryi Andropov and Konstantin Chernenko, all rejected this hard-line criticism and vigorously defended the established centrist policy. Limited détente, they argued, was a long-term trend that could be revived by dogged adherence to existing policies. As they saw it, skillful manipulation of political divisions within the West would ultimately compel western governments to return to a more conciliatory policy toward the USSR. In other words, time was still on the side of the Soviet Union rather than on the side of its western rivals.

The controversy over the proper response to the worsening international situation coincided with a sharp erosion of the ruling elite's confidence in the Soviet system's economic and political strengths vis-à-vis the West. Some hard-line analysts argued that socialism remained more capable than the West of withstanding an all-out arms race, but other commentators disagreed. Disputes over the superpowers' relative abilities to shoulder the burden of global competition led *Kommunist*, the party's main theoretical journal, to reprove "some Marxist researchers" for underestimating the West's technological dynamism and to point out that such estimates bore directly on the regime's foreign-policy decisions.[24]

This loss of economic confidence mingled with new fears about the political stability of the Soviet system. Chernenko, for example, voiced the anxiety that the Polish crisis might be repeated inside the USSR, and a few social scientists hinted that major reforms were necessary to avoid an internal political crisis that would be a greater threat than foreign military attack.[25] These unorthodox observations indicated that the party elite was steadily losing faith in the domestic system's capability and were beginning to sense that the system was overextended. The remarks, however, were far from being a coherent reform program, and none of the aging Soviet leaders was prepared to present a genuinely new political strategy for coping with the strains on the system.

Faced with such contradictory pressures, Brezhnev's immediate successors adopted a policy toward Third World involvements that was more cautious but not fundamentally different from Brezhnev's. Andropov evinced a new skepticism about the depth of the change in Third World clients that proclaimed themselves "socialist," and he declared that the USSR exerted its main influence on the world revolutionary process through its economic policy—and not, by implication, through military means.[26] Still, the Soviet leadership did not retreat from its existing Third World commitments or seek diplomatic resolution of Third World conflicts involving its established clients—for example, in Afghanistan and Syria. Instead it concentrated on protecting its increasingly beleaguered Third World clients.

Fragmentary evidence suggests that even this limited adjustment in policy provoked differences within the top leadership. During 1983, for example, Chernenko, who had recently lost out to Andropov in the contest to succeed Brezhnev, continued to defend an active commitment to Third World insurgencies despite Andropov's attempt to temper this commitment.[27] Perhaps Chernenko, as the most ardent politburo defender of Brezhnev's limited-détente policy, believed that with time western resistance could be overcome and the established Third World policy could again be pursued at little political cost. Or perhaps Chernenko simply saw Andropov's attempted retrenchment as a point of vulnerability to be exploited in the competition for support from hard-line elements within the ruling elite. In any event, because the political leadership had not yet faced up to the fact that the USSR was politically and economically overextended, the domestic preconditions for major changes in Third World policy did not yet exist.

The new element of caution in Soviet policy during the first half of the 1980s coincided with a continuing reappraisal of Soviet prospects in the Third World by Soviet foreign-policy intellectuals.[28] This reassessment had been under way since at least the mid-1970s, but heterodox analysts' views had not gibed with the triumphalism of the middle Brezhnev years and had therefore remained on the political periphery rather than receiving a serious hearing from party leaders and policymakers.

During the early 1980s, the efforts of some academics to warn against the Afghanistan invasion's dire impact on superpower relations evidently went unheeded.[29] Nevertheless, the war in Afghanistan, together with the USSR's other troubles, probably created the first serious attention to such heterodox foreign-policy views within the country's leadership, especially among younger leaders who had little personal stake in defending established policies.

Apparently the change in the international and domestic situations also provoked second thoughts among elements of the foreign-affairs and military apparatus, particularly the General Staff and the Ground Forces. Although the historical record is still far from clear, some evidence suggests that influential elements of the military establishment, particularly the General Staff, counseled against the intervention in Afghanistan and sought to minimize the Soviet combat role once the party politburo had taken the decision to intervene.[30] In any case, the impending U.S. INF deployments and changes in NATO military doctrine provoked alarm within the General Staff and must have inclined many military men to advise against Soviet involvement in additional Third World conflicts in order to concentrate on developments in Europe.[31] Although some naval officers resumed the campaign for a large navy in the early 1980s, this campaign was soon checked by the General Staff and subordinated to the drive to meet the perceived western challenge in Europe.[32] The military's brief but serious contemplation of Soviet military intervention in Poland to crush the Solidarity movement is further evidence of the renewed Soviet preoccupation with European developments.[33]

Not least important, the Afghanistan war had a major impact on the attitudes of the Soviet public toward involvement in Third World conflicts. The war gradually turned many citizens, especially the well educated, against the idea of foreign military intervention and gave rise to a widespread desire to reduce Soviet entanglements in the Third World.[34] This change in public opinion was of little moment to authoritarian Soviet leaders of the traditional stripe, but it became important once the struggle for democratization was launched in the second half of the 1980s.

The Gorbachev Era and the Change in Third World Policy

Ideology and Global Strategy

After 1985, Gorbachev and his political allies initiated a fundamental reevaluation of the Soviet regime's international strategy and domestic goals. Although strongly committed to maintaining the USSR's superpower status and ability to influence international developments, Gorbachev embraced a conception of the country's international role strikingly different from the notions of his predecessors. This conception laid an exceptional emphasis on cooperation with the West and was intended to focus the ruling elite's attention on the internal conditions that threatened the existence of the Soviet state. As it unfolded, the policy increasingly amounted to an effort to integrate the USSR with an international order dominated by western values and institutions. This strategy was pursued not only on a military level but also on the economic, cultural, and, to a large extent, political levels.

The emergence of the strategy of integration was foreshadowed by Gorbachev's early call to build a genuine system of international security that would entail "much more" than the 1970s version of East-West détente.[35] At first, his efforts to improve East-West relations centered on the arms race rather than on East-West commerce. Gorbachev came to power as an economic nationalist, and his initial emphasis on revitalizing the USSR's economic ability to compete against the West in traditional geopolitical terms was one source of his early appeal to Soviet national-security conservatives. Nonetheless, as his domestic reform program became more sweeping and the problems of the economy worsened, he abandoned the trappings of economic nationalism. Instead he evinced a growing desire for commercial ties with the West and for Soviet inclusion in such international economic institutions as the International Monetary Fund and the World Bank.

The strategy of integration had important cultural and political components as well. Early on, Gorbachev began to describe East and West as members of a single "world civilization"—terminology that implied that countries of the socialist and capitalist systems have basic values in common. His glosses on the doctrine of peaceful coexistence said almost nothing about the class struggle between East and West, which had been a key component of previous official interpretations of the doctrine.[36] Even more important, Gorbachev underscored the "colossal profundity" of the unorthodox proposition that "the interests of social development and common human values" have priority over "the interests of this or that class."[37] Although at first linked primarily with the need to avoid nuclear war, this theme gradually came to connote the policy of extending East-West cooperation to many international issues previously regarded as unyielding class struggles between the socialist and capitalist blocs.[38] Equally important, it became a major justification of the selective incorporation of western political values and institutions into the Soviet domestic order.

The new international strategy involved an abandonment of the traditional Soviet teleological view of history and a sharp reduction of the role assigned to military instruments of foreign policy.[39] Soviet policy, Gorbachev promised, would aim to avoid provoking other countries' "fears, even if imaginary, for their security."[40] In place of the expectation of an enduring contest for mastery between the socialist and capitalist worlds, the new approach emphasized the need for East-West accommodations and for efforts to arrive at a "balance of interests" between contending international parties. In essence, the formula amounted to an endorsement of the liberal tenet that all states have legitimate national interests that must be reconciled through compromise rather than military conflict. Whereas previous Soviet thinkers had traditionally assumed that international disequilibrium short of general war is both natural and desirable, the new strategy rested on an acceptance of international equilibrium as a Soviet goal. In contrast to the past, the new strategy made the search for international political stability a watchword of Soviet external policy.

In keeping with the accent on international integration, Gorbachev and other reform-minded politicians evinced a clear willingness to accept a direct link between East-West relations and a moderation of Soviet behavior in the Third World. Just as they accepted the linkage of domestic human rights and political reform with superpower relations, they acknowledged that relations with the West cannot be improved without consistent cooperation in reducing Third World conflicts. Reformist commentators condemned the past Soviet pursuit of "small change" advantages in the Third World as an impediment to East-West reconciliation and an obstacle to the transformation of the domestic system; class struggle, they now contended, was strictly "a matter for the people of each country" that should be excluded from interstate relations.[41] As guides to Soviet policy toward regional conflicts, these analysts embraced the notions of "national reconciliation" and "self-determination."[42] These slogans provided no ready-made formula for halting local interstate and guerrilla wars, but they did provide a philosophical basis for cooperating with the West to ameliorate such conflicts.

Prefigured by the withdrawal of Soviet military forces from Afghanistan, Soviet behavior during the Gulf War demonstrated the seriousness of the political leadership's commitment to this policy. It is quite true that the USSR sought to mediate between Iraq and the United States before the United States launched a military attack to force Iraq's withdrawal from Kuwait. It is also true that Gorbachev wished to protect the USSR's ability to play a leading role in any subsequent Mideast settlement—a role he knew would be jeopardized if the United States and other coalition members defeated Iraq militarily. Nevertheless, Soviet political support for the actions of the United Nations coalition was completely unprecedented. Without such support, the military operation against Iraq could never have been undertaken, let alone succeeded.

The International Correlation of Forces and the Domestic System

From the beginning, Gorbachev's new approach to international relations was linked to the elite's shifting appraisal of the Soviet system's socioeconomic strengths and weaknesses. During his first two years as party leader, Gorbachev repeatedly asserted that economic and technological growth must be accelerated to prevent the USSR from losing its superpower status, and he emphasized that a favorable international environment was necessary for this socioeconomic revitalization to succeed. After 1987, he went further, asserting that the Soviet system had slipped into a crisis that could be averted only through sweeping political liberalization as well as basic economic reform.

In highlighting the relationship between security policy and domestic affairs, Gorbachev and his supporters openly confronted a reality that the party leaders of the early 1980s hinted at but were afraid to face. In the eyes of many observers and officials, the Soviet system had reached a stage in which the internal socioeconomic threats to its existence exceeded the external threats. As one group of foreign-affairs analysts put it, domestic difficulties had become so acute that "possible dangers in the sphere of internal development" should be treated as a "problem of national security" no less than external threats.[43] According to another specialist, the old Soviet preoccupation with Lenin's question, "who [will destroy] whom?" "today simply 'doesn't work.' The 'center of danger' . . . has shifted from the interstate sphere to inside our system itself. And if we continue to use the formula, 'who [will destroy] whom,' then it is necessary to soberly realize that first of all, we [will destroy] ourselves."[44]

By choosing to respond to this danger with fundamental political reforms, Gorbachev reversed the customary Soviet approach to the relationship between external policy and the domestic system. In contrast to the Brezhnevian approach, Gorbachev's foreign policy was designed to promote domestic change, not to brake it. This entailed more than creating a propitious international environment for economic reform, although that was clearly one of Gorbachev's aims. As he told the June 1988 party conference, under the influence of the new approach to common human values "the USSR is . . . 'opening' anew for the outside world" and using expanded contacts with other societies to extract useful ideas and new understandings of such values as freedom and democracy.[45] Gorbachev and his supporters declared their intention of incorporating western economic and political ideas into a new model of socialism, and they sought to use extensive societal contacts with the West to modify the political culture associated with traditional Soviet authoritarianism.[46]

Despite its zigzag character, domestic reform seriously undermined the institutions and ideas that had traditionally sustained a confrontational Soviet posture toward the outside world in general and Third World conflicts in particular. *Glasnost* permitted heterodox civilian analysts to question previously sacrosanct foreign-policy commitments, in the Third World and elsewhere, as counterproductive. Radical critics of the regime's long-standing siege mentality began to assert that past descriptions of the western threat resulted not so much from genuine dangers as from the internal political needs of the dictatorship's institutions of coercion and from its militaristic impulses.[47] Together with such criticism, mounting domestic hardships crystallized antimilitary feelings within a good part of the general population, and opinion surveys indicated profound public skepticism about the reality of external threats to the USSR and strong support for cuts in the defense budget. Surveys also indicated widespread backing for cuts in the scope of Soviet military assistance to Third World countries.[48]

The new strategy of integration and East-West cooperation encountered doubts among some officials and commentators. When Gorbachev first articulated the notion of giving East-West cooperation higher priority than class conflict, Egor Ligachev, then a member of the party politburo, raised the objection that this policy would "confuse" the USSR's friends and clients in the Third World.[49] From 1989 onward, the policy of accommodation with the West came under increasing attack—particularly over the collapse of Soviet hegemony in Eastern Europe and the reunification of Germany—as the geopolitical costs of Gorbachev's policies became clear. In 1990, the chorus of complaint was swelled by bitter criticism of Shevardnadze over Soviet conduct during the Persian Gulf crisis. This criticism, voiced by a vociferous group of Supreme Soviet deputies from the "Soiuz" parliamentary faction, played a role in Shevardnadze's December 1990 decision to resign from his position as minister of foreign affairs.

As subsequent events proved, the contretemps over policy toward the Gulf War is not a harbinger of an abandonment of cooperation with the West in addressing regional conflicts. Despite Shevardnadze's resignation and Gorbachev's attempts to preserve some Soviet freedom of maneuver during the crisis, in the end the Soviet Union backed the U.S. military action against Iraq. Moreover, the criticism leveled at Shevardnadze did not imply a return to the policy of competitive activism that the USSR frequently followed in the Third World during the pre-Gorbachev era. Right-wing critics did castigate Shevardnadze for his policy toward the conflict in the Gulf, but they concentrated their attack on the accusation that he had advocated the use of Soviet military forces in the conflict. Although the affair illustrated right-wing distaste for international cooperation with the United States, it also testified to the persistence of the "Afghanistan syndrome" and a widespread desire, even among conservatives, not to become militarily entangled in another regional conflict. This outlook marked a substantial shift from the official attitudes toward Third World conflicts during previous decades.

Soviet politics crossed a major threshold in the spring of 1990, when elections in the Soviet republics produced democratic legislatures eager to push the pace of internal political liberalization faster than Gorbachev desired. The elections presented a new challenge to Gorbachev in the person of Boris Yeltsin, who was elected chairman of the Russian legislature and was later elected president of the Russian republic. The parliamentary elections also produced a grave new challenge to the Soviet state: mounting pressures in a series of republics for secession from the USSR. Attempting to shore up his position and counter these centrifugal forces, Gorbachev struck a tactical alliance with conservatives in the party, military, and police establishments. In the end, however, his attempts to achieve centrist goals by balancing antagonistic political forces failed. Instead, in August 1991, he became the target of an unsuccessful right-wing coup attempt that inadvertently precipitated the demise of the Communist party and the collapse of the Soviet state structure. A few months later, outmaneuvered by Yeltsin, Gorbachev resigned as president of the USSR.

The End of the USSR and Policy in the Post-Communist Era

The formal dissolution of the USSR and the establishment of the Commonwealth of Independent States (CIS) have further deepened the uncertainty about the future of Russia and the other nations that have emerged from the ashes of the Soviet Union. Proclaimed in December 1991, the commonwealth represents a decisive break with the legacy of communism and a formal espousal of national self-determination and multiparty democracy as the guiding principles of political organization within the new regimes. However, the commonwealth's political survival is endangered by political tension and instability within the member states, by the grave difficulty of coordinating the members' disparate approaches to economic reform, and by the risk that ethnic animosities will provoke sharp conflicts between the member governments. Together these factors make any predictions about the future especially hazardous.

Despite the existence of many imponderable factors, Russia's domestic politics and Russia's relations with other commonwealth states will be key determinants of future policy toward the Third World and Third World conflicts. Under almost any scenario, Russia will remain the dominant power within the territory of the former Soviet Union.[50] Of all the newly independent states, only Russia has a historical tradition of being a great power and possesses the material potential to play a great-power role in the future. Russia commands by far the largest share of erstwhile Soviet natural and human resources, and it stands to inherit the bulk of the Soviet regime's surviving military capabilities. Russia's international strategy and internal politics are therefore likely to be the most important factor shaping "post-Soviet" policy toward the Third World, even though the international strategies and internal politics of other commonwealth members will also have an effect. Much depends on whether Russia continues to evolve along a democratic, nonimperialistic path or reverts to an authoritarian, imperial pattern of behavior.

For Russian policymakers of any stripe, one salient feature of the new international landscape will be that elements of the former Soviet Union now count as parts of the Third World. Long suppressed by the authoritarian structure of the Soviet regime, ethnic animosities, particularly those in the Caucasus and also Central Asia, are likely to spark continuing violence and interstate tensions. The conflict within Georgia and the clash between Armenia and Azerbaijan over control of the Nagorno-Karabakh region exemplify this danger. Moreover, the achievement of independence by the former republics of the USSR will add a new complexity to the "traditional" Third World conflicts along Russia's periphery. The political evolution of the former Central Asian republics, for instance, will have an impact on the balance of forces in the Middle East, and several Middle Eastern countries are already involved in a competition for influence in the region. To date the political elites of the former Central Asian republics seem eager to establish ties with the West and with moderate Middle Eastern governments to prevent the growth of radical Islamic groups inside their societies. However, a major increase of Islamic radicalism in Central Asia would affect not only Central Asian relations with Russia but also political alignments and behavior in the Middle East as a whole.

Given Russia's internal crisis and the Russian public's current aversion to sending soldiers to die in non-Russian territories, a democratic Russia will probably strive to avoid becoming militarily entangled in the new Third World conflicts that emerge on its periphery. In a few cases, such as Kazakhstan, violent ethnic clashes involving many expatriate Russians could draw Russia into the conflict. The prevailing Russian impulse, however, is likely to be to follow a hands-off policy. Russia may seek western involvement, perhaps through the United Nations, as one means of trying to cope with interstate conflicts such as those in the Caucasus. In Central Asia it will probably welcome the involvement of prowestern or conservative Middle Eastern governments, such as Saudi Arabia, whose political and financial influence may enable Russia to reduce its Central Asian involvements without necessarily turning the region into a stronghold of radical forces hostile to Russia.

As for the Third World in the customary sense, in the short-to-medium term, a democratic Russia will almost certainly continue to reduce its commitments and will probably eschew independent Third World initiatives, particularly initiatives requiring any expenditure of blood or treasure. Still more than in the Gorbachev era, Russia and the other CIS members are pursuing the strategy of international integration to surmount the dangerous internal crises they face, and the explicit rejection of Marxism-Leninism by Yeltsin and many other post-Soviet leaders has further undermined the residual ideological motive for independent intervention in the Third World. As long as Russia and the CIS members continue to pursue the strategy of integration, cooperation with western Third World initiatives promises to be even fuller than it was in the late Gorbachev period. In effect, Russian policy will amount to a further drastic retrenchment of Third World commitments and increasing deference to U.S. and European initiatives in the Third World. Russia, for example, will probably abandon Gorbachev's already tenuous political commitment to the Communist regime in Cuba; in the Middle East, it is likely to continue to play the nominal role of superpower while consistently deferring in practice to U.S. preferences.

The short-to-medium term results could be quite different if Russian domestic politics veers onto a xenophobic, antidemocratic path. By blocking Russia's integration with the western international order and its access to large-scale western economic assistance, this turn of events would reduce the chances of a cooperative security system and the Russian leadership's incentive to cooperate with western initiatives in the Third World. On the other hand, it would probably also delay internal recovery and further intensify the acute pressures on the country's troubled economy. It therefore appears that in the short-to-medium term, a repressive Russian regime would probably turn inward and withdraw from involvement in most Third World conflicts rather than to pursue a vigorous role in opposition to western initiatives. Although this strategy would impede western efforts to build a consensus on traditional Third World conflicts through the United Nations, it would probably not entail Moscow's active involvement in traditional Third World conflicts remote from Russia. To the degree that an authoritarian Russia pursued an active role beyond its own borders, it would at first be more likely to strive to reassert influence over the most vulnerable of the USSR's former republics than to involve itself in Third World conflicts farther afield.

In the long run, once it recovers economically, a democratic Russia is likely to take a more active interest in the Third World regions outside the old Soviet borders. Even under a liberal democratic order, the country's great-power tradition will prompt it to seek a major role on the international stage, and the strategy of international integration will widen its economic linkages with Third World countries. Russia seems unlikely, however, to embark on a globalist Third World policy like the one pursued by the Soviet Union. The collapse of Marxist-Leninist ideology and the overthrow of the Communist party have eliminated the traditional ideological motives for challenging the West and promoting radical political change in the Third World. Moreover, a governmental system responsive to its citizens' domestic concerns and economic needs is unlikely to pursue a Third World policy not justified by real security challenges or economic benefits. Differences in geographical position and economic interest will no doubt generate some differences over Third World policy between a democratic Russia and the western democracies, but the possibilities for cooperation will remain much larger than in the heyday of Soviet power.

A xenophobic, antiwestern turn in Russian internal politics would lead to quite different long-term results. A highly nationalistic, authoritarian leadership that managed to revive Russia economically might not seek to compete vigorously with the West in some past areas of East-West rivalry, such as sub-Saharan Africa or Latin America. It would, however, be much more inclined to challenge western influence, and to exploit regional conflicts for that end, in regions closer to Russia's borders—particularly in the Middle East, Central Asia, and the Far East. In short, the future political complexion of Russia is likely to have a major impact on the long-term feasibility of efforts to resolve some of the planet's most enduring social conflicts.

Notes

1. Hugh Seton-Watson, *The Russian Empire, 1801–1917* (Oxford: Oxford Univ. Press, 1967), 41–62, 289–96, 438–45. During the late eighteenth and early nineteenth centuries, imperial Russia held colonial territories in North America, but it subsequently withdrew from them, selling Alaska to the United States.

2. The only arguable exception was the ill-fated attempt during the 1920s to foster an anticolonial alliance between Chinese Nationalists and Chinese Communists by providing military equipment and advisers.

3. Although Lenin's writings frequently criticized Tsarist Russia's imperialistic behavior toward neighboring peoples, Lenin's best-known exposition of the theory of imperialism, *Imperialism: The Highest Stage of Capitalism,* was directed exclusively against western imperialism. See Frederick Starr, "Tsarist Government: The Imperial Dimension," in *Soviet Nationality Problems and Practices,* ed. Jeremy Azrael [New York: Praeger, 1978), 13.

4. Stephen S. Kaplan, *Diplomacy of Power: Soviet Armed Forces as a Political Instrument* (Washington, D.C.: Brookings Institution, 1981), 154 and passim; Raymond Aron, *Peace and War: A Theory of International Relations* (New York: Doubleday, 1966, 515–20.

5. For the fullest account of this change, see Raymond Garthoff, *Détente and Confrontation: American-Soviet Relations from Nixon to Reagan* (Washington, D.C.: Brookings Institution, 1985).

6. *XXIV s"ezd KPSS* (Moscow: Politizdat, 1971), 54.

7. Andrei Gromyko, "Lenin's Peace Policy," *Moscow News,* 22 Apr. 1984, 5, translated in Foreign Broadcast Information Service, *Daily Report, Soviet Union* (hereafter *FBIS: SOV),* 27 Apr. 1984, R7.

8. George Breslauer, "Soviet Policy in the Middle East, 1967–1972: Unalterable Antagonism or Collaborative Competition?" in George, ed. *Managing U.S.-Soviet Rivalry,* 89–99.

9. Bruce Parrott, "Soviet Foreign Policy, Internal Politics, and Trade with the West," in *Trade, Technology, and Soviet-American Relations,* ed. Bruce Parrott (Bloomington: Indiana Univ. Press, 1985), 38.

10. L. I. Brezhnev, *The CPSU in the Struggle for Unity of All Revolutionary and Peace Forces* (Moscow: Progress, 1975), 182, 191, as quoted by Stanley Kober, "Changing Soviet Perceptions of the Threat: From Foreign to Domestic," unpublished paper, Washington, D.C. 1988, 2.

11. Leonid Brezhnev, *Na strazhe mira i sotsializma* (Moscow: Politizdat, 1979), 534; Francis Fukuyama, *Soviet Civil-Military Relations and the Power Projection Mission* (Santa Monica, Calif.: Rand Corporation, 1987), 8; Dmitri Ustinov, *Izbrannye rechi i stat'i* (Moscow: Politizdat, 1979), 271–72.

12. Bruce Parrott, *Politics and Technology in the Soviet Union* (Cambridge, Mass.: MIT Press, 1983), 232–35.

13. Joseph Brada, "Soviet-Western Trade and Technology Transfer: An Economic Overview," in Parrott, ed. *Trade, Technology, and Soviet-American Relations,* 3–34.

14. It is noteworthy that for several years after Soviet soldier began to die in Afghanistan, the official media systematically ignored the Soviet combat role and Soviet casualties.

15. See Robert W. Kitrinos, "International Department of the CPSU," *Problems of Communism* (Sept.–Oct. 1984): 54–56; Wallace Spaulding, "Shifts in CPSU ID," ibid.

(July–Aug. 1986); George W. Breslauer, "All Gorbachev's Men," *The National Interest* (Summer 1988): 95–96.

16. Stephen T. Hosmer and Thomas W. Wolfe, *Soviet Policy and Practice Toward World Conflicts* (Lexington, Mass.: Lexington, 1983), 34; Fukuyama, *Soviet Civil-Military Relations*, 17.

17. Fukuyama, *Soviet Civil-Military Relations*, 18–19. It is possible, although not certain, that these statements were part of a veiled elite debate about the proper level of Soviet support for North Vietnam.

18. See Michael MccGwire, "Soviet Naval Doctrine and Strategy," in *Soviet Military Thinking*, ed. Derek Leebaert (Cambridge: MIT Press, 1981), 133–46, 170–76 and Fukuyama, *Soviet Civil-Military Relations*, 24–25.

19. Eugene Rumor, "Soviet Professional Military Thinking," in *Gorbachev's Third World Dilemmas*, ed. Kurt M. Campbell and S. Neil MacFarlane (London: Routledge, 1989), 119–24.

20. Mark M. Kramer, "Soviet Arms Transfers and Military Aid to the Third World," in Campbell and MacFarlene, eds. *Gorbachev's Third World Dilemmas*, 90–91.

21. Ibid., 66, 71–72, 77–78, 90–92.

22. Roger E. Kanet, "Military Relations Between Eastern Europe and Africa," in *Arms for Africa: Military Assistance and Foreign Policy in the Developing World* (Lexington, Mass: Lexington, 1983), 87–89; and Melvin Croan, "A New Afrika Corps?" *The Washington Quarterly* (Winter 1980): 31.

23. Galia Golan, *Gorbachev's "New Thinking" on Terrorism* Washington Papers no. 141 (New York: Praeger, 1990), 19–32.

24. *Kommunist*, 1982, no. 12: 13, 20.

25. E. A. Ambartsumov, "Analiz V. I. Leninym prichin krizisa 1921 g. i putei vykhoda iz nego," *Voprosy istorii*, 1984, no. 4: 15–16, 23–25, and 28–29.

26. Iu. V. Andropov, *Iabrannye rechi i stat'i*, 2d ed. (Moscow: Politizdat, 1983), 215.

27. John Parker, *The Kremlin in Transition: From Brezhnev to Gorbachev, 1978–1989* (London: Unwin Hyman, 1990), 2 vols.

28. Jerry Hough, *The Struggle for the Third World: Soviet Debates and American Options* (Washington, D.C.: Brookings Institution, 1986).

29. See esp. the 1980 memorandum from Oleg Bogomolov, in *Literatunaia gazeta*, 16 Mar. 1988.

30. V. I. Varennikov, "Afghanistan: podvodia itogi," *Ogonek*, 18 Mar. 1989, 6. For a discussion of the reliability of various Soviet accounts of the decision to invade, see Jeanette Voas, *Preventing Future Afghanistans; Reform in Soviet Policymaking on Military Intervention Abroad* (Alexandria, Va.: Center for Naval Analysis, 1990), 10–13.

31. Bruce Parrott, "Political Change and Civil-Military Relations," in *Soldiers and the Soviet State*, ed. Timothy Colton and Thane Gustafson (Princeton, N.J.: Princeton Univ. Press, 1990), 65–66.

32. Rose Gottemoeller, "Intramilitary Conflict in the Soviet Armed Forces," in Parrott, ed. *The Dynamics of Soviet Defense Policy*, 104–5.

33. Richard D. Anderson, Jr., "Soviet Decision-Making and Poland," *Problems of Communism* (Mar.-Apr. 1982): 22–37.

34. For fragmentary opinion data covering the first half of the 1980s, see Ellen Jones, "Social Change and Civil-Military Relations," in Colton and Gustafson, ed. *Soldiers and the Soviet State*, 247–48. The depth of the trend in public opinion became obvious with the advent of *glasnost* in the second half of the decade.

35. Mikhail Gorbachev, *Izbrannye rechi i stat'i* (Moscow: Politizdat, 1987–), II: 134, 205.

36. Gorbachev, *Izbrannye rechi i stat'i*, II: 134. The notion of class struggle was subsequently omitted from the formula for peaceful coexistence included in the revised party program. *(XXVII s"ezd KPSS: Stenograficheskii otchet* [Moscow: Politizdat, 1986], I: 570.)

37. *Kommunist*, 1986, no. 16: 12.

38. For an account of this change, see my "Soviet National Security under Gorbachev," *Problems of Communism* (Nov.—Dec. 1988): 10–11 and passim.

39. Ibid., 7–8.

40. *Izvestiia*, 26 Feb. 1986, 8.

41. I. Usachev, "Obshchechelovecheskoe i klassovoe v mirovoi politike," *Kommunist*, 1988, no. 11: 110–12, 115–18; and V. Dashichev in *Literaturnaia gazeta*, 1988, no. 18. See also g. Shakhnazarov, "Vostok-Zapad: k voprosu o deideologizatsii mezhgosudarstvennykh otnoshenii," *Kommunist*, 1989, no. 9: 67, 69.

42. A. Kozlov, "Pereosmysleneie politiki v 'tret'em mire,' " *Mezhdunarodnaia zhizn'*, 1990, no. 4: 36–45. See also Igor Malashenko, "Printsip svobody vybora—mezhdunarodnyi aspekt," *Kommunist*, 1990, no. 7: 79–88.

43. Vitaly Zhurkn, Sergei Karaganov, and Andrei Kortunov, "Vyzovy bezopasnosti —starye i novye," *Kommunist*, 1988, no. 1: 43; Kober, "Changing Soviet Perceptions," 17.

44. O. Bykov in "Novoe myshlenie v mezhdunarodnykh delakh," *Kommunist*, 1989, no. 8: 102.

45. Ibid., 3.

46. See, in particular, V. Rubanov, "Demokratiia i bezopasnost' strany," *Kommunist*, 1989, no. 11: 46–47, 50–51, and passim.

47. Batalov, "Amerikanskii opyt i nasha perestroika," 5; Rubanov, "Demokratiia i bezopasnost' strany," 48, 54–55; Andrei Fadin, "Prokliat'e sily: magiia 'oboronnogo soznaniia'," *Vek XX i mir*, 1988, no. 10: 2–31; "Kruglyi Stol," *Vek XX i mir*, 1988, no. 3; "Voennyi protiv voenshcheny," *Vek XX i mir*, 1988, no. 11.

48. *Izvestia*, 4 June 1989, p. 1, cited in Archie Brown, "Political Change in the Soviet Union," *World Policy Review* (Summer 1989): 496–97; Karen Dawisha, *"Perestroika, Glasnost,* and Soviet Foreign Policy," *Harriman Institute Forum* (Jan. 1990).

49. *Pravda*, 8 Aug. 1988, 2. See also Nina Andreeva's attack on the idea of coexistence without class conflict in her infamous letter to *Sovetskaia Rossiia*, 13 Mar. 1988, 3; trans. in *FBIS*, 16 Mar. 1988, 51.

50. The main exception is the possible political disintegration of Russia itself, which is not probable but is conceivable.

PART THREE

Case Studies in Conflict Reduction

6

The Third World and Conflict Reduction

GEORGI MIRSKY

The Third World after the Gulf War

The study now under discussion concentrates mainly on sources of Russian and American conduct in situations of regional conflicts, prospects for cooperative security, opportunities for mediation within systems of world order, and so on. What has not been analyzed so far are the possible responses by the Third World to the superpowers' efforts at mediation and conflict reduction. In other words, it might be useful to look at the other side of the picture, to assess the mood of the "receiving end," to grasp the mentality of local actors faced with a prospect of lasting superpowers' involvement in what they may consider their internal affairs. To give just one example, let us look at the Middle East after the second Gulf war.

No single dominant local actor has emerged in the Gulf area after the dust has settled. This time the regional game is unlikely to be played only by home teams. The United States has entered the arena in a big way and is not likely to leave it. There is no way the Gulf Arab states can do without some degree of American military presence even when Saddam Hussein disappears. Deep distrust of Iran, if anything, provides ample justification for setting up a regional security system with western military might at the center of it. In this context American military presence in the region is believed able to exercise sobering and stabilizing influence.

Here we come to a question: Can the U.S. leading role be expected to gain regional acceptance? Will what is certain to be seen in many quarters as an attempt to impose pax Americana not be resented by local public opinion?

It is true that the Gulf blitzkrieg enormously enhanced American prestige, but mainly on the official level. In regard to Third World public opinion, deep-rooted, latent, long-standing anti-Americanism (or, to be more precise, resentment of U.S. power and suspicion of American motives) has, if anything, increased as a result of the war. Even more significant is the fact that the Third World reaction to the American intervention in Somalia, for humanitarian purposes, was much the same. While this chapter focuses on the Gulf, similar reactions in regard to Somalia should not be forgotten.

In October 1991, while on a visit to New Delhi and lecturing at the Institute of Defense Studies, I was surprised to hear local scholars voice their indignation about the allegedly arrogant way the Americans were handling the Gulf crisis. Why should the Americans have the right to decide who is to rule Kuwait? (The people who spoke like this were Hindus, not Muslims.)

The incredibly swift rout of the Iraqi armed forces shocked and aggrieved many people in the Third World, but did not basically change their opinion about the whole thing. Indeed, the very swiftness and brilliance of the American-led coalition victory has provoked dismay and anxiety. Public opinion was alarmed by what is seen by many as American arrogance and assertiveness as a result of this victory.

The new American position of global strength coupled with the weakening of the Russian influence has caused deep concern among wide sections of public opinion, particularly in Asia and the Middle East. At the same time, it should be borne in mind that fundamentalist forces are in the ascendancy throughout the area. They cannot help feeling frustrated now, after their poor showing during the Gulf crisis, when they proved to be totally unprepared to back Saddam.

However, such sentiments as frustration and humiliation usually breed anger and lust for revenge rather than resignation. Anti-American protestations from those quarters in the event of an obvious U.S. hegemony within the framework of a new security system are likely to be so loud and sound so convincing to broad masses ("the street") that one can hardly see local governments disregarding the new popular mood. No Middle East leader can afford to ignore mass discontent originating from the Gulf War (seen as a new Arab humiliation) and the then seemingly intractable Palestinian deadlock; for both issues America was to blame in the eyes of "the street" and the radicals.

It is only natural, because the louder the talk about America remaining the only world superpower, the stronger the resistance to growth of the U.S. power and influence in world affairs. Therefore it seems doubtful that the Americans can become chief architects and guardians of peace in any Gulf security system without causing severe embarrassment to the very governments they claim to protect.

Will the Third World recognize the United States after the Gulf crisis as the sole superpower or as a world policeman? It would be safe to assume that no single regional actor and no single outside power is likely to play a dominant role in the Gulf security structure or bear the main responsibility for preserving peace in the area. Logic seems to indicate the United Nations as the only force capable of directing efforts designed to ensure Gulf security. The United Nations has many shortcomings, and there is no denying that its record of failures appears impressive. Yet, mankind has not invented anything better and more efficient.

As Somalia, Rwanda, Cambodia, Angola, and Mozambique show, the UN can "count on getting asked routinely to sanction, shape or run a new form of global riot-control that none of the big powers, not even America, is ready to do alone."[1] Can the UN live up to these expectations, can it be trusted to rise to occasions in inevitable regional crises? It depends to a large extent on the international body's ability to transform and restructure itself, to initiate a kind of "perestroika" and adopt a new political thinking.

What kind of lesson can one learn from the history of regional responses to outside interference during the Gulf crisis? On the surface, at least, it all went very smoothly. Widely anticipated outbursts of pro-Saddam Arab nationalist feeling throughout the region leading up to popular uprisings and overthrow of existing regimes did not materialize. To be sure, there was widespread protest against the American military presence, violent expressions of pro-Iraqi sympathies, lots of angry demonstrations, but not a single action of revolt occurred nor were there any attempts at challenging the government.[2] No jihad-type crusade was mounted, no significant volunteer forces rushed to Saddam's aid. Even the Palestinians—Saddam's most ardent supporters—steered clear of the battle. Contrary to some predictions, King Hussein has managed to survive once again. No real domestic threat was posed to Saudi Arabia. The Baathist regime in Syria was able to get away with declaring its refusal to back Iraq even if Israel were to be involved in the war.

However, this picture of all but unanimous support of outside intervention in internal Arab affairs—support demonstrated, at least, on the official level—should not mislead us into believing that a new and positive pattern has already been set.

After all, the Gulf crisis initiated by the Iraqi invasion of Kuwait was probably unique, by no means typical, and can hardly be seen as a preview of things to come. It is difficult to imagine another Third World dictator behaving in such a blunt way. This attack on Kuwait was such a classic textbook case of a naked, clear-cut aggression as to be almost incredible at the end of the twentieth century. Saddam Hussein seems to have done almost everything, including simple annexation of a sovereign state, to antagonize even regional public opinion, to say nothing of the international community. That this local public opinion later turned against American military presence in the area does not contradict its early condemnation of Saddam's aggression. The Iraqi dictator's unprecedented arrogance, his total and unveiled disregard for all norms of civilized international behavior, is unlikely to be imitated by any other Third World leader, which is why it is difficult to expect a repetition of a grand international, UN-led coalition being set up to restore the sovereignty of a state fallen victim to aggression. Indeed, it would probably have been impossible even in the Iraqi case if Saddam were content to establish a puppet regime in Kuwait instead of outright annexation.

The UN-authorized expedition to drive Saddam out of Kuwait must be seen as an exception rather than the rule in international politics. We should not bank on this kind of almost unanimous support of outside intervention being reproduced in the future, as the Yugoslav case shows. Without a UN sanction and authorization, any international coalition against an aggressor would be very difficult if not impossible to organize.

In the hypothetical event of a new aggression modeled on that of Saddam Hussein but not as blatant and shameless, the United States and its allies, if they agree to undertake a joint action, are certain to be deprived of a UN umbrella legitimizing this action. As a result, their cooperation in conflict reduction is liable to be left open to criticism. Many accusations of superpower condominium are sure to be raised in the Third World. What we have here is a vicious circle: a UN commitment will be difficult to obtain without a particularly brutal and totally unprovoked act of aggression, and without such a commitment any action will lack legitimacy and will be regarded as a great power's attempt to impose its domination.

All this, however, is only one side of the coin. The problem has many aspects. For instance, is not the Third World itself interested in having—as a kind of guarantee against regional disorders—an international force always ready to intervene, to mediate, to prevent bloodshed? The answer seems to be: yes and no.

The "Saddam-type" pattern of conflict emphasizing a clear-cut case of aggression by a regional bully is liable to provoke strong responses by regional and international communities. Because the aggressor is clearly definable and unlikely to be stopped by local actors, outside interference is called for, given, and accepted. Let us imagine a UN-authorized or U.S.-led intervention during the first Gulf war, the Iran-Iraq war. There the initial ambiguity of the conflict and the difficulty of pinpointing the aggressor would have blocked all prospects of an international interventionist campaign. The same would be true, for instance, of the conflict between India and Pakistan (discussed in the chapter by Thornton and Bratersky), or that between China and Vietnam.

However, this kind of conflict—between more or less equally influential regional actors, each blaming the other for having started the quarrel, and regional public opinion divided on the issue—is much more frequent than a "neat" case of aggression à la Saddam. Consequently, outside intervention just cannot be a widespread phenomenon or a recognized pattern of conflict settlement.

Capability of a "world policeman," be it an individual state or a collective body, to act on behalf of the "civilized community" in conflict situations thus appears to be severely limited. Third World states will need international actions only when an unusually strong and expansionist regional center of power emerges in a given area, threatening not only its immediate neighbor/rival but also other states, or when a state collapses, putting its citizenry at risk. A regional center of power perceived as a threat can serve as a common denominator, as a mobilizing factor for neighboring states; if those cannot cope with the situation, outside intervention is certain to be called for. However, it should be stressed once more that this scenario of a conflict situation is not likely to be nearly as characteristic or typical of Third World regional conflicts on the whole as the case of state collapse. In both cases, the parties concerned will be reluctant to call for an official, impartial, UN-sponsored or superpower-led intervention, at the same time doing their best to get unilateral aid for themselves.

To understand reasons for this reluctance—which threatens to rule out or greatly diminish prospects of conflict reduction from outside—requires a closer look at the roots of regional conflicts in the Third World and at internal or intrastate conflicts, for it is there that roots of interstate confrontation usually lie.

Third World Conflicts: How Should the World Respond?

The upsurge of nationalist, religious, and sectarian feeling leads to constant radicalization of slogans and programs. Extreme factions that tend to prevail within a nationalistic movement do not, as a rule, advocate hatred only in relation to their local adversaries but do resort to xenophobia in a more general sense. Here comes imperialism ever ready to divide patriotic forces and undermine their strength by covertly supporting the opposing side.

Thus during the Iran-Iraq war both sides were accusing each other of collusion with imperialism (traditional western brand as well as "red").[3] Both India and Pakistan during their military confrontations claimed that only outside help to the enemy robbed them of decisive victory.[4] Ethiopia, Somalia, Rwanda, and Sudan provide examples of participants in intrastate and interstate regional conflicts bitterly complaining about crucial assistance from abroad given to the opposing side.

Therefore it would be difficult to expect a party to a regional conflict to appeal for help from America or Russia or even the United Nations (still considered by many to be a tool of the great powers) without risk of losing or at least seriously jeopardizing its nationalist credentials. There may be exception; after all, Saudi Arabia did send an urgent appeal for help to that archenemy of Islam and protector of Jews—America. The Saudis, however, were desperate, expecting every minute to become Saddam's next victim. This was an exceptional situation. Usually opposing sides reckon on achieving victory—or a compromise solution—by their own means, probably with outside military aid but without appeals to great powers either for intervention or mediation. It would have been inconceivable, for instance, for either Ayatollah Khomeini or Saddam Hussein to summon Washington or Moscow or both to their rescue.

The problem does not end, however, with local governments and their attitudes. What about public opinion? An important trend has been noticeable in recent years: popular frustration caused by poor performance of their government in the economic and social spheres is likely to turn more and more against national rulers. The old imperialist bogey appears to be less relevant as a scapegoat.

Strength and intensity of popular revolt against authority—and authorities—must make Third World governments even more susceptible to the "mood of the street." They can be expected to avoid doing things that might be seen. as antipatriotic and pro-Western. In this sense, government's interests will best be served by maintaining a distance from the great powers and stressing their complete independence. Antiimperialist rhetoric is certain to be resorted to, any outside interference being severely condemned.

On the other hand, this "revolt against authority" is not accompanied solely by the rise of chauvinism, xenophobia, and so forth. Some of the more mature elements of the population tend to become more sophisticated, less inclined to be guided by old traditional stereotypes. Calls for democracy are becoming widespread; some prerequisites for emergence of civil society are noticeable. Crude antiimperialist slogans and clichés look more and more obsolete; in the future it will not be so easy to make people believe that political initiatives coming from the "rich North" are suspicious by definition. Prospects of foreign mediation in regional conflicts will be viewed in a less hostile light by Third World public opinion, which, when faced with an alternative—to be engaged in a series of confrontations with a neighbor or have the conflict settled with outside help—would just possibly prefer the second option.

Prospects of successful conflict reduction are linked to patterns of democratization of the Third World. Dynamics of democratization and impact of freedom of speech and political activity tend to encourage open political debate. People are likely to adopt a less biased and rigid view of things, including new approaches to the issue of external involvement in domestic affairs.

It can be assumed, therefore, that in the future, as democracy (it is hoped) spreads in the Third World, it will be much more difficult for demagogic rulers to manipulate public opinion and frighten the masses with tales of imperialist plots. Crude and primitive "bloody shirt nationalism," so widespread in Asia and Africa in the early decades after independence, appears to have no serious chance of reasserting its former influence in those areas as dictatorial and totalitarian methods of rule are being denounced and discredited the world over. In this context, it is logical to expect more comprehension and tolerance for outside intervention by Third World populations in cases of brutal and naked aggression —which was exactly what we recently witnessed during the Gulf war.

It would be wrong to attach too much importance to democracy as a factor influencing the Arab countries' willingness to join the western powers in the fight against Saddam Hussein. Saudi Arabia, Egypt, and Syria took part in the war not because Saddam was a dictator but because he was an aggressor who attacked an Arab country and threatened the status quo in the whole area. Indeed, some of the regimes aligned against Saddam were only slightly less dictatorial and despotic. It can even be said that it is easier for a dictatorship than for a democratic government to make the population swallow any sharp roundabout, any volte-face in foreign policy. Still, in regard to the response to an outside interference in regional affairs, it is fair to assume that a more democratic, more sophisticated and enlightened society would be, on balance, more likely to condemn a brutal aggression and agree to outside help in combating this aggression than people under an oppressive, dictatorial regime. Such an assumption can be true only in case of a "first-degree" aggression of Saddam's kind.

Even in this case, plenty of hostile response can be expected coming from more extremist nationalist forces, as the Gulf war demonstrated, but one has to make a major distinction between the affective and effective responses from the Third World. What is striking in the aftermath of the Gulf war is the degree to which Arab resentment and the seething masses have settled down. We have seen very little effective response from public opinion to the Gulf operation. This episode demonstrates that fears of a massive, violent, and sustained Third World hostile response to any outside interference have probably been exaggerated all along. Once again, however, it has to be stressed that this was a clear-cut and shockingly arrogant aggression and the mainstream of the Arab public opinion, though obviously unhappy about the reappearance of western armed forces on Arab soil, had no deep inner conviction that allowing Saddam to swallow Kuwait would have been preferable to kicking him out even in collusion with the West. What was decisive in this respect was the unescapable fact that only the West had the physical power necessary to liberate Kuwait. This is not very likely to be the case next time, and not because Saddam Hussein is a unique figure in the Third World—there may be plenty of dictators like him around—but because other would-be aggressors, not least in view of what happened in the Gulf, are certain to be more cautious and mindful of both the probable UN response and the American resolve to combat aggression.

What we are likely to see in the future in the Third World is not a blatant and unprovoked aggression like Saddam's adventure in Kuwait but more ambiguous and complicated conflict situations. It will probably not be very easy to unmistakably pinpoint the aggressor or the cause of collapse when one instinctively feels which side is mainly to blame. Moreover, even in these cases one cannot always be expected to rush immediately to the rescue of the right party. Motives for such a reluctance may be different but largely linked to state reasons. For instance, at the start of the Iran-Iraq war it was known that Iraq's forces were the first to cross the frontier.[5] Still, nobody was anxious to brand Iraq as an aggressor, mainly because of political considerations and raisons d'état, Ayatollah Khomeini (not Saddam Hussein) being considered at the time the greatest danger. Anyway, even if these pragmatic motives could have been disregarded, it is highly improbable that any kind of international intervention against the aggressor—Iraq—could have been undertaken, if only for the reason that it would have been practically impossible to prove that this was unprovoked aggression.

One of the main difficulties in the initial phase of making a decision whether to intervene in a Third World conflict is that it is always extremely hard to obtain a consensus as to the extent of responsibility (or guilt) of any given party to the dispute. One has only to imagine, for instance, what it would have taken for the world community to agree on determining who was to blame for the start of any of the wars between India and Pakistan. Or, in another example, would it have been possible even once for the United Nations to declare that either Israel or the Arab states was the aggressive side? Or who was responsible for the collapse of Rwanda or Somalia?

This is a real problem. Most Third World conflicts are so complicated, so deeply rooted in history, so hard to evaluate in simple black-and-white terms (or in "good guys vs. bad guys" terms) that it is not realistic to expect either the world community as a whole or the UN or regional public opinion to take unequivocal side in any dispute. The Gulf exception only confirms the rule.

I had a chance to visit Azerbaijan at the very outset of the bitter dispute between Azeris and Armenians over Nagorny Karabakh.[6] Both sides did their utmost to convince visitors from Moscow that their cause was just and claims advanced by the other side were absolutely false if not outright ridiculous. Both pointed to the graves of their forefathers and to the remnants of old churches, mosques, monuments, and so on, allegedly destroyed by the other side, as proof of validity of their claim. I thought then that any impartial mediation attempt by the central authorities would be extremely difficult, for each side claimed to have a monopoly on the truth and was absolutely certain that its claim was one hundred percent right. This adamant, totally rigid, and maximalist stand precluded any compromise. In this situation it would have been almost impossible for Moscow to act as an honest broker even if Gorbachev wanted it (which was not exactly the case). What followed was direct interference of the Soviet army, which satisfied nobody, provoked resentment and hostility of both conflicting sides, and failed to prevent further bloodshed.

Looking at this situation in retrospect, it is hard to escape the conclusion that there were virtually no satisfactory options left to Moscow once the latent, deep-rooted hostility between Armenians and Azeris became an open confrontation and a violent conflict started to shape. Neither arbitrary transfer of Karabakh to Armenia nor introduction of direct presidential rule in the territory could have ended the conflict but would have antagonized both warring factions and led to emergence of new struggles, such as a two-front guerrilla war reminiscent of the one that had been waged in Palestine by both Arabs and Jews (against each other and the British) before the mandate expired.

Certainly situations occur when a great power chooses to disregard niceties and subtleties of a conflict, refuses to be drawn into a hopeless mess of historical and juridical claims and counterclaims and just chooses to back the party whose victory seems for some reason preferable. So it was with the Soviet Union in the difficult conflict between its client states Ethiopia and Somalia, as discussed in the Lyons chapter.[7] This case, however, was rather exceptional, because both adversaries were, before the outbreak of the war, members of the same political bloc and no superpower rivalry was then involved in the area. Somalia was doomed to lose before it had time to switch to the American side. The Soviet Union could afford at the time to ignore both the world public opinion and responses (not unanimous and not quite clear at that moment) of Third World countries.

The ambiguous and inconclusive response of those countries could be explained precisely in that they had to deal with a conflict involving both ethnic and frontiers issues, that is, the most sensitive issues of Asia and Africa as a whole. In those cases most Third World states prefer to choose maintenance of the status quo rather than open a Pandora's box. On the contrary, when about the same time the Soviet Union and Cuba again interfered in African affairs—in the Angolan civil war—the response of both world and African public opinion was almost unanimously hostile and quite strong.[8] If the western response can be easily explained in the cold war context, that of the African states must be attributed primarily to the general Third World antiimperialist, antisuperpower feelings. If the United States had been the first to intervene in Angola, the Americans would have been sure to be denounced as imperialist interventionists; as it happened, they were lucky to be seen as the defending, not the attacking, side.

The Changing Nature of Conflicts

Now that the cold war is over and there is no way Moscow can try to bolster radical "antiimperialist" regimes in the Third World (if any are left), attention must naturally be focused on intrastate conflicts rooted not in global ideological and geopolitical issues but in local ethnic and religious differences as well as in regional power games. These kinds of conflicts of state collapse (especially the ethnic-religious ones) are the most complicated of all. Compared with them, politico-ideological conflicts, based on cold war confrontational approach and linked to superpower rivalry, are relatively easy to evaluate, as shown in the examples of Ethiopian-Somali and Angolan conflicts.

Third World conflicts, as classified by Mitchell in the second chapter, are usually divided into two broad categories, interstate and intrastate. The first category, in turn, can be subdivided into border or territorial disputes of a more or less conventional (or traditional) type; and wars of conquest. The difference between these two—not always clear-cut or obvious at the beginning—is important for the purpose of this study. In border or territorial disputes, neither of the conflicting sides has as its explicit aim annihilation of the opposing party; both states are trying only to improve their respective geopolitical positions as well as to increase popularity of the regime at home. In Wars of Conquest, the real aim of one of the adversaries is to change the regional status quo drastically through a decisive defeat or even, if possible, destruction of the other side.

This difference—largely reflecting, at least in the twentieth century, the difference between nontotalitarian and totalitarian systems—can be seen on the global scale, for instance, in a comparison between the First and the Second World Wars. In World War I, neither of the warring states aimed at total destruction of the other and conquest of its land; in World War II, Nazi Germany's goal was total annihilation of many independent European states and outright annexation of territory of some of them. Similarly, the North Korean attack on South Korea in 1950 had all the features of the typically totalitarian war of conquest. It does not follow from these two examples that totalitarian states, when starting a war, necessarily have as their goal nothing short of total victory; China, when attacking Vietnam in 1979, had a more limited objective. Generally speaking, though, total victory and conquest, although not a prerogative of totalitarian states, is organic to their nature. Saddam Hussein's action against Kuwait falls entirely into this category. It would be hard to imagine any but a thoroughly totalitarian regime to undertake aggression of this kind.

Conversely, Saddam's attack on Iran ten years earlier can be considered belonging to the first subcategory because the aim of the invasion was not destruction of the Iranian state but humiliation and decisive weakening of a rival regional center of power. The territorial dispute, although essentially of minor importance, served both as a pretext and a catalyst. Also, different from Kuwait, Khomeini's Iran was no helpless victim of aggression; indeed, it may be argued that Tehran had its own aggressive, or at least subversive, designs on Iraq and resorted to some provocative actions. Classical conflicts of this category are the India-Pakistan wars.

Distinguishing between these types of armed conflict may seem unimportant; it is liable to be questioned from a theoretical viewpoint and found irrelevant in practical evaluation of concrete situations. Indeed, is it possible, or even necessary, to search for a precise definition of motivation when a war breaks out? Does it make much difference if we know, for instance, that a government, when attacking a neighboring country, has in mind merely acquiring part of its territory and not bringing down its regime?

For this study it does make a difference. What kind of response is to be expected from public opinion in the Third World to outside interference in a regional conflict? It greatly depends on perception of goals of the parties involved, on the kind of image these parties had in the eyes of regional public opinion before the outbreak of hostilities. Crucial here are these questions: How does public opinion perceive intentions and goals of the antagonists and prospects of regional security if these goals are achieved? What implications of the conflict are to be expected? What effect will the conflict have on the other countries of the region? Answers to these questions may be helpful in trying to forecast regional response to outside attempts at interference, intervention, or mediation in a local conflict.

Thus it can be presumed that a "total" aggression aiming at destruction of a neighboring state or its annexation, thereby drastically changing the regional status quo, and fraught with unpredictable dangers for regional security, is likely to be resented and opposed by local public opinion as well as by governing forces in the area, and external intervention will be accepted; a limited interstate war is likely to be more ambiguous and external intervention rejected. The previous comparison of the first and the second Gulf wars provides an example.

Does it mean that the great powers and the world community are to be advised to take a resolute stand on regional conflicts only should the Kuwait scenario be replayed somewhere else in the Third World? Such a conclusion would be erroneous and harmful. That outside intervention will be greatly facilitated if the conflict at hand is a war of conquest rather than a border or territorial dispute means only one thing, namely, that in this case one can be sure of support or tacit connivance of a significant section of both governing forces and public opinion in the Third World. The other scenario will not be that favorable, and one has to be prepared for much outcry, for whole series of veritable campaigns against intervention, even for actual resistance by both officials and volunteers. Nevertheless, the world community must meet the challenge, otherwise all hopes of establishing any kind of order on the planet will prove illusory.

It would be unrealistic to rely upon the United Nations except in cases of blatant and unprovoked aggression, such as the Iraqi invasion of Kuwait. The UN, dominated as it is by the Third World countries, is certain to reflect in its decisions all the innumerable divisions, rivalries, and alignments that bedevil Asia, Africa, and Latin America. This is why the great powers and nations ready to support them in combating aggression through a system of cooperative security will have to be prepared to act, in urgent cases, without formal UN approval. There is no need to exaggerate the scope of resentment and even resistance such actions are bound to produce in the Third World. After all, in the present international situation, hardly any government except the most extremist and irresponsible would be likely to challenge the United States and its allies, if only for economic reasons.

There is another side to the coin. It is relatively easy to involve oneself in a conflict but much more difficult to extricate oneself. Again, the lesson comes from the Gulf War. Much criticism has been voiced over President Bush's decision to halt the military operations in Iraq without achieving total annihilation of Saddam's armed forces. Undoubtedly, this decision allowed the Iraqi dictator to massacre the Shiites and the Kurds, and helped him weather the storm and survive as a ruler despite the disaster he had brought on his country. However, it is open to doubt whether Saddam would not have been able to crush both rebellions with troops he had in reserve even if the coalition forces totally destroyed the bulk of his army trapped beyond the Euphrates—unless the allies would have chosen occupation of most of Iraq, including Baghdad. If they had, the psychological shock to the Arab world would have been so strong and painful that its implications might have outweighed by far any advantages the coalition could have achieved as a result of its victory.

It seems in retrospect that, after having driven the Iraqis out of Kuwait, Bush had no really good option when it came to the vital issue: what next? He chose the lesser evil as he saw it maybe he was not as unwise as his critics believe. The important point is that it would be naïve to hope, in intervention in a conflict, to achieve maximum results, to definitely resolve the issue, to satisfy everybody, and to quickly get out of the whole mess without losses. Problems lying at the core of almost every Third World conflict are so deep-rooted, many-sided, intertwined, and not given to simple and definitive solutions that the maximum that can be achieved is to prevent or punish brazen, naked aggression, to save a state from extinction, to stop bloodshed and save human lives, and to give one more lesson to all potential aggressors, to assert once more the basic rule: aggression does not pay.

Intrastate conflicts, the second general category, have been subdivided into types: intrastate separatist of an ethnoconfessional or ethnocummunal nature; and intrastate replacement of a revolutionary (or counterrevolutionary or quasirevolutionary) nature. The first subtype is particularly painful and sensitive, most difficult to be solved with outside help. One of the best known examples is Sri Lanka where all attempts of an outside power—India—to mediate and reach a compromise solution failed dismally.[9] It can be argued that much of this failure was because India could not be considered an impartial force, for it had a whole province inhabited by Tamils. Still, would European or South American forces have achieved a better result? They could not even have been invited by the government in Colombo except if the issue were debated in the United Nations and the decision taken to send an international force. Experience shows that governments of sovereign states are as a rule averse to appealing to outside help, even (and in some cases especially) through UN channels.

However, ethnocommunal conflicts, usually being extraordinarily vicious and bloody, do not nevertheless present such a powerful threat to world peace and security as to warrant serious preoccupation abroad, except when they spill over into transnational conflicts between states (as, for instance, between India and Pakistan). Need for external help in these situations arises out of humanitarian motives to stop bloodshed, famine, and so on. Immediate help must surely be given in these cases; not only should humanitarian aid be provided (which is self-evident) but also steps should be taken to stop the fighting, however fiercely one or the other parties may resist foreign intervention.

The obstacle is the principle of noninterference in domestic affairs of sovereign states. Delicate though this principle is, it is time to do something about it. This principle made it possible for the Khmer Rouge and Idi Amin to exterminate hundreds of thousands of people, and nobody intervened until governments of neighboring countries, driven by their own political considerations, marched in and ended the massacres.[10] The world community has allowed Saddam Hussein, year after year, to commit large scale massacres of the Kurds. By contrast, in Rwanda, the massacres led to intervention by the UN, the U.S., and France.

Still, it would be unrealistic to expect that every time a government in the Third World faces revolt of an ethnic or religious minority, outside forces will be ready to rush to the rescue of the embattled and oppressed community. Generally, public opinion tends to regard with suspicion every kind of foreign interference, even if it is clearly motivated by humanitarian reasons. Just where does one draw the line? Where is the border between the legitimate right of a government to combat insurgency, thus safeguarding the nation's security, and its attempts to suppress an equally legitimate right of an ethnic or religious community to resist discrimination and oppression?

This applies also to intrastate replacement conflicts. It is not always easy to distinguish between rioting and revolutionary upheaval, or to determine which government truly represents the will of the population. Even where the despotic nature of a regime is clear, for the whole world to see, and not only are human rights being violated but also murders are being committed regularly, it is difficult to do anything with the criminal government, unless the population itself dares rise up against tyranny. Then, however, a new problem arises: how to handle unrest in a country where popular movement challenges the authority of a patently oppressive but formally quite legitimate government. Foreign intervention, even if welcomed by the population, may be condemned not only by neighboring governments but also by majority opinion in the Third World unless sanctioned by the UN or at least by some regional organization.

The argument points to a need for regional organizations. It would be quite wrong to see the world of tomorrow as consisting only of great powers (with their allies) and the rest, with the UN somewhere above. The best, and maybe the only, way to avoid giving an impression of a new domination of the world, with a privileged elite empowered to take the law into its hands, is to encourage creating regional security regimes, regional organizations or other effective regional structures that can handle aggression themselves and make the great powers' role, if not quite irrelevant, certainly much less prominent than it would be otherwise.

Setting up these organizations would greatly increase regional responsibility and foster feeling of independence among the Third World nations. The important thing is to make them feel masters of their own house, masters of their destinies. What would have been inconceivable for great western nations has already been accomplished by regional organizations, for instance, in Liberia, where the multinational forces of the Economic Community of West African States (ECOWAS) were sent to stop the civil war. Regional interference is usually preferable to that of totally outside forces. The desired effect of resisting aggression, preventing further bloodshed, and restoring order can be achieved if, on the one hand, the regional organizations can be trusted to handle things in an unbiased and coordinated manner, and, on the other hand, cannot be open to accusations of playing the role of stooges of the great powers.

The problem of conflict reduction in regional conflicts is not merely dealing with aggression but dealing with political change, something that will characterize the Third World for decades. Moreover, given inevitable aggravation of ethnic and religious passions and frictions as well as a low level of political culture, it would be fair to assume that change will largely be violent. Let us face it: we will have to witness many cases of violent and brutal sociopolitical changes without being able to do anything about it, for attempts to stop change are as absurd as they are doomed to failure. There is no way to try to keep social and political structures intact once they prove to be inadequate for new conditions.

This consideration is, however, necessarily too general to be of any use in concrete situations. Should we welcome any kind of change? Is everything new to be accepted and greeted simply because we know that such is the law of nature—the new must triumph? Both Hitler and Pol Pot, to take only two monstrous examples, represented forces of the new, forces of youth and vigor and rejection of the old, rotten order. Every revolutionary dictator emerging in the Third World, including Saddam Hussein, claimed to fight for a new, better life for people. These examples are sufficient for a rather pessimistic (or just realistic) conclusion, namely, that there is no recipe for dealing with change. Only in obvious genocide would it be possible to mobilize enough international support or prompt regional organizations to take urgent steps to end the intolerable situation.

There are, however, many ways to deal with the problem of political change. It does not occur only in violent forms, in coups and revolutions. Change also comes through evolutionary patterns. Because democracy is and must remain one of the paramount goals and guiding principles of any kind of new world order, evolution toward democracy in the Third World should be encouraged and promoted as vigorously and systematically as possible, beginning with an enunciation of standards and values. Democracy cannot be imposed by armed force, but there are positive means of encouraging democratic political trends. The economic weakness of the developing countries, their dependence on the industrial powers, although evil and harmful in principle, can nevertheless be used as leverage to influence and to a degree even control political development. One should not unduly fear all the hue and cry about imperialist meddling in the internal affairs of the Third World that is bound to follow any attempts to link, for instance, economic aid to democratic patterns of political development.

It is to be borne in mind that democracy is what is absolutely needed in the Third World and corresponds to the interests of its population. After all, what exactly are Third World interests? First of all is to build a strong, modern economy that can be a vehicle of transformation and modernization of society, to end the well-known ills of the less-developed countries. Democracy, as opposed to dictatorial government, appears to be, with all its faults, especially those originating from backwardness, the most reliable way to get rid of age-long misery.

However, problems of economic development and transition to democracy, vital as they are, matter less in Third World response to outside interference than such issues as national pride, self-esteem, urge to get rid of any remnants of inferiority complex, consciousness of solidarity with the oppressed and underprivileged in the whole world, and so on. Desire to make the world, especially the "rich white world," respect their sovereignty, their traditions, and so on, may be considered a priority for the peoples of the Third World. Indeed, this demand for respect, causing extreme sensitivity in dealings with the great powers, should be considered a legitimate interest of the Third World. It is an issue of such enormous importance and sensitivity as to deserve special and profound analysis. This factor, primarily psychological, must be always present in the minds of those who plan any kind of outside interference in the affairs of Third World countries, even with the best of intentions.

After all, it would be hard to deny that such a thing as a sense of belonging to the Third World does exist. The very term "Third World" has been called artificial and outdated, but in certain situations countries that seem to have practically nothing in common display a spirit of solidarity, a feeling of sharing a destiny, and having the same interests. Whatever the explanations of this phenomenon, it is always dangerous and counterproductive to disregard the possibility of such sentiments emerging when one is thinking over options in regard to Third World crises that demand some kind of intervention or mediation.

The Aftermath of the End of the Soviet Union

Finally, in regard to Third World responses to outside attempts to reduce regional conflicts, the very notion of "outside forces" capable of making such attempts has radically changed. A major and decisive role was to be played by the two superpowers, but now only one of them is left.

Until recently, the combined weight of the two superpowers could be counted upon in dealings with regional conflicts, evident of late in the second Gulf war. It is true that Russia played second fiddle to the United States, and Gorbachev gave Bush the green light to go to war against

Saddam Hussein, but no one can deny that the Russian contribution to resolving the crisis was both positive and important. Now, in situations of this kind, parties to a conflict as well as the Third World in general will virtually face only the western powers, Russia playing a largely symbolic role, as, for instance, in the Madrid talks. What implications can this new situation have?

First, some countries that could have yielded to outside pressure if it were brought to bear by both the USSR and the United States might be reluctant now to submit to pressure coming from the Americans and their allies because of the appearance of retreating before the imperialism. As a result, their intransigence might increase.

Second, however, the disappearance of the "second pole" in global politics means that the Third World countries can no longer reckon on playing one giant against the other, in the hope of balancing between them. There simply is no one to turn to in the event of confrontation with the United States. The alternative is gone, a counterbalancing force is not there anymore.

Which of the two trends can prevail? It is impossible yet to say. The hard fact is that for the first time in history the world has only one superpower, the United States. No single nation can hope to match or rival the United States in the future. It does not mean that long-standing fears of the international leftists have come true, namely, that the United States is on the verge of world domination, or that we are witnessing the advent of a pax Americana. However, for this study, the "one superpower in the world" situation means that from now on the task of reducing regional conflicts threatening world security will be, if by no means unilateral, largely a G-7 undertaking, whatever the reluctance of the western powers to dirty their hands or suffer casualties.

Previously, Third World response to conflict reduction was conditioned to a large extent by fear of a possible superpower dictate, of a new American-Soviet condominium. This is not so anymore. However, this fear can be replaced by a new one: a second edition of western imperialist domination. Asia and Africa are again facing the West, they are once more posed vis-à-vis with "the rich white world" without any counterbalance. Old nationalist, antiimperialist sentiment may again rise high, although perhaps tempered by the bitter realization that this time it is hopeless to expect support from any other quarter. This may lead to strengthening of that "tiers-mondisme," the feeling, previously mentioned, of belonging to a Third World community. The slogan of solidarity of developing nations, by now devoid of the former nonalignment rationale, may be revived. The north-south—or First and Third World

—confrontation may thus become more acute and pronounced than ever now that the third component of the global setup—the Second or Communist World—is no longer relevant.

On the other hand, common sense and economic interest may push the Third World ruling elites to accommodate the West, especially because profound differentiation of this large and disparate area has already highlighted divisions, frictions, and conflicts among the developing countries. It is becoming more and more difficult to find a common denominator that can unite the Third World. Motivations and prospects for the future are too far apart. Thus, for many countries, especially the more developed ones, cooperation with the West would look more promising than confrontation. However, for this pragmatism to prevail, meaningful economic and social progress must be achieved to pave the way for eventually eliminating the social ills at the root of popular discontent that constantly breed extremism and violence. To ensure this success, a wise, long-term strategy of cooperative security is needed by the industrially developed nations. Precisely on the success of this strategy will the chances of reducing social tension and thus minimizing the possibilities of conflicts in the Third World ultimately depend.

Notes

1. *The Economist* 27 Apr.–3 May 1991, 14.

2. James Ridgeway, ed. *The March to War* (New York: Four Walls Eight Windows, 1991), 102; John Bulloch and Harvey Morris, *Saddam's War: The Origins of the Kuwait Conflict and the International Response* (Winchester, Mass.: Faber and Faber, 1991).

3. Shahzem Chubin and Charles Tripp, *Iran and Iraq at War* (Boulder, Colo: Westview, 1988), 198, 206, 212, 218, 219; Dilip Hiro, *The Longest War: The Iran-Iraq Military Conflict* (New York: Routledge, 1991), 242–44.

4. Richard Sisson and Leo E. Rose, *War and Secession: Pakistan, India, and the Creation of Bangladesh* (Berkeley: Univ. of California Press, 1990), 46–54.

5. Chubin and Tripp, *Iran and Iraq at War*, 36, 39; Hiro, *The Longest War*, 40.

6. The Federal Institute for Soviet and International Studies, *The Soviet Union, 1988–89: Perestroika in Crisis?* (Boulder, Colo.: Westview, 1990), 78–79; John Maresca, *The International Communities' Efforts to Resolve the Conflict over Nagorno Karabakh* (New York: Carnegie Commission, 1995).

7. Michael MccGwire, *Military Objectives in Soviet Foreign Policy* (Washington, D.C.: Brookings Institution, 1987), 223, 286.

8. Willian Kintner, *Soviet Global Strategy* (Fairfax, Va.: New Books, 1987), 132–34; Alex P. Schmid, *Soviet Military Interventions since 1945* (New Brunswick, N.J.: Transaction, 1985), 102–10.

9. David E. Long, *The Anatomy of Terrorism* (New York: Free Press, 1990), 53–57.

10. Leo Kupez, *Genocide: Its Political Use in the Twentieth Century* (New Haven, Conn.: Yale Univ. Press, 1982), 17, 138, 150, 159–60, 165–170, 176.

7

War in the Gulf

Possibilities and Limits of the
Russian-American Cooperation

ALEXEI VASSILIEV

The second Gulf war was an acid test of the newly emerging system of international relations, a system in which Russian-American cooperation is a conspicuous new factor. Iraqi aggression against Kuwait was expected in neither Moscow nor Washington. Although Iraq had created the most powerful military machine in the Arab Middle East, nobody anticipated the invasion and purported annexation of Kuwait, which posed a challenge to the United States and the entire world community. Shortly before this crisis, the first Gulf war between Iran and Iraq, which sometimes seemed to have put the Saddam Hussein regime on the verge of collapse, had ended in a stalemate. The international climate had shifted toward cooperation and nonviolent settlement of international disputes. True, Washington made many more allowances than Moscow for the adventurist bias of certain Arab leaders. However, even Washington failed to gauge accurately the implications of Saddam Hussein's deplorable lack of understanding of the new U.S.-Russian realities.

For both superpowers the first international crisis since the end of the cold war became a test of their ability to institutionalize cooperation and mutual understanding, as well as of the limits of such cooperation.

The first meeting between Soviet Foreign Minister Eduard Shevardnadze and American Secretary of State James Baker III at the Vnukovo airport near Moscow on 3 August 1990 was used as an opportunity to outline the principles to which the two countries were to adhere during the months of crisis.

This crisis demonstrated that Russian-American interaction cannot be mere words when faced with a challenge to international peace and security. The two powers came out united against the Iraqi aggression in Kuwait. Each one turned to different sets of tools to respond to the crisis, each to the tools best suited in view of the very different situations in which the two found themselves with respect to the crisis. The United States froze the bank deposits of Iraq and Kuwait. Meeting the American request, the Soviet Union froze arms supplies to Iraq, nearly four-fifths of whose armaments were of Soviet make. Then the other two major arms suppliers, France and China, followed suit. This step by Moscow was of both practical and political value. The Soviet Union sided with the victim of aggression, irrespective of the Soviet-Iraqi Treaty of Friendship and Cooperation (a carryover from the period of East-West confrontation). Also, the Soviet Union maintained wide-ranging economic contacts and helped with dozens of national economic projects in Iraq. Secretary of State Baker set high store by this Soviet step and noted that it was not easy for Moscow to end them, bearing in mind the historic character of Moscow's relations with Baghdad.

"The Soviet Union and the United States as members of the UN Security Council consider it important that the council immediately and resolutely condemn the rude illegitimate invasions of Kuwait by the armed forces of Iraq," said the joint declaration.

The then-Soviet Union and the United States reaffirmed their appeal to Iraq for unconditional withdrawal of its troops from Kuwait. The sovereignty, national independence, duly established power, and territorial integrity of the state of Kuwait had to be fully restored and ensured.[1]

When the United States began to carry out an airlift of its forces, unprecedented in rate and scope, to the Persian Gulf area and to prepare for military operations against Iraq, cooperation with the USSR—even a debilitated USSR—proved indispensable. Without such cooperation, international consensus against the Iraqi aggression would have been unattainable. Without that consensus, the twelve UN Security Council resolutions, which laid the international law groundwork for antiaggression measures, in turn could not have been adopted.

The new cooperative security system of relations with the Soviet Union permitted the United States to leave vulnerable and exposed the European and, in part, the eastern Asian theaters, drawing down equipment and personnel—or potential reinforcements—from those areas to build rapidly the capability Washington deemed necessary in the Gulf. When the crisis entered the military phase, this new system of relations let the United States make short work of Iraq with no fear of the Iraq's receiving outside help, as Vietnam had fifteen to twenty years earlier. In turn, the Soviet leadership did not consider the emergent powerful American military grouping in the Persian Gulf zone a threat to the Soviet Union from the south, although the Soviet military voiced apprehensions from the very beginning.

The voice of the Soviet military could be heard from the pages of *Krasnaya Zvezda*.[2] In its most outspoken form it said: "The idea that Washington intends to play the role of world policeman is not devoid of proof. No doubt that the U.S. is a strong state. But it does not mean that it has the right to show arrogance and power to impose its will on the others. But such an effort is being felt."[3]

When the war started, new apprehensions were voiced by the Soviet generals, who were worried by American nuclear armaments in the region.[4] Some generals seemed to nourish wishes that there would be a replay of the Vietnam War and even expressed their belief in an eventual American defeat.[5]

The old stereotypes and rules of the cold war and world confrontation, however, were no longer in operation, marking a crucial and entirely new factor in the international situation. The meeting between the two presidents in Helsinki on 9 September became a watershed in the policy of the two powers at the time of the Gulf crisis. Officially, nothing was new compared with earlier developed positions; only the political meaning was new. President Gorbachev supported every crisis-related action of the United States, thus giving Washington a free hand in military matters, and reaffirming the general political view on nonadmissibility of aggression, as well as the joint line at the United Nations.

At the same time, differences between Moscow and Washington over the aims beyond liberating Kuwait were quite important, as were those over the ways and means of settling the crisis. The difference in viewpoint was a function of the differing geo-strategic situations of the two powers, their differing histories and relations with countries in the region, as well as their differing domestic situations.

The Soviet press clearly outlined those differences as early as the first weeks of the crisis. No "symmetrical" approach to the crisis was to be found. The Soviet approach emphasized that only within the UN framework and only under UN auspices were economic sanctions and the establishment of a multilateral force acceptable. Washington saw things differently. The American administration only used the Security

Council opportunities to introduce sanctions and, as far as everything else was concerned, insisted on getting a free hand outside the UN mandate. The airlifting of forces to the zone of conflict began not with the United Nations but with the consent of Saudi Arabia. When the Egyptian, Syrian, and Moroccan military units later entered the scene, the idea of allied military pressure and response developed in a form agreeable to Washington. Britain and France sent their forces to Saudi Arabia rather as members of NATO, instead of as UN members, though no NATO mechanism was involved in their decision. The efficient naval blockage of Iraq looked even more like a U.S.-NATO operation.

"American policy is a combination of principled nonacceptance of aggression and a strong regional, and global, practical interest," the daily *Investia* wrote. "Washington thinks not so much about punishability of aggression as about preserving and strengthening its influence in the Middle East. By landing troops in the desert and amassing a naval armada nearby, Washington backs up its 'friend' and ally Saudi Arabia against its old-time foe Iraq. In contrast, Moscow comes out against its own 'friend' in favor of a pro-American monarchy, thus sanctioning the American actions."[6]

By sacrificing its relations with yet another dictatorship, the Soviet Union reaffirmed its commitment to the new course—the abandonment of confrontation with the West—which dislocated external and internal policy priorities of the Soviet leadership and became a deep-seated cause of the historic crisis of Soviet society. A principal lever able to pull the Soviet Union out of crises seemed to be the new relations of cooperation and interaction, particularly with the United States.

It was supposed that the long-term advantages, both political and practical, to be gained in this direction would make up for the loss of Saddam Hussein's "friendship." The Soviet Union had pulled itself out of the global confrontation with the United States, seeking a new partnership and obliged in reality to make one concession after another. It badly needed to diminish its burden of racing armaments, to establish broader economic cooperation with the West, and to assure noninterference—at least in active form—by the West in the disintegration of the "socialist community" and the Soviet Union itself. If Moscow were to take the side of the doomed Saddam Hussein, or even if it were to hesitate in supporting the world community against the Iraqi aggression, the whole system of new relations with the United States could go to pieces.

Meanwhile, as far as practical diplomacy is concerned, Washington declared that it reserved for itself the right to decide what the interests of peace and stability meant. Despite the degree of interaction between the

United States and the Soviet Union, there neither was nor could be any similarity between their policies.

The drama of the crisis made it crystal clear who was the strongest, who was the superpower that could in practice stop and punish the aggressor. In the Middle East, the Soviet Union was saying good-bye to the superpower policy, and it was a painful process. The all-embracing internal crisis in the Soviet Union determined its policy but did not remove the specific goals and interests.

From the very beginning, Washington steered toward a military solution of the conflict. However, if Saddam Hussein had retreated before 15 January 1991, a military solution would have been impossible. For its part, the Soviet Union to the very end sought a political settlement. The two countries had very different crisis-related priorities reflecting their very asymmetrical interests.

For the United States, the regional interests boiled down to the "oil and liberation of Kuwait" formula. Clear enough, the principle of inadmissibility of aggression and punishing the aggressor operated because the oil interests of the United States and the West were in question. Hypothetical seizure of one African country by another would not have forced such a mechanism (or even a much smaller one) of military counteraction to get under way. (When Washington rushed to help Chad against Libya in 1982, it intended more to punish Qaddafi's regime than to defend Chad.) The combined oil wealth of Iraq and Kuwait, nearly equal to Saudi Arabia's, and the chance that the aggression might spread to the eastern provinces of Saudi Arabia (where oil deposits are located) presented the danger that an unpredictable force hostile to the West could snatch control of much of the Middle Eastern oil. That the force was not pro-Soviet did not matter much.

When the war was in preparation and then in process, additional American priorities surfaced, which lay, so to say, midway between oil and the liberation of Kuwait: particularly destruction of Iraq's military machine, including its embryonic mass-destruction weapons potential, and ensuring continued American presence in the region on a scale larger than before the crisis. The goal of destroying Iraq's military machine rose to full height during the war, when Saddam Hussein attempted to expand it and dealt missile strikes at Israel. The political restraint of the Israeli leadership was rewarded by the crushing defeat of Iraq, its most potent and dangerous foe in the Arab world, at the hands of the United States and the allied coalition forces.

In turn, for the Soviet Union, liberation of Kuwait by political means was most important. Moscow needed practical proof of the efficiency of the new approach to international relations. The so-called new political thinking included "balance of interests" instead of balance of force, priority of values common to all mankind, implanting of morality in international relations, and unconditional supremacy of international law. The enfeebled Soviet Union, more than the United States, was interested in putting this philosophy into international practice. Opposition to this philosophy, first by Iraq and then, to a degree, by the United States, which in practical actions went beyond the mandate given by the UN, impaired the national interests of the USSR and the prestige of the Soviet president.

Even in times of the cold war, the Soviet Union showed understanding for the West's oil interests. Supporting steps toward nationalization of concessions and foreign companies, Moscow realized the unacceptability (and hence the danger) of an erratic oil flow to the West. Moscow, however, did not care what part of Middle Eastern oil Iraq controlled. An oil-exporting country, the Soviet Union was more interested in higher oil prices. The general economic crisis, however, had led to oil production and export shortfalls in the country. Nevertheless, the oil price factor had no appreciable impact on the Soviet position.

Political settlement of the Middle Eastern crisis would have let the Soviet Union resume the embargo-interrupted economic cooperation with Iraq, which gave it nearly the most lucrative partnership in the Third World. The crisis also interrupted the Soviet's developing cooperation with Kuwait, which had given the Soviet Union a large credit.

Moscow's attitude toward possible destruction of Iraq's military machine, which was created mostly by the Soviet Union, was ambivalent. Iraq was no threat to the USSR or its allies, though the buildup of missiles and chemical and bacteriological weapons destabilized the regional situation and worried Moscow. Military defeat of Iraq, about which Moscow had no doubt, would deal yet another blow to the prestige of Russian weaponry. A military-enfeebled Iraq would clearly mean a stronger Iran, creating an unpredictable situation.

Lastly, the Soviet position was also influenced by serious internal factors, particularly the sentiments of the 70 million-strong Muslim population. The Soviet leadership had to consider the negative response of a large part of that population to military operations by the United States and its allies against Muslim Iraq.

A comparison of such elements in the Soviet and American positions in the crisis shows they were neither contradictory nor mutually exclusive —but they were different, which determined the different behaviors of, and even discord between, Moscow and Washington during the crisis. One difference was that one power had thrown its military, political, and economic weight on the scales in the crisis, while the other remained poised on the sidelines and could afford moralizing and appealing to common sense when the other's military mechanisms had already been triggered.

Leaving aside the first UN Security Council resolution that condemned aggression in principle, the twelfth council resolution (Resolution 678) aroused the greatest controversy in the Soviet Union and the Third World. It sanctioned the use of force against the aggressor and legalized war by the United States and its allies against Iraq. Many wondered, and continue to wonder, whether the Soviet Union's vote in favor was at variance with its sincere desire for political settlement. The following explanations were advanced by the Soviet Foreign Ministry:

> On November 29, the UN Security Council, adopting Resolution 678, made the last warning to Iraq on the inadmissibility of further ignoring the will of the international community. In letter and spirit, the resolution offers a real chance for preventing the worst turn of events—military explosion. The Security Council resolution sets the time frame, within whose limits the search for political, peaceful settlement of the conflict is possible and imperative. All must be done not to miss the chance and reverse the situation toward a nonmilitary option. The Soviet Union is convinced that now it is up to Iraq to decide. It depends on only the Iraqi leadership whether there will or will not be peace in the Persian Gulf. Iraq must soberly assess the world community resolve in favor of restoring international law observance and security in the region and display common sense and good reason. Baghdad must realize that further delay over fulfillment of the UN Security Council resolutions is inadmissible as posing a serious threat to Iraq and its people above all.[7]

Adoption of Resolution 678 in combination with the "pause of goodwill" until 15 January 1991 signified the desire for political settlement. The intent was to bring it home to Saddam Hussein that the world community was against him and that war would be inevitable if he did not get out of Kuwait. *Izvestia* wrote, "From the standpoint of Moscow, the resolution on the use of force was not a step toward war, but contrarily the last opportunity of preventing it."[8] Saddam Hussein, however, was not to be persuaded.

In the meantime, the Soviet Union could have avoided being involved, as China did, but the cooperation with the United States had gone so far that Washington would not have understood the step. Avoidance would have seriously complicated Soviet-American relations in other world policy areas more crucial to the Soviet Union.

Moreover, the internal struggles under way in the Soviet Union developed into criticisms against Eduard Shevardnadze over the extent of Soviet support for American military operations under the flag of the UN, or the American or allied flag. If the resolution did not pass, a solely American or allied, instead of UN, action would have been carried out with the Soviet Union staying out of it, in order to save face. This situation would be directly contrary to the basic interests of the Soviet Union as far as its American and European policies were concerned.

However, having sanctioned the use of force by the United States and its allies, the Soviet Union emphatically refused to be involved in military operations. In this respect, Foreign Minister Eduard Shevardnadze's report, circulated among USSR Supreme Soviet deputies on December 12, is indicative:

> Not one of our moves in the international arena, not one of our diplomatic steps, implied, nor could imply by any stretch of the imagination, any involvement of Soviet combat, auxiliary, or any other troops or formations in whatever military operation in the Persian Gulf region. Speculation to this effect was altogether groundless.
>
> We have not had, nor have we now, plans for becoming involved in any possible military conflicts in the area.
>
> I brush aside as naïve (I refuse to think they are malicious) the accusations by the people who would like to present things as if the Ministry for Foreign Affairs and the minister in person are steering the course toward war in the Middle East. We did not allow such thoughts to enter our heads for even an instant. We ruled it out altogether.
>
> But I think it my duty to tell the Supreme Soviet that as the foreign minister I can and will, in other possible situations, advise the Parliament to okay the use of force where and when the vital interests of the Soviet Union demand it. Of course, it is the Supreme Soviet and the president of the USSR who will decide on it.
>
> Indeed, I said quite intentionally in interviews that cases and emergency situations are possible when the executive power, without consulting with the Supreme Soviet—which it may not have time to do— is just forced to take extreme measures. We will do so when the life and security of Soviet citizens are in danger and if emergency measures are needed to save them.[9]

Even nowadays it is impossible to say to what degree the Soviet diplomacy in the Gulf crisis influenced attacks on Mr. Shevardnadze from the "right." Anyhow, feeling unbearable pressure he was obliged to resign on 20 December 1990. The new foreign minister, Mr. A. Bess-mertnykh, continued his line of cooperation with the U.S. State Department in crisis.

Even giving its sanction to the use of force against Iraq, the Soviet leadership never abandoned attempts to find a political situation. It put to use what remained of the "special relations" with part of the Arab world, including the remains of the mutual "credit of trust" with Iraq, and channels of personal contacts. In this context, the missions to Baghdad by the special presidential envoy, Evgeny Primakov, are noteworthy.

Yet, these missions, too, were seen differently in Washington and Moscow; Eduard Shevardnadze hinted that Saddam Hussein had misinterpreted them as signs of American concessions and possible compromise.

In my interview with him, he expressed his position more openly:

> The only correct way to deal with Saddam Hussein was to speak with him honestly, openly, and tough. He had to withdraw from Kuwait without any compromises. That is why to my mind Primakov's missions were useless. He planted in Saddam Hussein illusions that he could bargain—a piece of land, some financial gains, maybe a split in the coalition formed against him—to gain time. I met Tariq Aziz shortly after Resolution 678 was adopted on November 29 and explained that Iraq would be defeated in two or three days. Gorbachev said to him in a very tough way: "Get out of Kuwait immediately." Saddam Hussein could not listen to the voice of reason.[10]

Evgeny Primakov's missions did play a positive role in putting some sort of pressure on Saddam Hussein for the release of the Soviet citizens still staying in Iraq. Maybe there were hints on a possible Soviet role as a broker. Eventually, the Soviet Union's moral obligations toward the Arabs, Iraqi friends, and former allies called for peacemaking efforts. The Soviet leadership carried them out to the end, although many Arabs would have naïvely preferred the Soviet Union to return to confrontation with the United States and at least prevent war on land.

Although the responsibility for the failure of Soviet political initiatives to stave off bombing lies entirely with Saddam Hussein's gross miscalculations, the failure of the Soviet attempts to prevent land war came from the shrewd and precise calculations of President Bush. The chief executive needed a purely military, and inevitable, victory and rout of Iraq, personal triumph over Saddam Hussein, personal triumph in the

United States, and fulfillment of the obligations before Israel. For this reason irritable attempts by the Soviet Union to find a political solution in the pre-land-war days were smiled upon. Last-ditch agreement reached between Mikhail Gorbachev and Saddam Hussein on Iraqi troop withdrawal from Kuwait was turned down by the United States, which reciprocated with an ultimatum unacceptable to Iraq. The land war proved to be an ill-omen. Shortly after, the disillusioned Gorbachev even used the word "fragile" a propos Russian-American relations.

"The 'hot war' winds blowing from the Persian Gulf resuscitated specters of the cold war. Cracks of mistrust, suspicion, and alienation again began to widen," *Pravda* wrote.[11]

Illustrating the mood in the United States toward the Soviet peace moves, the Soviet press cited an article from the British *Sunday Telegraph*. Referring to an expert consulted by the American administration, it wrote of "annoying pseudomediatory" efforts by the Kremlin and "ill-intentioned intervention" by the Russians, which threatened to "split" the UN support for the United States. The Soviet peace move, it continued, touched off hostile commentaries in the mass media and by congressmen on a scope unprecedented since Gorbachev's coming to power.[12]

The Soviet press gave as good as it got and accused Washington of imperial ways, an outburst of militaristic sentiments, and the desire to overcome the "Vietnam syndrome."

Unlike the quick-tempered newsmen, diplomats remained cold-headed and reasonable. The UN Security Council continued to act in unison and, after the cease-fire, adopted a resolution that expressed an integrated approach to the aggressor.

Trying to make up for the overly undiplomatic American press, Secretary of State Baker said, in an NBC interview, that in his opinion the Soviet Union continued to play an extremely important political role in the Persian Gulf developments after August 2. "We'd hardly have been able to do what we have done within the given time frame if the Soviet Union had not been with us during all those months," he added.[13]

Possibly the connecting thread of negotiations with Baghdad has prevented the worst option—use of chemical and other weapons of mass destruction by Iraq—and helped preserve discretion, *Pravda* wrote in the same article. I would also put on the credit side of Soviet diplomacy the help in saving the lives and release of hostages and prisoners, including the American television reporters, and the Iraqis' renunciation of devastating street fights in Al Kuwait. Regrettably, Soviet peace initiatives were invariably belated at the time of the crisis. The Americans appeared

intentionally to create "offside" situations by hastening military decisions and presenting us with faits accomplis.[14]

One hour before the start of hostilities on the night of January 17,
Secretary of State Baker informed Foreign Minister Bessmertnykh. There
was no stopping the speeding flywheel of war. The same pattern was
repeated when the Soviet-Iraqi plan for the occupation force withdrawal
from Kuwait, submitted to the UN Security Council, was upset by the
start of the allied overland operations. Evidently, the new Russian-American relations, as repeatedly declared in Washington and Moscow, requires much more confidence and coordination.

During the crisis and the war, the background noise cast by the
Arab-Israel conflict was a source of definite friction between Moscow
and Washington. Russian proposals to seek approaches to an Arab-
Israeli settlement in a bid to facilitate an Iraqi-Kuwait solution were
viewed in Washington as an inadmissible linkage to which Israel would
never agree. To that, Moscow sensibly objected that the "Palestinian
card" should be knocked out of Saddam Hussein's propaganda pack.
The American administration, however, attached much more importance
to the position of Israel. In this sense, the fate of the Baker-Bessmertnykh
statement is indicative.

In this joint document, the Soviet Union and the United States declared that Persian Gulf hostilities could be ended if Iraq gave an unam-
biguous offer to get out of Kuwait, to be immediately followed by
concrete actions. They said that eliminating the causes of instability and
sources of conflict, including Arab-Israeli, would be of special importance. It was declared that removal of the sources of conflict and instability in the region was impossible without a full-scale peace process
conducive to a just peace, security, and genuine reconciliation among
Israel, the Arab states, and the Palestinians. Belief was expressed that
overcoming the Persian Gulf crisis would greatly facilitate and energize
Russian-American efforts taken in concert with other parties in the region toward Arab-Israeli peace and regional stability.[15]

The British Foreign Office welcomed the Baker-Bessmertnykh statement on the Persian Gulf. Its spokesman said at a press conference that
the statement reflected the British government's viewpoint. The French
Foreign Ministry official representative, Daniel Bernard, told newsmen
that France supported the Soviet-American statement.[16]

For its part, Tel Aviv viewed the "linkage" between Middle Eastern
settlement and ending the war in the Persian Gulf as hinting at the need
to convene an international conference, which the Israeli government
opposed. In turn Washington took to heart the Israeli sentiments, seeking
to restrain the Israelis from a retaliatory strike at Baghdad in return for

the Iraqi missile attacks. The results of this action were thought to be disintegration of the anti-Iraq coalition. Therefore, faced with the Israeli dissatisfaction, the White House and State Department representatives sought only to diminish the value of the document.[17]

As if to disavow the secretary of state, President Bush reiterated that his Gulf policy was not to be changed. State Department spokeswoman Margaret Tutwiler in a press conference said that the statement came as a surprise to everybody and that many in the administration lamented Baker's inappropriate words, uttered without approval from above and possibly promising more than they should.[18]

It was a very characteristic episode. The point was not that the Soviet and American positions on Middle Eastern settlement could come closer together, or even coincide, for the statement was vaguely worded and only well-wishing in form. Israel, though, rejected the very idea of Soviet involvement in a Middle Eastern settlement and the possibility of Washington voicing this matter in a tone different from that of Tel Aviv.

If the mainsprings of Soviet behavior at the time of the crisis are to be found, priority should be given not to the foreign-policy principles, or Soviet interests in the Middle or Near East, or the personal prestige of the president of the USSR. The episode may be the first in Soviet history where the Soviet leadership considered public opinion, the real spirit, and the deepening economic, social, and political crisis. Its prime concern became the protection of the lives and security of Soviet citizens in Kuwait and Iraq. An ad hoc group was set up, led by the USSR Council of Ministers vice-chairman, I. S. Belousov. A hot line for contact with the public was opened at the Foreign Ministry. The Soviet leadership had no illusions about the true status of the Soviet citizens in Iraq and Kuwait. They were mostly hostages and this necessitated a cautious and balanced tone in dealing with Saddam Hussein. It did not matter that many of them were unwilling to leave Iraq; for them the foreign trip was a chance to improve their material position, and they hoped that hostilities would not break out.

The cautious Soviet diplomacy, including the Soviet representatives' missions in Baghdad, yielded fruit. All 882 Soviet citizens in Kuwait at the start of the crisis were evacuated before 25 August 1990. Of the 7,791 people in Iraq before 2 August 1990, 7,673 returned to the Soviet Union. As of 15 January only 118 Soviet people remained in Iraq.[19] After some time the number was further reduced.

Although there was no difference of opinion in Soviet society as to the hostages' fate, sentiments of the Gulf crisis and the war against Iraq polarized public opinion. People may argue about whether the crisis deepened the divisions in Soviet society, or merely laid them bare, but this gaping polarization of opinion, at least in such an open form, was unprecedented.

For most people in a large, tormented country, the fate of Kuwait, Iraq, and Saddam Hussein's regime was a distant and irrelevant topic. At the poles, however, it was believed that many Soviets thought highly of Saddam Hussein, though nearly as many approved of the actions against him. In Muslim regions and in Russia proper, people volunteered to help the Iraqi dictator. Most letters to the editor of *Izvestia* on Gulf developments were skeptical about the Soviet Union's pre-perestroika and present Iraqi policy. It is noteworthy that this policy was centered on the right and on the left by those who believed the Soviet Union, made a wrong choice turning its back on a "friendly Arab state" as well as by the hotheaded, who insisted on joining the Americans who landed on the sands of the Arabian peninsula.[20]

Some said the Americans intentionally drew the Soviet Union into a "campaign against our ally, Iraq. In this way we will lose all our friends and remain face-to-face with the American bases around us. This is no good. People are right to ask: aren't we weakening ourselves by playing at giveaway with the Americans?" Muscovite A. Gubenko wrote.[21]

The "giveaway" thesis appeared serious, particularly when at the sitting of the USSR Supreme Soviet Committee for International Affairs late in August, the Defense Ministry spokesman declared that Soviet security was threatened by the plans of the United States to build up its military presence in the Persian Gulf.[22]

Other readers supposed that the Soviet Union, together with other permanent Security Council members, displayed a double standard toward the seizure of Kuwait. "I condemn Iraqi aggression against Kuwait, but I also condemn the drawn-out Israeli aggression against the people of Palestine," Muscovite I. Starostin joined in.[23]

Sometimes the "Soviet Atlantists" called for sending Soviet troops into the Gulf zone to support the Americans. Those who objected typically wrote the following: "I follow developments in the Persian Gulf. The American dictates and almost unanimously all states, including ours, have cracked down on President Hussein's actions. Why then was there, nor is there, unanimity when Israel occupied Palestine and waged war against Syria and Egypt?" A. Antonov of Yaroslavi asked.[24]

"Dear Editors, I beg to disagree with *Pravda* on the matter of Iraq's actions and their press coverage. Iraq is a friendly country and this should be remembered," S. Akhmedov wrote from Dushanbe.[25]

Hardly anybody in the Soviet Union would have really volunteered to go to Iraq to fight, but the voiced desire was indicative of the mood of much of the population. Stereotypes of deeply rooted anti-American propaganda had their effect, as well as the deeply felt sympathy for a Muslim Iraq hit by a giant Christian power, the United States. In this sense, the Soviet Muslim sentiments were little different from those widespread in the Third World. However, just as the "Muslim factor" proved overinflated in the entire Islamic world, in the Soviet Union it failed to become a serious force in the context of Gulf developments.

Crisis-related differences in Soviet society also showed up in another manner. The hard-line forces in the Communist party and the armed forces turned down the emergent sympathy for the United States in the regional crisis. The *Krasnaya Zvezda* publications were a clear indication of sympathy for Iraq and doubt over the success of the American forces. Such doubts lacked a strong foundation. Hard-liners did not like it that the Soviet political leadership gave the United States freedom of action in the Persian Gulf area. The self-centered American policy played into the hard-liners' hands.

"The Walburga's night of death and destruction has been continuing in the Persian Gulf for a month now," *Pravda* wrote.

> War's poisonous discharges poison the Gulf waters and the entire international situation. One dangerous aspect of this war is that the region is being converted into an unseen proving ground of military hardware. What took years and even decades to develop is being tested in practice. Just imagine the upsurge of activity of the generals, designers of armaments, and heads of the companies that produce them. Under the impact of the positive changes in the world in recent years, the military-industrial complex had to curtail its operations. Now it is back in the saddle, both in its status and business. Successful use of Patriot missiles gave a new lease on life to the once declining Star Wars programs.[26]

Such sentiments become a component of the hard-line forces' counteroffensives in the autumn-winter of 1990–91. They tried to take advantage of the Persian Gulf developments as part of a cover-up, carry out a sort of takeovers in the Baltic republics, and prepare the ground for a possible coup in Moscow. In the first half of 1991, however, the situation was so far more like a stalemate: none of the groupings could get the upper hand. To stir up anti-American feelings became fashionable in conservative circles of the country:

> Some of our people view Soviet-American cooperation in countering Iraqi aggression as betrayal of principles [*Pravda* went on to

write]. They would have preferred that we support Iraq in "the antiim-perialist struggle." It is beyond all doubt that the line of the Soviet Union really met principles of international law and elementary justice, as well as our own vital interests. It can be regretted that Washington failed to utilize the Soviet diplomatic efforts that paved the road toward the earliest fulfillment of the UN resolutions without having to launch overland operations. The boxer instinct was at work in the Americans: knock out the reeling opponent. As a result, there have been extra victims, destruction, and suffering. Will the American political leader-ship display enough realism to resist the temptation of neoglobalism?[27]

Beyond the Gulf

The Soviet leadership considered this factor when it sought to pre-vent hostilities and then the land war. Alongside the internal factors, however, there were also external factors. American victory, which none of the Soviet leaders doubted, could lead, and has led, to "arrogance of force." After the victory, the United States could have considered the Soviet Union even less: "The services rendered are nothing." Moscow, though, rejected the "one-polar world" logic.

The Soviet leadership believed that the Gulf crisis demonstrated both the possibilities and the limitations of Soviet-American cooperation in extreme situations, just as it demonstrated the idea that the outdated ideological East-West division of the world was fading and ceding ground to the new East-West division of the North. The previous bipolar world was being replaced by a multipolar, not a one-polar world. Here multipolarity means that even without confrontation and conflicts there could not be a dominating power in the world. The world poles of military, economic, demographic, and territorial might should shape the international scenery and relations among them, if not necessarily con-tradictory, would not be complimentary.

Bipolar-world disintegration was not symmetrical. The NATO bloc remains alive and active, although the Warsaw Treaty Organization had collapsed. From the Gulf crisis the United States emerged as an indisput-able military winner and the leader of a coalition of twenty-nine states. The Soviet peacemaking efforts were merely brushed aside. It appears that the weight and influence of Russia, beset with domestic crises, is diminishing.

Still, if not a superpower, renovated Russia remains a great power. The United States needs partnership with it in the Third World, in Euro-pean affairs, and in the Far East. Just as the second Gulf war was not to be won without approval from the Soviet Union, a strong, regional peace was not to be established from the positions of imperial arrogance. The post-Mideast crisis positions of Russia in the Middle and Near East are not as they had been before the crisis. "Ideological" allies, such as Syria, should now seek either a new basis for cooperation with Russia or a new patron in the "person" of the United States. Resumption of diplomatic relations with Saudi Arabia personified the Russian "de-ideologized approach."

When all was said and done, Moscow and Washington obtained freedom for cooperation at subsequent phases in creating a security system in the Middle and Near East. It was clear that Washington would play first fiddle in this regional duet, just as it was clear that the months of the crisis buried their rivalry in the region. Moscow and Washington shared, even if not fully, the new ideas of the future regional security system. The coinciding opinions had far-reaching effects.

Permanent and visible consultation by the head of the American diplomatic establishment with his Russian colleagues, combined with the American pledge not to leave behind an enhanced U.S. troop presence in the region, proved decisive in securing Soviet support for the American initiative. The Soviet Union argued with the Americans and the Arabs about American military depots in Arabia, joint war games, and somewhat lesser-scale naval presence. From the Russian leadership's standpoint, this does not mean return to the Dulles "pactomania," encirclement of Russia with American military bases. Nor would it seriously impair Russian security. True, a quiet American forces buildup on Russia's southern borders may create tension.

Russian considerations for a security set-up in the Persian Gulf area were given in a Ministry of Foreign Affairs document covering matters from regional security to arms limitations.[28] There were general ideas on noninterference in each other's affairs, abstention from the use of force, and so forth, as well as more concrete proposals. One of the main ideas was to put brakes on the armaments race in the region and to lower the level of military balance. Nonproliferation of mass-destruction weapons would become a specific part of the process. Some joint measures to show restraint in sending missiles to the region were considered. Foreign military presence in the region should not exceed the level existing on 1 August 1990, and any reinforcements should be sent within the UN framework and include Arab and Muslim contingements.

A navy under the UN flag was once again put forward and revitalization of the UN military-general staff committee was raised once more. Necessity to turn to the efforts to settle the Arab-Israel conflict was stressed together with creating a future security system in the Gulf as part of broader security arrangements.

These proposals taken in the context of the new international situation marked by the end of the cold war hardly contained elements that ran counter to American interest and plans. The question was how much Washington was interested in involving Moscow in Middle East affairs, whether the outmoded stereotypes predominated or new forms of partnership could be worked out.

If one asks the question, What is the future of Russian policy in the Gulf area? the answer will be interrogative: what *sort* of Russia? In the short run or in the long run? One may say that fifteen different former Soviet republics will have fifteen different foreign policies, but let us not kid ourselves. The former USSR was in reality Russia with peoples and countries united with it voluntarily or against their will. In the future, Russia with its allies in a federation or confederation is blessed or damned to be a greater power, and it is the Russian foreign policy with which we are concerned. Russia will be among the leaders of the world community because of its extraordinary potential—a demographic, territorial, nuclear, and economic (though it is sometimes a long way from potential to its realization). In the short run it will concentrate on its domestic affairs and diminish its involvement in world affairs in general and in the Gulf region in particular.

The Russian role in the region will be that of cooperation with the United States, the West, and local actors. Any return to confrontation or ideologization would be self-defeating. The danger of identification of Russia with U.S. interests, however, is real. Services rendered will not be paid. Russian "Atlantists" are forgetting the truth that Washington, with all its moral imperatives, esteems only force and principled positions. One-sided concessions could only help keep up with decorum and sweet declarations.

Although earlier the main question was whose allies ("friends," "clients") were engaged in a conflict and "my enemy's enemy" became automatically a friend,[29] now it would be truly in keeping with the renovated union's short-term and long-term interests to turn the Gulf area as well as the Middle East into a genuine zone of peace. However, it can be done only on acceptable terms (particularly in the Arab-Israeli conflict).

Russia thus must pursue its own policy and learn to keep aloof from the U.S.'s policy in the region without engaging in a conflict with it. The role of the U.S.'s junior partner is unsuitable for Russia, and nobody is going to "remunerate" its servility.

The stress in the regional politics will be on bilateral relations. Their economic component will play the main role, increasing with resolving the economic crisis in the former USSR and developing of an effective mechanism of foreign trade. True, it will take many years. Geographic proximity and the mutually complementary character of economies in the Gulf countries and some republics of the former USSR may provide a reliable basis of their cooperation, though both parties have yet to find their "pockets" in the world economy and international division of labor.

A sharp increase in economic ties between Russia and the Gulf countries is a problem for the future. Now the arms export remains a sizable part of cooperation of Russia with the countries of the region. The unconditional choice of the Russian government is nonproliferation of nuclear, biological, chemical, and missile weapons in the region and participation in all measures for its prevention. However, Russia should not refuse to satisfy the legitimate defense needs of some countries, if there are suitable conditions for military cooperation and controlled arms sales. A general decrease in arms supplies to the region is possible only if based on a collective agreement of the main arms exporters of the world under a strict international control. Besides, Russia must demand proper payments for its arms with currency, oil, or local goods, without delaying payment for many years. Nobody has ever repaid his old wartime debts. Nobody pays for a shot already fired, particularly when the bullet misses its target.

Russia and other republics will de-ideologize their relations with the countries of the region, giving up forever the messianic idea of the "communist future" and support to the models resembling Stalinism or Brezhnevism. However, ideology cannot disappear completely if it implies, for example, opposition to repressive dictatorships. At the same time, if Russia undertakes to give lessons in democracy, particularly that of western style, such lessons will hardly be convincing. The reason is not only that Russia is just beginning to get rid of the Stalinist-Brezhnevist totalitarianism but also that the Muslim society rejects the western system of values as the only universal one.

The present explosive fermentation in the region will continue. Various political trends will put forward various development models—liberal-democratic, Islamic, and new, original, until now unknown and undetermined ones. The Russian leaders had better follow the expedient policy of a bystander, with an equally benevolent and neutral attitude toward the sociopolitical experiments carried out there.

However, it will be quite natural if the Russian public opinion expresses its own sympathies or antipathies to various sociopolitical and religious trends abroad. The public opinion will influence political leaders and their foreign policy through ballot boxes and mass media.

Soviet-American cooperation in the Gulf crisis, though it had a sour taste, showed a real base for joint actions. It will be kept intact if Washington considers real Russian national interests. Both countries will do their best to settle already existing conflicts and at least not permit them to grow into hot ones. According to their economic, military, and political considerations, Russia as well as the United States will be ready to guarantee the free flow of oil and gas from the region and freedom of sea and air navigation. Both countries are interested in the nonproliferation of weapons of mass destruction in the region as well as in measures to save the fragile environment.

There are differences. Geographic proximity of the region to Russia (with or without buffer states in Trans-Caucasian and central Asia) dictates the need to continue its efforts to avert any military danger—even potential—from the South. No government in Moscow can approve or agree to a permanent stationing of foreign troops in the region, especially if and when they are armed with nuclear armaments that could reach the Russian territory. That is why Moscow should support aspirations of peoples and political elites in the region to strengthen its political independence and not to keep foreign military bases on its territory.

Their striving should be coordinated with the interests of the world community on the platform of cooperative security. Its mechanism is to be worked out, but it is already clear that it will be acceptable if it is created under auspices of the United Nations and not solely under control of the United States and its allies.

Notes

1. *Isvestia*, 4 Aug. 1990.
2. *Krasnaya Zvezda*, 17 Aug. 1990.
3. *Krasnaya Zvezda*, 25 Aug. 1990.
4. *Krasnaya Zvezda*, 31 Jan. 1991.
5. *Komosomolskaya Pravda*, 1 Feb. 1991.
6. *Izvestia*, 14 Aug. 1990.
7. *Pravda*, 4 Dec. 1990.
8. *Izvestia*, 1 Dec. 1990.
9. Ibid.
10. Interview with E. Shevardnadze, 21 Aug. 1991.
11. *Pravda*, 8 Mar. 1991.
12. Ibid.
13. Ibid.
14. Ibid.

15. *Pravda*, 30 Jan. 1991.
16. *Pravda*, Feb. 1, 1991.
17. Ibid.
18. Ibid.
19. *Pravda*, 18 Jan. 1991.
20. *Izvestia*, 15 Jan. 1991.
21. Ibid.
22. Ibid.
23. Ibid.
24. Ibid.
25. Ibid.
26. *Pravda*, 12 Mar. 1991.
27. Ibid.
28. Statement, Russian Ministry of Foreign Affairs, 15 Mar. 1991.
29. See Kautilya, *Arthasastra* (Mysore: Mysore Publishing House, 1960), 289–93.

8

U.S.-Soviet (Russian) Conflict
Resolution in the Gulf

CHARLES F. DORAN

After a short theoretical discussion of the premises of U.S.-Soviet cooperation in the reduction of conflict, this chapter examines the recent conflict experience in the Gulf for insights into the maintenance of stability in the area. The roles of the United States and the former Soviet Union in underwriting that stability are also considered, however secondary those roles are to the impact of indigenous regional factors and to the internal regional balance of power. An attempt is then made to project forward this recent experience in the Gulf against the theoretical backdrop of U.S.-Russian conflict resolution efforts. The objective here is to discern what is likely over the next few years, what is possible, and what is not.

Theoretical Premises of Conflict Resolution Roles

Foreign policy role is grounded in state interest. Role is not defined as though many options are available to the actor in some cornucopia of unconstrained choice. Each foreign policy role is imbedded in restrictions imposed by capability, traditional foreign policy practice, domestic elite and party imperative, and what has been accepted as legitimate and conventional by other actors. State interest is only one part of this assemblage of influences on role, but it is a large part, indeed along with capability, perhaps the largest influence. Because state interest changes slowly over time, it transmits even more impact. One reason state interest changes so slowly, and has so much impact on role, is that geostrategic factors in turn affect state interest deeply. As boundaries become sacrosanct in the modern world, these tendencies toward geostrategic rigidification, if not permanency, are nonetheless partly offset by the rapidity of technological effects in commerce as well as security.

For some, national interests are subjectively determined.[1] Different regimes, even different leaders, define them differently. Further, over time the same regimes and the same leaders often redefine their national interests. How then can national interests change slowly and have a base in objective international political reality?

Analytically, the starting point for state interest assessment is admission that there is a subjective component to the definition of state interests. Total subjectivity would yield a meaningless concept, but a polity may prefer a specific state interest or interpretation of that interest involving some subjectivity. Its government may assert a state interest, or brand of state interest, as "vital." Ultimately, however, the international system will determine, as well, whether that interest is "legitimate." Ultimately, the corrosiveness of world politics begins to strip away the subjectivity of state interest.

Moreover, a nation's history, its geography, and its political traditions affect the determination of state interest. That is the principal reason such interests change slowly even though regimes, ideologies, and governmental leadership may change radically and abruptly. German reunification was a German interest even though the two governments, West and East, had radically different political philosophies. Great Britain had an interest in the freedom of the seas and in naval power throughout its history because it was not only an island state but also a market-oriented, trading state.

Under Leonid Brezhnev and his predecessors, Soviet foreign policy sought justification in the "balance of forces." Under Mikhail Gorbachev, Soviet foreign policy was legitimized in a "balance of interests." Intervention in Afghanistan was criticized because it abused the balance of interests, including the interests of nearby states such as Iran and Pakistan. Alliance with Iraq nonetheless was a Soviet interest under Brezhnev, even as it was under Gorbachev, and probably will continue to be in the state interest of Russia after Boris Yeltsin.

What may change abruptly and significantly is foreign policy role.[2] The foreign policy role of both the Soviet Union and the United States was altered decidedly after the 1960s. For the Soviet Union foreign policy role was turned upside down, not so much because the interests of the

166 CHARLES F. DORAN

two polities changed as because their relative ability to achieve these interests changed. Likewise, their strategies for employing capability, including their respective ideological outlooks, altered dramatically. Role should not be confused with state interest from which role is in part derived. In contrast to state interest, role is a far more labile element of foreign policy architecture.

Of the total set of possible foreign policy roles contemplated by the state, the roles of conflict mediator or conflict dampener are an important subset, particularly for a state possessing great leadership potential and salient interests at stake within the region of conflict. Quite a number of potential roles of conflict mediation have been delineated. The key observation is that the choice of conflict resolution roles is not determined only by the "demand" side of the conflict equation, namely, what is demanded by the conflict situation and seems most relevant to speedy and effective resolution. The "supply" side is equally crucial. What resolution role is feasible given the capability and state interests of the actor attempting the mediation or resolution? Not to give sufficient attention to the supply side of the resolution effort is to doom the analysis and indeed the ensuing policy.

An essential truth about conflict resolution at the level of the international system is that it is mostly conflict avoidance. Conflict avoidance is the best way among sovereign states to achieve a resolution of conflict. No other technique among powerful, decentralized, independent entities is likely to have as great a record of success. Once the war clouds are on the horizon, techniques of mediation, postponement, or conflict reduction are already at a great disadvantage. Analytically, the problem here is demonstration that conflict (major war) would have occurred anyway had the effort to deter war not been attempted. This is a difficult analytic problem. It is no problem at all for the policymaker, however, who will have observed plenty of signals of oncoming war close-up to convince him of the validity of a "near miss" and of the likely value of the earlier prophylactic measures. The policymaker may be guilty of false positive judgments (asserting that war was imminent when it was not) but fewer false negatives, for these quickly are recorded by history whatever their outcome as to victory or defeat. Conflict avoidance encompasses many techniques of traditional diplomacy and of structural analysis long associated with a harmonious international system.

U.S.-Soviet Interests and Conflict Resolution in the Gulf

If state interest is crucial in determining the conflict resolution role, then identifying American and Soviet interests is a useful first step in understanding the roles the two countries attempted to play in the recent Gulf crisis. In particular, both a study of capability and interest are necessary in understanding why the crisis occurred at all, in keeping with the admonition that the best form of systemic resolution is conflict avoidance in the first place.

From the American perspective, two objectives stand out above all others in the Gulf region.[3] First, the oil must flow. This statement should not be interpreted narrowly. It does not mean that the United States is trying to protect its own oil supply to the disadvantage of others. On the contrary, simple arithmetic will show that many importers are more dependent upon Gulf oil than the United States, including, for example, Germany and Japan and a number of Third World countries. Nor is the United States trying to obtain oil at "bargain basement" prices at the expense of the interest of the oil exporters. The United States produces almost as much oil domestically as it imports (principally from Venezuela, Canada, and Mexico) and therefore, if for no other reason, has an interest in price stability. Insofar as possible, market prices ought to prevail, or an orderly incremental increase in the real price of crude ought to take place. Oil exporters have as ingrained an interest in the protection of oil fields and supply lines as the oil importers. The mutuality of interest here transcends partisan division into importers and exporters.

Second, the United States has a commitment both to the resolution of the Arab-Israeli conflict and to the security of Israel. That these two objectives are different does not mean that they are necessarily incompatible, certainly not for Washington or for Moscow, nor ultimately, as must be demonstrated, for Israel itself. Long-term security of Israel is impossible outside a resolution of the conflict with the Palestinians and with Israel's Arab neighbors. The Camp David Accords are seen as a step in the right direction, but only a step. Although Gulf stability is regarded for some purposes as a separate matter, in other ways the fate of the Arab-Israeli question hangs over the Gulf, affecting attitudes and initiatives. Without progress in the Arab-Israeli question, for example, all efforts at stabilizing the peace in the Gulf are hampered, especially insofar as the United States, with its special relationship with Israel, is involved. This at least is the American understanding of the Gulf situation and of its own interests therein.

In short, the overriding American interest in the Gulf is in territorial security and peace. Territorial aggression by any of the states internal to the region is seen as a threat to this overriding goal and to either or both of America's subordinate concerns.

From the American perspective, the main Russian interests in the

Gulf look somewhat different from U.S. interests. Self-reliant in oil production, Russia is naturally less concerned than the United States about
access to Gulf oil. First among Soviet interests was to protect its southern
border from aggression. Having recently withdrawn from Afghanistan in
a disappointing effort to secure by force this long, vulnerable border, the
Soviet Union remained nonetheless concerned about the stability of the
border and of the countries adjacent to it. Iraq, an erstwhile ally, and
earner of scarce foreign exchange, had badly overreached itself in
annexing Kuwait, imperiling not only itself but also those that to some
extent in the past had abetted it. Stubborn and parochial, Saddam Hussein, facing harsh internal challenges, refused to heed the advice of President Gorbachev to withdraw (indeed to have the "guts" to withdraw
according to translations in the English press of Gorbachev's admoni-
tions). A weakened Iraq was as much a threat to Soviet interests in the
Gulf as a too strong and adventurist Iraq. Iraq's adventurism brought a
foreign military presence even closer to the Soviet border, despite the
multinational character of that presence and its commitment to military
withdrawal from land areas along the Gulf after engagement.

Second, again from the American perspective, the Soviet interest was
not to take any action, or to allow any action in the Gulf to occur,
that would exacerbate the Soviet nationalities problem, or would further
contribute to internal Soviet political weakness. With more than 80 million Moslem citizens, the Soviet Union could not afford to regard ideological questions, and questions of Kurdish nationalism, or of Shiite
fundamentalism, as irrelevant to its internal political situation.

Third, the Russian interest in some kind of "presence" in the Gulf,
through negotiations or coalition formation, in economic interaction or
in political contact, dates from the days of the Tsars. Defined in European terms as an interest in "warm water ports," an interest now sur-
mounted by modern ice-breaking and submarine technology, this
traditional Russian and Soviet interest in physical or political access to
the Gulf region may be exaggerated abroad but has geostrategic roots.
In its simplest manifestation, this interest is merely a desire to participate
politically in events and deliberations in the Gulf that affect the Soviet
Union (Russia) directly.

How do these interests relate to foreign policy roles? The Soviet and
the American foreign policy role in the Gulf region were each based on
sound state interests. The roles are not to be regarded as "peripheral."
Yet neither government has an interest in Gulf affairs so vital that its
foreign policy role there becomes paramount in defining its generalized
security outlook. The United States and those it sought to represent could

lose access to some 4 million barrels of oil per day in present markets and still continue economic activity virtually unaffected. An eight-year-long war could rage on the Soviet border between Iraq and Iran without threatening Soviet security so much that it felt compelled to intervene. Thus both external governments enjoyed some flexibility in the roles that they sought to adopt in the Gulf area.

Moreover, the relationship of the interests of each external government to their Gulf roles has been changing. For the United States, by 1989 the Soviet Union was no longer looked upon as a potential threat to American interests in the area and as a potential aggressor. Part of the explanation for the new outlook stemmed from Gorbachev's new foreign policy and revised military strategy. Part was due to the perceived internal political weakness of the Soviet Union and the distractions away from outward initiative that these seemed to promise. Tactical military policy changes reinforced this new perception by U.S. military planners. Forward planning was, according to the American press, being modified in the Gulf. Likewise the pro-Iraq stance by the United States during the latter years of the Iraq-Iran war was being shifted toward "evenhandedness" once again.

Similarly, the Soviet Union no longer saw the United States as the principal rationale for its policy in the Gulf. Dropping a heavy ideological focus, the Soviet Union began to appreciate the complexity of political and cultural factors in the Moslem and Arab worlds. It recognized how unreasonable was the contention that the Arab world was "ripe for revolution" and that Soviet assistance could further that process. Indeed, local regimes had learned to govern or at least to control. Stability was more the norm than instability. Moreover, the Soviet Union saw how unproductive direct competition with the United States for alliance affiliation had become. It could not outspend the United States. Subsequent demands for hard currency in arms sales to Syria and other countries in the region revealed the new impact of market thinking on Soviet foreign policy and the new constraints on expenditure at home.

Jewish emigration from the Soviet Union created a twofold situation vis-à-vis state policy. On the one hand, it weakened the Soviet Union internally as some of its best scientists and most productive citizens chose to leave. On the other hand, this emigration stood to improve its relations with Israel as the new emigrants continued to retain ties with relatives and friends in the Soviet Union. Moslem Asia had to come to terms with Jewish Europe, inside the Soviet state. Soviet foreign policy was gradually tilting toward a more balanced role between Israel and its Arab neighbors just as Soviet policy had, like the United States, selected a more balanced policy toward Iran. Primary affiliations were slowly yielding to what some in the Kremlin undoubtedly would label opportunism.

In short, both the United States and the Soviet Union by the last decade of the twentieth century had adopted new foreign policy roles in the Gulf dictated by changing capability, interest, and other factors. Chief among the reasons for the new role was the changed attitude of the two countries toward each other, not the new circumstances found in the Gulf. In fact, not that much had changed in the Gulf politically or militarily. Yet at the end of the long Iraq-Iran war, and the Afghanistan debacle, both the Soviet Union and the United States seemed to look forward to an interval of unbroken peace in Gulf affairs.

New Peacekeeping Roles?

If foreign policy roles for the United States and the new Russia were changing in the Gulf, how were their attitudes and policies toward peacekeeping affected? Were new conflict resolution roles evident as well? Most conspicuous was the detachment of the external governments from Gulf matters. It was almost as though they had bought the Third World propaganda regarding their own prior roles, namely, that war stemmed not largely from internal regional quarrels but from the rivalry between the United States and the Soviet Union that had been imposed on the region. The Soviet Union and the United States were practicing conflict resolution by *self-abnegation and detachment*. By winding down their own competition for power and status, they hoped that tension would be reduced as well inside the Gulf region among potential contestants for dominance. By releasing steam from the pressure cooker of global politics, they hoped that such steam would be released from regional politics too.

For the United States, conflict resolution by self-abnegation and detachment came easily. In the aftermath of the Iraq-Iran war, the United States, like other western states, found delusion comfortable. First, Washington thought Iraq and Iran were tired after their long war. Each had taken heavy casualties. Neither had obtained major gains. Surely this lack of territorial success was a sufficient deterrent to new aggression by either state.

Second, in the view of Washington was the imperative of internal economic reconstruction for each government. The war had devastated their economies. Iraq was heavily in debt not only to Saudi Arabia and Kuwait, who would probably not exact repayment, but also to western governments who would. For reconstruction to proceed, Iran and Iraq needed time and an opportunity for undivided developmental activity. This left little place for militarist campaigns. Because economic reconstruction and aggression were incompatible, Washington believed that Iraq and Iran would each choose the route that promised the greatest long-term gains for the state. Because militarism had failed in the opinion of most foreign observers, the two governments would choose a rebuilding of their economies.

Third, many in Washington believed that they now understood the Gulf better and in particular the Gulf policies of Iraq. After all, they had assisted Iraq during the Iraq-Iran war. They believed that they had figured Saddam Hussein out and could work with him. They did not minimize his ruthlessness and brutality, but they thought he would listen to reason, American reason.

Fourth, oil was in a surplus position in 1990 and price seemed stable. No immediate threat to oil availability at acceptable prices seemed on the horizon. Without a specific threat to oil accessibility, the American strategic mind tends to drift away from Gulf politics and security to other apparently more pressing issues and areas.

For an American analyst, fathoming Soviet thinking about the pre-Kuwait invasion attitudes toward Gulf conflict resolution is quite difficult and subject to correction. However, several observations appear plausible. First, above all floated the recent memory of the Afghanistan debacle. The reality that only partial use of Soviet military might occurred (casting discredit on the notion of military defeat), and the tactical success of extracting itself from the quagmire, may have softened some of the bitterness. The Soviet Union, however, did not want to get itself into a situation where it would soon again be obliged to intervene with force.

Second, there must have been some complacency in Moscow about its relationship with Iraq. After all, Iraq used predominantly Soviet weaponry, relied upon Soviet military advisers for instruction, and often consulted with the Soviet Union about alliance matters. Iraq had come out of its war a putative victor in the eyes of Iraq's citizens and other members of the Arab world. Therefore, by association, the Russian standing in the Arab world seemed in the ascendancy. If Mr. Gorbachev did not believe he could control Saddam Hussein, he at least believed that the Iraqi president would not embarrass the Soviet Union on the world stage.

Third, the Soviet Union must have had some confidence that it could reinforce the peace in the Gulf through diplomatic counterpoising of Iran vis-à-vis Iraq and vice versa. The success of Soviet policies during the Iraq-Iran war, despite its Afghanistan handicap, must have encouraged the Kremlin to think that its obstreperous neighbors could be cajoled into postures that at least were not anti-Soviet and at best were peaceful. Like the United States, the Soviet Union must have had few forebodings about the policies of Iran or Iraq in an era of oil glut and economic reconstruction.

All of this added up to policies of disengagement for the United States and the Soviet Union regarding the Gulf. Not having each other to fear as principal adversaries, the United States and the Soviet Union took their eyes off the Gulf itself. Pursuing conflict resolution at a distance or through disengagement meant that the major powers had lost touch not only with certain intelligence monitoring functions but also with any possible leverage they might have had with respect to possible Gulf aggressors. They had no arms control policy or discussions in place. They had withdrawn most of their military capability from the area because of cost and local opposition as well as their comparative bureaucratic indifference to Gulf stability. They relied on past interactions with the Gulf states, and a local balance of power that was precarious, to keep the possible belligerents in line. Moreover, more attention was given to a reopening of the Iraq-Iran war than to possible belligerence elsewhere in the Gulf.

Kuwait did not make these matters easier by denying offshore actors land bases from which to operate in the defense of Kuwaiti territory. Its arrogance over its luck at avoiding calamity during the Iraq-Iran war contributed to the Kuwaiti resistance to a "foreign military presence" that it assumed would have destabilizing domestic political implications. Kuwait's attempt to play off the superpowers during the reflagging operations in the last phase of the Iraq-Iran war earned it neither sympathy nor confidence in Moscow and Washington.

In short, if international conflict resolution is essentially conflict avoidance, such resolution failed because the roles the external powers adopted were not sufficient to maintain the peace.[4] Moscow could not constrain Baghdad by its weak levers and its persuasion. Washington could not deter Baghdad militarily because most of its naval and air capability had been removed from the area.

Conceptually, however, conflict avoidance did not occur because a vacuum had emerged in power inside the Gulf. Détente had made the United States and the Soviet Union less suspicious and less watchful. Saddam Hussein had a huge army in place that was not disbanded after the previous war and that had been organized with borrowed money. If he could have taken Kuwait successfully he would have doubled his oil revenue without increasing the size of the Iraq OPEC quota, that is, without upsetting the base of oil price stability. With twice the revenue, he could have accelerated his arms production and acquisition policies. Neither constraint applied by Moscow, nor opposition put into place by Washington, led to a prudent Iraq.

In the wake of détente between the former Soviet Union and the United States, the lesson for conflict avoidance is that detachment by one or both states is likely to lead to increased belligerency in many Third World areas.[5] Local demagogues, long bottled up by attentive action higher on the power hierarchy, may now seek to vent hostility toward neighbors and local rivals. In an age when powerful weaponry quickly diffuses, the apparently easy dispatching of Saddam Hussein's army by the more sophisticated technology in the American arsenal might also not be perpetuated. Thus the way to preserve territorial integrity is not to try to reverse aggression once it has occurred, but to negate the grounds of the aggression in the first place. Conflict avoidance through intensive interaction with smaller allies, through active and passive deterrence, and through an intelligent understanding of the potential and limits of local balances of power remains the key to regional stability. Decompression at the top of the system is likely to lead to expansion of conflict in many places lower on the international political hierarchy, unless an improved strategy of conflict avoidance is implemented by the United States and the other powers, such as Russia, in this interval of systems transformation.

Charting Future Cooperation in U.S.-Russian Conflict Resolution

Puzzlement had greeted the phrase "new world order" articulated by the White House during the Gulf crisis. *What* new order? is the normal response.[6] What are its guidelines, where is its substance? For whom is it defined, and why?

Two long-standing principles of conservative statecraft have been reestablished in the aftermath of the Gulf crisis. Both Washington and Moscow subscribe to them. Other great powers, such as Japan, Britain, France, and Germany have associated themselves with these principles through word, action, and financial contribution. More than anything else, the two principles provide the foundation for an emerging new world order.

First is the principle that territorial aggression not only violates international law, and the integrity of the state system, but that the reward for such aggression will be an overwhelming military response from the international community. That the United States and the new Russia, each in its own way—one passively, the other actively—and each in conjunction with its own interests and ability, have backed opposition to territorial aggression through UN resolutions, gives this principle of statecraft muscle and credibility. Without the UN backing, any unilateral actions would have far less legitimacy. Without the willingness and capability to use force when faced with territorial aggression, the declaration of principle would have had little pungency.

Second is the principle of nonintervention into the domestic affairs of another state. No one doubts the capability of the allies to have mopped up the Revolutionary Guards and other Iraqi military units, bereft as they were of air cover and effective armor. The decision not to destroy the Iraqi military, and the government it supported, however, was a political decision with its roots as far back as the noninterventionist policies of British Foreign Secretary Castlereagh after the Napoleonic wars.

Castlereagh refused to heed the cry for intervention on behalf of the Greek nationals, who were being slaughtered by the Ottoman Empire, for fear that such intervention would lead to a return of European-wide war. Likewise Mr. Bush refused to intervene militarily on behalf of Shiite units or Kurdish forces deep in Iraqi territory, despite aversion for Saddam Hussein, not only because the American president did not want to get bogged down in a civil war that could expand but also because he did not want to set a precedent for forceful intervention by the superpowers into the domestic affairs of smaller states in volatile regions. Just as Mr. Gorbachev had foresworn the Brezhnev doctrine of military intervention into the affairs of the Eastern European states, so the United States and the United Nations have reinforced the principle of nonintervention in the Gulf.

Nonintervention does not preclude extension of humanitarian aid. Hence the policy of most of the allies to help the Kurds. Nor does it imply unwillingness to set up limited peacekeeping forces in the way that Canada and other countries, for example, have been prepared to do along the Iraq-Kuwait border.

Oil politics may have guaranteed that the United States and the former Soviet Union would take the Gulf more seriously than other global arenas, but no matter that oil politics became the fulcrum for an exposition of the new world order. The international system is in transformation, rapid transformation. Lest more massive instability begin to unravel the long peace experienced since 1945, the big powers have reinforced two principles underlying collective security that may serve the world well, perhaps through the end of the century.

Conflict Avoidance and the Cycle of Power and Role

Conflict avoidance, that is global conflict resolution, during systems transformation, will require more than the joint application of the two principles, however. Conflict avoidance will require awareness in Moscow and Washington that each country is on its own cycle of relative power and that (1) these cycles have a relationship to each other and (2) each country is at a place on its own cycle of power, relative to the system. Put very simply, both the former Soviet Union and the United States were "mature" international political actors at, or perhaps slightly past, the peak of their respective cycles of relative power. Each government faced a challenge in its future role and security projections, derived from the position on its cycle of relative power. The Soviet Union peaked in its power by an attempted partial *political* reform from above to stimulate a massive *economic* reform from below. Instead, these attempts led to internal convulsion and eventual fragmentation of the Soviet state. Imminent Soviet decline in power brought domestic reforms that came too late, were wrongly implemented, and convulsed the polity. The international system, however, was very lucky. Instead of imploding, the Soviet Union under different leadership well might have exploded upon its neighbors. The crisis of peaking could have been directed externally, rather than internally, and with far more violent consequence for world politics.

The United States faced an earlier peak in the late 1960s, at a higher level of power, but it did so in a more gradual fashion, cushioned by an economy and by political institutions that acted as "shock absorbers" for the crisis the government and society were undergoing. Fortunately the dual incidence of this peaking process, in these two huge polities, did not occur in a fashion that was reciprocal and escalatory. Now the passage through critical points of radical structural change is moving toward other governments in the system, toward Japan, Germany, and, at a different level, China, all of which must contend with the same foreign-policy tensions that the former Soviet Union and the United States faced contemporaneously.

In addition, on the rising side of the power cycle, and on the declining side, the relationship between power and role tends to be different but similarly problematic for international political equilibrium, that is, conflict avoidance. On the rising side, increases in role tend to lag increases in power for the ascendant state, because other actors in the system refuse to "move over" fast enough to prevent gaps between power and role from developing for the ascendant state. Likewise on the declining side of the curve, decreases in role tend to occur more slowly than decreases in power, because powerful but declining states either refuse to yield role fast enough or find that they cannot disengage from dependent allies. Such declining states become "overextended," meaning that they suffer from a gap between power and role (too much role, too little power). Power-role gaps in the system emerge and are destabilizing because one nation's surplus of role is another nation's deficit. Elimination of power-role gaps yields a system in rough equilibrium, and is therefore peaceful and comparatively secure.

Power-role gaps tend to emerge at points on the power cycle where everything changes, that is, where the tides of history seem to shift against the state. A state passing through such a critical point on its power cycle finds that its future suddenly looks drastically different. When several states pass through such critical points at about the same time in history, the system itself is in transformation. Structural change is at a maximum. The likelihood of major war is at a maximum as well.

Unfortunately, as the system moves from bipolarity to some future condition of undefined characteristics, precisely this type of transformation is occurring. Given its current economic crisis, and its effort to rebuild, Russia faces a situation today where its role exceeds its usable power; its enormous nuclear arsenal exceeds its ability to implement foreign policy on the scale required. Its international obligations in Asia exceed its ability for coordination and mediation.

This is why management of conflict requiring involvement of the United States and of Russia is potentially full of contradiction. This is also why such management is ever more important, for the international system is in transformation. Maintaining an international political equilibrium of power during systems transformation is more difficult than when the structure of the system is more settled. Equilibrium during systems transformation, however, is for this very reason more crucial than at other times.

Thus for conflict avoidance to proceed at the regional level, it must prevail at the global level. Elimination of power-role gaps, and management of passage through critical points on the respective power cycles, is challenge enough for both state and system. Conflict resolution that endures is possible only in this structural context of general international political equilibrium, even (indeed especially) during turbulent periods of system transformation, such as the one that the international system now faces.

Restoring Regional Equilibrium After Conflict

Some have posed the question, "Can efforts to restore regional balances of power upset by conflict resolve conflict?" The short answer is restoration of regional balances can enable regional governments to avoid war in the future if the equilibrium, as articulated above, is genuine. Hidden within this question, however, are two contradictions. The first involves the term "restore." The problem with the old balance was that it was not a balance. Iraq, fueled by the influx of enormous military assistance, combined with focused austerity, became suddenly far more powerful than its neighbors and was not content to remain within its borders; it started two wars. Thus key to peace is a new balance in which (a) Iraq is relatively less powerful militarily than in the past (or its neighbors become relatively more cohesive and powerful) and (b) its government forgoes force to alter its territorial boundaries. The new balance must be "new," not an attempt to restore the old flawed balance of the past.

Second, the question contains a contradiction from the perspectives of both contemporary American and contemporary Russian foreign policy thought. A true equilibrium requires, as power cycle theory avers, a balance not just of power but of interests—"legitimate" interests—as well. Insofar as Iraq, on the basis of its internal economic development, becomes a more major actor regionally and globally, it has a right to greater salience, more status, a larger role in OPEC decision making. That larger role, however, cannot be based on the artificiality of billions from friends never to be repaid, and with military might as the vehicle for Iraqi territorial expansion. Ultimately both Iraq and Iran have a right to a larger relative regional role insofar as (1) their internal national capability justifies that role, (2) that role does not threaten its neighbors both as to means and ends, and (3) that role is a positive leadership function addressing regional as well as national interests. A new peaceful equilibrium in the Gulf must emerge from a better matching of power with interests. Until the regional actors can sort this out for themselves, the presence of the larger external powers, in diplomatic counsels as well as in more material ways, will continue to be a very important factor in Gulf stability.

Notes

1. For a revealing discussion of the Russian concept of state interest, see Udalov, "The Concept of Balance of Interests."

2. Charles F. Doran, *Systems in Crisis: New Imperatives of High Politics at Century's End* (Cambridge: Cambridge Univ. Press, 1991) 30–33.

3. Edward N. Krapels, "U.S. Energy Interests in the Gulf in the 1990s," in *The Gulf, Energy, and Global Security: Political and Economic Issues,* ed. Charles F. Doran and Stephen W. Buck (Boulder, Colo.: Lynne Rienner, 1991), 13–26.

4. On the problem of coordinating regional policy from abroad, consider Phebe Marr, "The United States, Europe, and the Middle East: An Uneasy Triangle," *The Middle East Journal* 48, no. 2 (Spring 1994): 211–25.

5. Part of the problem is that assumptions about the causes of war differ. Alexander George, for example, emphasizes the challenge of the "rogue state" in *Bridging the Gap: Theory and Practice in Foreign Policy* (Washington, D.C.: United States Institute of Peace, 1993) 45–60. Alternatively, consider the 'security dilemma' posed by Robert Jervis, "Perception and Misperception: The Spiral of International Insecurity," in *Theory and Practice of International Relations,* ed. William Olson, David McLellan, and Fred Sondermann, 6th ed. (Englewood Cliffs, N.J.: Prentice-Hall, 1983), 201. John A. Vasquez holds that the "underlying cause" is "territorial contiguity" in *The War Puzzle* (Cambridge: Cambridge Univ. Press, 1993), 293. For an excellent overview of all this literature, see Greg Cashman, *What Causes War?* (New York: Lexington, 1993).

6. Zbigniew Brzezinski provides a pessimistic account in "The Premature Partnership," *Foreign Affairs* 73, no. 2 (1994): 67–82. Richard Rosecrance supplies a more optimistic account of the possibilities for collective security in "A New Concert of Powers," *Foreign Affairs* 71, no. 2 (1992): 64–82.

9

India and Pakistan
The Roots of Conflict

THOMAS THORNTON AND MAXIM BRATERSKY

Historic Background

The dispute between India and Pakistan, focused on Kashmir, is the oldest dispute between any Third World countries. It is so by definition, for India and Pakistan were the first nations to emerge in the postcolonial era after World War II, and the status of Kashmir was in violent dispute from the very beginning. More fundamental, however, the roots of the conflict—of which Kashmir is a symptom rather than a cause—lie in centuries-old rivalry between Hindus and Muslims on the subcontinent. Few other ethnic disputes between Third World states have such a long-documented history, going back to the Muslim invasions more than a millenium ago. This conflict is often described as a communal, or religious-communal conflict, a term that embraces a whole set of simultaneous and interconnected religious, civilizational (cultural), economic, social, and linguistic conflicts. In its essence, however, it may be described as a Hindu-Muslim conflict.

Except, no doubt, for the Muslim invasion, rivalry between Hindus and Muslims in India never was an open war, because the peninsula was divided into hundreds of small states that rarely represented a specific community. In the absence of "nationalism" in the modern sense, Hindu-Muslim antipathy was "antiforeignism" directed against all "aliens" (aliens were determined not in religious or ethnic terms, but as people

179

not indigenous to that place). Hindu-Muslim differences were not only at the abstract level; centuries of intimate contact had left the two communities with specific grievances, imagined and real, that had persisted for more than a thousand years.

During the *raj*, the British played an important role in containing the conflict by separating and dividing the rival communities and monopolizing the use of state violence. At the same time, however, the British policy of divide and rule produced still greater alienation between Hindus and Muslims. The rise of Indian nationalism in the later nineteenth century, which was frequently manifested in specific Hindu and Muslim nationalisms, coincided with the incipient industrialization and urbanization of India that physically brought the two communities together in new and unsettling ways. This combination provided ready tinder for new forms and levels of conflict in more explicit and violent forms.

As the *raj* drew to an end, the British were less and less able to contain the conflict. By 1946, London realized that it lacked both the means and the will to keep its hold on India. In the following year, it reached a similar realization about holding India together, as Hindu versus Muslim passions swept the subcontinent and split historic India into two. The intense violence of that partition determined the relationship between the successor states, India and Pakistan. For the first time, the rival ideologies of Muslim nationalism and an Indian secularism richly colored by Hinduism had organized state power behind them, and they helped push the two nations toward international conflict. Because of the size and power of the two antagonists, the conflict was highly asymmetrical.

Partition was based on communal factors and these form the substratum of hostility between the countries. Its more specific, symptomatic form came to be the dispute over the status of Jammu and Kashmir (hereafter simply called Kashmir), a dispute that is itself deeply rooted in the two state ideologies. Pakistan argued that because more than two-thirds of the Kashmiri population is Muslim, and because British India had been divided between Hindus and Muslims, Kashmir should belong to Pakistan. India argued that the ruler of Kashmir had the legal right to join his state to India and that the religious composition of the state was irrelevant, because India is a secular nation.

Thus the Indo-Pakistani conflict emerged—a conflict between rival communities, a geopolitical conflict between neighboring powers, and a conflict between state ideologies, which was the major characteristic of the conflict at the beginning: Is religion the basis of the nation or are historic, geographical, and cultural circumstances? Is there one nation in the subcontinent or two? What criteria—the will of the people or formal legal decisions—are legitimate to resolve a territorial dispute that involves a provisional regional system?

Early Stages of the Conflict

The first Indo-Pakistan conflict, focused on Kashmir, erupted into violence shortly after independence and soon became a concern to the international community.[1] The fledgling apparatus of the United Nations was invoked and the Security Council spent much of its time in 1948 trying to end the fighting and bring about a solution. Success was achieved on the first point when a cease-fire was implemented, but a permanent solution to the status of Kashmir—and hence a major alteration in the underlying ideological and communal conflict—was made the subject of further negotiations.

It was generally assumed that the Kashmiris would be permitted to settle their future through a plebiscite. There is no need to follow the dreary history of these attempts at settlement as, over the next decade or so, the Indian position progressively hardened and Kashmir became an institutionalized international issue; instead, we shall focus on the role of the United States and the Soviet Union in that evolution.

At the beginning, neither of the two was anxious to play a significant independent role in addressing the problem. The Kashmir dispute was precisely the kind of issue that the UN was supposed to handle, and both Washington and Moscow were apparently willing to leave the matter there. This description masks, however, some of the reality of the situation. At the beginning, the Soviet Union did in fact take little or no interest in the matter. Its role in the debates was small and it abstained on important votes. In Stalinist terms there was presumably little to choose between Indian and Pakistani cryptoimperialists. It was not until September 1951, after New Delhi was showing signs of nonalignment in Korea, that the Soviets began to shift toward the Indian position on Kashmir and the issue became linked to cold war politics. The linkage was completed by 1957 on the Soviet side when Khrushchev gave unqualified support to India and later vetoed UN Security Council resolutions embarrassing to New Delhi.

Washington also showed relatively little interest in the early stages of this remote dispute, but given its dominant position in the UN and close ties to the United Kingdom, it was soon a prominent actor in the Security Council on Kashmir issues; it is hard to imagine that the UN would have taken any action to which the United States seriously objected. The United States saw itself as evenhanded in the matter and had no interest in merging it in cold war politics, for, unlike Moscow, it sought good relations with India and Pakistan. Increasingly, however, America's close security relationship with Pakistan made it seem that the United States had taken Pakistan's side.

The United States pushed for implementation of UN resolutions calling for a plebiscite; later (and especially when the Chinese invaded India in 1962) it sought to bring the two sides together on any reasonable basis. All these efforts came to naught. The Indians were adamantly opposed to any outside involvement in South Asian affairs (a central tenet of Indian foreign policy) and the Pakistanis felt that the United States failed to favor them to the extent that their alliance relationship warranted. No outside party had the kind of leverage needed to bring to bear to force a settlement of the Kashmir dispute and, a fortiori, the underlying enmity between India and Pakistan. By the mid-1960s, it had become a seemingly permanent part of the international environment— troublesome but not sufficiently acute to force serious negotiations. In particular, in the fullness of the cold war, there was no basis for cooperation between the United States and the USSR on the issue; such could have been the case when both Moscow and Washington were worried about the threat to South Asia posed by the Chinese invasion—and indeed, the two superpowers ultimately followed parallel courses, but since the Cuban missile crisis was going on at the same time, overt cooperation was hardly likely.

The 1965 War

Causes

After the 1962 war with China, Pakistan saw India as weakened, loosening the asymmetry. At the same time, however, India was starting a major military build-up, this time with the help not only of the Soviet Union but also of Pakistan's American and British partners. In several years this collaboration promised to confirm the asymmetry and push Pakistan into a subordinate role in South Asia, and it also showed Pakistan that it cannot rely on its western friends in confrontation with India. Time was clearly running against Pakistan; if it were to force a favorable outcome in Kashmir, it would have to act soon.

Besides disagreements over the Pakistani policy toward India, Pakistani president Ayub Khan and American president Lyndon Johnson held opposite views on Chinese policy in the region. The United States was inclined to see a more active Chinese role in the region as a sign of Communist aggression, while Ayub believed that China should be regarded as a powerful country with legitimate interests in the region and a potential ally in Pakistan's conflict with India.

At the same time, Washington was undertaking some moves that Pakistan regarded as interference in its domestic affairs. Americans were recommending improvement in the political and economic situation in East Pakistan, and had established some contacts with the opposition in both West and East Pakistan.

In a situation where a weakened India was becoming rapidly stronger and former friends were more concerned with containing China than supporting Pakistan against India, Pakistan decided to move closer to China to employ its weight in its own interests, and to improve its relations with the USSR as a counterbalance for fading American support. Moscow, under the new Brezhnev-Kosygin leadership, was ready to respond—mainly because of its concern to counterbalance China. There was an exchange of high-level visits and Soviet policy became markedly more balanced. When Indian and Pakistani forces came to blows in the Rann of Kutch crisis in early 1965, Moscow professed neutrality in the dispute, which both worried India and strengthened Pakistan's self-confidence. Eventually Ayub and then-Foreign Minister Zulfiqar Ali Bhutto launched a policy of "leaning on India"—a policy of pressure through contacts with great powers and China in particular, closer relationship with the Third World countries who provided India with legitimacy as a leader of Afro-Asia, and more aggressive military behavior in Kashmir.

India, in turn, suspected that a secret military alliance had been established between Pakistan and China, with Sukarno's Indonesia as a co-conspirator. The feeling of growing pressure from Pakistan pushed India to a more aggressive policy. It responded with a demonstration of force and a rapid military buildup. These political developments coincided with a general unrest in Kashmir and deep political crisis in both India and Pakistan.

Both Ayub and Lal Bahadur Shastri (who had succeeded Jawaharlal Nehru as prime minister in 1964) desperately needed a success, and as their difficulties lay primarily in political-ideological sphere, the success had to be of the same nature. An external solution to their problems appeared to be exploitation of the Kashmir problem; both hoped that a success there would not only solve a major foreign policy problem but also calm the political opposition at home and raise their popularity with the people.

In 1964, either as a retaliatory action, or more likely as a demonstration of its commitment to Kashmir, India dropped the old Nehruvian idea of granting some kind of autonomy to Kashmir in special constitutional provisions and moved to integrate Kashmir fully with India.

For its part, Pakistan launched ill-disguised guerrilla attacks in Kashmir. India responded forcefully, and an escalatory process led to the outbreak of full-scale war, first in Kashmir and then across the established Indo-Pakistan frontier. It was the first real war between two Third World countries. Fighting dragged on for three weeks, neither side gaining a decisive advantage, although India was in a much more advantageous position because Pakistan was running out of supplies and its attempt to stimulate a revolt in Kashmir had failed miserably. Neither side had an interest in continuing the conflict, the stalemate was beginning to hurt, and the time for mediation was at hand.

Positions and Roles of the United States and the Soviet Union

Uncharacteristically for those years, the United States and the USSR took practically parallel positions, thus removing the dispute from the cold war context. This fact can be explained partly by the superpowers' firm opposition to the growing role of China in the region and partly by the absence of their deep involvement in Pakistan and India. For these and other reasons, they adopted impartial positions on the conflict, supported the UN resolution on the cease-fire in Kashmir, and pressed India and Pakistan through their own channels for a cease-fire and negotiations.

By banning arms supplied to both parties, the United States had alienated India and Pakistan and was not acceptable in a mediation role. Britain and the UN were also, for varying reasons, unacceptable to the parties. As the USSR was no longer committed solely to India and was the only great power that had a demonstrable interest in peace near its southern borders, it turned out to be the natural and the only possible mediator. (Technically, the Soviets offered "good offices"; India rejected mediation in the technical sense.)

The USSR and the United States found themselves in a strong position to influence the behavior of the sides. They were the major suppliers of arms to the combatants; they (the United States in particular) were the main source of foreign economic aid; they were the members of the UN Security Council; and each had a very strong voice in the international community.

Why India and Pakistan Went to Tashkent

In a military sense both India and Pakistan found themselves in dynamic balance, neither of them having been able to win the war. The position of Pakistan was, however, weaker. It had lost more territory; it was running out of spare parts; and it could not replace armor and aircraft lost in battle. (The last two factors were the effect of U.S. sanctions; India was less dependent on American arms and was receiving regular though modest supplies from the USSR, France, and some other countries.)

India had established military control over the strategic mountain passes in Kashmir and threatened Lahore, Pakistan's principal city. India could not, however, advance further for political reasons: (1) India would have encountered the opposition of the world community; (2) the superpowers made it clear that they expected a reestablishment of the status quo in Kashmir and on the Indo-Pakistani border; (3) India would have undermined its peaceful and progressive image in the developing world on whose behalf it claimed to speak; and (4) India would have alienated its Arab oil suppliers who have close links with Pakistan.

Besides the military stalemate, both Ayub and Shastri faced domestic difficulties: they were sharply criticized for the inability to win an expensive war; the political and economic crisis grew more acute in their countries; and the suspension of the foreign military and economic aid that counted much in their development programs increased economic and social burdens. Although several weeks previously they had sought a major political success in Kashmir through military means, now they needed a success in Kashmir by ending war and by trying to bargain at the negotiation table for some of the things they were unable to get on the battlefield.

The Tashkent Conference: Results and Lessons

There is a modest but solid enough body of literature on the Tashkent conference,[2] to which one may refer. Hence there is no need to elaborate here on the behavior of the sides, their demands, the procedures of the conference, or the tactics of Kosygin. It is worth emphasizing, however, that the Pakistani side pressed for a package approach to the problem, that is, an outcome that would settle the Kashmir conflict permanently along lines acceptable to Pakistan. The Indian side kept the scope of negotiations narrow.

The conference dealt only with the impact of the war itself and resulted in restoring the status quo in line with the existing politico-military balance. It did not address the fundamental issues at dispute nor even their Kashmir manifestation. The hurting stalemate that brought the parties to Tashkent was limited to the battlefield situation. Neither side was hurt to the point where it would negotiate or settle profound ideological differences, and the net effect of the Tashkent mediation was to perpetuate the conflict even while defusing the crisis. The 1965 war demonstrated that the Indo-Pakistan conflict was protracted, and though periodic crises in the form of Indo-Pakistani wars can be contained, the conflict itself could not be diffused.

Finally, it should be noted that neither the United States nor the Soviet Union could build on the success at Tashkent to deal with other problems between India and Pakistan. In fact, the U.S. readiness to allow Kosygin to mediate between the parties signaled in practice the American abandonment of its attempt to act as security manager in South Asia. Moscow made some attempt in the following few years to bring the parties together but with no effect. The Soviets also resumed their court-ship of Pakistan in the late 1960s, but the events of 1971 soon brought home to them as well how difficult it is to follow a balanced policy in South Asia.

The 1971 War

Causes

The 1971 war marked the crisis of ideology as the basis of the Kashmiri problem, the basis of conflict, and the cornerstone of the Indo-Pakistani relations. With the split of Pakistan into two Islamic states on nationalist principles, the relationship of India and Pakistan was shifted away from its religious origin and evolved toward becoming a "pure" interstate conflict.

A domestic crisis broke out in Pakistan. The broad autonomy that the Bengali nationalist movement in East Pakistan demanded would have entailed a breakdown of the ideological foundation and ultimately the very existence of the Muslim state. Simultaneously the opposition in West Pakistan, headed now by Z. A. Bhutto, refused to accept rule by the majority Bengalis, and the military leadership of Yahya Khan proved inept in holding the situation together. In the spring of 1971, the crisis began taking the shape of a civil war and Islamabad sent the army to suppress the Bengali national movement. The Mukti Bahini (Bengali

resistance forces) put up a spirited resistance, however, and civil population fleeing from atrocities flooded North-Eastern states of India. By
summer, India reported some eight million Bengali refugees on its
territory.[3]

India began a series of political and military maneuvers: training and
arming Bengali partisans, complaining about the flood of Bengalis to
India, and at the same time objecting to any UN intervention in the
events on the Indian–East Pakistani border. Although Indian motivations were ambiguous at first, New Delhi increasingly concluded that it
had little choice but to intervene directly and in the process achieve some
long-held goals: (1) to weaken Pakistan physically and establish beyond
dispute its own regional predominance; (2) to improve its strategic positions in the troublesome North-East where Pakistan had been supporting
anti-Indian insurgences; and (3) to weaken Pakistan ideologically by
undermining the two-nations theory—depriving it of the right to claim
Kashmir on the grounds that all Muslim-majority areas of the subcontinent naturally belonged to Pakistan.

In August, Indira Gandhi made a tour of foreign countries to prepare
world opinion for Indian intervention in East Pakistan, and India got
ready to go to war. Foreseeing a very strong negative response to its
policy from the United States and China, India signed a friendship treaty
with the USSR. Soviet motivation for the support of India was mainly
the containment of China, which had already turned into the Soviets'
bitter rival in Asia, the Third World, and the international Communist
movement, and was building up its political and security positions
through its rapprochement with the United States and Pakistan.

Pakistan had little choice but to continue repression in the East. It
had gone too far to start negotiations with the rebels on some kind of
autonomy; neither could it yield to their demands for secession. As the
fighting continued, Indian troops openly entered East Pakistan in late
November and soon crushed Pakistani resistance there. In a desperate
move, Pakistan launched a preemptive attack on India on the western
border in the hope that the UN, the United States, and China would
intervene and save not only West Pakistan but also the integrity of the
whole country. None came. Indian forces easily withstood the Pakistani
attack but showed little interest in a counterattack that would penetrate
deep into Pakistan. In that sense, a sort of military balance was reached.

The Roles and Responses of the United States and the USSR

As distinct from the 1965 Indo-Pakistani war, the superpowers this time took classical cold war stances. The Soviet Union was at the beginning of an intensified Third World policy that would lead it through Angola and Ethiopia ultimately to Afghanistan. The United States, while still bogged down in Vietnam and seeking to reduce its own Third World involvement, was engaged in an extremely complicated set of global political maneuvers that entailed a firm stand on the South Asian situation.[4]

Thus instead of the tacit cooperation of 1965, open rivalry determined the relationship between the United States and the USSR in the 1971 conflict. At the same time, however, some kind of understanding on the key problems of the situation in the subcontinent existed even between the rival superpowers. Neither side wanted a war to take place, and the Americans made strenuous efforts to find a way of preventing conflict and, when that failed, of ending the fighting. The USSR followed a much more ambiguous policy through the autumn, but once it saw that the Indians were determined to go to war, it threw its support behind its long-standing ally and protected the Indians from pressures in the UN to bring about a cease-fire before the Indians were ready.

Neither side, however, seriously contemplated military intervention in the region. Soviet political involvement plus India's greater strength counterbalanced Chinese and American commitments to Pakistan—which in any event were only symbolic—so that the conflict developed without effective foreign interference. In addition, not only the Americans and Chinese but also probably the Soviets established certain boundaries to a victorious Indian advance in the West; it was made clear that India would not be permitted to occupy Kashmir or to launch a major offensive on the West Pakistani territory. Although such representations were not made jointly, the 1971 case suggests that even a minimum understanding or, more probably, a parallelism of interests between the United States and Russia could help prevent, or at least limit, major violent changes in the subcontinent.

The superpowers had, however, no direct role in the peacemaking process that followed the 1971 war. A cease-fire was negotiated and observed and for several months the two sides held back from further discussions, primarily because Pakistan, now defeated and truncated, needed time to reassess the entire basis of its existence and redefine its identity abroad as well as at home. At the end of June 1972, however, Indira Gandhi and Z. A. Bhutto, now Pakistan's leader, met at Simla to discuss a settlement.[5] Unlike Tashkent, there were no outsiders present; the negotiation was strictly bilateral. Also in contrast to Tashkent, India pressed for a package settlement that would include Pakistani acceptance of Indian rule in Kashmir; Bhutto, on the other hand, sought an outcome that dealt only with the aftermath of the war.

The outcome of the meeting was, like Tashkent, a shallow compromise. The status quo ante was essentially restored in Kashmir and along the Indo-Pakistan border. Rumors that Gandhi and Bhutto reached a secret agreement to settle the Kashmir problem are apparently unfounded, although there is little doubt that Bhutto was looking for ways of removing the problem from the agenda of Indo-Pakistan disputes. Significantly, Bhutto acceded to Gandhi's demand that all future disputes (including any over Kashmir) would be settled bilaterally, without the involvement of outside powers. This "bilateralism" was a key element of Indian policy and, if followed consistently, would be severely disadvantageous to Pakistan as the weaker of the asymmetrical parties.

Thus although Simla, like Tashkent, could not do more than alleviate the symptoms of conflict (that is, the aftermath of the war) and could not make any good headway on the underlying issues, it did create a somewhat more promising framework, one in which both sides hoped to find ways to bury the Kashmir dispute and recognized that only they themselves could do so. The inability of outside parties to gain leverage over fundamental issues was clear; it remained to be seen whether Bhutto and Gandhi could do any better. Not surprisingly, the course of the 1970s showed that they were not. The remainder of the decade was, however, one of the most stable in the history of Indo-Pakistan relations.

Evolution of a New Structure

1965 and 1971: Some Lessons and Conclusions

The events of 1965 and 1971 reflect, as we have said, two levels of conflict: the first is seemingly unchanging; the second has to do with three specific episodes of fighting.

The conflict over Kashmir in 1947 offers few lessons, for neither the United States nor the USSR had entered the subcontinent by that time, nor they did have any interests there as their attention was concentrated primarily on Europe. In the years following—indeed up to the next outbreak in 1965—the underlying conflict simmered on and despite much exertion by the United States and the UN, no solution was found.

In most of this period the USSR was not helpful, preferring to cultivate its tie to India through fairly blind support of the Indian position. Nor was the situation helped by the fact that the United States, in aligning with Pakistan, reduced Pakistan's incentives to settle the issue on a "realistic" basis. In dealing with this level of conflict, then, superpower involvement ranged from ineffective to harmful.

As for the superpower role in the armed conflicts of 1965 and 1971, it is clear that no international efforts could stop the parties from going to war, for these were an ineluctable outgrowth of the underlying struggle and of pressing situational factors. However, the efforts of the United States and the USSR usefully supplemented the natural course of events and the military-political situation in and around the subcontinent in discouraging India and Pakistan from engaging in protracted, large-scale war.

Six interesting commonalities appear on a list of major factors that work to contain a large-scale war between India and Pakistan:

1. In both wars the United States openly and the USSR tacitly pointed out to India that it would not be permitted to take over Pakistan.

2. India is not interested in the balkanization of Pakistan as it would result in chaos along the borders and provide external forces with the chance to manipulate the politics of new small bordering states. In any event, few Indians have any interest in undoing partition.

3. India has always shown some sensitivity to the position of the international community and the UN, especially in regard to violence and the results thereof.

4. Another restraining factor is the Non-Aligned Movement. Though today it is less important in the international politics than in the 1960s and 1970s, still India aspires to be its spokesman; hence, it is inconsistent for India to maul another nonaligned country.

5. India is loath to aggravate its relations with the oil-rich Arab countries, which maintain close relationships with Pakistan. India gets a major amount of its oil imports from the Gulf and earns substantial hard-currency income through the export of its labor force.

6. As for Pakistan, it can be argued that it was and still is restrained by (a) the superior Indian military might that precludes a Pakistani victory on the battlefield; and (b) American and Russian determination to restrain conflict. In 1965, the major pressure was suspension of economic aid and, especially, arms and spare parts by Washington. In 1971, the USSR exercised a formidable pressure on Pakistan and the United States on India, but each on its own client as well.

On the evidence of this unfortunate history, we can make some observations as to how this dispute fits into broadly applicable criteria.[6]

1. The conflict is a *continuing* one, ranging from near dormancy to high tension: from *incipient* to *hot.*

2. The conflict is rooted in a rich variety of sources, including *ethno-national* factors, *territorial* rivalry, and attempts to assert and resist *regional hegemony.* The issues in dispute are deeply entwined in the *internal politics* of India and Pakistan. Above all, it is *ideological* in content.

3. However, *economic* and *developmental* factors are not directly relevant to the dispute or how the parties approach it.

4. It is a dispute that has been affected by superpower involvement, but only marginally (and not always negatively).

5. It is a dispute where the power positions of the two parties have been asymmetrical in favor of India, with wars occurring at crucial points to redress or augment that asymmetry.

6. Although specific conflicts have resulted in hurting stalemates and have resulted in successful conflict termination, neither India nor Pakistan has ever been sufficiently "hurt" to be prepared to make fundamental concessions to settle either their broad range of conflict or its symbol —control over Kashmir.

Finally, it can be argued that a large-scale war in the subcontinent was restrained by both political and military factors, interior and exterior, and without drastic changes in the subcontinent it is likely to be restrained in the future.[7] It is also clear, however, that only the manifestations of the disease have been restrained. The disease itself, involving strategic, psychological, and ideological dimensions, remains intact.

We can also make some assessment of the potential for amelioration of the conflict by the so-called four D's.[8]

1. *Democratization* comes a cropper here. A democratic regime in India has done nothing to restrain its actions, and Indian claims that Pakistani military rule is at fault are not at all convincing. In fact, authoritarian governments in each country might be better able to force on their own publics the kinds of concessions that will be needed to deal with the Kashmir issue.

2. *De-ideologization* is probably an essential interim step toward conflict resolution, but little progress has been made. The real conflict is at levels extremely difficult to reach. Until then, the best that can be hoped for is conflict management and control—that is, keeping the situation quiescent.

3. *Demilitarization,* although no panacea, is highly desirable. It needs very careful definition, however, for simply cutting off foreign supplies of military equipment would be a blatantly pro-India policy. Getting the parties to think in less dangerous ways about their military

(including nuclear) capabilities is extremely important; even more so is prodding them toward a recognition that military posturing and accumulation of huge armories is not acceptable behavior. The United States, Russia, and the major aid donors have some role in these matters (see below) but they must recognize that both India and Pakistan are highly sophisticated countries who do not need, for example, to be lectured on the costs of conflict.

4. There may be some long-term, abstract sense in which economic *development* would reduce the volatility, or even alter the substance, of the Indo-Pakistan dispute. Realistically, however, little is to be expected along these lines in any relevant future. A prosperous India and Pakistan would not necessarily be any less bellicose than they are today—and prosperity is not likely to arrive for a very long time in any case.

1987: A War That Never Happened

Pakistan and India came close to conflict again in 1987 when the two armies engaged in extensive maneuvers (code-name "Brasstacks" on the Indian side). The reasons for the dangerous upsurge of activity are obscure—in part probably because of India's anger over Pakistani support to Sikh dissidents in the Punjab and to a more general demonstration of strength by an activist Indian military commander. After some posturing, the crisis was defused by active bilateral diplomacy between India and Pakistan, apparently without any direct inputs from Moscow or Washington aside from expressions of concern.[9]

In a sense, the handling of the affair fitted the stipulations of the Simla agreement—bilateralism was the final solution. At the same time, however, the way that the contretemps arose and developed reflected changes that had taken place in the intervening decade. India had made dramatic strides in developing the power of its armed forces; Pakistan, because of the Afghanistan crisis, had once again obtained access to American money and equipment and had also developed a much more impressive military machine (and considerably greater self-confidence) than it had in the mid-1970s. The possibility that either or both sides even then had a deliverable nuclear device lurked in the background. In a changing international environment, India and Pakistan had become more substantial and more autonomous international actors.

Similarly, it was evident that the United States and the USSR had no desire or will or both to be directly involved in South Asian conflicts anymore. India and Pakistan concluded that in case of war neither side would likely be given any preference. The superpowers are interested first of all in stability, and hence they will throw their weight into preventing either side from violating the status quo.

The 1990s: A Changed International Environment

A New Crisis

At the beginning of the new decade, India and Pakistan once again seemed to come near to war. How that conflict arose and how it was handled provide important clues to the new situation within the subcontinent and, especially, the international environment that affects India and Pakistan.

The crisis arose once again over Kashmir, and specifically over Pakistani involvement in supporting unrest in the disputed state. In sharp contrast to 1965, however, this time the impetus came from within Kashmir itself as the hitherto docile Kashmiri Muslims rose up against an Indian regime that they saw as corrupt and oppressive. Pakistan, of course, soon began to give both moral and material support.

Although the conflict was once again centered on Kashmir, it was in a new context. It was more geostrategic, rather than primarily ideological. Pakistani intervention was responsive rather than aggressive, a mixture of a necessary response to public opinion and an opportunity to embarrass an India that was increasingly beset by domestic problems, including severe separatist threats in Punjab as well as Kashmir. In a way, Kashmir had moved from being the cause of tension to a manifestation of an entrenched conflict between the nations' self-images and divergent political cultures.

The reactions of the United States and the USSR also reflected elements of stability and of change. Both Moscow and Washington were clearly opposed to the war and soon started sending signals to both sides, discouraging them from large-scale fighting. The real danger that nuclear weapons might be used was particularly compelling. The critical act was the mission of then-Deputy National Security Adviser Robert Gates. Gates had been in Moscow for discussions on the Afghanistan situation and proceeded directly to Islamabad and New Delhi to express opposition to the conflict in the strongest possible terms. The two sides pulled back from their confrontation, though once again doing nothing to address the underlying causes of the problem.

On the face of it, this appeared to be a representation on behalf of both the United States and the USSR, a significant exercise in joint crisis reduction. In fact, however, the Gates mission was a unilateral American endeavor; the Indo-Pakistan crisis had not been discussed at the Moscow meetings. Certainly the position of the Soviet Union (and the international community generally) was clear and lent authority to Gates's representations, but Moscow was much preoccupied with other matters and apparently chose not to involve itself directly in conflict reduction exercises. Thus the United States assumed the responsibility for conflict reduction. The analogy to the parallel but distinctly separate United States and Soviet roles in the Persian Gulf crisis of 1990–91 is obvious. Cooperative security was not yet in place.

Changes within South Asia

The dynamics of the Indo-Pakistan relationship are not reassuring in terms of conflict reduction. As we have said before, Kashmir is only the symptom, not the cause, of the disease, and despite the current centrality of Kashmir in Indo-Pakistan affairs, this remains the case. The dynamics of the conflict in South Asia have progressed so far that both countries perceive the conflict as constant, independent of its historic roots and the problems that previously underlay it. Ideology has moved to the background, the foreground is occupied by rivalry, suspicions, disbelief, the mentality of violence. The conflict is whipped up by communalism and Muslim as well as Hindu nationalism. To maintain credibility, India and Pakistan try to prove their strength and toughness, leading to more toughness in bilateral relations than is necessary.

During the last decade the situation in and around the region has been stirred up by the arms race. Afghanistan, the Iran-Iraqi war, and the Gulf War constantly kept India and Pakistan on alert, affecting both the ruling elites and mutual perceptions of the threat from the neighbor. Fears have been added to the situation by the Indian and Pakistani nuclear programs.

More important, perhaps, it is evident that the domestic problems of India and Pakistan have altered markedly. Both are undergoing the travails of democratization, separatist forces threaten national unity, and severe economic pressures have developed. These various difficulties make both countries vulnerable to outside pressure and ever more in need of a settlement of the conflicts between them. Yet these same pressures make it doubtful that either could evoke the strength to accede to international pressures to reduce conflict in South Asia.

This question is particularly salient in the case of India. For perhaps the first time in its history, and certainly the first time since its defeat by China in 1962, India may be hurting sufficiently to consider whether a more forthcoming approach to Pakistan—including on Kashmir—is necessary to offset other pressures. Significantly, not an inconsiderable part of that pressure comes from the current unrest within Kashmir. India may be at the point where costs of maintaining the status quo in Kashmir exceed the benefits. On the other hand, because Pakistan's hand is seen in the unrest, it is more difficult for India to make the kinds of concessions that Pakistan would find adequate, even if the government could otherwise summon the capability to do so—which is in itself questionable.

The situation within Pakistan is less striking, but equally ambivalent. Although Pakistan is beset by many troubles, it is not in a qualitatively worse position than it has often been in the past. Pakistan can ill afford the expense of keeping up with India militarily and its foreign sources of support are drying up, but the unrest in Kashmir is seen as a morale-building factor in difficult times. The weakness of the Pakistani government impels it, too, to a harder line on Kashmir rather than toward compromise. Thus in Pakistan as well as India, important conditions for accommodation are objectively present but situational factors make it questionable whether any progress is possible.

Changes at the Global Level

The rearrangement of global power relationships has profound implications for South Asia. In the broadest sense, the end of the cold war changes the context in which almost any regional conflict can play itself out, and South Asia was one of the areas most tied into the cold war nexus. More specifically, both India and Pakistan looked to superpower patrons for support in their conflict and these factors, too, have changed.

The breakup of the Soviet Union and the dramatic decline in Moscow's involvement in international affairs impinges primarily on India. New Delhi never needed Soviet assistance to defeat Pakistan but counted heavily on Soviet moral support, the Soviet veto in the United Nations Security Council, and the Soviet Union as a counterbalance to any support that China or the United States might give to Pakistan. There is now no more Soviet Union and the will and the capability of Russia and the other successor states in the Commonwealth of Independent States to perform these roles is negligible.

The United States has emerged over the past several years as a seemingly unchallenged global force, proclaiming its interest in the creation of a new world order. This term is vague at best, and in the South Asian context, it appears to be quite empty. For the past quarter century, the

U.S. interest in South Asia has been strictly derivative of its global rivalry with the Soviet Union. Now that this rivalry has abated, there is even less reason for the United States to play any high-posture role in South Asia.

As one looks farther into the future, it is likely that the present American preeminence will fade, if less abruptly than has the Soviet. The United States is hardly likely to bear the burden of global security manager for very long; historic inclination and economic and political realities tend in quite other directions.

Nor would India or Pakistan seem to be positioned to play any important role in a Washington-designed new world order, except to the extent that one or both of them can contribute to stability in the Persian Gulf or upset the idea of order through expansionist or nuclear-backed, or both, foreign policy initiatives. The word "marginalized" occurs with increasing frequency in discussions of South Asia in the global order. This marginalization also means that India and Pakistan are now more likely to be left to pursue their own devices than has hitherto been the case.

In a more positive sense, however, to the extent that either Washington or Moscow is interested in South Asia, both would favor, even more than they have in the past, reducing conflict in the region and have little or no incentive to play a role in support of one or the other of the regional protagonists. This fact weighs particularly heavily on Pakistan, for it must look to the outside for help against a stronger India. (And, it might be noted, there seems little inclination by the Chinese to support Pakistan against India.)

Thus developments at the global level also can be characterized as mixed: positive in U.S. and Russian support for conflict reduction, but negative in either party's proclivity to play an active role.

The Situation in Central Asia

Following the breakup of the Soviet Union, Russia no longer shares a border with South Asia; it is now separated by a huge buffer zone extending some thousand miles south towards Afghanistan. Issues that appeared pressing now recede into a more comfortable distance. By the same token, the military pressure that the Soviet Union was able to bring to bear on Pakistan (never very credible in any event) will no longer be a factor. We do not believe, however, that whoever rules in Moscow will over the long run be able to ignore events in the subcontinent. The imperatives that caused the tsars to look southward will continue for the successors of Lenin and Brezhnev. As those successors seek to reestablish Russia in the international role commensurate with its size and importance, South Asia will inevitably be an area of interest to them.

Nevertheless, at least for the foreseeable future, Moscow will have markedly less interest in South Asia and the rest of the Third World than it has had in the past. The business of survival and rebuilding, together with an extreme shortage of money, will limit the attention that can be given to all but the most pressing international issues. The prestige that the Soviet leadership derived from its relationship to India will be of little relevance. The economic ties that have bound the two countries are already fraying, as each looks to the West for markets and technology. Only with great difficulty can something resembling the trade relations of the past two decades be restored.

Much depends on how the central Asian republics will relate to the Russian state. Quite possibly they would seek to maintain close ties with Moscow for economic and political reasons, rather than submit to wooing by Turkey, Iran, and China. In this case, interest in South Asia could grow again as the CIS had to pursue security interests right up to the Afghan border.

More novel configurations are at least as likely to emerge. Should the new Muslim states in central Asia fall out among themselves and with their Slavic neighbors, an extremely complicated and potentially dangerous situation could arise as a new international subsystem emerged, embracing central Asia, South Asia, Iran, and Turkey, with China an interested participant. Might Uzbeks, for example, find a community of interest with their Afghan neighbors? Or might they fear Afghanistan and seek reinsurance through ties to Pakistan? Or might they look farther afield to India, should the perceived threat come from an Islamist Pakistan-Afghan combination? Might Pakistan join Iran and Turkey to fish in the troubled waters of central Asia? What are the prospects for an Islamist movement sweeping the area and forcing Christian, Hindu, and Confucian neighbors to find common cause?

There are probably dozens of such hypothetical contingencies, any of which could impinge on how Moscow perceives its role in South Asia. It is pointless for us to do anything beyond point to the fact that new configurations are in the making and there may be unknown dangers ahead. Few of these contingencies would appear to have any direct impact on the Indo-Pakistan dispute as such, and although India and, especially, Pakistan hope to turn economic and political profit from new openings in central Asia, probably none will alter much the balance of forces in South Asia. In the changing world of the 1990s, however, it seems that nothing can be excluded and we will do well to keep this in mind.

Toward 2000: Can Moscow and Washington Help?

The analysis of the major events in Indo-Pakistani conflict over forty-five years, as well as different patterns of superpower behavior during Indo-Pakistani crises, lead to several conclusions in regard to the conflict itself and to the attitudes of the superpowers in this radically new international situation.

The Indo-Pakistani conflict itself is a protracted geopolitical conflict with an important ideological dimension. It is not a Kashmiri conflict as such: Kashmir is a symbol—a place where broader conflict is manifested. The conflict was aggravated several times. None of the peace settlements afterward remedied the conflict, and solutions adopted at different peace conferences addressed only manifestations of the conflict. It made no difference whether these were bilateral or brokered settlements.

Against this background it seems unlikely that relations between the countries will radically improve in the near future. Technically, there are two models for such an improvement: either a breakthrough of the Gorbachev-Reagan type or deep integration like that in the European Union.

Until now there hardly has ever been a situation when India and Pakistan simultaneously enjoyed domestic stability and popular innovative leadership—the prerequisites for a breakthrough (The closest approaches were in the late 1950s and the middle 1970s and these were in fact times of relative quiet and stability.) The second option might also work someday, but it may take decades and it demands that none of the sides try to impede the integration. The existence of the South Asian Association for Regional Cooperation (SAARC) offers a structure within which such a rapprochement might take place but it is still a very fragile entity with little direct political impact.

It can be argued that though in many aspects the Indo-Pakistani conflict became more complicated than it was in the 1960s and 1970s, the possibilities of control over the conflict from the outside improve as it becomes less ideological—that is, the issues in dispute, relating to power, are increasingly of a nature that permit outsiders to play a role. The great short-term economic problems that plague India and Pakistan also provide substantial leverage—not only to the United States and Russia but also but also to other aid donors and international lending institutions that would prefer a peaceful South Asia. On the other hand, economic leverage is not readily applicable where matters of supreme national interests are perceived to be at stake. In addition, as the two nations become more politically autonomous, the opportunity for external pressure is reduced. Finally, we have to reckon with Washington's and Moscow's declining interest in the region.

On balance, then, we remain skeptical that there is much scope for any fundamental change in the situation in the short term. This does not mean, however, that the United States and Russia could not play important roles, as they have in the past, in containing and ending specific episodes of conflict, nor that pressure from them, especially in a broader international context, can reduce regional arms spending and development of unconventional weaponry.

There are some lessons for the United States and Russia that may be useful for their policies in the subcontinent and in other conflict regions as well.

1. The experience of Indo-Pakistani conflict and its aggravations in 1965, 1971, 1987, and 1990 show that for India and Pakistan there is a very complicated but stable asymmetrical balance—or in Stephen Cohen's apt phrase "balanced imbalance"—between the countries. It is military-political and it involves regional actors (China, the Gulf countries) and international structures (UN, Non-Aligned Movement) as well as the United States and Russia. The history of the conflicts also shows that after the peak of U.S.-Soviet involvement in 1971, the relative role of the United States and, especially, Moscow in the conflict has been growing less. Further *controlled* disengagement of Russia and the USA from the region is desirable—not in an economic or political sense, but in a military sense, arguably to the point of no military commitments at all.

It is emphatically not desirable, however, that the United States and Russia disengage completely from South Asia. At least as far as specific conflict reduction and nuclear matters are concerned, each has a useful role to play, and no other external force is discernible that could replace that role. More broadly, Moscow and Washington must act to contain any crises that threaten to trigger a nuclear exchange.

2. A particular form of the military commitments of the United States and the USSR was the arms trade, and history shows that arms supplies to either country provided for the defense against some third parties can be eventually turned against India or Pakistan.

In this balanced imbalance between the countries, there is no immediate military danger from any outside power to the subcontinent. We believe that the major arms suppliers should reassess the real defense needs of the two countries and keep a low profile in arms supplies and not violate the balance through arms shipments. This injunction takes on particular importance because large amounts of weaponry will soon become surplus to the needs of the United States and, especially, the nations of the former USSR. The temptation to unload this surplus at a profit will be strong.

At the same time, it should be noted that a modest arms supply program gives the United States and Russia certain leverage on Indian and Pakistani policies. Also, some provision should be made for Pakistan, which does not have an important indigenous military industry. The possibility that Pakistan should be allowed to buy arms in Europe rather than from the United States has merit, although there are impediments, because the Pakistan military infrastructure and military hardware are mostly American-made.

3. The most effective instruments for influencing India and Pakistan in case of crisis are different.

Pakistan is relatively more dependent on foreign economic and military aid. An important share of foreign aid is represented by American aid, so in the situation of Russian and, especially, Chinese disinvolvement from future possible crisis, the United States will be in a good position to influence Pakistan (if the nuclear issue is resolved and the United States can resume its aid to Pakistan). Such a policy demands not only supportive policies from the United States, Russia, and China but also noninterference from Arab Gulf states.

India is less dependent on foreign economic and military aid today than is Pakistan, although in the short term at least, its economic situation remains difficult. Because of its geographic and political position it is vulnerable to pressure from (a) the UN Security Council including the United States, Russia, and China; (b) the IMF and World Bank and other donors; (c) oil-rich Arab countries; (d) the Non-Aligned Movement. The experience of the past Indo-Pakistani wars shows that the United States and the USSR were able to influence to some extent Indian decision making, particularly when the two countries employed both direct communication and adequate efforts through the above-mentioned international entities.

4. In regard to direct political involvement of the United States and Russia in crisis reduction on the Indian subcontinent, it should be pointed out that because of the very complicated domestic politics in India and Pakistan, both countries are very sensitive to foreign pressure or even contacts with foreign powers especially when they involve domestic political opposition. Thus all channels of communication for crisis

reduction should be kept confidential. In addition, these are important countries with international options; thus the United States and Russia must not be seen to be discussing them as simply objects of international relations. This is particularly important in addressing nuclear regimes for the subcontinent since Pakistan and, especially, India are extremely sensitive to the appearance of dictation from outside. Simple terminology can also be important: "mediation" as such, from whatever source, is unacceptable to India. By defining his role at Tashkent as "good offices," Kosygin was able to achieve more than any other outsider has ever done.

5. There should also be an understanding between the United States, Russia, China (and any "security regime" in South Asia, but especially one dealing with nuclear weapons, must include China) that aggravations of the Indo-Pakistani crisis are related to their domestic political and economic crises. At such times the United States, Russia, and China should be very cautious and they should enter into consultations with India and Pakistan and between each other.

6. In an increasingly multipolar world, a world where economic influence carries a growing weight, there are new tools for bringing pressure to bear on conflict situations and new actors to wield those tools. Washington and Moscow must consider closely how their joint and several conflict reduction activities in South Asia (and more broadly) can best be associated with those of others, notably Europe, Japan, the UN, and the international financial institutions. Pressures from a variety of sources, not just memories of the Gates mission, have helped keep India and Pakistan back from the brink of war over Kashmir in the 1990s. With Moscow's influence greatly eroded and Washington's uncertain in the longer term, conflict reduction needs all the help it can get.

7. Another source of help is the activity of individuals and non-governmental organizations that seek to bring Pakistanis and Indians together as modest steps towards breaking through the frozen communications between the two countries. Expectations must be limited and such activities would hardly be feasible at times of crisis. Nonetheless, the process which has begun at American initiative deserves help from the Russian side.

8. Finally, the United States and Russia must be clear as to their own relationships regarding the subcontinent. Russia still has the greater interest in South Asia; for the time being at least, the United States has the greater capability to act. Although both sides have greatly lowered their regional posture, and it is hard to see why there should be any need to compete, there can still be room for disagreement and even potential conflict. Each must clarify for itself and for the other what it sees as its

minimum interests in South Asia and define the threat to those interests. The greatest policy challenge now will be to ensure that both Washington and Moscow remain constructively engaged in South Asia. There is a real danger that the United States may lose interest, and the decline of the Russian role is already evident. This should be discussed between Moscow and Washington—hardly among their highest priorities, but also one that must not disappear completely.

In terms of the C5-I actions,[10] the following observations can be made.

Consultation and communications are extremely important, as the preceding paragraphs indicate. Fairly good procedures have been in place between Moscow and Washington for discussing issues in Third World areas; it will be important to ensure that these are continued. Discussions on South Asia have focused particularly on the situation in Afghanistan; as that disappears these talks should be continued to deal with broader South Asian questions, with due care for South Asian sensitivities.

Condominium and collaboration are not appropriate or necessary at this time—if ever. Even collaboration may put an excessive load on U.S.-Russian relations and be inappropriate in view of our respective ties to Pakistan and India. It is also far from certain that Russia or any of the CIS states will for some time be able to play such ambitious roles.

Concert is an interesting concept that needs much closer definition in the South Asian context (for example, the geographic extent of the "membership"). India is likely to resist anything that threatens to dilute its unilateral advantages over its neighbors; over time, however, some version of SAARC could be beneficial and it would be in the interest of all concerned if Moscow and Washington played at least supporting roles. Again, the issue may be one of keeping Moscow and Washington constructively involved.

Isolationism could well be the most likely outcome, at least in regard to the security involvement of the superpowers in South Asia. As indicated above, this is a possible course of action, but, in its widest sense, an undesirable one. Extending "isolationism" across the board would make no sense; South Asia is too important a region to be neglected. In the most fundamental security terms, outside powers cannot walk away from the region until the nuclear problem has been solved.

Neither the United States nor Russia can hope to end Indo-Pakistani conflict. To improve the atmosphere in the subcontinent they can give a positive example by slowing down the arms race in the subcontinent, by influencing both countries through bilateral channels and international structures, and, above all, by continuing and strengthening their nonproliferation efforts—one of the few areas affecting South Asia where there had been good U.S.-Soviet cooperation over the years.[11]

At the same time, historic experience shows that in the past, even under much less favorable circumstances, Washington and Moscow with the help of some regional actors and international bodies were able to contain a large-scale war. With the cold war now history, they should be able to do it even better—assuming that they remain willing and able to exert the effort.

Notes

1. For an understanding of the early years see Sisir Gupta, *Kashmir: A Study in Indo-Pakistan Relations* New York: Asia, 1966); Josef Korbel, *Danger in Kashmir* (Princeton, N.J.-Princeton Univ. Press 1954); William J. Barnds, *India, Pakistan, and the Great Powers* (New York: Praeger, 1972); and Philips Talbot and S. L. Poplai, *India and America* (New York: Harper 1958.)

2. Notably Thomas Perry Thornton, "The Indo-Pakistani Conflict: Soviet Mediation at Tashkent, 1966," in *International Mediation in Theory and Practice,* ed. Saadia Touval and I. William Zartman (Boulder, Colo.: Westview 1985), and Amer Kayani, *The Kashmir Conflict: Soviet Mediation at Tashkent, 1966* (Pittsburgh: Pittsburgh Univ. Press, 1987).

3. The definitive study of the 1971 war is Sisson and Rose, *War and Secession.*

4. The strategic picture according to which the U.S. government claimed to be working is presented in chapter 16 of Henry Kissinger's *The White House Years* (Boston: Little, Brown, 1979).

5. The Simla Negotiation is examined in Imtiaz H. Bokhari and Thomas P. Thornton, *The 1972 Simla Agreement: An Asymmetrical Negotiation* (Washington, D. C.: School of Advanced International Studies, 1988).

6. The present list is derived from R. Craig Nation, *Conflict Reduction in Regional Conflicts,* 9ff.

7. The debate over whether nuclear proliferation in the subcontinent would encourage or restrain extensive conflict is a lively one but goes beyond the scope of this study.

8. Nation, 16ff.

9. In contrast, the U.S. and U.S.S.R. intervened much more energetically to avert a war between China and India that threatened at the same time. See Stephen P. Cohen, "Superpower Cooperation in South Asia", in Kanet and Kolodziej, eds. *The Cold War as Cooperation.*

10. Nation, 16ff.

11. See Cohen, "Superpower Cooperation in South Asia," 288.

10

The Crisis in the Andes
A War at the End of the World

ILYA PRIZEL

Peruvian novelist Mario Vargas Llosa, in one of his shorter works, predicted the total disintegration of the fabric of an imaginary—but clearly Andean—country. In a truly Latin American surrealistic fashion, the society falls into an ever-deepening quagmire as it is bedeviled by every imaginable natural and human-made calamity; ultimately a spreading plague of random violence plunges the society into endless, bloody anarchy.[1]

Tragically, Llosa's work was less of a prediction than a reflection of an existing reality in several Andean countries. The rapid disintegration of all their state institutions presages potentially calamitous results—for both the region and, ultimately, the international system.

The primary force at work is not territorial disputes, although all Andean countries have had such disputes and armed conflict has indeed resulted. (Episodes include the war of the Pacific between Bolivia, Chile, and Peru in the late nineteenth century; the Chaco War between Bolivia and Paraguay in the 1930s; and repeated armed clashes between Peru and Ecuador.) Interstate clashes in the Andean region are, nevertheless, rare and do not constitute a major threat to the countries in question.

The key threat to the peace and stability of the Andean region, particularly with respect to Peru, and to a lesser degree, Bolivia, Colombia, and Ecuador, is the increased marginalization of these countries within the international system. It may be said that since the 1960s all of the Third World (except the oil producers and some newly industrialized countries [NICs] on the Pacific rim of Asia) has undergone marginalization, yet nowhere has the result of this process been more acute and more painful than in the Andean region of Latin America. Virtually all Third World economies are integrated with the international system, but the case of the Andean region is truly unique. In other parts of the Third World, integration with the global division of labor has been relatively recent and limited to particular sectors of the economy. The integration of the Andean economies, however, began more than a hundred years ago, and it created a set of economies extraordinarily dependent on and, indeed, distorted by, events over which these countries have no control.

The heavy reliance of all the region's economies on mineral exports to the industrial world, along with the introduction of a plantation agricultural economy aimed at serving foreign markets, created a situation in which every sector of the region's economy was held hostage to the whims of the world economy. Because of the export orientation of these economies, the region's rail system and many other infrastructure projects were undertaken almost exclusively to serve the export market, without creating a viable internal market.[2] Thus movement of the world's industrial economies into the postindustrial age, which required far less input of primary commodities into production, had a devastating effect on the economies of the Andean region.

The decline in the price of extractive products came on the heels of changing patterns in the world's agricultural trade. Historically, the economic well-being of Latin America's agriculture has depended heavily on monocultural development aimed at serving the European market and, to a lesser degree, that of North America. The formation of the European Economic Community (EC) with its highly protective Common Agricultural Policy (CAP), dealt a terrible blow to the agricultures of the region. The emergence of an increasingly integrated Europe has changed the former relationship with the Andean region, a relationship in which Argentine wheat and beef producers could count on a stable British market, and in which Argentina, Brazil, and Colombia could rely on Italy as a large buyer of leather for its famed shoe industry and could depend on much of northern Europe as a long-term buyer of sugar. Hefty subsidies and closed frontiers have reversed these traditional patterns of trade, often leading to bizarre results. Because of the CAP, the United Kingdom has not only ceased to buy grain from Latin America but, since 1986, has become a net exporter of grain (for the first time in at least seven hundred years). Because of the internal European preferences, the

Italian shoe industry must now buy costlier Spanish leather, and Britain must rely on expensive continental beef.

The deterioration of Latin America's global terms of trade, brought about by the growing reluctance of Europeans to buy Latin American agricultural goods, only deepened when Europe, under the provisions of the CAP, entered the world markets as a competitor. Today, western Europe is a major exporter of such commodities as sugar, a pillar of many of the region's economies since the eighteenth century. Even in the sphere of tropical and subtropical fruit, such as bananas, citrus fruits, and coffee, Europe's preference for the produce of its "associate" states in the Mediterranean, and of its former colonies in the so-called PAC (Pacific, Africa, and the Caribbean), has resulted in a radical decline in the Andean region's presence in the international division of labor.

Although international trade has been growing at a rate of from 5 to 7 percent per annum since the early 1950s, Latin America's share has declined from almost 18 percent of world trade to less than half that figure. The drop in the Andean countries' share of world trade has been sharper still. Peru's economy, for example, has shrunk by 25 percent in the last three years alone. In fact, it is becoming increasingly evident that Latin America's efforts to move its economies into the international mainstream during the last decade have resulted in almost universal economic contraction and a massive increase in poverty.[3] One may better appreciate the magnitude of the change in the trade of the producers of primary commodities by noting the following: whereas in 1914, almost 90 percent of the value of world trade was in primary commodities, with manufactured goods accounting for the remaining 10 percent, by 1985, the situation had virtually reversed itself, with commodities accounting for about 15 percent and manufactured goods for about 85 percent. These figures would be even more polarized if oil and natural gas were to be excluded from the basket of primary commodities traded.

This reversal in the world trade pattern affected most developing countries, but the impact on Latin-American countries —with their absence of internal markets—and extreme specialization as a commodity supplier was indeed tragic. Between 1980 and 1987, Latin America's income per capita fell by 7 percent: Peru's 1989 per capita income fell to 48 percent of the level attained in 1970.[4] It should also be borne in mind that during the 1950s, the Andean countries appeared to be within reach of what W. W. Rostow referred to as the "staging point" for "self-sustained growth."[5] Millions of people who considered themselves middle class, or nearly middle class, have found themselves slipping back in income and status to the levels of their grandparents. Therefore the sense of failure from within, as well as of rejection from without, is far more profound than in many developing countries elsewhere in the Third World. This sense of failure has contributed to the emergence of an entire generation of anarchist rebels.

In a perverse way the end of the cold war and the fading of fears of Communist expansion into the region has only heightened the fears of further marginalization in the Andes and in Latin America as a whole. Even the United States, the sole major international actor who paid a modicum of attention to the region, is being drawn to more "exciting" regions of the world, such as the Persian Gulf and eastern Europe, a tendency leading to what Jorge Castañeda calls the "Africanization" of Latin America.[6] This fear is not unfounded. Despite the precipitous decline in the region's standard of living, the supply of capital available to the region from without has declined. Japan has cut its loans to Latin America from $10 billion over the next five years to $4 billion (the remaining $6 billion having been retargeted to eastern Europe).[7] The United States first forgave Egypt's $7 billion debt and then took a lead in pushing the Organization for Economic Cooperation and Development (OECD) members in cutting Poland's debt by 70 percent, but it has offered no relief to the Andean countries, despite a far more desperate decline in economic conditions there. Increasingly, many in the Andes are coming to believe that because they are neither near the fault line of the cold war nor a vital strategic asset, such as Kuwait, "Lebanonization" may occur in the region without eliciting much of a response from the international community.

This collapse of the region's link to the international system, on which the region's economy has depended for the last one hundred years, is a bad situation made worse by a succession of natural disasters: a series of devastating earthquakes (in Colombia, Ecuador, and Peru); droughts lasting several years, only to be followed by floods and massive mud slides; outbreaks of epidemics (the recent outbreak of cholera in Peru being but the latest of several calamities); and a shift in the pattern of Pacific ocean streams, which has resulted in a sharp decline in Peru's vital fishing industry.

The combination of these relentless waves of natural disasters and the region's growing exclusion from the international division of labor has led to the near collapse of the region's official economies and the virtual disintegration of the mechanism of the state (a fragile institution in the Andes under the best of circumstances). The "Culture of Violence," rooted in deep class and race divisions and endemic to most of Latin America—and having a history of particular virulence in Central

American and the Andes—has reemerged in the region with greater strength than ever.

Although political violence has been prevalent in all countries of the region, Peru and Colombia face the severest degree of violence and disintegration of state institutions. Many similarities exist between the sources of violence in both countries, and in both cases the destructive illicit drug trade plays an important role. The two countries, however, are very different and follow sufficiently differing paths in dealing with their dilemmas to warrant a separate discussion of each case.

Peru

No country in Latin America has suffered greater deterioration in the state of its economy during the last twenty years than Peru. Its economy has been contracting with no interruption, and by the late 1980s its inflation rate was raging at the pace of more than 1,700 percent per annum. Natural calamities have ranged from the devastation of the fishing industry, caused by the disappearance of anchovies off the coast, to massive floods destroying more than 25 percent of wheat crops, to an outbreak of cholera that affected more than 260,000 people and killed nearly 5,000. The collapse of the Peruvian economy has affected different social strata of the country to varying degrees. Social tensions owing to the distribution of wealth, very skewed even by Latin American standards, have created an explosive situation and thrown Peru into a state of nearly permanent civil war. This situation is worsened by the tendency of class differences to follow racial patterns, the Highland Indians being the poorest group, the mixed race mestizos of the coastal plain being marginally better off, and the urban criollo elite being the wealthiest.

Peru's extreme economic disparity, its deteriorating economy, and the region's culture of violence produced two distinct forms of conflict. First, there has been an outbreak of "traditional" guerrilla violence in the country. On the Left the Túpac Amaru Revolutionary Movement (MRTA), drawing its inspiration from Castro's Cuba, launched an offensive whereby, for the most part, wealthy industrialists have been abducted and food or money for the poor has been demanded as ransom. These activities provoked a right-wing response in the form of a death squad, named the Rodrigo Franco Front, which proceeded to assassinate leftist journalists and lawyers representing leftist defendants.

Besides this kind of violence, which has bedeviled nearly every country in Latin America, Peru faced the far more challenging threat posed by the Maoist Sendero Luminoso. Members of the Sendero Luminoso—

sharing only a vague notion of Maoist ideology and a sense of grievance against outsiders for crimes committed against the Indian heritage of Peru—have no agenda besides conducting a genocidal war against the regime and randomly terrorizing the population, regardless of race or class. Because much of the violence is totally random and is waged by small, self-contained cells, it has been difficult either to fight the insurgents militarily or to negotiate with them. Remarkably, during over a decade of uninterrupted struggle between the forces of the government and those of the Sendero, very little was known about its organization, structure, and ultimate goals.[8] Led by a former professor, "President Gonzalo" or Abimael Guzman, it adhered to this basic ideology: the regime in Peru is a fascist entity that must be destroyed, and no dialogue whatsoever is warranted. The war, according to the doctrine of the Sendero, must aim at the total destruction of all state institutions; it must begin—much as it did in China—in the countryside and ultimately engulf the coastal cities.

Unfortunately, the Sendero tactics of killing local officials, attacking foreign businesspeople and aid workers, assassinating Peruvians of Japanese descent, and intimidating local peasants from voting were very effective. By September 1992, when Guzman was finally captured, twenty-seven thousand people had died, and more than $20 billion in property damage had been inflicted on the country.[9] The Sendero's repeated attacks on foreign-aid workers forced the Catholic church to reduce the number of foreign social workers it sent to Peru and the government of Japan to withdraw all aid workers. With its successes the Sendero had become far bolder in its attacks, moving beyond remote rural areas and carrying its warfare to Lima itself, increasingly targeting state institutions and relying on criminal gangs and restless and unemployed youths from the ever-growing shanty suburbs around the capital. However, an even more dangerous development was gradually threatening the viability of the Peruvian state. Indication was mounting that the Sendero was progressing toward the establishment of a de facto independent state in the Upper Huallaga Valley, using the region's vast coca lands as a base.[10] Guzman's arrest stopped but did not eradicate the Sendero.

The ideology and method of violence pursued by the Sendero make it a movement without analogy in the history of contemporary guerrilla movements except, possibly, the Pol Pot regime in Cambodia.[11] Following a strict Maoist model of rural warfare, the Sendero was totally self-reliant, receiving no support from the outside. Consequently, there was no external power either to act as mediator or to act, at least on occasion, as a moderating influence (as the government of Iran has done in the case of the Hizbollah in Lebanon). In Lebanon, chaos notwithstanding, the war is waged by clearly identifiable groups with reasonably clear agendas and with obvious foreign patrons who can at times play a moderating and restraining role. This is not the case in Peru, where terrorism and violence often appear to be as random as they are purposeless.

Over fourteen years of unfocused terrorism and the regime's obvious impotence to restrain it, Peru has experienced both a flight of capital and a massive emigration of its most able and talented people. In 1990 alone, 328,000 Peruvians (one in every 65) permanently left the country. Because most emigrants have been from Peru's professional and educated classes, this movement has accelerated Peru's isolation within the international system.

Although the region's culture of violence must be recognized as a major cause of Peru's national disintegration, it is equally clear that the collapsing economy is greatly intensifying these tendencies. Taking it a step further, the economy's collapse is directly linked to the region's exclusion from the international division of labor. The same may be said of the growth of the illicit drug trade.

The growth of what is virtually uncontrolled illicit drug trade and production is indeed undermining the social ecology of the region. What started as a minor problem twenty years ago has mushroomed to the point that the illicit drug trade now represents the largest segment of the Peruvian economy, accounting for a profit of $1.2 billion per annum. As Peru's president, Alberto Fujimori, noted, illicit drugs are the only opportunity that the Peruvian peasant has left by which to participate in world markets, and until the region's decline in the global trade pattern is reversed, no amount of police action will stem the cultivation and processing of drugs on a massive scale.[12] Given that 15 percent of Peru's work force is employed in the cultivation of coca leaves, and in light of Peru's unemployment rate of more than 40 percent, it is doubtful that rapid progress in eliminating the coca leaves can be attained.[13]

The destructive effect of the illicit drug industry is not limited to the fact that many young Latin Americans are growing up to be addicts. The industry is also contributing to the further destruction of the state mechanism throughout much of the hemisphere. The massive inflow of billions of dollars in illegal drug money has caused the near collapse of the state mechanism in the Andean countries. With more than 40 percent of the country's gross domestic product produced by an "underground" economy, Peru is in danger of sliding into an anarchy that "exports" its chaos and intimidation to the rest of the Western Hemisphere.

Peru is both a country that for long found no common ground with its various, highly violent political factions and a country that has continued to fail to find a niche within the international system. President Fujimori, addressing the Peruvian people in 1990, stated: "We have failed to reinsert Peru into the international financial system." It seems quite clear that unless the United States, the European Union, and Japan make a concerted effort to help Peru (and other primary commodity producers) find a new niche in the world order, the country may well face continued deterioration that not only will exact a tragic price from the Peruvians but that will also ultimately have a catastrophic effect on the entire hemisphere.

Colombia

After Peru, Colombia is the most violent of the countries of South America. As mentioned earlier, the differences between the countries are profound despite similar problems of guerrilla warfare and illicit drug trade. In comparison with Peru, a country divided by race, language, and a very weak sense of national identity, Colombia is a far stronger national entity. It is true that there is a white criollo elite in the cities, a black population along the Caribbean coast, and a preponderant mestizo majority throughout the country, but virtually all Colombians are Spanish-speaking and identify themselves as Colombians. Further, Peruvian violence is very much a war of the castes, attempting to settle a cultural sense of grief. Colombia's culture of violence is a product of a violent past—in which vast lands were colonized across impassable terrain and with no semblance of a legal authority—and to the resulting tradition of banditry and lawlessness. It also derives from an exclusive political system, which disenfranchised most of Colombia's people. Commenting on the exclusivity of Colombia's politics, one analyst observed: "If according to Karl von Clausewitz, war is the continuation of diplomacy by other means, then it might be said that in nineteenth century Colombia there was not always a clear distinction between election campaigns and revolutionary violence."[14]

During most of the twentieth century, Colombia was governed by two political parties, the Conservatives and the Liberals—an uneasy coexistence of two oligarchies, which led to repeated cycles of violence over power, the status of the Catholic church, and land colonization. The bloodiest cycle occurred in 1946–66, a period known in Colombian history as La Violencia, when more than 200,000 Colombians died in the power struggle between the parties. In 1966, the two parties agreed to a new modus vivendi, whereby both parties would rotate power and assure representation within the government for the party out of power. This agreement, however, did little to bring in the masses disenfranchised from Colombia's exclusive power structure.

In fact, it was precisely the emergence of this new, "closed" political system (which offered no political space to other players) as well as the inspiration of the Cuban revolution that led to the emergence of leftist guerrilla movements, such as the FARC (Fuerzas Armada Revoluccionarias de Colombia), ELN (Ejército de Liberacíon Nacional), and EPL (Ejército Popular de Liberacíon). These three movements, drawing inspiration from Che Guevara's "foco"[15] doctrine, pursued a policy aimed at the overthrow of the government; the FARC concentrated on the countryside and waged a campaign of rural armed colonization, while the ELN tended to be an urban phenomenon.

A later and much different actor in the Colombian guerrilla movement was the M-19. The M-19 emerged in 1972 as a result of the accusation that the governing parties "stole" the 1970 election from Rojas Pinillia's (ANAPO) opposition party. Unlike the other guerrilla movements, the M-19 movement was almost entirely an urban movement, prone to spectacular, daredevil actions, such as the seizure of the Dominican embassy and the takeover of the Colombian supreme court.[16] The purpose of the M-19 was to inject itself into the political process of the country and thus force the oligarchy to open the political structure to new players. The attack on the Palace of Justice in 1985 weakened the M-19, killing many of the movement's members and forfeiting public support. However, the disruptive urban campaign had greatly debilitated the government. Both sides had reached the "ripe moment" for a negotiated settlement. After prolonged negotiations between the M-19 and President Virgilio Barco, the government committed itself to rewrite the constitution, making Columbia more open to new political actors. The M-19, despite the murder of its initial presidential candidate, Carlos Pizzaro, fielded another candidate, Antonio Navarro Wolf, who scored 12 percent of the vote for the presidency and thus attained a respectable presence for his party in the constituent assembly.

If the administrations of president Virgilio Barco and his successor, Cesar Gaviria, were successful in their effort to bring the M-19 into the country's political life, they were far less successful in trying to pacify the Marxist FARC and the ELN. Although the government started negotiations with an umbrella organization representing those groups, Coordinadora Nacional Guerrillas Simon Bolívar (CNGSB), the talks soon broke down, and the Catholic bishops of Colombia, who at first played a mediating role, withdrew from the negotiations.

Why did the government succeed in its negotiations with the M-19 and fail in dealing with the Marxist renegade movements? The answer may lie in the history of a previous attempt by President Belisario Betancur to arrive at a negotiated settlement during the mid-1980s. The FARC through its political wing, the party Union Patriotica (UP), fielded candidates for local officials and other posts and scored impressive victories. What followed was virtually the wholesale murder and assassination of its elected officials, including the UP's presidential candidate, Bernardo Jaramillo Ossa. The Colombian Marxists fear, much as the guerrillas in El Salvador do, that arriving at a political settlement with the government will expose them to the fury of the army and the police, which the civilian government does not control in any event. As if to underscore that point, on the day that President Gaviria was about to start talks with the CNGSB, the armed forces raided the headquarters of the FARC, thus aborting the negotiations.

The situation is further complicated by Colombian drug barons and their private armies. Because the Marxists (who might themselves be involved in the cultivation of coca) are determined not to allow their rural strongholds to become controlled by the drug cartels, they are reluctant to disarm. They are convinced that if they do so, radical death squads controlled by the drug lords and the army will wage a genocidal war against them and the campesinos in the regions where the Marxist exercise control. Thus the current CNGSB position is that under present conditions a negotiated settlement will not lead to an "open" political system but to the wholesale destruction of the leftist opposition. As things stand, the situation in Colombia is deadlocked. In 1990, there were 1,451 political abductions in the country and several thousand deaths, with no relief in sight. In November 1991, talks with the government broke down, and the government issued arrest warrants for the entire leadership of the CNGSB.

Despite the very high level of Colombia's violence, the situation in that country is not nearly as tragic as that in Peru. Unlike the Sendero in Peru, the Colombian guerrillas are not attempting to carry out either a genocide or even a Kulturkampf against any specific segment of the country's population; nor do they question the intrinsic legitimacy of the Colombian state. Another source of potential strength for Colombia is that Colombia is the world's largest coffee exporter, as well as a substantial exporter of energy (oil, low-sulfur coal, and natural gas) and has thus managed to avoid the kind of marginalization within the world economy that Peru has experienced. In fact, Colombia's economy grew by 2.5 percent in 1991, and was predicted to grow by 4.5 percent in

1992; similar economic strength enabled Colombia to be among the only three Latin-American states to service their foreign debt without interruption during the 1980s.[17] This relatively robust state of fiscal health gives the Colombian government the ability to continue to govern, even when facing the dual challenge of left-wing guerrillas and right-wing narco-death squads. What continues to fuel Colombia's growing violence is the maldistribution of wealth in the country as well as the decline in prices of virtually all its official exports.

Thus while the immediate prospects for the end to guerrilla activity in Colombia are glum, long-term prospects for peace in that country are far better than those in Peru. Colombia's Marxist rebels, deprived of external help from either Cuba or the former USSR, are anxious to find a political solution to their warfare. It would seem that if Colombia's government could assure the guerrillas represented by the CNGSB that they would not fall prey to the army or the narco-lords, a political solution might well be at hand. The current negotiations in El Salvador (where the FMLN had similar concerns to those of the FARC and the ELN) may well provide an appropriate model for a peace settlement. Further, there is the possibility that an international organization, such as the United Nations, the Organization of American States, or the Andean Pact, will be useful as both an ombudsman and an honest broker. The decision by the United Nations secretary, Boutros Ghali, to send four hundred UN "Blue Helmets" to El Salvador may inspire a similar solution for Colombia. What makes the Colombian situation more complicated than the one in El Salvador is this: whereas in El Salvador the government must assure the FMLN that it can control the army and the right-wing death squads associated with the army, in Colombia the government will also have to assure the leftist rebels not only that it can control the army but also that it can protect the rebels from the armies of the narco-barons. The previous record of Colombia's governments in controlling the drug lords is not reassuring; it would be difficult to convince leftist rebels that the government can provide a secure return of the Left to the country's political mainstream.

A far more serious challenge to the long-term viability of the Colombian state than guerrilla warfare is the power of the illicit drug trade. The Colombian drug barons have managed to establish private armies, which, at times, may be better equipped than government troops. With their multibillion-dollar purses, the drug lords have managed to corrupt, intimidate, or do both to the judicial systems of large parts of the hemisphere. The corrupting power of this wealth has been evident in the judicial systems of countries as remote from the Andes as Mexico and the Bahamas. Furthermore, the governments of several smaller countries of the hemisphere, such as Panama, the Bahamas, and probably Cuba, have become willing partners of the region's powerful drug families.

The impact of drugs has not only perverted the judicial and the administrative mechanisms of the state but also destroyed the ability of several of the Andean states to conduct a fiscal policy. With narco-dollars at times exceeding the official gross national product of some area economies, it is difficult to imagine how a government could set an economic agenda for its country. Although there may be no accurate statistics about the scope of drug exports from Colombia, all analysts agree that coca earns far more than coffee, Colombia's largest official export. The governments of presidents Barco and Gaviria scored only a cosmetic "victory" in forcing the Medellin cartel to curtail its activity and even allow some of its leaders to face nominal arrests for a promise that the kingpins would not be extradited to the United States. The lower supply of drugs by the Medellin cartel was easily replaced with the wares of the Cali cartel. Furthermore, with the increased reliance of the Colombian cartels on coca grown in Bolivia, Brazil, and Peru, the ability—and the will—of Colombia's government to control the export of drugs is limited at best.

The drug problem, along with its associated conflict, is made less susceptible to resolution because of the absence of agreement about its origin and who must take responsibility for enacting solutions. In the case of guerrilla insurgencies, it is clear that the ultimate resolution will have to be arrived at by the parties themselves; outside players can at best act as either an honest broker or a facilitator. In the case of the illicit drug trade, the degree of interaction between the consumer and producer countries, and the violent impact of this illicit trade both on the Andean region and the inner cities of the developed world, makes it clear that both the producers and the consumers have a strong interest in the issue. Furthermore, given the economics of the narco-trade, neither the producers nor the consumer countries can hope to attain a solution and curb the violence alone. Unfortunately, as of now there is no consensus among the producers and consumers about the strategy needed to deal with the ever-deepening crisis. To the producer countries the proliferation in drug output has two causes: first, the industrial north appears to have an insatiable appetite for illicit drugs; second, export of drugs is but a manifestation of the region's exclusion from the international economy. To the governments of the consumer nations, such as the United States and countries in Europe, the drug problem is primarily a law enforcement issue for the producer countries to solve.

U.S. policies are an example. Although the United States continues to insist that it wants to help Peruvian peasants find alternative crops to coca, in 1990 the United States allocated $6 million to help the Peruvian farmer abandon a crop that had generated an estimated $1.3 billion in revenue. Despite the glaring failure of interdiction attempts, Washington continues to view the narcotics problem almost entirely through a law enforcement lens, a policy severely straining the fragile state institutions in the Andes. By agreeing to supply nearly $2.2 billion in aid to the area's military establishments, it strengthens one of the most corrupt and brutal institutions in the region. Furthermore, U.S. insistence that eradication and "counterinsurgency" measures against leftists be carried out in tandem splits the law enforcement agencies of the Andes. Thus, the Peruvian army, which sees the Sendero as its key nemesis, avoids challenging the peasants involved in coca cultivation, for such action will force the peasants to support the Sendero. The police, on the other hand, have little interest in battling the Sendero and are anxious to "combat" the drug trade, given the access to bribe money. The result is nearly open warfare between the police and the army, which is further eroding state institutions.[18]

Given that much of the challenge to the security and stability of the region is internally generated, the role of outside players is very circumscribed. It is not unimportant, however. Because the source of the region's growing anarchy is its marginalization within the international system, and because the region, owing to its economic weakness, can play only a responsive role, the future of the region's stability will depend on how outside players manage the reintegration of the region into the international system.

The world clearly cannot afford to continue its policy of benign neglect of the region, especially when the corrosive effect of narcotics-driven economies has started to undermine state institutions throughout the Western Hemisphere and beyond. The conflict-resolution roles of outside players will naturally vary according to how each is affected by the Andean crisis. At present the United States—most directly affected by the flow of drugs and immigrants from the Andes—is most concerned; the EU, preoccupied with a somewhat analogous situation in North Africa and, potentially, eastern Europe, is less concerned, although it is increasingly alarmed by the flow of drugs from Latin America to Europe; Japan, feeling virtually immune, is showing little interest in getting involved.

The crisis in the Andean region is complicated by what may well be considered historically anomalous times. In the past, economic power tended to go hand in hand with military power; great economic powers tended to be great military powers as well, with a vested interest in the stability of the international system. Today, of the three major economic blocs in the world, (the United States, the EU, and Japan), only the United States has a sense of a global responsibility.

Both the EU and Japan, notwithstanding their status as economic giants during the last forty-five years, have become increasingly parochial powers whose defense and economic policies show little interest in stability beyond their immediate perimeters. The EU does pay some attention, though by no means enough, to the countries of eastern Europe and the Mediterranean and to the Middle East and the Maghreb, but it shows virtually no interest in the stability of the global system as a totality. Similarly, Japan's capital exports are totally directed either at other developed countries or countries on Asia's Pacific rim. both Japan and the EU continue to invest huge amounts of money in protecting indigenous sunset industries, such as coal mining, textiles, and lumber processing, and compete head-on with the rest of the Third World in their subsidized agricultural exports.[19] Some observers in western Europe, particularly in Portugal, Spain, and the United Kingdom, seem to recognize that the disintegration of Andean state institutions will ultimately affect Europe, whether because drugs from the region will increasingly be directed toward Europe's porous frontiers or because collapse in the Andean region may distract United States attention from other areas of the world that the EU considers vital to its security. The European voices warning that the EU's parochial attitude toward global stability is dangerous, however, remain a faint echo of a minority view.

The situation is even more discouraging when it comes to Japan. Because Japan, thus far, is unaffected by the flow of drugs and other criminal activities resulting from Andean disintegration, and because Japan seems to feel that it has no role to play in upholding international order (especially in a geographically remote region with few strategic minerals essential to its mighty industries), the country has chosen to be a bystander and ignore the region altogether. Thus, despite Japan's mammoth economy, its trade with the region remained stagnant during the 1980s. Japan has proved to be a poor source of financial aid, even when facing such ecological disasters as the deforestation of the jungles of the Amazon. The tiny Netherlands has given more economic and technical assistance to the countries of the Andes than has mighty Japan.

Because the Andean conflict is an internal conflict, which was not caused by the superpowers even during the cold war, the United States and Russia could play any of three basic roles. They could attempt to fish in the region's troubled waters and exploit the region's problems to bolster their positions in the context of the cold war (assuming the crusader role). The end of the cold war and the collapse of the USSR, coupled with deep economic problems in the United States, makes this role unlikely. They could ignore the region and hope thereby to have a calming effect on the crisis and to avoid exposing themselves to a potential confrontation in a marginal region (assuming the bystander role). Or they could try to influence key trading powers, such as the EU and Japan, to do more toward the integration of the region with the international division of labor (assuming the ombudsman role).

Historically, Russia and the United States, although occasionally extending their cold war competition to the region (especially between 1960 and 1967),[20] have often tended either to ignore the region or, at least, to show restraint. Therefore even when such regional governments as the "leftist" military in Bolivia, Ecuador, and Peru attempted to induce a superpower competition, the response of the "excluded" superpower tended to be tepid and restrained. Despite Peru's nationalization of U.S. properties, strong anti-American rhetoric, and some flow of Soviet weapons to the country's armed forces, the USSR showed no appetite for creating yet another area of confrontation with the United States. The United States, in turn, despite the rhetoric and the nationalization, never attempted to isolate these regimes within the international community or even to impose the Hickenlooper amendment, which would have forbidden any further U.S. aid or credits to the countries that nationalized U.S. assets.[21] Similarly, despite the often misconceived role of the United States as a gendarme in the ejection of the Allende regime from power in Chile, Washington played a very minor role, a fact conceded by Soviet and Communist analysts.[22]

If the superpowers showed an impressive degree of self-restraint in the Andean region during the cold war, this restraint turned into cooperation with the end of the cold war. To begin with, there is no evidence that Moscow has given any material or rhetorical aid to the Túpac Amaru guerrilla movement, despite that movement's pro-Cuban position and declared adherence to Marxist-Leninist doctrines. Although the military of Chile once alleged that the USSR had provided material aid to the Communist-dominated Manuel Rodriguez Front, since 1988 even Chile's rightist generals have ceased to make any such claims. The turnabout in the Soviet position was even more dramatic in the case of Central America. Not only did the USSR discontinue military aid to the Sandinistas in Nicaragua and the FMLN in El Salvador, but it also cooperated with the United States in encouraging both Salvadoran parties to pursue a negotiated settlement. In addition, the USSR, along with the United States, played the role of ombudsman between Nicaragua's FSLN and UNO, facilitating the smooth and "clean" elections in 1990. By mutual denial of military assistance to their respective clients, the superpowers established a "hurting stalemate," which led to the "ripe moment" that enabled the democratically elected government of President Violeta Barrios de Chamorro to take office.[23] In the U.S. case, despite pungent rhetoric by the Reagan administration vis-à-vis the Sandinistas in Nicaragua, the U.S. Congress became increasingly reluctant to continue to support the "contras" in Nicaragua, and progressively more vocal in its criticism of the armed forces of El Salvador. A decline in U.S. military aid to El Salvador could create a painful stalemate in that country that might lead to serious negotiations.

If indeed the Andean region must be reintegrated into the international system to avert the complete collapse of the state institutions in a group of countries, the role that Russia and the United States can play is one of ombudsman within the international system. The critical needs of the Andean region are markets and capital. Russia, its economy in shambles, is in no position to provide either capital or markets. As the world's largest commodity producer, however, Russia could use its diplomatic weight to keep world markets open to commodity producers. The United States, although in a much better position than Russia, is nevertheless a constrained power. Facing two huge deficits, both in internal deficits and current account, Washington has a limited ability to provide capital, especially when its source is public coffers. Although the U.S. market is relatively open to the products of the Andean region, structural factors have been causing its size to shrink for more than twenty years.

The U.S. market is problematic for the Andean producers for two reasons. As for the region's agricultural products (except sugar, an industry in which local producers insist that a 40 percent share of the market be reserved for domestic producers), much of the U.S. market is reasonably open to Andean products. The limiting factor in additional sales to the United States is that in many spheres, such as beef, U.S. domestic producers are highly competitive, and in other regional products, such as bananas and coffee, the U.S. market is fully saturated and will continue to grow very slowly. In a sector vital for the economies of the region, mineral exports, several factors constrain potential growth in sales to the United States. Although the United States has no trade barriers on raw materials, it can provide only limited markets for these goods, being a very efficient producer of coal and copper (both of which are major Andean exports). Furthermore, as the U.S. economy moves further and further into the "postindustrial" era, the United States' consumption of primary minerals is declining.[24]

Although the United States may not be a perfect trading partner for Andean countries, and although many nontariff barriers continue to govern the U.S.-Andean economic relationship, North America nevertheless remains the only part of the developed world where Andean exports have avoided major deterioration. The great unknown in the U.S.-Andean relationship, which may either help reintegrate the Andean region with the world economy or cause its greater marginalization, is the impact of the North American Free Trade Area (NAFTA), which includes Mexico, Canada, and the United States. Many Andean analysts believe that the inclusion of Mexico is a first step toward the inclusion of the rest of Latin America into this wealthy trade bloc and, thus, that NAFTA will facilitate the reintegration of the region with the world economy. Others in South America worry that, by including Mexico as a privileged partner of Anglo America and establishing a preferred economic zone under the banner of the Caribbean Basin Initiative, the United States is creating an exclusive zone that will further marginalize the region in the world economy. What most observers from the Andean region find reassuring is that the United States will not be able to ignore the region's travails for long—given the region's nearness to the United States and given that North America is already suffering from the fallout of the collapse in the Andean region, including a massive inflow of drugs and illegal immigrants. The United States, as a global power and the leading power in the hemisphere, cannot long remain indifferent to the prospect of spreading Lebanonization in its own backyard.

Although it is folly to believe that the crisis in the Andean region has only local fallout, few countries besides the United States seem prepared to realize that the international system cannot endure state disintegration bound to engulf almost the entire hemisphere. Paradoxically, because of the blind spot that much of the developed world has toward the region, Russia and the United States, each serving its own national interest, may jointly assume the role of the region's ombudsman in the international forums. The benefit to the United States in attracting western European and Japanese interest to the region is self-evident, in view of the limited economic resources of the United States and because the United States is the country most affected by the collapse of the state system in the Andean region. Russia's interest in applying its residual diplomatic pressure to increase the access of the Andean region to the world economy is somewhat more obscure but no less important.

First, if the former Soviet economy is ever to recover from its precipitous decline, it will need greater access to world markets. As mainly an exporter of minerals and primary commodities, Russia would be well advised to see that such key industrial blocs as the EU and Japan do not become closed trading blocs. Any such international regime would severely restrict the prospects for greater integration of Russia with the international system. Russia can reenter the international division of labor only if world trade continues to expand and semi-industrial producers have access to the lucrative markets of Europe and Japan. Furthermore, the United States has historically been the strongest supporter of relatively free trade, and it is not in the interest of Russia to see the United States become so preoccupied with its internal difficulties and with instability in its own hemisphere that it becomes less of a global advocate of free trade. Although the United States is a minor trading partner for Russia and although Washington remains the most conservative member of COCOM concerning technology transfers to the former USSR, the United States is still the most consistent advocate of free trade. It would be a tragedy for reform in Russia if the United States followed the lead of Europe and Japan and retreated to a parochial cocoon.

Despite their economic decline, the United States and Russia remain the world's largest military blocs, most directly responsible for the stability of the current international system. Thus it is their duty, and their self-interest, to prevent the international system from breaking up along the fault lines of the countries that can participate in the international system and those that cannot.

If there is a ray of hope for integration of the countries of the Andean region, it is in the experience of Czechoslovakia, Hungary, and Poland. These three countries discovered, after a series of false starts, that the only way to get international attention was to stop competing with one another and, instead, to negotiate with the EC/EU and other economic bodies in unison. The result has been very encouraging, indeed. By forming a bloc of nearly 60 million people, they have greatly improved their bargaining position. Recently the Andean Pact expanded, from a loose paper organization to a common market, including besides the weak Bolivian, Colombian, and Peruvian economies, the powerful economies of Chile and Venezuela. This development may well prove to be the key that will enable the region to assert itself in the international forums, and to assure that the people of the Andes do not become the forgotten tribe of the international system.

Notes

1. Mario Vargas Llosa, *Historia de Mayta* (Barcelona: Seix Barral/Ediciones Norte, 1984).

2. For an insightful critique of Latin America's economic development as it has related to the industrial world, see Raul Preibish, "Commercial Policy in the Underdeveloped Countries," *American Economic Review* (May 1959).

3. Stephen Fidler's report on the Inter-American Development Bank's latest study, "Latin American Poverty 'Deepened' by Reforms," *Financial Times* 8 Apr. 1991.

4. David Scott Palmer, "Peru's Persistent Problems," *Current History* (Jan. 1990): 5–33.

5. See W. W. Rostow, *The Stages of Economic Growth* (New York: Cambridge Univ. Press, 1960).

6. Jorge Castaneda, "Latin America and the End of the Cold War," *World Policy Journal* (Fall 1991): 469–92.

7. Ibid.

8. For one of the best analyses of the Sendero, see David Scott Palmer, "Terrorism as a Revolutionary Strategy: Peru's Sendero Luminoso," in *The Politics of Terrorism*, ed. Barry Rubin (Washington, D.C.: Johns Hopkins Foreign Policy Institute, 1988).

9. Palmer, "Peru's Persistent Problems," 8.

10. See *Latin America Report*, 24, Jan. 1991.

11. For a comparative study of the Sendero and its chief Marxist rival, MRTA, see William A. Hazleton and Sandra Woy-Hazleton, "Terrorism and the Marxist Left: Peru's Struggle Against Sendero Luminoso," *Terrorism* 11, no. 6 (1988): 471–90.

12. See Cynthia McClintock, "The War on Drugs: The Perivian Case," *Journal of Interamerican Studies and World Affairs* 30, nos. 2 and 3 (Summer/Fall 1988).

13. See Peter Andreas et al., "Dead End Drug Wars," *Foreign Policy* 85 (Winter 1991–92).

14. David Bushnell, "Politics and Violence in Nineteenth-Century Colombia," in *Violence in Colombia: The Contemporary Crisis in Historical Perspective*, ed. Charles Bergquist, Ricardo Penaranda, and Gonzalo Sanchez (Wilmington, Del.: Scholarly Resources Books, 1992), 19.

15. The foco doctrine generally associated with Che Guevara and the experience of the Cuban revolution is based on the belief that a revolutionary situation can be induced among a poltically inert peasantry through the activities of a small group of revolutionaries.

16. For a good discussion of Colombia's guerrillas, see Eduardo Pizarro, "Revolutionary Guerrilla Groups in Colombia," in Bergquist et al., eds. *Violence in Columbia*.

17. Only Colombia, Chile, and Uruguay managed to remain current in servicing their foreign debt during the 1980s. The Colombia export of drugs played an important role in enabling Colombia to service its foreign debt.

18. Andreas et al. "Dead End Drug Wars," 115.

19. For a review of a GATT (General Agreement on Tariffs and Trade) evaluation of EC trade practices, see William Dullforce, "Poor Marks for EC External Trade Practices," *Financial Times,* 17 Apr. 1991, 6.

20. For example, see Bruce D. Jackson, *Castro, Kremlin, and Communism in Latin America* (Baltimore: Johns Hopkins Univ. Press, 1969). for a study of U.S. behavior in the region, see Cole Blasier, *The Hovering Giant* (Pittsburgh: Univ. of Pittsburgh Press, 1980).

21. See Ilya Prizel, *Latin America Through Soviet Eyes* (New York: Cambridge Univ. Press, 1990), chap. 7.

22. It should be noted that even Soviet analysts never ascribed the collapse of the Allende regime to U.S. interference. Instead, they attributed it to mismanagement of Chile's internal affairs by Salvador Allende. For example, see Boris Ponomarev, "The World Situation and the Revolutionary Process," *World Marxist Review* 6 (1974), and *1000 Dnei Revoliutsii: Rukovoditile KPCh ob Yrokakh Sobytii v Chili* (Prague, 1978).

23. See Michael Kramer, "Anger, Bluff, and Cooperation," *Time*, 4 June 1990, 35–45; Zartman, *Ripe for Resolution*.

24. For example, until the mid-1960s the United States was the world's largest producer of steel; by the late 1980s it ranked third behind Japan and the USSR. Although the United States has lost about a third of its steel-producing capacity in the last decade alone, the decline of the U.S. steel industry is far from over.

11

The Russian-American Stake in Southern Africa

VITALEY VASILKOV

The unique colonial rule in southern Africa, more than five-hundred years long, emerged earlier and was eliminated later than its counterpart in the rest of the continent—only with the declaration of Namibian independence in March 1990. Continuing and protracted conflicts, however, are left over from the colonial order and the anticolonial struggle, challenging the capabilities of any cooperative security efforts involving the United States and Russia. Although the experience in U.S.-Soviet cooperation for conflict reduction had its accomplishments and its lessons, they tend to indicate the limitations on cooperative security rather than its opportunities in the coming era.

History has marked southern Africa with a strong regional structure. During the struggle for hegemony over southern Africa in the seventeenth to nineteenth centuries, even Great Britain during its highest supremacy failed to eliminate its opponents in the subcontinent and become the absolute winner. Because of the absence of any predominant colonizer in the region, external powers had to start experimenting with cooperative forms of colonialism. Southern Africa saw the first attempts to transform classic colonialism into some new type of postcolonial relations of partnership. A genuine local force—the white settler state—was formed, with its own interests and dynamics. During several centuries and influenced by these factors, a strategic entity was formed in southern Africa that cannot be artificially divided.

224

Thus southern Africa has become a sort of world proving ground for innovative (and often successful) concepts of Third World regional orders. That distinction did not make its history unclouded, but it predetermined a unique stability of the order in southern Africa, stability that recently even prevented making the necessary reforms in due time. True, as distinct from America, the white settlers failed to build the "United States of Southern Africa." They did build a special type of economic, political, and strategic space, which makes it an inseparable single whole.

East-West Competition in Southern Africa

This situation notwithstanding, when the Soviet-American competition in the form of East-West, or communist versus capitalist, confrontation reached the southern tip of Africa, both great powers inevitably made mistakes. Viewing Africa through an ideological prism, they at best took the traditional approach to conflicts in the region, as a chain of classical colonial (or postcolonial) cases. Southern Africa, however, was not just another regional case; it was a strategic entity, demanding an absolutely new approach. Instead, both great powers came to southern Africa with their global interests and their burden of ideological and strategic rivalries. These prevented them from reckoning with the local peculiarities, which did not correspond to their schemes of world order. In this sense Soviet-American confrontation in southern Africa was just a legacy of the Vietnam War. It started immediately after the 1974 revolution in Portugal and even before the signing of the Paris agreements in Vietnam. One should also note that it was begun in Mozambique, not in Angola, as it is usually thought.

In Mozambique, Henry Kissinger placed his main hope in the right-wing Portuguese settlers in Maputo, headed by the millionaire of Portugese origin, Jorge Jardin, and their supporters in Lisbon. There were also several weak black African groups, the best-known of which was headed by Paolo Gumane. He admitted later to have contacts with the CIA since the 1960s and to have received certain covert CIA financing in spring 1974 to start activities against the Front for the Liberation of Mozambique (FRELIMO),[1] although the mutinies organized by these forces in Maputo and Lisbon in September 1974 failed. The civil war in Mozambique did not come about mainly because FRELIMO was fortunate enough not to have real opponents in the country as opposed to the situation in Angola.

These circumstances, however, seriously affected the decisions of all the participants in the Angolan drama. True, the situation in that country at first had been developing quite positively. On 15 January 1975, in the Portuguese city of Alvor, three Angolan groups—the Popular Movement for the Liberation of Angola (MPLA), the National Liberation Front of Angola (FNLA), and the National Union for the Total Liberation of Angola (UNITA)—reached an agreement with the government of Portugal on the date and conditions of independence for Angola, and also on the division of power and on the scheduling of elections right after independence. However, on 22 January the U.S. National Security Council's "40 Committee," the Washington interagency group responsible for the CIA covert operations, authorized a covert grant of $300,000 to the FNLA. UNITA did not receive U.S. covert aid until July, because, according to some American estimates, MPLA and UNITA could then find common ground and form a united front against FLNA.[2] The 40 Committee's decision, according to Marcum,[3] was based on past U.S. connections with FLNA and on "an irrepressible habit of thinking in terms of 'our team' and 'theirs', which enticed the Administration into choosing sides."

Moreover, in September 1975, the CIA directly rebuffed the appeal of UNITA's leader, Jonas Savimbi, to explore the possibility of reaching a negotiated settlement with the MPLA. "We didn't need soft allies," explained John Stockwell,[4] the former head of the CIA Angolan Operational Team. Thus one cannot help agreeing with Wayne S. Smith's conclusion. "The United States, then, was responsible for setting in motion actions that destroyed the Alvor Agreement and that touched off a bloody civil war that was to rage in Angola well into 1976. It was not a move that served U.S. interests. To the contrary, it proved unnecessary and foolish."[5] At the same time, it was quite natural, considering that "both during the final weeks of the Vietnam War and during the Angolan crises of 1975, the Secretary and the President seem to have believed that it was better to roll the dice against the longest of odds than to abandon the competition against our great adversary. The Secretary would freely acknowledge, I believe, that he saw Angola as part of the U.S.-Soviet relationship, and not as an African problem."[6]

In such a situation the USSR and Cuba felt they had no choice except to take appropriate countermeasures, which helped ensure the MPLA's victory in early 1976. It is only fair to admit that after the MPLA victory, the Soviet Union missed a more farsighted, wise, and courageous— though more difficult—policy option. Encouraging conciliation between the MPLA and UNITA would have given a more proper answer to the needs of the Angolan people, for if successful, it would ensure more representative government and conditions for peaceful development of the country. This move would have strengthened the government, as UNITA got its support from southern Angola, and would be the most favorable contribution to Luanda's prestige. Finally, it would deny any legitimacy to the speculations about East-West "victories" or "defeats," would make senseless any further confrontation, and would create conditions for constructive United States-USSR cooperation during the Rhodesian settlement.

Instead, at the XXV Communist Party Congress in February 1976, Secretary-General Leonid Brezhnev explained the MPLA victory by "the current state of world class forces." The Soviet-Mozambican communiqué, adopted in May 1976, read: "The present epoch is characterized by the mounting peoples' fight for national and social liberation." The Soviet-Angolan statement of 14 October 1976 proclaimed "the loss by imperialism of its positions in southern Africa," and noted its intention to take "a revenge."[7] So, southern African events were interpreted in asymmetrical terms, solely as a "victory" of the East and a "defeat" of the West, as a result of the global power equilibrium favorable for socialism, and simultaneously as a factor for strengthening it and ensuring further "intensification of the fight" against imperialism.

There is no documentary confirmation, either, that the USSR made any effort to discuss the Angolan case with the United States or to promote a rapprochement between the MPLA and UNITA. The only exception is a short note: "After consultations between President Ford and Soviet Ambassador Anatoly Dobrynin, the Soviet Union halted its airlift to Angola" on 4 December 1975 but "resumed" it on 25 December.[8] The exact circumstances are still unknown, but it is possible to speculate that the U.S. covert aid to the FNLA and UNITA, disclosed in the American press in December, made the USSR feel betrayed. Cuba twice made unilateral reductions in its forces in Angola (maybe with Soviet advice) in 1976 and 1979, thus taking steps toward reconciliation in the region. The opponents decided "not to understand" these hints and did not show reciprocal restraint. According to Marcum, as the first withdrawal, as early as April 1976, proceeded, "The Carter Administration missed an opportunity in early 1977 to accord relatively uncontroversial recognition to the government. Soon afterward, the exodus of Cuban troops was ended and reversed because of overflights of South African aircraft and mounting antigovernmental insurgency."[9] Probably that tense situation demanded not "a diplomacy of hints" but some deeper agreements, especially between the USSR and the United States.

Nor did the Soviet government take seriously the change in U.S. policy, declared by Kissinger at Dallas on 22 March 1976, where he came out with "two equally important principles: support for majority rule in Africa and firm opposition to military intervention."[10] True, this change kept two strong elements of what even friendly observers called "an attempt to save by diplomacy something which [was] failed to be saved by force."[11] However, an underestimation of the opportunities contained in the concept of negotiated settlement on Rhodesia and a failure to consider the possible Soviet-American cooperation in solving this problem, at least during a next administration, were serious miscalculations.

Nothing changed during the Carter years, either, although his initial program contained some constructive ideas besides the inherited Republican concept of negotiated settlement. "The basis of our position in Africa," Secretary of State Cyrus Vance noted, "is the African perception that we see them and their problems in their own terms, and not as an arena for East-West differences. . . . We would welcome Soviet help—which we regret we have not had—in achieving a peaceful transition to majority rule in Rhodesia, Namibia and elsewhere in Africa."[12] Nevertheless, the chairman of the Presidium of the Supreme Soviet of the USSR, Nikolay Podgorny, during his visit to Africa stated in Maputo on March 29 that Angola and Mozambique form "the crest of [a] powerful anticolonial, antiracist wave," their boundaries with Rhodesia and South Africa "being not just interstate but the class frontiers." With respect to a possible peaceful solution in Rhodesia, Namibia, and South Africa, he could say "just one thing, gentlemen: transfer the power to the majority of the population, that is, to the Africans in the person of their genuine representatives, eliminate the apartheid policies, and the problem will be eliminated."[13]

Soviet-American relations under the Carter administration were troublesome from the very beginning, but Carter's approach to southern-African problems stood out against the background of general U.S. policy for its realism and readiness for necessary compromise. This might well be explained by pure pragmatic estimates of the situation in Rhodesia (though not by them alone). However, Moscow's willingness to hold a constructive dialogue on the Rhodesian issue would probably have given an impetus to favorable changes in the atmosphere of the Soviet-American relationship as well, and would have helped weaken or even eliminate the consecutive outbreaks of confrontation between the two powers in 1977–78 during the uprisings in the Zairian province of Shaba or the conflict on the Horn of Africa. It cannot be excluded that, had there been some cooperation in Africa, the situation in Afghanistan might have developed in an entirely different direction.

Both sides ran the danger of having détente tested to the utmost, though, as was known, it had not been prepared for such a stress. The complex of Soviet-American agreements of the early 1970s did not contain any direct reference to regional conflicts. The extension of the agreed-upon general principles in the sphere of regional conflicts demanded too broad an understanding, which each side could interpret in its favor: the Soviet Union, as U.S. agreement to consider peaceful coexistence (hence, the détente too) as a class struggle; and the United States, as Soviet obligation to abstain from the support of national-liberation movements and to give the United States carte blanche in the Third World in return for détente. Neither of these misinterpretations were acceptable to the other party. Instead of searching for more profound agreements to sweep this time bomb under détente, both sides preferred to intensify confrontation.

As a result, despite the declaration of Zimbabwean independence in 1980, with an informal U.S. Soviet agreement, the late 1970s and early 1980s became "conflict rebirth," provoked, in many ways, by superpower behavior: by the Reagan Doctrine, directed toward escalating East-West contests in the Third World, and by the "ministerial reshuffle" in the USSR, during which the Soviet Union could at best keep inertially afloat its previous policy of response to the "imperialist intrigues." Both moves paralyzed political will, turning the United States-USSR occasional discussions on regional issues into talks of the deaf. All this precluded attempts to build a mechanism of such negotiations, particularly undermining the United Nations' capabilities in this respect. All this not only helped raise conflict situations and widen their geographic, temporal, and military scales, but also provoked local forces, being generally in a very irreconcilable mood, to reach for their objectives by military means. In the end, the Namibian settlement was blocked, reform in South Africa was stopped, Pretoria's destabilizing efforts against the Front Line States were raised, and the internal conflicts in Angola and Mozambique became irreparable.

The situation was made more dangerous by the direct engagement of the superpowers' air or naval forces around Africa. The fact that Africa ranked low in the priorities of both the USSR and the United States might increase, not decrease, the chance that either wished "to teach somebody a lesson" through confrontation with a client of the other, or a clash between clients of the two. Something of this kind appears to have happened: "When the military pressure from South Africa and . . . UNITA reached its peak in late 1983 . . . a Soviet naval detachment composed of an aircraft carrier and three other major surface ships called at Luanda in November and then rounded the southern tip of the continent for a stop at Maputo. This constituted the most powerful naval detachment from the USSR that had ever sailed past the Cape of Good Hope."[14] That move resembled a similar voyage of the American Navy near Angola in 1975.

A new political approach was required to give impetus to the political settlement of regional conflicts. The new Soviet orientation broke the deadlock of both Soviet and American policies in southern Africa. Mikhail Gorbachev could declare before the United Nations on 7 December 1988, "The year 1988 has brought a ray of hope in this sphere of our common concern. It touched upon almost all the regional crises and somewhere there are shifts for the better. We welcome them and have encouraged them within reasonable limits of our capabilities."[15] Among these shifts were the agreements on Namibia signed in New York two weeks later, negotiated in less than a year after six years of vain effort.

The Fundamentals of Successful Political Settlement

The seemingly fast success of political settlement in southern Africa —a showcase for other regional conflicts—was not only because the superpowers no longer had any directly conflicting interests there, once the ideological constraints were lifted. The real key of success seems to have been that both superpowers pursued policies that reflected the strategic integrity of southern Africa, as already noted. The southern-African conflict was the summation of several conflict situations—dismantling of apartheid in South Africa, independence of Namibia, cessation of destabilization activities against a number of Front Line States. On a deeper level, conflict reduction in South Africa was the central issue in the region, and the rest was derivative or peripheral. Besides, some problems were inherited, others were introduced from abroad. All of them, however, were so closely interconnected that one could examine them separately only in theory.

This is not to say that a simultaneous solution to all these conflicts was the only workable way. On the contrary, settlements of the Namibian, Angolan, Mozambican, and other peripheral problems necessarily preceded the most complicated decisions on apartheid and in a sense served as a prerequisite for them. At the core of the problem lay the fact that settling these peripheral issues should include at least some preliminary arrangements for solving the central problem. Otherwise any settlement could be only temporary.

Another side of the problem was the need to consider the legal national interests of South Africa, the central power in the region. Among these were defense of the state from outside armed intervention, elimination of apartheid through cooperation between the majority and the minority, and preservation of its regional interests. Finally, a principle of U.S. Assistant Secretary of State Chester Crocker's intervention was that the conflict should be settled in reverse order of its emergence, that is, first, eliminate direct and indirect foreign intervention, and, second, settle internal problems.

Phase One: Angola-Namibia

The Angolan-Namibian settlement of 1988 constituted the first stage in reducing conflict in southern Africa, and it was important that the remaining two stages went on almost simultaneously, not subsequently. Before they could take place, however, the United States had to undergo the undermining of its constructive engagement policy because of sanctions against South Africa in 1986; and the USSR had to deal with the deadlock of the so-called Brezhnev Doctrine. For the first time, the problem of southern African was touched upon during the Soviet-American summit held in the United States in December 1987, during which Michail Gorbachev said: "We paid attention to the necessity of discussing a common approach to the settlement of regional conflicts. Though we did not go too deeply in this respect, the discussion helped to clear up the issues and gave hope for continuing the dialogue." [16] The dialogue was continued in 1988 during the talks between the USSR deputy foreign minister for Africa, Anatoly Adamishin, and Secretary Crocker, followed by Adamishin's shuttle negotiations with Fidel Castro in Havana (28 March 1988) and Dos Santos in Luanda (31 March 1988). In Havana, the two sides "confirmed the identity of the Soviet and Cuban positions" on the southern African issues "in the light of some new possibilities. In Luanda, Adamishin "came out for the keeping up of the dynamics of the peaceful settlement of the South of the continent." [17]

During the next Soviet-American summit in Moscow, at the end of May, Secretary Gorbachev stated that in southern Africa "an outcome is possible" because "some new possibilities have been opened. . . . There was an interesting, substantial and realistic exchange on Angola. Both our side and the Americans ascertained a possibility of advancing to the settlement of this conflict." [18] It was clear that during that year the Soviet leadership decided to support the new initiatives in southern Africa. Consequently four-party talks began between Angola, Cuba, South Africa, and the United States, with a Soviet observer, and continued for ten sessions between May and December 1988, an interim agreement reached in July.

The head of the third African department of the USSR Foreign Ministry, Vladillen Vasev, the Soviet observer at the negotiations, assessed this agreement as a "considerable concession" by South Africa. "To keep face," he said, South Africa on the eve of the Cairo session came out with an absolutely unacceptable proposal. The result was a deadlock. The Soviets then asked Crocker to convey to South Africa the need to abandon several unacceptable points, particularly a special status for the UNITA and a "security zone" in southern Angola. Thus before the July session two documents emerged: a ten-point and a fifteen-point proposal. Together, they became the basis for the final fourteen-point Governors Island agreement on the principles of peaceful settlement in South-West Africa signed in July.[19] This first common document created during the talks constituted a complex of operational guidelines for subsequent agreements, including a timetable of troop withdrawals, methods of verification, and a procedure to disengage five local armed forces. Important problems remained, but they became technicalities after the fundamental political decisions made during the summits.

Finally, on 22 December 1988 the four parties signed the New York agreements under which South African and Cuban troops were withdrawn from Namibia (in 1990) and Angola (in 1991). The end of foreign intervention opened the way to Namibian independence, which was proclaimed on 21 March 1990 after the first free and just elections in the country.

Cooperation of both powers was a key to the successful result of the Angolan-Namibian problem, as has been stressed by then-Secretary of State George Shultz: "The Soviet Union has played an important and constructive role in the peace process in southwestern Africa. The parties themselves made the sovereign decisions for peace, but, in doing so, they have been encouraged and strongly supported by both the United States and the Soviet Union. Though our roles have been different, our close cooperation has made an effective contribution to the achievement of this agreement." Similar words were expressed by Secretary Crocker.[20]

With the goodwill of all the parties, especially the USSR and the United States, the process moved rapidly. Technically, the success is due to learning the right lessons from previous mistakes. In these circumstances Crocker's remarks, made shortly after his resignation from office, that the Soviet Union "has adopted major tenets of U.S. policy and explicitly endorsed a regional settlement designed in Washington over eight years ago" and that "in the name of 'new thinking', the Soviet

leadership has adopted the functional equivalent of Western policy toward this most troubled and perplexing region,"[21] resembled some cold-
war patterns. They also reflected real feelings in Washington, which had
been earlier expressed more frankly though not less self-deceptively by
Lt. Gen. Colin Powell, assistant to President Reagan for national security: "Where the West had stood firm, the Soviets clearly are reassessing
their foreign policy."[22] Even neutral observers had to note that "despite
tacit cooperation between the superpowers on facilitating the Angolan-
Namibian peace accords . . . the Bush administration seemed initially
to be cautious and reactive, reluctant to undertake broad new
initiatives."[23]

Such estimates left an impression that at first the United States had
wanted to achieve nothing more than the withdrawal of Soviet and
Cuban forces and once they reached this aim they lost any incentive to
push the settlement to the end. The impression was strengthened by the
agonizingly slow pace of talks to resolve internal Angolan problems, not
to mention Mozambique. Several rounds of negotiations between the
MPLA and UNITA in 1989–90, held under the auspices of African
states, failed, including the Gbadolite Declaration mediated by Zaire's
President Mobutu Sese Seko in September 1990. Since 1989, the United
States had become UNITA's main external supplier, providing it with an
estimated $50 million in annual covert military assistance, most of it
spirited into UNITA territory through Zaire's United States–built air
base at Kamina.[24]

Fortunately, realism prevailed. The efforts of Soviet and American
diplomats contributed to the success of negotiations, but mediation by
Portugal as a mender in 1990–91 deserves credit for the management of
the conflict.[25] As a former colonial power, Lisbon had the best knowledge
of the situation in the field, which enabled it to help overcome the lack
of confidence between the MPLA and UNITA, and to reach the final
agreement. That is a good illustration of the great and often indispensable role that only global and European powers can play in mediating
African conflicts, an application of cooperative security. The real breakthrough in this field was made in December 1990, during talks between
the Soviet foreign minister and the American secretary of state in Hous-
ton. In their joint statement Eduard Shevardnadze and James Baker
agreed that both states would end military supplies to Angola immediately after a cease-fire. A week later the new situation was discussed in
the "cross-negotiations" of Shevardnadze with Savimbi, and of Baker
with Angolan Foreign Minister P. Van Dunen. Once again the superpower intervention acted as a decisive dampener, providing the condi-

tions for peace. The final agreement on restoring peace in Angola was signed at Estoril, near Lisbon, on 31 May 1991 by President José Eduardo Dos Santos and Jonas Savimbi.

Unfortunately, conflict management was not conflict resolution. The conflict between the two movements—and particularly between Savimbi and Dos Santos—shifted to the electoral field, and when the latter won a near-majority in the September 1992 elections, Savimbi broke the agreement and returned to the battlefield. Two more years of mediation by the United States and the UN produced a new agreement at Lusaka with many of the necessary details about disarmament and power-sharing now filled in. The two sides were by then so suspicious of each other that they would not trust an agreement, and so burdened with sunk costs that they both kept pushing for one final escalation to victory; thus, the agreement remained unsigned and the bloody war dragged on, independent of its former external supporters, until 20 November 1994.

Phase Two: Mozambique

The situation in Mozambique has been much worse than in Angola and Namibia. If this country, as distinct from Angola, was fortunate enough not to have had several antagonistic nationalist movements, it instead experienced great misfortune in being a hostage first of Rhodesian and then of South African politics. Rhodesia left the Mozambican National Resistance (MNR) as its heritage, and South Africa continued destabilization efforts toward Mozambique. Western pressure and South African business interests in the Mozambican market produced the Nkomati Accord in 1983 to lower the conflict and its cost between Mozambique and South Africa, but not to resolve it. The capture of the the MNR's Gorongosa base in central Mozambique in 1985 revealed that the South African military had not abided by the agreement to end aid to the MNR. The so-called Vaz diary discovered at Gorongosa contained embarrassing details of South African Defense Forces (SADF) support for the MNR. It quoted the then-SADF chief, Constand Viljoen, as advising the MNR "not to be fooled by the schemes of [South African Foreign Minister] Pik Botha because he is a traitor" and contained other references to Botha as being a "Soviet nark" and a stooge of Chester Crocker.[26] The mysterious circumstances of President Samora Machel's death in an air crash over South African territory in late 1986 added to the impression of Pretoria's unwillingness to respect the Nkomati agreements. Reports in 1988 that the South African Department of Military Intelligence was pushing ahead with a new strategy to rebuild support for the MNR[27] followed the damaging U.S. Department of State Gersony Report, which attributed a hundred thousand deaths and widespread brutality to the MNR, and compared it with Pol Pot's Khmer Rouge.[28]

Both the United States and the Soviet Union saw no military solutions to the war and preferred a quiet diplomacy to help establish contacts between the government and the MNR, supporting mediation variously by Zambia, Kenya, and Malawi. In 1990, when the peace process deadlocked, Washington came out with the seven-point program, which recognized the legitimacy of the Frelimo government. The MNR rejected the proposed terms, although it agreed to continue talks in Rome, under the aegis of the Saint Egidio community, with Italy, Portugal, Russia, and the United States as observers. Two years of mediation finally bore results in an agreement in October 1991 and elections in October 1994.[29] The reason seemed to be that the Mozambican situation differed diametrically from that of Angola.

For Savimbi, a political settlement was the outcome for which he had been fighting, while bargaining relentlessly during the talks for more favorable conditions. For Afonso Dhlakama, it was something different. His "movement" was artificially created to fight not for political power but for destabilization. He did not begin with the goal of political power in a normal sense; he was frightened by it. His normal state was "fighting" with peasants, robbing and killing them, which is why any diplomatic process was doomed to failure until Renamo was "retrained" by long negotiations to revise its goals. Dhlakama learned in the process; Savimbi only confirmed his goal of winning by any means, and the weak disarmament program in the Bicesse agreements left all means intact. The U.S. had some leverage in this process in Mozambique but little in Angola, and Russia had lost its sources of influence.

Phase Three: South Africa

All the negotiation and agreement would have not been possible without the cooperation of the Republic of South Africa. Nevertheless, it was not always the case that the great powers considered its interests. Probably the reason was that they did not seriously look at the prospect of political solutions in the region. Marcum, Kitchen, and Spicer talk of the "leap of faith assumption" as a "weakness shared by anti-apartheid and conservative activists, legislators and businessmen." Few, if any, had done much strategic thinking or feasibility testing of their policy prescriptions. It seemed to matter only that one took the "right" stance.

The moral climate, suffused by racial or anticommunist emotion or both, was largely intolerant of deliberate or deliberative processes. There was no sense of obligation to expand upon and "reality test" the logic of why one's strategy would work, and at what costs, over how much time or by what criteria for success.[30]

The sanctions imposed by the American Congress against the will of the Reagan administration remained the most contradictory measure for the Bush administration too. The maintenance of sanctions was its obligation under the law and certainly an instrument of influence on Pretoria. Once President Frederick W. de Klerk announced his reformist course in February 1990, and the process of managing the collapse of the apartheid state moved to the National Peace Accord in September 1991 and the Congress on a Democratic South Africa in December, the creation of a new state appeared to be irreversible. Thus careful monitoring of the process caused President Bush to decide to lift sanctions in mid-1991.

The USSR found itself in a similarly delicate position when a decision was taken to switch from a military-political to a political-military settlement in South Africa. It was clear that having no official and economic contacts with South Africa, the USSR could contribute to the settlement mainly by trying to encourage the African National Congress (ANC) leadership to switch from military to political struggle. It was equally important to convince them that it was neither betrayal nor coercion to suspend arms supplies. They had to understand that for Russia it was a move toward restoring its real national interests and eliminating their ideological substitute, and that such a shift was for the black South Africans too. The problem was further complicated in that those in power in Moscow hardly understood what those real national interests were.

Despite the ANC statements welcoming positive foreign influence but rejecting any foreign interference in the negotiations, Russian behind-the-scenes influence was exerted and contributed to the ANC's official rejection of armed struggle as a policy and its agreement to sit at the negotiating table without any preconditions. The United States had also made part of the deal when Secretary Shultz first met with ANC President Oliver Tambo in 1987, and when Nelson Mandela visited Washington during his triumphant world trip in May 1990. Those contacts helped convince black South Africans that political settlement was really much more favorable for their interests.

To be sure, the ANC decision had been most powerfully influenced by positive developments within South Africa itself and its fair assessment of them. Soon after President de Klerk came to power, all main prerequisites for a nationwide roundtable in the country were in place. As of 1991, the main apartheid laws were eliminated, all black-African organizations were legalized, the 1985 state of emergency was lifted, almost all political prisoners were released, and investments to increase the black population's living standards had grown. Still, the path from confrontation to dialogue had been difficult.

During the initial rounds of National Party–ANC talks, some very promising understandings were reached, including the cease-fire, release of political prisoners, and repatriation of political emigrants.[31] Unfortunately, but quite understandably, progress was blocked by persistent differences in goals. De Klerk's government, while trying to keep the support of the white community, had to be cautious to escape any moves that the white electorate might interpret as excessive concessions or that might provoke further development of ultra-right groups. The moderate elements in the ANC leadership, in turn, could not forget the black radicals, preferring to negotiate from the position of strength and threatening to resume fighting in case of any setbacks during the talks. Though the predominant popularity of the ANC was beyond question, its leaders also had to reckon with the competing black African organizations, especially the radical Pan-Africanist Congress (PAC) and the Zulu Inkatha Freedom Party (IFP).

Therefore it was very important that Russian-American cooperation covered contacts with South African government too. For the United States, this meant the lifting of sanctions in mid-1991. For Russia, it meant building positive bilateral relations with a country that had been practically unknown. Besides normal interstate interests, this rapprochement was considerable in helping Pretoria and the white community to realize that moving away from apartheid gave very real political benefits, particularly in breaking through international boycott. This process, a sort of "expert diplomacy," went cautiously from the Soviet side and with many excessive expectations from the South African one. Through several meetings of scholars and diplomats, first in the third countries, then in Moscow and South Africa, and through tours of journalists, both countries had slowly passed through the initial phase of a new relationship as early as 1985–88.

Officially Soviet position of that period was explained by the chief of the African Department of Foreign Ministry, Yury Yukalov: "The Soviet policy is based on realism and on denial of confrontation in regional conflicts. This policy now will help the others abandon a contrary approach to southern African crises too. We are ready to respect the interests of any sides in the region. The stability there will meet even our economic interests. We prefer the problem of apartheid to be settled by political means. That is why we do not stress the need to support armed struggle." Yukalov added that because of the boycott against South Africa, the Soviet Union also suffered certain losses. "We are ready to restore diplomatic relations with South Africa," he said, "and reestablish cooperation in various fields. But under only one condition: if it becomes a democratic republic, where human rights will be respected and the practice and politics of apartheid will be canceled."[32]

That policy made possible official contacts between the countries. The talks on Namibia gave a chance for contacts of Soviet Deputy Foreign Minister Adamishin with Foreign Minister Botha and his colleagues. In April 1989, a Soviet diplomat for the first time since 1956 came to Capetown to take part in the work of the Joint Commission on South-West Africa. In March 1990, in Windhoek, a sensational meeting between President de Klerk and the Soviet foreign minister dispelled groundless hopes and fears that the Soviet Union was abandoning its long-standing antiapartheid policy. A year later, establishing interest sections in the Austrian embassies in both countries was soon followed by restoring the consular relations that had existed in 1941–56, as agreed upon during the unofficial visit of Foreign Minister Botha to Moscow in November 1991. Full diplomatic relations soon followed.

Yet, as noted, the primary impetus for the evolution of events in South Africa came from within, and interested and well-meaning powers abroad had little role to play once the initial decision to negotiate a transition from apartheid had been made. Instead, both superpowers have concentrated on normalizing state-to-state relations in consonance with their interests and in preparing for a smooth transition of those relations to a new South African government. Although the ANC, in July 1992, called for a UN role in the interrupted negotiations and the South African government on occasion mentioned an international presence, there was no role for a superpower mediator either directly or behind the scenes in the South African conflict, as there was in Namibia, Angola, and Mozambique. The only role left open was that of an unofficial "midwife," as thousands of foreign private individuals under various auspices–including the UN–contributed to a final resolution of the South African conflict by monitoring the elections of 26–29 April 1994, and five foreigners–including an American–were members of the Independent Electoral Commission which oversaw the electoral process.

. . .

As the world slips from an ideological cold war to a greater realization of national interests and conflict reduction, the roles of the global powers in the southern African conflicts have paradoxically diminished. In Namibia, Mozambique, and Angola, an active mender was needed, and mending began with the relations between the external patrons of the parties to the regional conflict. As cooperation was established between the superpowers, they could turn to the regional conflict and mediate its interstate and then intrastate aspects. Their role as a mender was more direct in interstate than in intrastate aspects, however, where they were at most "midwives," and not always successful ones at that. In the fourth conflict, within South Africa itself, the global powers were essentially powerless and their role was reduced to looking after their own interests in their relations with the evolving South African government. Thus both the need for superpower cooperation and the limitations on their leverage in conflict reduction are the two lessons from southern Africa.

Projecting beyond the southern African conflicts, what can appear is not a South African empire but some new type of commonwealth of the twenty-first century. Having been a proving ground for new types of Third World relations in the past, southern Africa may also play the same role in the future. With the collective help of all the nations of the world, it may show the path to new forms of black-white, North-South relations—the priority of the coming century.

Notes

1. *Observer* (London), 23 Mar. 1975; *Expresso* (Lisbon), 10 May 1974.

2. Rene Lemarchand, ed. *American Policy in Southern Africa: The Stakes and the Stance* (Washington, D.C.: Univ. Press of America, 1978), 75, 78, 79.

3. John A. Marcum, "Lessons of Angola," *Foreign Affairs* 54, no. 3 (1976): 414.

4. John Stockwell, *In Search of Enemies: A CIA Story* (New York: W. W. Norton, 198), 193.

5. Wayne S. Smith, "A Trap in Angola," *Foreign Policy* no. 62 (Spring 1986): 68.

6. Nathaniel Davis, "The Angola Decision of 1975: A Personal Memoir," *Foreign Affairs* 57, no. 1 (1978): 123–24. See also Stockwell, *In Search of Enemies,* 43; William Colby and P. Forbath, *Honorable Men: My Life in the CIA* (New York: Simon and Schuster, 1978), 439–40; "The Pike Papers," *Village Voice,* 20 Feb. 1976; Roger Morris, "The Proxy War in Angola: Pathology of a Blunder," *The New Republic* (Jan. 1976): 21; Marcum, "Lessons of Angola," 414ff.

7. *Materialy XXV s'ezda KPSS* (Materials of the 25th CPSU Congress) (Moscow: Politizdat, 1977), 13; *SSSR i strany Afriki: Documenty i Materialy,* 1971–76, pt. 2, 149, 228.

8. "The United States and Angola: A Chronology," *Department of State Bulletin* 89, no. 2143 (1989): 17.

9. John A. Marcum, "Africa: A Continent Adrift," *Foreign Affairs* 68, no. 1 (1988/89): 161.

10. Henry Kissinger, "Foreign Policy and National Security," *Department of State Bulletin* (12 Apr. 1976): 664.

11. *NATO's Fifteen Nations* 23, no. 3 (1978): 35.

12. Statement of Cyrus Vance, State Department Subcommittee on Foreign Relations press release, 10 June 1978, 5.

13. *Pravda,* 31 Mar. 1977.

14. David E. Albright, "The New Trends in Soviet Policy Toward Africa," *CSIS Africa Notes,* 29 Apr. 1984, 9.

15. *Pravda,* 8 Dec. 1988.

16. Mikhail Gorbachev, *Izbrannye rechi i stati'i,* 5:534, 555.

17. *Vestnik MID SSSR* (Bulletin of the USSR Foreign Ministry), 1988, no. 8, 40–41.

18. Soviet-American summit, Moscow, 29 May–2 June 1988, 137, 154.

19. *Novoe Vremya* (New Times), 29 July 1988, 10. For an account of the negotiations and of the evolution of the Namibian conflict, see Zartman, *Ripe for Resolution,* chap. 5, 230ff. on the interim agreement and 231–36 on the final agreement and implementation.

20. "Angolan/Namibian Accords," statement by Secretary Shultz and remarks of Assistant Secretary Crocker, *Department of State Bulletin* 89, no. 2143 (1989): 10, 12.

21. Chester A. Crocker, "Southern Africa: Eight Years Later," *Foreign Affairs* 68, no. 4 (1989): 147, 149.

22. "U.S. Foreign Policy in a Time of Transition," address by Assistant to the President for National Security Affairs Powell, National Press Club, Washington, D.C., 27 Oct. 1988, *Department of State Bulletin* 89, no. 2142 (1989): 31.

23. Donald Rothchild and John Ravenhill, "Retreat from Globalism: U.S. Policy Toward Africa in the 1990s," in *Eagle in a New World: American Grand Strategy in the Post-Cold War Era,* ed. Kenneth A. Oye, Robert J. Lieber, and Donald Rothchild (New York: Harper Collins, 1992), 390.

24. Richard W. Hull, "United States Policy in Southern Africa," *Current History* 89, no. 547 (1990): 228.

25. On the Angola negotiations, see Donald Rothchild and Caroline Hartzell, "The Road from Gbadolite to Lusaka," in *Elusive Peace: Negotiating an End to Civil Wars,* ed. I. William Zartman (Washington, D.C.: Brookings Institution, 1995); Shawn McCormick, "Angola: The Road to Peace," *CSIS Africa Notes* 125 (6 June 1991).

26. *South Africa at the End of the Eighties: Policy Perspectives* (Johannesburg: Center of Policy Studies, Univ. of Witwatersrand, 1989), 66.

27. *Africa Confidential,* Sept. 1988.

28. R. Gersony, *Summary of Mozambican Refugee Accounts of Principally Conflict-Related Experience in Mozambique* (Washington D.C.: Department of State, 1988), 41.

29. On the Mozambican negotiations, see Ibrahim Msabaha, "Stalled Negotiations in Mozambique," in Zartman, ed. *Elusive Peace.*

30. John Marcum, Helen Kitchen, and Michail Spicer, "The United States and the World," in *A Future South Africa; Visions, Strategies, and Realities,* ed. Peter L. Berger and Bobby Godsell (Boulder Colo.: Westview, 1988), 249.

31. On the South African negotiations, see I. William Zartman, "Negotiating the South African Transition," in Zartman, ed. *Elusive Peace.*

32. *Moscow News,* 16 Apr. 1989, 10.

12

Great Powers and Conflict Reduction in the Horn of Africa

TERRENCE LYONS

Conflict and External Power Involvement

The Horn of Africa, consisting of Ethiopia and its immediate neighbors —Somalia, Sudan, Kenya, Djibouti, and since 1991 Eritrea—has been a region of endemic interstate and intrastate conflict for decades.[1] The many conflicts are interlinked in a regional "security complex"[2] that blurs the lines between internal and interstate struggles. Somali policies to create a "Greater Somalia" state that includes Somalis living in Ethiopia, Kenya, and Djibouti have led to conflicts and subversion since Somalia's independence to 1990. The clash between Somali irredentism and the commitment to territorial integrity of its neighbors led to border fighting with Ethiopia in 1963–64 and Somali support for insurgents in Kenya in the early 1960s. After a coup in Somalia that brought Siad Barre to power in 1969 and the Ethiopian revolution that led to Mengistu Haile Mariam's rise to power in 1977, the two states fought a major war in the Ogaden in 1977–78. Further intervention by both Somalia and Ethiopia through proxy forces continued during the 1980s. Ethiopia's other neighbor, Sudan, supported Eritrean insurgents seeking independence in the 1970s and 1980s; Ethiopia, in turn, supported southern Sudanese rebel movements. The complex interlinking of these internal and regional conflicts tied each actor's security to the others' and created obstacles for conflict reduction.

241

During the cold war, this regional security complex was complicated further by superpower competition for clients. The region attracted the attention of the great powers because of its strategic location and because Ethiopia played an important role in African affairs. More important, neither superpower was willing to concede the region to the other.[3] In the 1960s, the United States provided Haile Selassie with military and economic assistance while the Soviet Union armed Ethiopia's regional rival, Somalia. After the Ethiopian revolution, relations between Addis Ababa and Washington cooled. Moscow, after trying to preserve its influence in Somalia while improving relations with Ethiopia, eventually decided to back the revolutionaries in Addis Ababa. From 1977 to 1990, the Soviet Union provided very generous support for Mengistu, supplying the military equipment needed to pursue internal wars and to repel the Somali invasion of the Ogaden. After losing its position in Ethiopia, the United States developed patron-client relations with Somalia, Kenya, and Sudan. The enduring cleavages between Ethiopia and Somalia, Ethiopia and Sudan, and Somalia and Kenya provided the entry point for external powers seeking to introduce themselves into the regional security system. Vulnerable regional leaders sought to "borrow power" from beyond the region to reinforce their positions. The great powers were invited in because the prospective clients hoped that in this way they could improve their position vis-à-vis their regional rivals.[4] Although external patronage fed these conflicts, the primary sources clearly were rooted in the competition among the states for contradictory visions of regional security, complicated by internal conflicts that spilled over borders.

In the late 1980s, the internal changes in the Soviet Union unleashed by Mikhail Gorbachev's policies of *perestroika* transformed cold war relations between the great powers and the Horn of Africa. Moscow gradually disengaged itself from Ethiopia; Washington, no longer concerned with Soviet activities in the region and troubled by the undemocratic policies of its clients, followed suit in Sudan, Somalia, and Kenya. Without cold war competition, external interests in the region were marginal. This disengagement, however, did not resolve the heated struggles for change in each of the regional states. Post-cold war U.S. policy toward the region soon was tested as the old regime in Ethiopia neared collapse. The United States seized the opportunity to encourage a less violent transition after insurgent military victories. The old imperatives of competitive patron-client relationships clearly had ended but new patterns and their implications for conflict reduction still were evolving.[5]

Patron-Client Politics and Conflict Reduction during the Cold War

During the cold war, the superpowers assumed the position of patron to regional clients in the Horn of Africa. The United States and the Soviet Union on occasion tried to assume the status of "monopoly patron," providing assistance to both sides of regional disputes. Washington endeavored to bridge the regional divisions and support both Addis Ababa and Mogadishu in 1963; Moscow sought to do the same in the period immediately before the Ogaden War of 1977. Neither attempt succeeded because the intense regional cleavages mattered more to regional leaders than external linkages. Consequently both the Soviet Union and the United States functioned as partisan patrons and adopted policies that supported opposite sides in regional conflicts. Sometimes they acted as sheriffs, providing direct military assistance to one party in a conflict. In 1977, for example, the Soviet Union airlifted military equipment and advisers to defend Ethiopia from Somalia, an effort that approached the crusader role because Moscow also was motivated by its desire to defend the Ethiopian revolution. During most of the cold war the two superpowers played the role of umpire, each attempting to reinforce the rights and position of its client indirectly through assistance programs and by supporting favorable regional initiatives. Washington served as Ethiopia's supplier and advocate, while Moscow promoted Somalia in the 1960s and early 1970s; the alignments reversed in 1977 after the Ethiopian revolution, but the pattern of superpower rivals supporting regional competitors endured. When each superpower had a client in the region, Washington and Moscow tended to emphasize their resolute commitment to their client's security and subordinate conflict resolution goals to the requirements of the patron-client relationships. As a result, the superpowers left conflict resolution efforts to regional organizations, such as the Organization of African Unity, or to individual African leaders. So long as the peace initiatives were not perceived as benefiting their superpower or client's rival, both Moscow and Washington acted as umpires and endorsed these efforts. Finally, on several occasions, Washington and Moscow acted as dampers, constraining their clients to prevent conflict escalation and to avoid crises that might endanger a direct superpower conflict.

The United States and the Soviet Union possessed far more aggregate power than their clients in the Horn but their influence over regional policies and conflict behavior was limited. Ethiopia, Somalia, and Sudan all demonstrated their ability to use external patronage for their own regional advantages, refusing advice and ignoring pressures from the superpowers when it threatened their own perceptions of security, and expelling their patrons when the relationship no longer benefited them.[5] Emperor Haile Selassie regularly played the "Soviet card" by threatening to improve relations with Moscow, a strategy that worked in the late 1950s and early 1960s to win more assistance from Washington but failed in 1973 when U.S. interests in Ethiopia declined.[6] Kissinger tried to get the revolutionary government in Addis Ababa to call off the 1976 Peasants' March against Eritrean forces without success. The Ethiopians felt free to ignore their arms supplier and soon shifted their military ties to the Soviet Union. Somalia similarly ignored Soviet pressures to cooperate with Ethiopia in 1977 and invaded the Ogaden. Despite the asymmetry of power, the patron-client associations were mutually agreed-upon exchange relationships that did not give the patron veto power over the client's policies, particularly on matters of vital concern to the client, such as internal security. The availability of alternative patrons allowed the regional states to persist in their conflicts and disregard any superpower pressure to negotiate.

The depth of regional cleavages prevented either superpower from developing cooperative relations with both regional rivals at the same time. In 1963, the United States offered Somalia military assistance while maintaining its patronage to Ethiopia.[7] Addis Ababa was alarmed and Mogadishu rejected the offer and accepted a more generous package from the Soviet Union. Similarly in 1977, after the Ethiopian revolution and improved relations between Moscow and Addis Ababa, Cuban President Fidel Castro and Soviet President Nikolai Podgorny tried to construct a "Pax Sovietica" federation based on a common Marxist-Leninist ideology among Ethiopia, Somalia, and South Yemen. This scheme quickly failed when Mogadishu insisted that Eritrea and the Ogaden receive independence first.[8] Fundamentally, neither the commitment to Marxism-Leninism by Ethiopia and Somalia nor the regional dominance of Soviet influence were sufficient to overcome the intense regional divisions.[9] Washington and Moscow made these efforts in the hope of excluding their rival from the region. In addition, if the regional competitors had accepted a common patron, the superpower might have been able to limit conflict. In both cases, however, the importance of the local issues in conflict exceeded the benefits perceived in Addis Ababa and Mogadishu to such an arrangement. The client states refused to cooperate with a patron whose loyalties straddled regional cleavages and the availability of a rival patron prevented unilateral imposition of conflict limits.

The 1963–64 border war between Ethiopia and Somalia demonstrates that when conflict threatened to undermine a patron-client relationship, the superpower responded by reassuring its client and increasing its patronage with less regard for the impact of its actions on the conflict. In late 1963, after Somali rejected Washington's offer of military assistance and the establishment of military relations with Moscow, a major border conflict broke out between Ethiopia and Somalia.[10] Ethiopian armed forces at first performed poorly, and panic-stricken military leaders presented Washington with a costly new shopping list of additional military equipment needed on an emergency basis. When the United States was slow to respond because it feared an arms race in the region, Minister of Defense General Merid Mengesha vented his anger and stated that "the United States must either give us the assistance we require or we might have to deal with the Devil himself to save our country."[11]

Once the conflict threatened the patron-client relationship, Washington abandoned restraint and provided additional military assistance. Somalia and the Soviet Union had signed a military agreement in 1963, and United States interests in the Horn were to maintain its relations with Ethiopia and prevent Moscow from expanding its influence in the region. U.S. attempts to act as patron to both sides had failed and countering Soviet moves in Somalia by reassuring Ethiopia—rather than conflict reduction—became the imperative.

The politics of patronage led Washington and Moscow to defer action on conflict reduction to African institutions and actors. The superpowers gave verbal support and an occasional push to their clients to encourage them to pursue these conflict management efforts but generally remained bystanders. In 1964, Sudan, operating under the aegis of the Organization of African Unity (OAU), mediated a disengagement after the 1963–64 Ethiopia-Somalia border conflict. In 1967–68, Zambian President Kenneth Kaunda facilitated conflict management talks between Somalia and Kenya.[12] The 1972 Addis Ababa Agreement, which ended the Sudanese civil war for a decade, was mediated by the All-Africa Council of Churches backed by Ethiopian Emperor Haile Selassie.[13] Ethiopia and Somalia agreed to a disengagement in 1988 at meetings held under the auspices of the Intergovernmental Authority on Drought and Development (IGADD), a regional organization headquartered in Djibouti. All these examples are of conflict management that left underlying issues unaddressed, often to flare again when one party or the other perceived new opportunities. A new regime in Somalia in 1967, the domestic consequences of a coup attempt in Sudan in 1972, and internal security concerns in Ethiopia and Somalia in 1988 motivated regional leaders to accept these management efforts. In the Somalia-Kenya case, management turned into resolution as the importance of the conflict issue faded with time. The political chaos in Mogadishu and Addis Ababa in the early 1990s may make the 1988 disengagement endure as the actors' interests turned inward.

The superpowers acted mainly as supportive bystanders in these processes, urging their clients to take advantage of the opportunity but not willing to risk their access by taking the lead. In some cases the superpower helped by reinforcing a leader already inclined to reduce conflict. For example, Moscow offered expressions of support for Somali Prime Minister Ibrahim Egal when his policies of détente with Kenya encountered criticism in Mogadishu in 1967.[14] The United States and Soviet Union also encouraged Ethiopia and Somalia to de-escalate their conflict in 1988.[15]

The two superpowers did act successfully to prevent local conflicts from escalating into superpower crises, most notably during the dramatic *renversement des alliances* after the 1977–78 Ogaden War. As Zartman has pointed out, despite all the opportunities to get in each other's way during this transition, the United States and the USSR managed to switch clients in the middle of revolution and interstate conflict while avoiding each other in an ad hoc coordination like pedestrians passing on a sidewalk.[16] In February 1978, the Ethiopian army advanced across the Ogaden toward the Somali border, raising fears that the Soviet Union and Cuba would use force to create the "Pax Sovietica" in the Horn that they failed to establish using diplomacy in March 1977. Washington sought to deter any consideration of such a plan by Moscow by threatening to arm Somalia if there were a Soviet-Ethiopian attack.[17] Secretary of State Cyrus Vance received promises from the Soviet Union that Ethiopia would not invade Somalia. Deputy National Security Adviser David Aaron received similar assurances from Mengistu in Addis Ababa.[18] The superpower actions to assure that the Ethiopian army stopped at the Somali border did not constrain Addis Ababa, because Mengistu never intended to take the fight into Somalia. The joint Moscow-Washington diplomatic moves, however, were important in sanctifying the end point of the war and making the results clearer and cleaner. It is notable that superpower diplomacy took place only after military facts on the ground made the outcome of the Ogaden War evident, a pattern we will see again in Washington's actions toward the Ethiopian transition in 1991. Furthermore, this exercise in superpower crisis prevention succeeded in avoiding direct conflict between the United States and the USSR but did not address the conflict issues between Ethiopia and Somalia.

During the cold war, therefore, the two superpowers played only a marginal role in conflict reduction. The depth of regional divisions provided few opportunities. The patronage provided by the superpowers, particularly the very generous support Moscow provided Somalia until 1977 and Ethiopia thereafter, did not encourage leaders to seek negotiated settlements. In principle the superpowers wanted conflict reduction because it lessened demands from clients for ever-increasing assistance, because conflict provided the excuse for the other superpower to become more involved in the rival regional party, and because regional conflict always risked escalation into superpower conflict. As long as the cold war played out across the Horn of Africa, however, Moscow and Washington made maintaining ties to their clients first priority and conflict reduction a clear second.

Post-Cold War Conflict Reduction

The politics of competitive patronage declined in the late 1980s when the Soviet Union began to signal its desire to disengage from the region. This new Soviet policy transformed the basic assumptions of cold war patron-client relationships and provided the rationale for limited but important U.S. activities designed to promote conflict resolution. The clearest example of this change was seen in Ethiopia. Former President Jimmy Carter and later Assistant Secretary of State Herman Cohen organized talks between the Ethiopian government and the Eritrean insurgents in the late 1980s and early 1990s. The Soviet Union supported these efforts but played a minor role in what was a unilateral U.S. effort. When the old regime collapsed in Addis Ababa, Cohen took the lead and helped broker an agreement for a transitional government.

Background to Conflict Resolution in Ethiopia

After the overthrow of Emperor Haile Selassie by a military committee known as the Derg in September 1974, Ethiopia underwent constant armed conflict over the nature and leadership of the postimperial state.[19] The most enduring conflict was in Eritrea, where Addis Ababa fought to preserve the territorial integrity of the state while Eritrean nationalists struggled for independence. Eritrea was a former Italian colony federated with Ethiopia in 1952 and absorbed into Haile Selassie's imperial domain in 1962. The conflict began against the emperor but escalated under the leadership of the Marxist-oriented Eritrean Peoples' Liberation Front (EPLF) after the revolution.

Other rebel groups in other parts of Ethiopia joined the Eritreans in a complex, interrelated, but uncoordinated struggle against Mengistu's central government. The most successful insurgents organized on the basis of ethnicity or regionalism, such as the Tigray People's Liberation Front (TPLF), which formed the dominant component of the multiethnic Ethiopian People's Revolutionary Democratic Front (EPRDF), and the Oromo Liberation Front (OLF). Growing rebel strength, a coup attempt on 16–18 May 1989 by military officers frustrated by the endless war, and increasingly clear signals from Moscow that its patience and willingness to supply massive military assistance were running out made resolving the internal conflicts essential for Mengistu's survival.[20]

A long series of failed bilateral peace initiatives and attempts at mediation preceded the U.S. involvement in the early 1990s. In the early days of the Ethiopian revolution, General Aman Michael Andom tried to end the Eritrean rebellion by appealing over the heads of the insurgent leadership and offering reconciliation within a reformed Ethiopia.[21] Aman's plan was never articulated fully and was rejected by both the Eritrean exile leadership and hard-liners in the Derg. In April 1976, the military regime offered a Nine Point Peace Plan that called for integration of Eritrea into a Marxist-Leninist Ethiopia. This effort coincided with the Peasants' March that attempted to solve the problem militarily. Both the Nine Point Plan and the Peasants' March failed.[22] During the complex and often violent politics in Addis Ababa after Haile Selassie's overthrow, leaders identified as "soft" on Eritrea lost power and their lives to hard-line factions.[23] Militants also dominated the EPLF, as indicated in their January 1977 program that contained little to indicate a desire for compromise and reconciliation.[24] Mengistu launched a series of progressively larger military campaigns against Eritrea in the late 1970s and early 1980s but only succeeded in alienating the Eritrean people and driving new waves of recruits into rebellion.[25] In 1987, Mengistu tried to institutionalize his control over the region by promulgating a new constitution that offered some measure of autonomy to Eritrea and other regions but this offer was insufficient to end the EPLF's struggle.[26]

Besides these unilateral initiatives and attempts to get bilateral talks started, many possible mediators have tried to broker an agreement. The East German government organized a meeting between the Ethiopian government and the EPLF in 1978 but the Eritrean insurgents rejected this mediation because they believed, with good evidence, that the East Germans simply were supporting the Ethiopian position. During a brief détente between Ethiopia and Sudan, Jaafar Nimieri offered his good offices and access to the Eritrean leadership to promote a negotiated settlement, but this effort failed because of Eritrean disunity and renewed tensions between Addis Ababa and Khartoum.[27] EPLF officials claim they met Derg representatives no fewer than ten times in various European capitals between 1982 and 1985, all without substantial progress. According to EPLF officials, Addis Ababa used these talks to stall for time and prepare for new military offenses. In 1985, the EPLF refused additional talks unless they were public, with a third party observer, and without preconditions.[28]

All these talks failed because both the EPLF and Mengistu believed they could achieve their objectives by defeating their opponent through unilateral military actions. Both sides perceived that time was on their side. External powers, in particular the Soviet Union, fed this perception during the late 1970s and 1980s. Ethiopia received an estimated $4.1 billion in military equipment between 1984 and 1988, almost all from the Soviet Union or its Eastern European allies.[29] This tremendous patronage encouraged Mengistu to believe that he could defeat the Eritreans without compromising his designs for centralized, unchecked power. The EPLF also sought and won external support for its cause in Arab capitals seeking to expand their influence along the Red Sea. The most important supporter was Sudan, which provided vital supply routes and a secure hinterland for the insurgents. Military support to the EPLF was less clear: by the late 1980s most of their equipment was captured from the Ethiopian military, but supplies, financing, and diplomatic support also came from Saudi Arabia, Iraq, and other Arab sources at various times. The ability to extract resources from the international economy—arms, food aid/famine relief, and remittances from overseas workers—allowed both the government and the insurgents to persist in military operations far beyond the capacity of their local resource bases.[30] The vital issues at stake in Eritrea were not created by external powers, and the patrons often had only limited leverage over their clients. The point here, however, is that the willingness of external sponsors to bank roll the conflict encouraged efforts to win unilaterally by securing additional external assistance rather than compromise with their opponent.

After more than a decade of generous military support, the Soviet Union began to reconsider its support for Ethiopia's policies, at least as pursued by Mengistu.[31] Mikhail Gorbachev's reform program at home provided him with incentives to reduce his involvement in clients overseas. Soviet analysis of regional conflicts began to reflect a new awareness of local social sources of conflict, although some military writers clung to old patterns and continued to support military assistance.[32] Soviet economic experts recommended reforms in a report ignored by Addis Ababa.[33] In March 1989, a Soviet diplomat in Addis Ababa criticized

Ethiopian military effectiveness to a *New York Times* reporter,[34] and articles critical of Mengistu began to appear in Soviet journals.[35] During the spring of 1989, the Soviets told Mengistu to reform, seek a nonmilitary "just resolution" in Eritrea, and improve relations with the West.[36] By signaling their intention to limit future assistance, the Soviets forced Ethiopian officials to recognize that unilateral military escalation to unconditional victory was impossible, thereby encouraging Addis Ababa to seek a negotiated solution. The change in patron-client relationships instigated by the decline of the cold war prompted regional leaders to reconsider their policies regarding conflicts.

Carter's Talks

In the context of the new message being sent from Moscow to Addis Ababa, former President Jimmy Carter offered his services and organized talks between Ethiopia and the EPLF. Carter had established the International Negotiation Network specifically to resolve civil conflicts around the world to fill the lacuna left because the UN, the OAU, and other international organizations refused to play a role in internal conflicts.[37] The two sides met in Atlanta in September 1989 and two months later in Nairobi. They seemed genuinely interested in talking and succeeded at first in setting an agenda.[38] Both the EPLF and the Ethiopian government sought to build their international image as the party most committed to seeking a peaceful settlement. Neither side felt they could afford the political costs of being labeled the obstructionist party.[39] This concern for world opinion gave Carter leverage over both sides by threatening to go public if either proved uncooperative. Although Carter acted as a private citizen in organizing these talks, he kept in close contact with and had the support of both the United States and the Soviet Union.[40]

Carter focused the talks on procedural issues in an attempt to construct a process acceptable to all parties. The substantive issue of what a settlement might look like was left for a later stage.[41] The talks soon faltered, however, over the selection of observers and EPLF perceptions that Carter favored Addis Ababa.[42] These procedural obstacles, however, were only a cover for more substantive differences on which the parties remained immovably far apart.

The Carter talks failed principally because both parties were not yet convinced that military victory was impossible. The conflict had not reached a "hurting stalemate" because, although the pain both sides endured was extraordinarily high, neither perceived a stalemate.[43] The EPLF took to the offensive during the Carter talks and seized control of the port of Massawa (February 1990), demonstrating that they believed their objectives could be more easily achieved on the battlefield than at the negotiating table.[44] This offense represented an escalation in the conflict, not a move to reinforce a stalemate or force the opponent to the table.[45] Both sides participated in the talks in order not to be perceived and castigated as recalcitrant, but both stated their belief that the other side was not interested in compromise.[46]

Another fundamental problem with the Carter talks was that they began after the bilateral Eritrean conflict had been transformed into a new multilateral struggle for power in Ethiopia. The military successes of the TPLF/EPRDF in 1989 dramatically altered the structure of the crisis in Ethiopia. The TPLF began talks with Ethiopian officials in Rome while the Carter talks took place, indicating the linkage between these conflicts from Ethiopia's security perspective.[47] The Ethiopian-Eritrean conflict became intertwined with the struggle for control of the Ethiopian state, and the EPLF had little incentive to compromise with the faltering Mengistu regime. The identity and relative power of the actors and the issues at stake remained too undefined for resolution in 1989 and 1990.[48]

Cohen's Initiative

Despite these new developments that increased uncertainty and suggested that the time was not propitious for a settlement, officials in Washington saw sufficient evidence that both sides were looking for a way out of their conflict to justify a limited diplomatic initiative. After the Carter talks derailed, U.S. State Department officials began to meet and explore various issues with both Addis Ababa and the EPLF. Washington decided to focus on the EPLF-Ethiopian government conflict and encouraged the Italian government to pursue similar exploratory talks with representatives from the TPLF and Addis Ababa in Rome.

In October 1990, the U.S. assistant secretary of state for African Affairs, Herman Cohen, chaired a meeting between Ethiopian Foreign Minister Tesfaye Dinka and the EPLF representative in the United States, Hagos Ghebrehiwet.[49] Cohen raised the issue of peace in Ethiopia when he met his Soviet counterpart, Yuri Yukalov, in Rome. Cohen traveled to Addis Ababa in November and declared that he was "very pleased in my discussions with the foreign minister and the president to learn that there is a continuing commitment to a peace process."[50]

The talks resumed in Washington on 21–22 February 1991.[51] Despite favorable pretalk hopes and the high level officials present at the meeting, the talks ended with little progress.[52] Both the Ethiopians and the Eritreans accused each other of offering nothing new.[53] As had happened immediately after the Carter talks, the insurgent movements began major new offensives while the meetings took place. So long as military fortunes on the ground remained undetermined, neither set of talks made progress.

The thoroughly demoralized Ethiopian army could not resist the major joint EPRDF-EPLF offensive.[54] A cabinet reshuffle in April 1991 proved to be far too little too late and Mengistu fled to exile in May. Mengistu's departure in the face of successful insurgencies made it clear that Ethiopia was undergoing an historic transition of great uncertainty. The caretaker government left behind in Addis Ababa and the principal armed opposition movements all asked Washington to reconvene talks to develop a cease-fire and a nonviolent transition. Cohen accepted the request and called the principal actors to a meeting in London.

U.S. Motivations

The United States took on the organizing of transition talks because the continuing humanitarian tragedy in Ethiopia, as famine in one part of the country was followed by famine in another, led to an increased sense among both Ethiopians and foreign observers that "someone" must do "something." The United States had been heavily involved in the relief operations, and the more than $1 billion in food relief sent to Ethiopia since 1984 demonstrated that reducing hunger in Ethiopia was an important goal to Washington. As shown in the 1984–85 famine, pictures of starving children on the evening news were too compelling to allow for U.S. government inaction. U.S. officials became convinced that without progress in resolving the various conflicts in Ethiopia, the food aid would not bring relief to the suffering people. U.S. officials felt ready to act on behalf of the world community frustrated by its inability to do anything other than pour famine relief into the country.[55]

The recent disasters in Liberia and Somalia showed the damage and destruction that could result from U.S. reluctance to become involved in regional political crises.[56] Rather than stand safely on the sidelines and watch Ethiopia disintegrate into violence, Washington hoped that, by expending a modest amount of diplomatic resources and dangling a few carrots of future cooperation, it could facilitate a "soft landing" by acting as "midwife" to the transition.[57] Cohen's October 1990 and February 1991 talks with the Ethiopian government and the EPLF convinced U.S. analysts that they could help the combatants find a desperately needed peaceful solution. Rebel hostility to the Soviet Union and Moscow's loss of influence in Addis Ababa after Mengistu's overthrow eliminated them as a potential facilitator.

In addition, domestic politics were critical in encouraging the United States to act. Immigration to Israel for Ethiopia's Jews (also known as Beta Yisrael or Falashas) mobilized an important constituency in the U.S. Congress and gave Ethiopia a higher salience in Washington than otherwise would have been expected. The Caucus for Ethiopian Jews included more than a hundred members of Congress, including several very powerful members with influence over foreign policy. The American Association for Ethiopian Jews and many of the U.S. groups that had worked tirelessly on behalf of emigration for Soviet Jews adopted the Ethiopian Jews' cause, making Ethiopia an issue of unusually high domestic attention.[58]

Before talks about the new political order in Addis Ababa took place, Washington intervened to help settle the emigration issue. President Bush sent former Sen. Rudy Boschwitz to Addis Ababa as his personal representative to try to negotiate an airlift of Ethiopia's Jews to Israel. In the confusion after Mengistu's departure, the Israeli government paid $35 million to the interim government that then permitted Israel to organize a dramatic airlift that brought fourteen-thousand Jews to Israel on 24 May. Supporters of this action argue that the Ethiopian Jews risked becoming caught in the cross fire of the transition, making this extraordinary operation necessary. Others criticized the action, arguing that the United States and Israel had put the well-being of a few thousand Jews ahead of the fate of 50 million Ethiopians.[59]

The London Talks

Because of Cohen's work in late 1990 and early 1991, the United States was in position, knew the principal players, and had talks already under way. This allowed the United States to act quickly when insurgent military advances and Mengistu's flight created new opportunities for conflict resolution. It is suggestive of the nature of the post-cold war world that all the critical parties in Ethiopia looked to the United States to assist them and legitimize creating the post-Mengistu political order. After some delay, Meles Zenawi and the Ethiopian People's Revolutionary Democratic Front (EPRDF), Isaias Afewerki and the Eritrean People's Liberation Front (EPLF), Lencho Letta and the Oromo Liberation Front (OLF), the remnants of Mengistu's old regime in the person of Prime Minister Tesfaye Dinka, and Cohen began their meetings on 27 May 1991.[60]

By the time the talks commenced, the military facts on the ground made Tesfaye Dinka and the delegation from Addis Ababa marginal players with little choice but to sue for peace. The EPLF used the opportunity of the confusion after Mengistu's departure to seize Asmara and the few remaining towns in Eritrea still in government hands and declare that they would establish a separate provisional government.[61] The EPRDF marched to the outskirts of Addis Ababa but honored U.S. requests to refrain from entering the capital until the talks commenced.[62] Cohen, after receiving reports from U.S. Chargé d'Affaires Robert Houdek that the caretaker government was losing control of its troops and hoping to prevent the chaos that recently had devastated Monrovia and Mogadishu, publicly "recommended" that the EPRDF enter Addis Ababa "in order to reduce uncertainties and eliminate tensions." EPRDF troops moved into Addis Ababa during the night of 27–28 May, assumed "state responsibility," and the change of government effectively took place.[63]

The next day, Cohen met with the leaders of the EPRDF, EPLF, and OLF together. Because of EPRDF control of Addis Ababa, the United States, according to Cohen, no longer mediated but served in a "de facto advisory role for the three opposition groups."[64] Cohen justified sanctioning the EPRDF move into Addis Ababa on the basis that it was the only group "capable of going in and maintaining law and order." The EPRDF, however, was put on notice that if it wanted to continue to receive Washington's blessings it must deliver on its promises of reform. Cohen said, "You must go democratic if you want the full cooperation to help Ethiopia realize its potential. . . . No democracy, no cooperation." The United States, according to Cohen, was acting as the "conscience of the international community," suggesting that more was at stake than just U.S. assistance.[65]

Besides providing an important boost to the EPRDF by accepting its move into Addis Ababa, Cohen also bolstered the EPLF's position on the always contentious Eritrean issue. Cohen stated that the United States "favor[s] an act of self-determination by the people of Eritrea who have never been consulted on their desires."[66] This statement stood in stark contrast to earlier U.S. pledges supporting Ethiopia's territorial integrity.[67] Cohen, however, was concentrating on guaranteeing the broadening of the ruling coalition and did not want to alienate either the EPLF or the EPRDF, which accepted Eritrean self-determination.

Many observers were surprised by the outcome of the London talks. Some sharply criticized Washington's role. Anti-American demonstrations broke out in Addis Ababa after the Voice of America's Amharic service broadcast statements by exile leaders. Some labeled the change of government "Cohen's Coup."[68] The critics, especially Ethiopian exiles in Washington, believed that the United States had double-crossed them and replaced Mengistu with a government that would be just as oppressive and narrowly based.[69] Other analysts conceded that Cohen could have done little to change the two most important facts—the EPRDF and EPLF controlled their respective parts of the country. These critics, however, questioned the high-profile role Cohen played and his statements that suggested that the United States had more influence in the proceedings than it did. By placing U.S. prestige so clearly behind the EPRDF with only verbal promises of democracy in return, Washington risked losing the goodwill it had in Ethiopia if the new leaders reneged on their commitments.[70]

Cohen's acceptance in London of the EPRDF and EPLF takeovers as a *fait accompli* reflected his belief that U.S. interests in democratization and famine relief for Ethiopia would best be served by working with the forces in control. He realized that he could do nothing to change the military facts on the ground: Mengistu's army was shattered, the EPRDF completely surrounded Addis Ababa, and the EPLF occupied all of Eritrea. Rather than oppose what he could not change, he decided to make a virtue of *Realpolitik*.[71] The EPRDF occupation of the capital was due to the collapse of the Ethiopian armed forces and the insurgents' military victory, not a prize bestowed upon them by the United States. Cohen believed that he increased U.S. leverage over the transition process and served humanitarian interests by taking the EPRDF leaders' declared commitment to democracy at face value. If outside powers treated the rebels as a responsible governing power, it would become more likely that the EPRDF would act as such. Cohen plainly stated "no democracy, no assistance," making it clear that the new regime could expect no cooperation unless it delivered on its promises of reform.

U.S. officials described their role as a "midwife," intervening diplomatically to facilitate the transition to a new political order, without mediating a reconciliation or changing the nature of the victory. Cohen urged the opposition groups to accept a democratic basis for the new political order by employing two forms of leverage. First, Ethiopia and Eritrea desperately needed western economic assistance to rebuild the war-ravaged country. Without Washington's blessing, few were likely to provide such assistance. Second, the United States had leverage as an umpire that established the rules of the game. The new leadership in Addis Ababa and Asmara understood that international legitimacy and recognition depended on Washington's acceptance of the transition process. As one newspaper editorial put it, "America has established the rules of the game, and placed itself in the ring as a referee no Ethiopian government can afford to ignore."[72]

One of the unusual features of the U.S. role in the transition in Ethiopia was that Washington became involved even though it had minimal relations with any of the parties.[73] Relations with Mengistu were terrible until a very minor warming in the early 1990s and Washington never sought to save him. U.S. relations with the opposition movements (EPLF, EPRDF, OLF) were also minimal during the 1980s when Washington shunned the groups as Marxist and secessionist. Assistant Secretary of State for African Affairs Chester Crocker reportedly said, "I have no interest in taking sides between a bunch of Marxists; let them fight it out among themselves."[74] The United States was interested in conflict resolution and humanitarian issues more than it was concerned about the fate of any of the parties.

Cohen's actions in London demonstrate the degree to which, in regard to Ethiopia at least, the new world order was unipolar. The Soviet Union's role ended with Mengistu and none of the opposition parties looked to Moscow for support. The Soviet role was that of a bystander, limited to not interfering in the process and not providing those dissatisfied with the outcome an external source of encouragement and support. Ethiopians and Eritreans recognized that the United States was the only truly global power and wanted Washington's blessing on their transition. The United States therefore served as the umpire who proclaimed the rules and determined the kind of future political order that would be acceptable to the international community. Cohen made clear in London that democratization was the necessary condition for this sanctification. To receive legitimacy from Washington, Ethiopian parties were willing to meet Washington's stipulations. Cohen's conditioning of future cooperation on the new government's delivering on commitments to democracy and human rights had elements of the crusader in it, but there was never any consideration that the United States would use military force to impose a new government.[75] Because the leaders of the Ethiopian opposition movements sought U.S. support, nothing more than the carrots and sticks of diplomacy was required.

Cohen's role in brokering the London talks indicates that the United States can take certain actions to facilitate conflict resolution. The adept use of diplomacy reduced the potential for violence associated with the departure of the Mengistu regime and the coming to power of the new leaders in Ethiopia and Eritrea. Washington's role, however, was limited. The outcome of the military struggle was determined on the ground before the London talks began. As in the Ogaden War, the United States sanctified, legitimated, and thereby made cleaner and less violent an ending that it did not create and could not change. By reducing the uncertainty of such an inevitable end point, such actions may usefully facilitate conflict resolution.

Besides the collapse of Mengistu's regime creating a rare opportunity for quick results, Ethiopia enjoyed an unusually high salience in Washington as a result of the 1984–85 famine and the issue of emigration for Ethiopia's Jews. The costs of the mediation were marginal beyond Cohen's time and attention. When solutions have required sustained attention or significant expenditures for development assistance or peacekeeping forces rather than simply limited diplomatic actions, Washington has been far more reluctant to become engaged.

U.S. Policy Toward Conflict in Somalia and Sudan

As in Ethiopia, the end of cold war competition prompted new thinking and innovative initiatives to conflict management in Somalia and Sudan. In Somalia, the United States disengaged from its client Siad Barre in the late 1980s as his regime grew increasingly authoritarian and U.S. interests in access to Somali ports decreased. The United States suspended assistance in 1989 and did nothing to prevent Barre's overthrow in January 1991. Opposition groups fought each other to succeed Barre and, in the ensuing chaos and violence, the Somali state collapsed.[76] The United States and the rest of the international community largely ignored the growing catastrophe, except for funding some relief operations through non-governmental organizations. A series of diplomatic efforts in 1991 and 1992 to broker an end to the Somali impasse failed and media reports of massive starvation outraged audiences in the United States and elsewhere. In November 1992 President George Bush decided to offer a large U.S. force to lead a United Nations operation to Somalia.[77]

The United States intervention, however, evaded the fundamental challenge of Somalia. Although the catastrophe came to the general public's attention when the media aired heart-rending pictures of starvation, and although Bush justified his decision to send troops on humanitarian grounds, the core problem in Somalia was political—the collapse of the state. Vulnerable Somalis were starving not due to a lack of food but because of the absence of political and social structures capable of securely managing its distribution. By denying the political nature of the intervention, Washington had a partial policy that did not meet the challenge.[78]

In an effort to limit its mandate and responsibilities, Washington left the contentious problems of political reconciliation, demilitarization, and economic rehabilitation to the United Nations. The UN, however, lacked the capacity to manage this complex burden. By mid-1994 the United Nations forces that remained in Somalia largely had given up their efforts to provide security and promote political reconciliation. The potential for a new round of violence and insecurity of the type that caused the 1992 humanitarian emergency seemed high.[79]

In Sudan, the international community faced an even more daunting challenge of trying to play a constructive role in ending what was one of the world's worse internal conflicts, complete with massive starvation, displacement of people, and human rights violations on a nearly unprecedented scale.[80] The United States deferred to African attempts to mediate the conflict, first in Abuja, Nigeria under the auspices of the OAU and later in talks sponsored in Nairobi by IGADD. Washington reduced its relations with Sudan to the bare minimum. All bilateral assistance expect humanitarian was cut off and Sudan was added to the list of states that sponsored terrorism, making Khartoum a pariah state in Washington's judgment. None of these sanctions were sufficient to end the conflict and in mid-1995 the war continued to rage.

Prospective U.S. Policy Toward Conflict Reduction in the Horn of Africa

Creating sustained interest in Washington for conflict reduction policies in the Horn of Africa will be difficult. All initiatives in Africa struggle for attention in Washington in the face of generally low and declining interest, competition for resources from regions of higher salience such as Eastern Europe, the limited leverage the United States has over the states in the region, and the absence of well-organized domestic constituencies pressuring the government on behalf of Africa. Even the small yet useful role played by the United States in the London talks on the Ethiopian transition represents an exception to the more general pattern of remaining a bystander. Despite these obstacles, however, several potential roles are worth outlining briefly. In all these efforts, the United States can expand its impact by cooperating with other actors, such as the United Nations, the European community, Japan, and international financial institutions. The roles sketched below require diplomatic leadership and relatively small financial contributions. They therefore should be possible despite tight budgets and competing international commitments.

Midwife: Remain engaged in the transitions in Ethiopia and Eritrea.

In mid-1994 the Ethiopian and Eritrean transitions were far from complete. Whether their outcome will be more peaceful, democratic states or a new cycle of violence will depend on the actions of the new leaders and people of the region. The challenges are enormous but if the changes in Ethiopia and Eritrea indicate they are moving toward more broadly representative and democratic forms of government that respect human rights, the United States and other international actors should remain engaged. As of mid-1994, transitions in both states seemed open to democratization efforts and therefore received considerable international assistance.

Since the beginning of the Ethiopian transition in May 1991, the United States has acted to encourage a successful consolidation of a new, sustainable political order. The United States, European donors, and international financial institutions have provided generous financial support for rehabilitation and development projects. Washington instituted a small but significant program to encourage democratization and respect for human rights.[81] This program assisted and organized an observer delegation to regional elections in June 1992, but intimidation led to an opposition boycott, making the elections largely meaningless.[82]

Washington similarly tried to assist the peaceful transition toward greater democracy in Eritrea. The Eritrean People's Liberation Front, acting as the provisional government of Eritrea, held an internationally supervised referendum in April 1993 that resulted in an overwhelming vote for independence.[83] The United States and other nations quickly moved to recognize the new state and establish friendly bilateral relations. The Eritrean transitional government continued to move, if slowly, toward promised multiparty elections and the ratification of a new constitution.

Mediator: Follow through on conflict reduction efforts. Washington continued to play its role as mediator in Ethiopia's conflicts. After the July 1991 National Conference and the formation of the EPRDF-led transitional government, armed conflict broke out between the EPRDF and the Oromo Liberation Front (OLF), another party in the government at that time. The fighting threatened to derail the transition and throw Ethiopia back into full-scale civil war until talks co-chaired by the Provisional Government of Eritrea (which maintained strong ties to both groups) and the United States in February, April, and May 1992 resulted in a cease fire and encampment of forces. A further, brief civil war broke out after the failed June 1992 elections, and the EPRDF destroyed the OLF's military capacity. The United States and other donor states tried on a number of occasions to encourage talks between the OLF and the transitional government without success. In February 1994 a number of Ethiopian opposition groups met with former president Jimmy Carter in Atlanta to explore opportunities for a new round of talks. Despite encouraging signs from the opposition, the transitional government in Addis Ababa declined Carter's offer to mediate.[84]

Umpire: Encourage new regional order and international norms. In the long term, the Horn of Africa will break the cycle of internal and regional conflict only when a new order, both within the constituent states and across the region, is constructed, accepted as legitimate, and institutionalized. This process will take years to sort itself out and the outcome will be determined largely by forces within the region. Outside powers, and particularly the United States, can, however, encourage this process and accelerate new thinking about regional order. The example of the Association of Southeast Asian Nations (ASEAN) suggests that regional organizations can play important conflict reduction roles by establishing and structuring rules of state behavior. The Economic Community of West African States (ECOWAS) has demonstrated the ability to become involved constructively in Liberia when the conflict threatened regional destabilization. The Intergovernmental Authority on Drought and Development (IGADD) in the Horn of Africa offers a nascent regional organization that has increasingly taken on a leading role in conflict management. IGADD sponsored talks in 1994 on the Sudan conflict and has served as the principal forum for regional security discussions. Other continentwide organizations, such as the Organization of African Unity and the important new process for a Conference on Security, Stability, Development, and Cooperation in Africa (CSSDCA), may play a larger role in the future.[85] It is not clear, however, how the international community can participate in strengthening such regional organizations whose purpose is to exist independently. A global cooperative security system will have to consider the role it can play with regard to these organizations and the most effective relationships between regional arrangements, such as the OAU and CSSDCA, and subregional groupings, such as IGADD and ECOWAS.

In addition, there are questions relating to the architecture of a new international order that do not apply specifically to the Horn of Africa but may have important conflict reduction implications in that region. Arms limitations agreements do not remove the underlying conflict issues but may reduce violence and prevent leaders from becoming tempted by runaway means to risk conflicts. Recent initiatives to create a disaster relief coordinator at the United Nations may eliminate some of the friction over humanitarian assistance programs in conflict zones that have plagued the Horn.[86] New guidelines that redefine the role of the interna-

tional community, especially international organizations such as the UN
High Commission for Refugees, in responding to and preventing humanitarian disasters when sovereignty is at issue will help reduce the degree
to which the politicization of humanitarian relief has hampered efforts
in the past.[87]

.   .   .

The dynamics of competitive patronage in the Horn of Africa during
the cold war led the United States and the Soviet Union to relegate
conflict resolution to a secondary goal. In the 1990s, after Moscow's
disengagement from the region, the United States has new opportunities
to emphasize its interests in humanitarian goals, such as conflict resolution, democratization, human rights, and economic reform. Washington's acceptance of a small but catalytic role of midwife in the transition
in Ethiopia/Eritrea demonstrates that external powers can encourage
conflict resolution, if only under unusual circumstances. The United
States has opportunities to assist the peoples of the Horn of Africa build
a more peaceful region by remaining constructively engaged, building on
the successes in Ethiopia and Eritrea, and encouraging the development
of regional institutions and new international norms that will reduce
conflict. Although the most important actors in the complex task of
building less conflictual systems of governance are the peoples and leaders of the region, external powers can use their limited leverage to encourage this process.

Notes

1. Terrence Lyons, "The Horn of Africa Regional Politics: A Hobbesian World," in
Wriggins, ed. *The Dynamics of Regional Politics;* Terrence Lyons, "Internal Vulnerability
and Interstate Conflict: Ethiopia's Regional Foreign Policy," in *The Political Economy of
Ethiopia,* ed. Marina Ottaway (New York: Praeger, 1990); Hizkias Assefa and Gilbert
Khadiagala, eds. *Conflict and Conflict Resolution in the Horn of Africa: A Regional Ap-
proach* (Washington, D.C.: Brookings Institution, forthcoming).

2. Barry Buzan, *People, States, and Fear: The National Security Problem in International Relations* (Chapel Hill: Univ. of North Carolina Press, 1983), 106.

3. Shimshon Zelniker, *The Superpowers and the Horn of Africa,* Center for Strategic
Studies Paper no. 18 (Tel Aviv: Tel Aviv Univ., 1982), 35–38.

4. S. Neil MacFarlane, "Intervention and Security in Africa," *International Affairs*
60, no. 1 (Winter 1983/84): 53–74; Colin Legum, "Communal Conflict and International
Intervention in Africa," in Colin Legum, I. William Zartman, Steven Langdon, and Lynn
K. Mytelka, *Africa in the 1980s: A Continent in Crisis* (New York: McGraw Hill, 1979),
55.

5. Marina Ottaway, "Foreign Economic Assistance in the Horn: Does It Influence
Horn Government Policies?" paper presented at the Woodrow Wilson International Center
for Scholars Conference on Crisis in the Horn of Africa: Causes and Prospects, Washing-

ton, D.C., June 1987; Marina Ottaway, "Superpower Competition and Regional Conflicts in the Horn of Africa," in *The Soviet Impact in Africa,* ed. Craig Nation and Mark V. Kauppi (Lexington, Mass.: Lexington, 1984), 175.

6. Terrence Lyons, "Reaction to Revolution: United States–Ethiopian Relations, 1974–1977," Ph.D. diss., Johns Hopkins Univ., 1991; Terrence Lyons, "The United States and Ethiopia: The Politics of a Patron-Client Relationship," *Northeast African Studies* 8, nos. 2/3 (1986): 53–75; Jeffrey A. Lefebvre, *Arms for the Horn: U.S. Security Policy in Ethiopia and Somalia, 1953–1991* (Pittsburgh: Univ. of Pittsburgh Press, 1991).

7. Saadia Touval, *The Boundary Politics of Independent Africa* (Cambridge, Mass.: Harvard Univ. Press, 1972), 147.

8. Robert G. Patman, *The Soviet Union in the Horn of Africa: The Diplomacy of Intervention and Disengagement* (Cambridge: Cambridge Univ. Press, 1990), 203, 213.

9. Christopher Clapham, *Transformation and Continuity in Revolutionary Ethiopia* (Cambridge: Cambridge Univ. Press, 1988), 226–27; Rene Léfort, *Ethiopia: An Heretical Revolution?* (London: Zed, 1983), 210.

10. See Ted Gurr, "Tensions in the Horn of Africa," in *World Politics and Tension Areas,* ed. Feliks Gross (New York: New York Univ. Press, 1966), 316–34; Lyons, "Reaction to Revolution," chap. 2.

11. A-295, airgram from Addis to State, "Transmittal of Memorandum of Conversation Between Representatives of IEG Ministry of Defense and Members of the Country Team," 11 Dec. 1963.

12. Touval, *Boundary Politics,* 212–45.

13. Hizkias Assefa, *Mediation of Civil Wars: Approaches and Strategies—The Sudan Conflict* (Boulder, Colo.: Westview, 1987). For an important firsthand account, see Abel Alier, *The Southern Sudan: Too Many Agreements Dishonored* (Exeter U.K.: Ithaca, 1990).

14. Patman, *The Soviet Union in the Horn of Africa,* 89; Touval, *Boundary Politics,* 244–45.

15. Patman, *The Soviet Union in the Horn of Africa,* 302.

16. I. William Zartman, "Superpower Cooperation in Northeast and Northwest Africa," in *The Cold War as Cooperation,* ed. Roger Kanet and Edward Kolodziej, (Baltimore: Johns Hopkins Univ. Press, 1991).

17. Larry C. Napper, "The Ogaden War: Some Implications for Crisis Prevention," in George, ed. *Managing U.S.-Soviet Rivalry,* 234.

18. David A. Korn, *Ethiopia, the United States, and the Soviet Union* (Carbondale: Southern Illinois Univ. Press, 1986), 50.

19. John W. Harbeson, *The Ethiopian Transformation: The Quest for the Post-Imperial State* (Boulder Colo.: Westview, 1988), 2–9.

20. A good overview of these organizations and their development is Patrick S. Gilkes, "Conflicts in Ethiopia: Roots, Status, and Prospects," paper presented at the Woodrow Wilson International Center for Scholars Conference on Crisis in the Horn of Africa: Causes and Prospects, Washington, D.C., June 1987.

21. "Defense Minister Cites Causes for Suppression in Eritrea," *Ethiopian Herald,* 29 Aug. 1974; "General Aman Is Informed That People of Eritrea Seek Peace, Security," *Ethiopian Herald,* 31 Aug. 1974; "Gen. Aman Visits Eritrea for Second Time," *Ethiopian Herald,* 11 Oct. 1974.

22. Haggai Erlich, *The Struggle over Eritrea, 1962–1978: War and Revolution in the Horn of Africa* (Stanford, Calif.: Hoover Institute, 1983), chap. 9.

23. Aman, Sisay Habte, and Teferi Banti all lost power after pursuing peace efforts in Eritrea.

24. The program is printed in Basil Davidson, Lionel Cliffe, and Bereket Habte Selassie, eds. *Behind the War in Eritrea* (Nottingham: Spokesman, 1980), 143–50.

25. For details on the Red Star Campaign, see Dawit Wolde Giorgis, *Red Tears: War, Famine, and Revolution in Ethiopia* (Trenton, N.J.: Red Sea, 1989).

26. Edmond J. Keller, "Constitutionalism and the National Question in Africa: The Case of Eritrea," in Ottaway, ed. *The Political Economy of Ethiopia*, 104.

27. I. William Zartman, *African Insurgencies: Negotiations and Mediation*, Intelligence Research Report no. 206 Washington, D.C.: U.S. Department of State, Bureau of Intelligence and Research, 1989), 8–10.

28. See the interview with EPLF Gen. Secy. Issayas Afewerki, "EPLF Chief: War to Continue; No More Talks," *Le Monde*, 23 Nov. 1988, translated in Foreign Broadcast Information Service, *Daily Report, Sub-Saharan Africa* (hereafter *FBIS-AFR*), 29 Nov. 1988, 3.

29. U.S. Arms Control and Disarmament Agency, *World Military Expenditures and Arms Transfers 1989*, 115.

30. See the excellent discussion in Christopher Clapham, "The Political Economy of Conflict in the Horn of Africa," *Survival* 32, no. 5 (1990): 403–20.

31. Mark Webber, "Soviet Policy in Sub-Saharan Africa: The Final Phase," *Journal of Modern African Studies* 30, no. 1 (1992): 12–14.

32. Melvin A. Goodman, *Gorbachev's Retreat: The Third World* (New York: Praeger, 1991); Celeste A. Wallander, "Third-World Conflict in Soviet Military Thought: Does the 'New Thinking' Grow Prematurely Grey?" *World Politics* 42, no. 1 (1989): 31–63; Richard B. Remnek, "The Soviet Union and the Quest for Peace in the Horn of Africa," paper presented at the Conference on Peace and Security in the Horn of Africa, Michigan State Univ. 29 Apr. 1988; Remnek, "Translating 'New Soviet Thinking' into Practice: The Ethiopian Case," manuscript.

33. Paul B. Henze, *Ethiopia: Crisis of a Marxist Economy: Analysis and Text of a Soviet Report* (Santa Monica, Calif.: RAND Corporation (R–3677–USDP), 1989).

34. Jane Perlez, "Ethiopia Starts to Come Unglued after String of Military Setbacks," *New York Times*, 22 Mar. 1989.

35. See G. A. Krylova, "Socialist Orientation: Reality and Theory: The National-Democratic Revolution in Light of the New Political Thinking (With Ethiopia as an Example)," *Narody Azii i Afriki*, 1989, no. 1, translated and annotated in Paul B. Henze, *Glasnost about Building Socialism in Ethiopia: Analysis of a Critical Soviet Article* (Santa Monica, Calif.: RAND Corporation (N–3022–USDP), 1990).

36. "USSR Government Issues Statement on Ethiopia," *Pravda*, 14 June 1989, translated in *FBIS: SOV*, 14 June 1989, 13. See also "Ethiopia: Dark Days for Mengistu," *African Confidential* 30, no. 4 (1989). Soviet officials also opened channels with the EPLF. See "Soviet Union Holds Discussions with Rebels," *Indian Ocean Newsletter*, 22 July 1989.

37. David B. Ottaway, "Carter Opens Peace Talks Between Ethiopia and Eritrean Rebels," *Washington Post*, 8 Sept. 1989.

38. Carter said, "I don't think there's any doubt that they both know that the other side is sincere in trying to make progress toward peace." "Ethiopia Talks Build Trust, Carter Says," *Washington Post*, 10 Sept. 1989.

39. "Ethiopia: Talks Start at Last," *Africa Confidential* 30, no. 17 (1989).

40. Ottaway, "Carter Opens Peace Talks."

41. "September Preliminary Peace Talks Between the Government of Ethiopia and the EPLF Resume in Nairobi on November 18," *International Negotiation Network News* 1, no. 3 (1989).

42. See interview with Isaias Afewerki in *Al-Khalij* in Arabic, 10 July 1990, translated in *FBIS-AFR*, "EPLF's Afewerki on Battles, Arab Relations," 12 July 1990, 7.

43. On a "hurting stalemate," see Zartman, *Ripe for Resolution.*

44. Todd Shields, "Rebels Said to Take Port in Ethiopia," *Washington Post,* 11 Feb. 1990. Carter blamed this offensive for scuttling the talks. See "EPLF Withdraws from Peace Talks; Carter, Nyerere Call for Unilateral Ceasefire," *News from the Carter Center,* 14 June 1990.

45. I. William Zartman, "Strategies of De-escalation," in *Timing and De-escalation* ed. Louis Kriesberg and Stuart J. Thorson (Syracuse, N.Y.: Syracuse Univ. Press, 1991).

46. On the EPLF side, see Robert M. Press, "Ethiopia Edges Toward Peace Talks," *Christian Science Monitor,* 10 Aug. 1989, quoting EPLF spokesman Tesfai Ghermazien; interview with Isaias Afewerki in *Adulis* (July–Aug. 1989). On the Ethiopian side, see Ethiopian Foreign Ministry statement in *FBIS-AFR,* 6 June 1990. See also "Ethiopia: Talks Start at Last," *Africa Confidential.*

47. "Ethiopia: An Elusive Victory," *Africa Confidential* 31, no. 14 (1990).

48. Marina Ottaway, "Eritrea and Ethiopia: Negotiations in a Transitional Conflict," in *Elusive Peace: Negotiating an End to Civil War,* ed. I. William Zartman (Washington, D.C.: Brookings Institution, 1995).

49. Clifford Krauss, "U.S. Aides Meeting Foes in Ethiopia," *New Your Times,* 24 Oct. 1990; "USA/The Horn: All Federalists Now," *Africa Confidential* 31, no. 25 (1990), 7.

50. "Ethiopia Said Willing to Seek Peace," *Washington Post,* 15 Nov. 1990.

51. Eritrean People's Liberation Front, "Report on the Deliberations of the Exploratory Talks for Peace Negotiations in Washington, D.C.," Feb. 1991. This document contains the EPLF transcript of the talks. See also Jennifer Parmelee, "Ethiopia and Eritrean Rebels to Open Peace Talks Today," *Washington Post,* 19 Feb. 1991; Clifford Krauss, "Conflicting Peace Plans Offered in Ethiopian Strife," *New York Times,* 24 Feb. 1991.

52. U.S. Department of State, statement by Margaret Tutwiler, "Ethiopia: Exploratory Talks," 22 Feb. 1991 (press release).

53. Eritrean People's Liberation Front, "Report on the Deliberations."

54. Jennifer Parmelee, "Rebels Launch Attacks in Ethiopian Provinces," *Washington Post,* 27 Feb. 1991; Jane Perlez, "As Rebels Surge in Ethiopia, Government Seems Near End," *New York Times,* 23 Mar. 1991.

55. See the address by Dep. Asst. Secy. of State for African Affairs Irvin Hicks to the African American Institute 1990 Forum Series, 18 Nov. 1990.

56. According to Cohen, the Liberian disaster was very much on his mind as he formed policy toward Ethiopia. He reportedly said, "I kept telling my staff we didn't want another Monrovia." See Neil A. Lewis, "His Vineyard in Shade, Africa Hand Stays Cool," *New York Times,* 23 Mar. 1992.

57. Neil A. Lewis, "U.S. Plans to be 'Midwife' to a New Rule in Ethiopia," *New York Times,* 26 May 1991.

58. Ellen B. Laipson, "Ethiopian Jews," *Congressional Research Service Issue Brief,* 26 June 1990, details congressional actions.

59. John M. Goshko, "U.S. Plea for Ethiopian Jews Led to Mediator Role," *Washington Post,* 30 May 1991; Richard H. Curtiss, "Airlift Culminates 17 Years of Secret Israeli

Links to Mengistu Government," *The Washington Report on Middle East Affairs,* (July 1991): 48–50. For background and accounts of earlier efforts to assist emigration, see Teshome E. Wagaw, "The International Political Ramifications of Falasha Emigration," *Journal of Modern African Studies* 29, no. 4 (1991): 557–81.

60. For more details on these talks, see Terrence Lyons, "The Transition in Ethiopia," *CSIS Africa Notes* no. 127 (Aug. 1991).

61. Blaine Harden, "Eritrean Rebels to Form Own Rule, Separate from Ethiopian Government," *Washington Post,* 30 May 1991.

62. Clifford Krauss, "Ethiopia's Dictator Flees; Officials Seeking U.S. Help," *New York Times,* 22 May 1991; Jennifer Parmelee, "Ethiopian Regime, Residents Await Attack on Capital," *Washington Post,* 24 May 1991.

63. Clifford Krauss, "Ethiopia's Leader Agrees to Give Up Capital to Rebels," *New York Times,* 28 May 1991.

64. Statement of Asst. Secy. of State Herman J. Cohen before the House Foreign Affairs Subcommittee on African Affairs hearing on the Political Crisis in Ethiopia, 18 June 1991.

65. Transcript of press conference of Asst. Secy. Herman J. Cohen and Rudy Boschwitz, London, 23 May 1991.

66. Cohen press conference, 23 May 1991.

67. Secy. of State James Baker reportedly was prepared to rebuke Cohen's statement on Eritrea because it made the administration's policy against the breakup of the Soviet Union look inconsistent. See Lewis, "His Vineyard in Shade, Africa Hand Stays Cool." For implications regarding Yugoslavia, see Blaine Harden, "Yugoslav Crisis Raises Questions about Nature of National Security," *Washington Post,* 20 June 1991.

68. "2 Ethiopian Protesters Are Killed As Rebels Fire on Anti-U.S. Rally," *New York Times,* 31 May 1991.

69. Richard Dowden, "Addis Ababa Tricked into a 'Soft Landing,' " *Independent* (U.K.), 31 May 1991; Richard O'Mara "Eritreans' Intent for Sovereignty Mars Agreement," *Baltimore Sun,* 2 June 1991; Daniel Teferra, letter to the editor, *Washington Post,* 2 June 1991; Darrell Morris, "Marchers Protest U.S. Policy in Ethiopian Civil War," *Washington Post,* 15 June 1991.

70. Editorial, "From One Dictator to Another?" *Washington Post,* 12 June 1991; editorial, "New Deal for Ethiopia," *London Times,* 29 May 1991. For a supportive view, see Paul B. Henze, "Off the Sidelines and Discreetly into the Fray," *Los Angeles Times,* 29 May 1991.

71. Michael Binyon, "West Acts as Midwife at Birth of New Leadership," *London Times,* 29 May 1991.

72. See the *London Times* editorial, "New Deal for Ethiopia."

73. Contrast this with Zartman's statement that *"interest in conflict management* is dependent above all on the relations that outside party has with the conflicting parties and on the degree of hurt and opportunity caused it by the conflict; humanitarian interests (the degree of hurt caused by the conflict to the conflicting parties themselves) run a far distant second" (see p. 14 above).

74. Colin Legum, "Ethiopia: Test for American Foreign Policy," *Third World Reports,* 5 June 1991.

75. Cohen's statement about acting as the "conscience of the international community" had more than a hint of the crusader to it.

76. I. William Zartman, ed. *Collapsed States: The Disintegration and Restoration of Legitimate Authority* (Boulder, Colo.: Lynne Rienner, 1995).

77. For details on the intervention see Ken Menkhaus and Terrence Lyons, "What Are the Lessons To Be Learned From Somalia?" *CSIS Africa Notes* no. 144 (Jan. 1993); Ken Menkhaus, "Getting Out Vs. Getting Through: U.S. and U.N. Policies in Somalia," *Middle East Policy* 3, no. 1 (1994); and Ahmed I. Samatar, ed., *The Somali Challenge: From Catastrophe to Renewal?* (Boulder, Colo.: Lynne Rienner, 1994).

78. For a more complete consideration of the political imperatives of intervening after state collapse see Terrence Lyons and Ahmed I. Samatar, *State Collapse and Multilateral Intervention in Somalia: The Lessons for Political Reconciliation* (Washington, D.C.: Brookings Institution, forthcoming).

79. Keith B. Richburg, "Somalia Slips Back to Bloodshed," *Washington Post,* 4 Sept. 1994.

80. Khalid Medani, "Sudan's Human and Political Crisis," *Current History* (May 1993).

81. J. Stephen Morrison, "Ethiopia Charts a New Course," *Journal of Democracy* 3, no. 3 (1992).

82. National Democratic Institute, *An Evaluation of the June 21, 1992 Elections in Ethiopia* (Washington, D.C.: National Democratic Institute, 1992): Terrence Lyons, "The Transition to Democracy in Ethiopia: Observations on the Elections in Welega, June 1992," testimony before the House of Representatives Subcommittee on Africa, 17 Sept. 1992.

83. African-American Institute, *Eritrea: A Report on the Referendum on Independence* (Washington, D.C.: African-American Institute, 1994).

84. "Carter Center Statement on Ethiopia Negotiations," *News from the Carter Center,* 23 Mar. 1994.

85. Obasanjo, Olusegun, ed. *The Kampala Document: Towards a Conference on Security, Stability, Development, and Cooperation in Africa* (New York: African Leadership Forum, 1991).

86. Paul Lewis, "Disaster Relief Proposal Worries Third World," *New York Times,* 13 Nov. 1991. For a detailed critique of existing mechanisms, see Jeffrey Clark, *The U.S. Government, Humanitarian Assistance, and the New World Order: A Call for a New Approach* (Washington, D.C.: U.S. Committee for Refugees, 1991).

87. Francis M. Deng and Larry Minear, *The Challenge of Famine Relief: Emergency Operations in the Sudan* (Washington, D.C.: Brookings Institution, 1992).

13

Moscow-American Interaction in the Arab-Israeli Conflict

IRINA ZVIAGELSKAIA

The history of Soviet-American interaction in the Middle East is in some respects beyond comparison. It has long been characterized by both acute rivalry and a certain amount of cooperation, along with widely differing forms and mechanisms of conflict management used by the USSR and the United States. Management as a model of behavior did not necessarily contribute to conflict reduction, as this goal had not always been perceived by the superpowers as their main priority in the region.

A unique situation when one actor, such as the Soviet Union, ceases to exist and is replaced by a Commonwealth of Independent States, with each member seeking a foreign course of its own, may invite asking if we are witnessing the end of history. In other words, will a long, dramatic period of Soviet-American relations in the Middle East have any impact on the future, and who in the former USSR will ensure a measure of continuity of the foreign policy after the collapse of the Soviet empire? It is also important to trace new elements that would characterize perceptions of regional interests of the new states, and to estimate their abilities in carrying out independent policies.

Right now there are more questions than answers. The commonwealth is seen by many observers as a transitional model where the pattern of interaction among the member-states is not yet clear.

The agony of the unitarian state lasted long enough to give way to many concerns about its possible consequences. The quest of the republics for sovereignty and independence was greatly advanced by an abortive coup d'état of August 1991. First, by demonstrating the real threat posed by the central government to the members of the Soviet Union, the coup gave a new impulse to the idea of secession. Second, by constituting a successful revolt of the Russian authorities against the Soviet political structure, it set an example. The victory of the Russian leaders turned out to be a mixed blessing. On the one hand, it undermined the regime, which though weakened still had enough power to impede reforms. On the other hand, it speeded up the disintegration of the state, including the Russian federation itself, where autonomous republics and regions began to demand sovereignty.

The efforts to find a new formula for the Soviet Union that would recognize the sovereignty of the republics and preserve a relatively strong and influential center, failed. It was already too late for renovation. The disintegration was gaining momentum. As the last leader of the Soviet Union, President Mikhail Gorbachev, said in his address to the Mideast Peace Conference: "Of late the world has been confronted by yet another crisis of tremendous proportions. What I have in mind is my own country. It became inevitable as a result of latent contradictions building up over a long period of time. A great country is going through a great transformation. It is a painful and arduous process which has brought about personal tragedies and inter-ethnic and regional conflicts. Much in the world depends on how our crisis will be resolved."[1]

The USSR had many international commitments. It was responsible for the control of arms, including nuclear weapons, on the territories of the republics; it was represented in the UN Security Council and in other international organizations; it was a party to many international agreements and treaties. These functions cannot be performed by the republics' ministries of foreign affairs without Russia, which has become the legitimate successor of the USSR. Moreover, a new entity coming into being needs a basis. A coordinated foreign policy in the most important fields reflects the reality: the independent states, despite isolationist currents, will need, along with their own foreign endeavors, some solid and authoritative international representation.

For the authorities in the former republics, a foreign policy is acquiring a special importance. It might legitimize newly elected presidents and secure recognition of sovereign republics. The former Soviet republics are still newcomers in international relations. Whatever their interests are and how much they might differ from the interests of the Soviet Union and from those of the Russian Federation, they possess comparatively limited means to support a desired international status. In the commonwealth not many states are ready to formulate and to implement a regional policy of their own, let alone a global one. What they are doing now and will have to do for a long time is establishing and developing bilateral relations, mostly with the countries that are geographically, historically, ethnically, and culturally close to them.

The peculiarity of the domestic situation in the former USSR is determined by the fact that claims for independence and sovereignty often acquire ethnic dimensions. For example, an assembly of Turks from the Russian Federation and from several republics was convened in Kazakhstan on 18–20 December 1991. The main issue oat the assembly was the possible creation of Turkestan, an independent state uniting the Turks of the former Soviet Union. The border problem was left unresolved but it was agreed that branches of the assembly would be formed in certain regions of Russia, in the Caucasus and Transcaucasus, in Kazakhstan, and in central Asia. The basis of the proposed state is purely ethnic, as many Turks are not Muslims.[2]

Ethnic currents often go hand in hand with nationalism and politicization of religion, however. These factors in turn cannot help having an impact upon foreign policies of the republics. As there are more than 55 million Muslims in the former USSR, these trends are especially relevant in the Middle East.

The last point is well illustrated by the events in Chechen-Ingushetia republic, which has been a member of the Russian Federation. The Chechen population proclaimed its independence as a sovereign Chechen republic. Presidential elections were organized by a former air force general, Jofar Dudaev, and his followers, who in August 1991 had supported the Russian government in its fight against the junta. Jofar Dudaev was named the president of the Chechen republic, though only a few citizens voted for him. His behavior outraged Russian leaders, who after the failure of their talks with Dudaev introduced the state of emergency in the republic. Later, on facing growing destabilization, the Russian parliament did not support such strict measures. But the harm was already done and a Russian invasion destroyed the capital in 1995.[3]

A domestic conflict between the Russian and the newly elected Chechen authorities immediately drew the attention of some ethnic and Muslim communities abroad. Observers from Iran and Syria attended the presidential elections. Anxiety was felt among the influential Chechen clans in Jordan. Dudaev himself referred to forces in Turkey that, according to him, are ready to extend their support to the republic.[4] On the one hand, the republics themselves are making foreign-policy choice;

on the other, they are also being chosen by external forces and states, interested for their own ends in cooperation with the former periphery of the USSR.

This conclusion can be applied to Turkey, Iran, and Saudi Arabia. Turkey is especially active. There are ideas in the country of creating a "Turkic Commonwealth," which will incorporate the southern tier of the former USSR. The basis must be provided by the Organization of Economic Cooperation comprising Turkey, Iran, and Pakistan.[5]

Historical, ethnic, and religious ties with the neighboring states and some Arab and non-Arab Muslim states will no doubt have their impact on the attitude of the republics toward the Middle East conflict. To an extent, depending on the amount of assistance and support they can expect from their partners, they will have to consider how Muslim states approach the problems of the region.

The behavior of the former Soviet Muslim republics in the international arena will be also dictated by purely pragmatic considerations. All of them, despite differences in the level of development, are now facing grave economic problems. Any leader in power will have to solve them first to ensure social stability. Probably for some of them Muslim recipes of boosting economy may seem inviting, but it does not deny the importance of applying technology and know-how of the West and of the most developed Oriental countries, such as South Korea and Taiwan, which do not belong to the Muslim world. From this point of view, the Turkish example is now considered a good model by authorities in Azerbajan and in central Asian states. Turkey is a secular state with a relatively high level of development, a member of NATO, and integral to the Muslim world. What is also important is that the Turks, unlike the Iranians and the Saudis who are primarily busy in religious sphere, are ready to invest in infrastructure in the former republics.

Practically all the former Soviet Muslim republics, after having acquired independence and sovereignty, will have to adapt to a very modest and humble existence in the international community. It will be psychologically difficult for them to accept the fact that the standards of underdeveloped countries is the maximum they night count on. Eager to overcome economic and political barriers, they will have to combine traditionalism and modernization. The Muslim republics are turning their faces to the Muslim world but they can hardly afford at the moment the price of alienating the West. Pragmatic considerations may counter some of the most extreme manifestations of Islamicism during a transitional period.

The Islamic factor in the former Soviet republics should be analyzed at different levels. At the domestic level, it is, no doubt, growing. The revival of Islam is a response to the long suppressed national identity under the Soviet rule. Despite all changes, societies in the Muslim republics remained traditional, and Islam remained for them a way of life. The official "clergy" did not have the trust of the population; Islam went underground becoming less intellectual but more popular. It is this unofficial Islam that prepared the soil for Islamist movements, including fundamentalists. Islam is now filling a vacuum left by the collapse of the Communist ideology.

At the external level, it would be incorrect to automatically project growing Islamist current into a foreign policy. They cannot be treated as the only factor that will determine the Muslim republics' political behavior even in the most sensitive area, namely, in the Middle East.

In this context it is no wonder that Tadjikistan, Uzbekistan, Kazakhstan, and Azerbajan are eagerly developing economic ties with Israel despite a drift to the Muslim world. The activity of Israel itself is an important factor, as it tries to neutralize possible negative aspects of the growing Islamic trends in the former USSR by offering advantageous economic cooperation.

Though certain forces in the republics might become an obstacle to efforts at conflict reduction in the region through their connections with Muslim extremist groups, still it is out of the question that the republics as a whole would come out against the peace process. Stability in the region is now in their best interest, for it will facilitate a realization of their pragmatic goals and will also save them in the future from a difficult and uncomfortable choice. Besides, the situation in the Middle East has drastically changed. The Arab-Israeli confrontation is here and will surely go on for an indefinite period, but as even Saudi Arabia has found it possible to sit at the negotiation table with Israel, why should the republics be more royalist than the king?

Their ties and various connections in the region might be useful for a behind-the-scenes diplomacy, which will also boost their self-esteem, though fine-tuning the activities of different republics will be extremely delicate.

Russia in the Middle East

The main actor collaborating with the United States in conflict reduction in the Middle East is the Russian Federation, whose participation in the peace process is dictated by its national interests and its status as the legitimate successor of the USSR. A partial withdrawal of the USSR from the region did not mean a loss of prestige and authority. Repudiation of the old ideology made it possible to carry out a much more balanced regional course. Diplomatic relations were established with Israel in 1991, and contacts with this country acquired a previously unheard-of dynamism. Diplomatic relations with the Arab world were expanded; Soviet embassies now bearing the Russian flag opened in the United Arab Emirates, Oman, Qatar, and Saudi Arabia, which provides the Russian authorities with new opportunities for mediation in the Middle East conflict.

The existence of such opportunities does not mean that they will be easily implemented. Moscow is not ready yet to shoulder the whole Soviet foreign-policy heritage, because of economic difficulties, political tensions, and unresolved problems within the commonwealth. Moreso, the last Soviet performance in Madrid was not impressive and did not provide a point of reference for the successors. In *Izvestia*, Stanislav Kondrashov called the Soviet efforts to be a co-chair "the last tango."[6] The United States made the conference possible; the Soviet role was marginal. In fact, the American president gave his Soviet co-partner a chance to preserve the image of a superpower, of an indispensable participant in the peace process, in circumstances where this status was already gone for good. The Middle East proved once again that American-Soviet interaction had changed dramatically. The two countries are no longer adversaries nor equal partners, as the former Soviet Union is now desperately seeking the patronage of the United States.

It is true that after the Gulf War the United States acquired very strong positions in the region. If not for the swift victory in the Gulf, there probably would be no Madrid. By demonstrating its indispensability for Middle East security, the United States got an opportunity to use coercion safely to bring reluctant actors to the negotiations. The Soviet performance during the Gulf crisis proved that, despite all domestic limitations, such as the "Afghan syndrome" and internal political controversies, the Soviet Union remained a player in the Middle East scene, using not military but diplomatic means.

Russia cannot afford to be a bystander in the Arab-Israeli conflict, as it has interests in the region. Some of them are traditional, the others are new. Moreover, diplomatic efforts in the Middle East and, foremost, a role of mediator might give an impetus to forming the Russian regional policy, confirming its status as the legitimate successor of the USSR, and contributing to a closer political coordination within the confederation. The Arab states, for their own reasons, are interested in the Russian participation, at least in order not to be left alone with the United States.

Formulating national interests of the Russian Federation in the Middle East along with recognizing the U.S. national interests in the region will determine the prospects of superpower cooperation for security in the Arab-Israeli conflict.

The Bases of Soviet-American Rivalry

Historically, American interests in the Middle East have focused on four major issues, as formulated by Graham Fuller:

1. Protection of Middle East energy resources and their unrestricted commercial flow to consumers

2. Preservation of the security and welfare of Israel

3. Assistance to friendly regimes in the region to enhance regional stability

4. Maintenance of U.S. political influence and commercial access in the region[7]

When put into practice, these declaratory goals had some internal contradictions. "Indeed, all American administrations have recognized that exclusive and uncritical acceptance of all aspects of Israel's own security policies at some points begins to create incompatibilities with other U.S. regional goals, including good relations with Arab states and the exclusion of Soviet influence from the region."[8]

It seems that during the "zero-sum game" played by the United States and the USSR in the Middle East, American administrations hoped that a monopoly in the peace process would help undermine the positions of its global rival to an extent when the above-mentioned incompatibility would cease to be a nuisance. Without the Soviet spoiling influence, Arab states, with an American assistance, would find a modus vivendi with Israel, which in turn would create a more solid base for U.S. presence in the region.

The specificity of Soviet and American approaches to the Middle East stemmed, first, from the geographic factors. "The Soviets thought of the region as contiguous to their borders and therefore, as an area to be kept free of military threats. For the same reason of proximity to the Soviet Union, the United States thought to project power from bases and facilities in the Middle East."[9]

Geostrategic motives traditionally were dominant in the decision making about the Middle East. The region was being turned into an arena of superpowers' struggle for spheres of influence; the Arab-Israeli conflict, whose participants were divided into Soviet and American allies, became an instrument in this struggle.

Soviet-American rivalry in the Middle East was conditioned by considerations of practical policy but also by an ideological tenor. There is no doubt that the leadership of both countries sought to create conditions of reliable security, but their determination of the nature of the threat reflected an ideological view of the world.

The Soviet concept of the system of international relations was based on the premise that such relations were the continuation of class struggle in the special forms inherent in the given system. The strife between socialism and capitalism, personified by the leaders of the two opposite blocs, was considered the central contradiction of the epoch. The expansion of one's sphere of influence was regarded as a reliable means of undermining the position of one's adversary.

At the theoretical and ideological level, the division of the world into two sociopolitical systems was regarded in the USSR as evidence of the doubtless successes of socialism. Both systems were considered not only antagonistic but also autonomous. This approach ignored the interdependence of various subjects of international relations and made it possible to practically disregard the adversary's interests. The result was many adventurous actions in which U.S. behavior raised apprehensions and responses by the USSR, and vice versa.

The USSR's attitude toward the processes taking place in the zone of the newly free countries was not rigid. Recently many Soviet experts, analyzing the Soviet policy of that time, have been eager to present it as one formed under the exclusive influence of ideological dogmas. Ideological preferences did play their negative role. Still, the Middle East course of the USSR, even at the height of the cold war, was pragmatic and underwent an ideological evolution under the impact of realities. Communist parties were practically considered the only reliable pro-Soviet forces for a long time. That belief did not prevent Stalin and his colleagues from ruthlessly exterminating their "class friends" or closing their eyes to their tragic fate in many countries. In the early 1950s, Soviet leadership had volubly cursed the national movements, especially those where the army, regarded as an instrument of oppression, was the leading political force. Later it became clear that in the Arab countries, Egypt first of all, the nationalists were the real political force to deal with. Accordingly, the pendulum of Soviet policy swung to the other side—not the attitude of the authorities to Communists inside the country, but their attitude toward imperialism and neocolonialism, became the criteria for choosing local allies.[10]

It was not solely the Soviet leadership that initiated or imposed such cooperation. Certain Arab regimes were strongly interested in the support of a superpower, using it in the struggle against their regional rivals or, at least, for balancing the American influence in the region.

Speaking Arab-Soviet collaboration, mention should be also made of the Soviet Development model. Not all Arab nationalists found it appealing or acceptable; Nasser, for instance, spoke quite critically about it. Still, the example of the USSR for many years served as a bearing for the local radical nationalist forces. On the one hand, there was a lack of information about the true state of affairs. On the other, Soviet totalitarianism and authoritarianism, so repulsive to a western democrat, were regarded in a completely different light in the East. Moreso, in the 1960s, the administrative system of the government had not yet demonstrated its insolvency. The signs of the crisis, perhaps visible to economists, evaded the attention of nonspecialists and were regarded as individual errors against which no economic organism was insured. The desire of the Arab countries for a strong centralized power was a result of the influence of traditions, the economic development, and the characteristic features of political culture. As Soviet scholar Georgi Mirsky put it:

A society with the incomplete process of class differentiation, multitude of economic forms, prevalence of small producers, little or not at all involved in the system of capitalist commodity production, such a society is a favorable nutrient medium for a mighty state power. Diversity, mosaic, torn and heterogeneous nature of that society, precariousness of the pyramid the bottom of which has not yet left the pre-capitalistic social relations and the top has already adopted the way of life and thought of the second half of the 20th century, the weakness of "internal cohesion" between the components of the nation in the state of formation, all that leads to the independence of the superstructure elements, strengthens authoritarian tendencies.[11]

Thus the copying of elements or even of the whole Soviet model not always was a result only of the desire of the Soviet leaders to impose it on their local allies. In the least-developed countries of the Middle East, to the greatest extent dependent on the Soviet Union, attempts to build the society following the Soviet model were in fact made. For instance, a vanguard party was established in South Yemen;[12] it was an experiment that failed under the pressure of local conditions and finally was buried after the unification of the two Yemens. Behind this ideological crusade, there was primarily an idea of military and political presence in the vital part of the region.

Taken together, these approaches decisely affected the Soviet-American interaction in the Arab-Israeli conflict, accounting for rather sharp tactical turns. The history of the conflict may be divided into several stages.

The first stage (1948–69) was marked by the struggle for the spheres of influence, a search for allies, and establishment of strong patron-client links. That period saw the subjection of the regional confrontation to the zero-sum game.

The second stage (1969–79) was marked, besides by continuing rivalry, by the attempts of the USSR and the United States to achieve, under the conditions of détente, the lowering of tension in the region and a political settlement of the conflict. The unsuccessful joint efforts in that field resulted in the deepening of mutual distrust.

The third stage (1979–88) was characterized by the failure of détente, by a new spiral of confrontation between the powers, which was projected upon the Middle East. Only at the end of that period did expansion of contacts on the settlement take place under the impact of positive global shifts.

The fourth stage (1988–94) was marked by improved Soviet-American relations, unprecedented cooperation during Iraqi aggression, and joint action at the Madrid conference and its sequels in Washington.

The Arab-Israeli conflict started when neither the USSR nor the United States had any firm positions there; both powers needed time to formulate their policies and to impose upon the Arab-Israeli confrontation an additional burden, their own rivalry. Only after 1967 did the conflict, because of regional developments and outside influence, acquire its dimensions. Consequently, in the 1970s the two powers formulated their approaches to conflict reduction.

It seems that the United States realized much earlier than its global adversary the political importance of a Middle East settlement for its own interests. Washington's perception of the issue had a bearing of ideology as well. Anxious to stem the spread of Communist (Soviet) influence, the administration concluded that, by promoting peace, the United States might not only make its positions in the region militarily secure but also undermine a basis of the Soviet presence. As Henry Kissinger put it: "We sought to draw the Middle East into closer relations with us at the Soviets' expense."[13]

Though not always dominant, settlement has been a priority in the American Middle East policy for a long time. It has stimulated a search for conflict reduction measures.

The approach of the Soviet Union was somewhat different. The Soviets have had a distinct interest in stability near its borders. Still, the leaders preferred to differentiate between political and military stability and eagerly welcomed political stability if it could lead to a further radicalization of the region. Interest in military stability became clearly manifest only in the early 1970s. The main threat to Soviet security was associated with American policy, and the Arab-Israeli conflict was regarded as an instrument of that policy, not an independent phenomenon with its own destabilizing functions. Until the 1967 war dispelled illusions, official circles were of the opinion that Arab states armed with Soviet weapons and using the services of military advisers would be able to rebuff the Israeli army. Few believed that the Six-Day War would be such a strong shock to the Arab world. Arab leaders themselves helped create such false notions, stressing their strength and resoluteness: "We, Arabs," Egyptian journalist Mohammed Hasanein Heikal subsequently admitted, "have ourselves done much damage to our cause politically in the eyes of both the enemies and the friends. Israel spoke about peace and was readying itself for war. We spoke about war but were not prepared for it. . . . The world saw the actions of the Arabs before the aggression as irresponsible and after the war as impotent."[14]

Time was needed for the USSR to realize that the Middle East conflict and permanent military instability were detrimental to its own interests. This realization, however, did not automatically lead to its readiness to collaborate with the United States.

Although the Soviets were aware that U.S. peace activities had been directed against their influence in the Middle East, the United States believed that Soviet peace plans, which reflected the maximalist stand of the Soviet allies, had no chance for success and could only spoil the American game. This point is well illustrated by Robert O. Freedman, who described three main schools of thought that analyzed Soviet policy in the Middle East and made recommendations for the American administration. Somewhere between the "offensive-successful" and "defensive-unsuccessful" schools, he located the approach that more adequately depicts Soviet goals and achievements. It is called the "offensive-unsuccessful school."

> This school of thought argues that while Moscow is essentially offensively oriented in the Middle East and will seize upon virtually any opportunity to weaken Western, and particularly American, influence there, the USSR has been basically unsuccessful in extending its influence in the region because of the independence of the local actors and their resistance to Soviet control. This school . . . is wary of inviting Moscow to participate in any peacemaking efforts, arguing that while there might well be tactical compromises by the USSR in specific situations, the USSR cannot be trusted to fulfill its parts of any agreement in the long term, and point to past Soviet behavior in crisis situations and

to the Soviet peace plan for settling the Arab-Israeli conflict to support its argument.[15]

It was not so much the asymmetry of interests of the two superpowers that precluded in the past their cooperation in conflict reduction (the irony is that both of them were interested in a political solution), but self-imposed restrictions. Among them were perceptions of threat as coming mainly from a global adversary, not from the conflict itself; exaggeration of outside powers' abilities to influence the course of events; and mutual distrust.

It would be wrong to assert that the history of Soviet-American interaction in the Middle East knew no cooperation in conflict reduction. Such cooperation became possible when relations between the global rivals had been improved and when development of conflict had led to military and political deadlocks thus inviting conflict management.

The first détente that managed to soften the cold-war approaches opened doors to Soviet-American cooperation in the conflict settlement. In the early 1970s, it developed on a narrow basis, involving only the strategic arms limitations talks. New philosophy of the international relations was lacking and it make détente processes weak and brittle. Positive trends in Soviet-American relations, however, were regarded by the two sides as important, and in the first half of the 1970s, they tried to preserve them. The 1973 war in the Middle East, which created an acute international crisis, accentuated the destabilizing function of the conflict, which ended détente. The necessity of joint USSR-U.S. actions to find political solution also became evident. Henry Kissinger's visit to Moscow was used to formulate UN Security Council Draft Resolution N338, adopted on 22 October 1973. In that resolution the call for a cease-fire in the Middle East coexisted with the demand of practical implementation of the UN Security Council resolution; it also called for immediate political talks between the parties under the proper auspices.[16]

In December 1973, the Geneva Peace Conference on the Middle East was convened with the USSR and the United States as its co-chairmen. The conference marked a breakthrough in the protracted Soviet-American confrontation in the region, but did not bear the expected results. First, efforts of both superpowers to play a simultaneous role of an umpire with opposite goals in mind precluded the elaboration of parallel or compatible courses. Second, not all participants in the conflict were ready for a compromise either politically or psychologically. Kissinger's diplomacy was perceived in Moscow as a U.S. attempt to act as the only arbitrator, to strengthen its positions by expelling the Soviet Union, the more so as Kissinger had previously stated it quite frankly.[17]

Carter's initial statements[18] and his loyalty to the idea of the Geneva conference, as well as the continuing détente, established a basis for a closer USSR-U.S. cooperation for the settlement; it peaked with a joint statement of 1 October 1977.[19] Both sides, their interests coinciding, realized that the eventual resumption of hostilities in the Middle East might lead to a clash between themselves and create additional difficulties in their relations with local allies. There was also a wide diversity of views as far as the settlement was concerned, each power pursuing its own goals. According to Cyrus Vance, "Without question, the bedrock of the Carter Middle East policy would continue to be our commitment to Israel's security. We agreed, however, that the critical importance of stable, moderate, pro-Western regimes in the Middle East and access to the Arab oil meant that a return to a passive U.S. posture was not realistic."[20] Ultimately, the new system of relations that could be established in the region in case of successful progress of the settlement was to set up a more reliable basis for the strengthening of American positions.

To ensure the extension of its influence in the Arab world was no less important for the Soviet Union. The USSR, its interests still linked up with the Arab radicals, saw its role in the settlement as a defender of maximalist demands of its allies. Such divergences in interpreting the ultimate goals of the settlement made both powers regard the Soviet-American actions as precluded not only by specifics of their bilateral relations but also by the negative attitude of the main local actors (Egypt and Israel) to the prospect of Soviet participation in the peace process.

Soviet negative perspective of the Camp David agreements was based on the postures of most of the Arab countries stigmatizing Egypt for its capitulation. Solidarity with the Arabs made it possible for the Soviets to capitalize on the U.S. failure to apply the Camp David model to other Arab countries and thus to partly weaken the impression created by the international success of the Carter administration, who, for the first time in the history of the Arab-Israeli relations, was able to bring about the signing of a peace treaty between Israel and a leading Arab country. The mediation activities of Washington in the Middle East added new friction to the Soviet-American interaction in the region. Moscow felt that, despite the détente, Washington was not going to reckon with its role in the region and, in fact, did everything to deny its participation in the peace process.

By the late 1970s, Soviet-American relations again acquired a confrontational nature. Both sides were impairing détente. The last shattering blow was delivered to détente by the Soviet invasion of Afghanistan. The USSR-U.S. contradictions became especially aggravated after the Reagan administration assumed the White House. Soviet-

American relations were back at the level of the cold war with the Middle East becoming a kind of focal point for the confrontation. For the first time in many years, there was a build-up of the direct military presence of the two powers along the region's periphery. The Soviet forces in Afghanistan were regarded in Washington as an evidence of the USSR's traditional expansionism, as a thrust to the warm seas in order to control the area's main communications and oil routes. The United States responded by setting up a rapid deployment of forces focused on the Persian Gulf, and later began to bring its navy closer to the area.

No joint efforts in the Middle East could be feasible. In the early 1980s, both powers were clearly losing interest in the settlement. The Soviet Union was getting more and more involved in a bloody and protracted conflict in Afghanistan. The United States was in no hurry to start new mediation for the following reasons. First, the fall and subsequent stabilization of oil prices and the general change in the oil market, which was favorable to consumers, excluded oil as a factor and required that the United States consider the postures of the pro-western Arab regimes in the conflict. Second, the return to Egypt of the rest of the Sinai meant the end of the Egyptian-Israeli confrontation. If the United States moved further, it would have inevitably faced the opposition of the Begin government, which ruled out compromises on the West Bank, Gaza, and the Golan Heights. After the collapse of the Shah of Iran's regime, Israel was regarded as the only reliable American ally in the region, and Washington was eager not to worsen that relationship. Third, the Arab-Israeli confrontation no longer was perceived in the United States as the primary source of instability. It was shadowed by the Iran-Iraq war started in September 1980.

The American administration, placing in the foreground the task of countering the Soviet threat, apparently concluded that the balance of forces in the region permitted involving Israel and moderate (Arab) regimes to oppose the USSR. According to Robert G. Newmann, a well-known expert on the Middle East, "Haig knew enough about the Middle East to realize that an agreement between the Arabs and Israel on a common defense against the Soviet Union was not possible. But he thought that official or unofficial agreements with each individual Middle East country concerned might be possible."[21]

A new stage of Soviet-American confrontation put new obstacles in the way of conflict reduction. In the 1980s, there appeared an American peace plan and Soviet peace initiatives.[22] Though they were not devoid of positive elements that could have been useful for the settlement, they were not intended to become a basis for a collaboration of the two powers. Each of them acted along its own course, either ignoring peace proposals of the opponent or strongly criticizing them.

The position of the USSR claiming to participate in the peacemaking in the Middle East was complicated by its link to Arab radicals, at times becoming a hostage of their postures. The interest in conflict reduction prompted the USSR to use its channels to try to lure Arabs away from extremism. Much was done in this respect vis-à-vis the PLO. Although the Arab allies showed no inclination to be realistic, Soviet diplomacy continued to officially support their demands, not necessarily in line with the task of searching for peace. All this made the Soviet posture both too inert and rigid. Thus the USSR more than coldly responded to the Fahd Plan of November 1981, although it did not contradict the Soviet approaches or even their interest in the normalization of relations with Saudi Arabia. It was because the radical regimes, Syria first, rejected Saudi proposals, not wanting to yield to the Saudis the role of leaders of the Arab world. Later, the Fahd Plan became the basis of the common Arab platform elaborated at Fez in September 1982, which was favorably received by the Soviets.

Mention should be also made of the Soviet response to the Amman agreement reached by King Hussein and Yasir Arafat in February 1985, which envisaged a joint settlement strategy. It was negatively assessed in the press, not only because of fears that the United States might use the opportunity to revive the peace process without the USSR's participation but also because of the attitude of the radical leftist forces in the PLO, who subjected Arafat to biting criticism and made him denounce the document.

Soviet policy in the conflict was far from being balanced, but its support of the Arab radicals had its limitations. Politically the USSR, irrespective of its relations with Israel (nonexistent for many years because of the former's willingness to please Arab allies), never questioned Israel's right to existence and was highly critical of the extremist calls of that kind. Militarily a leading supplier of arms to the Middle East, the USSR never delivered to its allies the most sophisticated offensive and destructive weapons, despite repeated requests. Terrorist activities also found no support in the USSR, though sometimes they were met with a milder response than deserved.

The end of the confrontation period in Soviet-American relations in the Middle East, which witnessed steps aimed at opposing each other, irrespective of what was involved—peace proposals or military-political measures—became evident in the second half of the 1980s. The coming to power in the USSR of political leaders voicing the concept of a new political thinking had long-term implications. De-ideologization of inter-state relations and broad Soviet-American contacts were conducive to the gradual removal of the Middle East from the influence of Soviet-American rivalry, though not excluding it completely.

Some American experts believed that two factors were responsible for the increasing confidence in the USSR's policy in the Middle East: the withdrawal of Soviet forces from Afghanistan and the beginning of Jewish emigration from the Soviet Union.[23] These changes of Soviet policy were not instantaneous, but the readiness to introduce them was becoming more and more evident to Washington. The language of Soviet-American interaction also changed. For instance, the USSR's response to the 1988 Schultz plan was critical, but reserved and differing from the earlier immediate rejection of American initiatives. The Baker plan was already formulated in the context of a constructive Soviet-American dialogue on the Middle East problem, and the Soviet attitude toward it not in the least echoed that of the Arab radicals.

Still, the new approaches to the Middle East did not always facilitate pursuing the Soviet course. Many Arab allies felt deserted, even betrayed. They were worried about whether the USSR would be willing to continue its support to the national-liberation movement and its military aid as well. Additional friction in relations with the Arabs were caused by massive Jewish immigration to Israel, which, in their opinion, made it easier for Israel to maintain its hold on the occupied territories. Some former Soviet allies still dream of the old days when the Soviet-American confrontation made them especially important for the USSR's military-industrial complex and when they were readily exploiting that situation. Their hopes that the Soviet Union might again become an adversary of the West were demonstrated during the tragic days of August 1991 in Moscow. The coup d'état was happily supported by Saddam Hussein, Moammar Qaddafi, and some radical Palestinian leaders, who felt much better under the patronage of the previous Soviet regime.

New Middle East priorities of the former Soviet republics are being formulated. The geostrategic factor suggests that, with the American threat gone, there are regional developments that might undermine the security of the commonwealth member-states. Hostilities in the region where enormous military potential was acquired by the actors, including the most sophisticated weapons of mass destruction, are especially dangerous for the southern periphery of the former USSR (both militarily and ecologically).

At the same time, efforts to overcome economic problems as fast as possible and to acquire hard currency may have a destabilizing effect.

Reportedly, Iraq and Libya have sought access to nuclear materials and experts in some central Asian states. Russia is going to remain an arms supplier. On the one hand, the policy can provide leverage over the Middle East recipients; on the other hand, if peace talks fail or come to a standstill, Russian arms supplies might also add fuel to the developments.

An economic interest shadowed in the past by ideological considerations has vividly increased. It comprises trade and economic exchanges, credits, and investments. It is possible that the republics will become importers of Middle East oil, as there is a fall in oil production in the confederation because of its backward technological base, to the disintegration of the economic ties between the republics. Ultimately, when the economic situation in the confederation depends on collaboration with the West, its member-states cannot afford again the region becoming a scene of rivalry and confrontation.

The importance of historical, ethnic, and religious ties with the countries of the region has grown. On the one hand, there is the Muslim connection mentioned above; on the other, massive Jewish immigration to Israel has created a new situation. As the immigrants are allowed to have double citizenship, they are becoming an important factor in shaping relations with Israel. In the transitional period, conflict reduction may help preserve some form of common foreign policy and demonstrate its viability.

· · ·

The history of Soviet-American interaction in the area has given birth to some positive trends. First, the widely recognized responsibility of both powers to cooperate for peace and security in the Middle East results from their longtime involvement in regional affairs. Russia is still viewed in the Middle East as a player that can contribute to these ends. Second, it is a tradition of the United States and the USSR to co-chair the Middle East peace conference.

Still, the future of Russian-American collaboration in the conflict reduction will not be totally cloudless. Misunderstandings are likely to appear because of the separate interests of the two players. As stated in the first chapter, "A degree of autonomy is useful but it should be complemented by full access and encouragement along diverse paths to an agreed-upon goal. Such tolerance and coordination does not come naturally, and the combination of diplomatic autonomy and cooperation contains enough contradictions to invite mixed signals and bad feelings." The history of Soviet-American interaction with its deep rooted mutual distrust may have a negative impact on the future. One may recollect, for example, anxiety aroused in the United States by Primakov's mission to Iraq. As the Russian authorities are interested in having their own course in the region, because of national interests of the country and a tactical goal of demonstrating to domestic and foreign audiences their indispensability as the USSR's successor, there will be enough room left for "mixed signals and bad feelings." Policies of sovereign republics with their special ties to the local actors can produce not only cooperation but also conflicts and concerns, thus making the Middle East situation less manageable, as Russian nuclear sales to Iran in 1995 show.

It is obvious that reduction of conflict in the Middle East will be a long and painful process. The diplomatic breakthrough achieved at Madrid and Oslo has created new dynamics in conflict reduction. However, this trend is not necessarily irreversible. It is in the best interests of the global powers and regional actors to keep the negotiations going, for unpredictability of the future developments both in the region and in the confederation is now greater than ever.

Notes

1. Address by Soviet President Mikhail Gorbachev to the Mideast Peace Conference, Madrid, 30 Oct. 1991; transcribed in *Federal News SVC*, 3.

2. *Commersant*, 1991, no. 49.

3. *Izvestia*, 1 Nov. 1991; *Literaturnaya Gazeta*, 13 Nov. 1991.

4. Ibid.

5. *Izvestia*, 10 Jan. 1991.

6. *Izvestia*, 30 Oct. 1991.

7. Graham E. Fuller, "The Middle East in U.S.-Soviet Relations," *Middle East Journal* 44, no. 3 (Summer 1990): 419.

8. Ibid.

9. William B. Quandt, "U.S.-Soviet Rivalry in the Middle East," in *East-West Tensions in the Third World*, ed. Marshall D. Shulman (New York: W. W. Norton, 1986), 20.

10. R. A. Ulianovski, ed. *Revulytsionny protsess na Vostoke. Istoria i sovremennost* (Revolutionary process in the East: history and the present time) (Moscow: Politizdat, 1982), 22.

11. G. I. Mirsky, *Trety Mir: Obshchestvo, Vlast, Armiya* (The Third World: society, power, army) (Moscow, 1976), 374–75.

12. *Politicheskie Partii* (Political parties) (Moscow, 1986), 191–92.

13. Henry Kissinger, *Years of Upheaval* (Boston: Little, Brown, 1982), 594.

14. Cited in Y. M. Primakov, *Anatomy of the Middle East Conflict*, trans. H. Vladimirsky (Moscow: Nauka, 1979), 124.

15. Cited in a paper by Robert O. Freedman, "Moscow and Middle East Peace Settlement: From Breznev to Gorbachev," provided by Dr. Freedman.

16. See William B. Quandt, *Camp David: Peacemaking and Politics*. (Washington, D.C.: Brookings Institution, 1986), appendix A, 341–42.

17. See Stanley Hoffmann, *Dead Ends: American Foreign Policy in the New Cold*

War (Cambridge, Mass.: Harvard Univ. Press, 1983), 33; *Middle East* (London: Zed, 1990), 109.

18. *Towards Peace in the Middle East* (Washington, D.C.: Brookings Institution, 1975).

19. Quandt, *Camp David*, 45–46, 48.

20. *Pravda,* 2 October 1977.

21. Cyrus Vance, *Hard Choices* (New York: Simon and Schuster, 1983), 163.

22. Robert G. Neumann, "United States Policy in the Middle East," *Current History* 83, no. 489 (Jan. 1984), 2.

23. Official text of President Reagan's address on the Middle East peace process at the American Embassy, *Moscow,* 1982, no. 152; *Pravda,* 30 July, 1984.

PART FOUR

Conclusions and Implications

14

U.S.-Russian Regional Cooperation
Redefining Mutual Expectations

EDWARD A. KOLODZIEJ

This chapter has two aims. The first, and principal, aim is to review briefly U.S.-Soviet regional cooperation to reduce regional conflicts during the cold war and to identify the underlying rationale on which their limited cooperation was based.[1] The second is to explore the argument that the brittle and unreliable forms of cooperation of the cold war era, built on the shaky grounds of mutual distrust and counterbalancing threats, can be replaced by cooperation that increasingly integrates these two powers within a shared security framework. This cautious optimism rests on the counterintuitive but reassuring cold war experience and, more important, on growing evidence of a convergence of political, security, and economic interests and aims between the United States and Russia, the principal inheritor of the Soviet Union's power and international responsibilities.

A cooperative security system, resting on integral rather than threat-based cooperation, would require, at a minimum, the conformity by the members of the system to agreed-upon principles, rules, and norms for peacefully reducing conflict between them as well as for their intervention—alone or in combination—in the conflicts of states outside of their sphere of cooperation.[2] As progress toward this new security structure is made, in necessary tandem with the political and economic reforms among the republics of the former Soviet Union on which the success and stability of such a system would have to depend, the basis will also be laid for resuming and subsequently expanding U.S.-Russian cooperation in regional conflict reduction.

Transition to integral cooperation will not be smooth or sure; nor, realistically, will it be an entirely reliable basis for formulating national security policy for either the United States or Russia in all instances of regional conflict in which their interests are engaged. Furthermore, it is not sensible to assume that the interests of the United States and those of whatever governing structure—at best a loose and tension-torn confederation of states—that will eventually emerge from the current turmoil among the former Soviet republics will see eye to eye in pursuing those national interests affected by regional conflicts. Even preserving the fragile cooperation developed during the cold war cannot be assured, as the failed August coup of 1991 in the Soviet Union suggests. The possibility of future attempts to reverse the current trend toward market reform, democratization, and political openness cannot be ruled out any more than armed clashes—witness Armenia and Azerbaijan—between the divergent national republics that have reappeared out of the ashes of the Soviet Union. The legacy of cold war mistrust, only partially offset by instances of cooperation, as well as the memory of past grievances and of war-threatening crises between Washington and Moscow are not automatically effaced just because the current political climate encourages working together. Changing a tire on a moving car is never easy.

Russia remains the principal center of decision and power, but others will very likely crystallize among the peoples of the vast continental expanse that was once the Soviet Union. The United States and its allies may well have to reckon with several regimes. In any event, the military capabilities of this emerging grouping or groupings will remain formidable in the near future and beyond, even if the divergent national peoples previously making up much of the Soviet Union do not achieve the cohesion of their recent Communist or previous Tsarist past. Indeed, the West's assignment of a clear role to Russia for regional conflict management in the post–cold war era—in Europe and in the developing world—would arguably contribute to its restoration as a unified nation resting on democratic principles and shared national purpose and to its rapid reintegration within an international society of states dedicated to the promotion of a cooperative security system.

Russia's problems, and those confronting the United States and the international community, can be understood best by comparing them with those of France in 1815 and 1945. In 1815, after the Napoleonic wars, a former revolutionary France, which had sought hegemonic control of Europe and the global Eurocentric system, had to be reintegrated within a European concert to keep the peace. Europe's security could be assured only within a security framework in which each of the major states of Europe accepted both a limited role in defining Europe's governing arrangements and constraints on the use of its military power to press its demands. Hegemony was ruled out of order. Adjustments in regime rules or the resolution of crises (for example, the Belgium issue) were to be made consensually and not imposed on member-states. Even small states were to be accorded a say on matters of vital interest to them.[3]

In 1945, after World War II, the international community faced quite a different problem in reintegrating France within the international society of states.[4] A defeated France had to be internally bolstered, as Charles de Gaulle and Winston Churchill understood,[5] by treating it as a great power—if it were to eventually play a supportive and constructive role in rebuilding itself and postwar Europe. Anglo-American assignation of big power status to a divided France proved critical, particularly after de Gaulle's return to power under the Fifth Republic, in subtly promoting long-term internal national self-confidence, reconciliation, and cohesion through France's gradual resumption of a significant role in international politics, however diminished in proportion to its imperial past.

With respect to Russia, both tasks—taming a revolutionary power and according it a great-power role within a common security framework shared by its former rivals—have to be accomplished simultaneously. A once-revolutionary Soviet Russia and now a gravely weakened Russia in turmoil need to be placed on an equal moral and political footing with the western powers victorious in the cold war, pending harness of the powerful forces that have been unleashed by internal revolution and the subsequent implosion of the Soviet Union. Treating Russia as a great power, on a basis like that which a defeated France enjoyed before, would bolster domestic political and economic reform and constructively focus reemergent national sentiment as preconditions for Russia's participation in managing and resolving regional conflicts in Europe and elsewhere.

What also lends encouragement to the long-term prospect of successful Russian integration within an international system, progressively based on integral rules and norms of cooperation, is the record of U.S.-Soviet cooperation during the cold war. Under the most trying of circumstances, in which these continental giants competed in deadly earnest for global ascendancy, cooperation to avoid a mutually fatal war between them and to restrain regional conflicts between their clients was still possible. This experience, if understood by the leadership and populations of both nations, bolsters belief that Moscow and Washington can enlarge and deepen regional security in moving from a threat-based to a consensual framework of cooperation that increasingly integrates both powers in a shared and mutually defined security system responsive to their differing security needs.

The Cold War as Cooperation: U.S.-Soviet Cooperation in Regional Conflict Management

By the start of the twentieth century, the empires of the European states had created a global international society for the first time in history.[6] The United States and the Soviet Union, as victorious powers in World War II, replaced the European power in their attempt to organize the world community on terms congenial to their divergent interests and values. In their search for allies around the world, both were compelled —by national interest, regime imperatives, revolutionary experience, and ideological commitment—to pit themselves against the surviving remnants of the Eurocentric system. Despite serious lapses in their support for the principle of national self-determination as the organizing principle of the world society of states, Washington and Moscow essentially converged in their opposition to the European imperial system in much the same way that they struck on alliance of convenience to block the German-Japanese bid for global ascendancy. This revolt against the Eurocentric system was inevitable, for the very principles of national independence and self-determination which drove the European states to construct empires in their global struggle for dominance carried the seeds of their own devolution. The cold war superpowers catalyzed and ensured the final success of the decolonization process.

If the U.S.-Soviet rivalry speeded the collapse of the European imperial systems, the two powers did not possess equal advantages. The Soviet Union initially had the upper hand, as Hedley Bull explained: "Since it [was] the established ascendancy of Western Europe and North America in Asia, Africa, and Latin America that the Third World ha[d] been struggling to overthrow, the alliance of the Third World and the Soviet Union against the West . . . [was] natural and perhaps inevitable."[7] The United States had to support its European allies to meet the Soviet threat in Europe, yet it was compelled to distance itself from their futile efforts to retain their colonies. The United States invariably choose either to side with the developing state against its former master—witness Soviet-

American cooperation to frustrate the French-British-Israeli attack on Egypt—or to replace the former European hegemony as the dominant power in the region.

The cooperation of the United States and the Soviet Union in catalyzing the decolonization of the developing world was occasioned, paradoxically, by their conflict. Each sought to prevent the influence of the other from expanding. Each was induced to support independence movements to forestall the loss of what each perceived were strategic assets in the struggle to impose their preferences on the global system. Parallel to the cold war's performance of this midwife function, Washington and Moscow also cooperated to create regional structures of power that regularized and managed their conflict, short of armed hostilities between them.

Although it can be argued that their rivalry sparked and spurred regional conflicts and fueled arms races, it is no less true that they were able to adapt their struggle (until the collapse of the Soviet Union) to the globalization of the nation-state as the principal unit of legitimate political organization of the diverse peoples of the world society. They were also to learn, at great expense in Vietnam and Afghanistan, that they would have to accommodate their preferences to those of smaller states and local sentiment in constructing postwar regional security systems. To avoid war and to contain the human and material costs of pressing their aims and interests unilaterally, both sides learned to cooperate to check the hegemonic ambitions of regional clients and, not always successfully, to limit the destructiveness of hostilities. They were often induced to constrain the aims and violence of their local allies, whose conflicts, like those in South Asia or the Middle East, were driven by factors quite independent of those animating the superpower competition. These fragile regional security regimes, tenuously supported by often hastily constructed understandings and temporary convergences of interests, are one of the legacies of the cold war, whose passing raises their continuance into question.

Even if the cold war had persisted, the stability of these regional arrangements might well have been unsustainable. Defection by Moscow or Washington was always tempting and often a preferred choice in regional conflicts, given the deep distrust and perception of unreliability of the rival-partner, not to mention their profound and seemingly intractable ideological differences. U.S.-Soviet limits on regional conflict rested on cooperative compromises that were induced by the costs and risks confronting them, if they relentlessly pressed their regional claims without inhibition or limit. The prospect of mutually damaging outcomes acted as a brake, even when losses could be differentially calculated by the antagonists in varying absolute or relative values.

What is useful to recount, however, is that regional cooperation between the United States and the Soviet Union was greater than one might have supposed from a cursory examination of the magnitude of their global struggle and of the distance between their ideological positions. Without depreciating the enormous cost and deadly seriousness of the cold war, both Washington and Moscow gradually fashioned a reliable, though fragile, set of understandings, more tacit than explicit, to guide their behavior and power in limiting the scope, aims, and means to be employed in regional conflicts. Even as they armed their allies, they also exercised restraints on them during crises and worked behind the scenes to lower tensions or to preclude hostilities from getting out of hand.

The case for extending U.S.-Russian regional cooperation in a post-cold war environment rests to an important degree on an appreciation of the stabilizing role that the cold war played in regional conflict. A brief review of this experience not only serves this aim but also identifies more concretely some of the limits on regional conflict that must be sustained or for which substitutes have to be found as Washington and Moscow refocus their resources and priorities on domestic reform. If threat-based cooperation proved viable and lasting during the cold war, the prospect now arises that the United States, Russia, and the other great powers of the international system can go beyond threat-based cooperation and engage in creating regional security regimes that may be able to enlist former regional rivals in their support.

Regional Cooperation During the Cold War

Cooperation in Europe and in undermining the Eurocentric system. The cold war provisionally resolved three chronic European security problems. First, it organized the continent into two military blocs and two spheres of influence under the leadership of Moscow and Washington. In retrospect, this was a remarkable achievement and underwrote the long peace between East and West.[8] Neither Washington nor Moscow at first sought this outcome, but in their unilateral pursuit of the Europe they wanted, they got a divided Europe as their unintended second preference. Despite repeated crises, particularly centered on Berlin, the global war which had hung over the continent for a century gradually evolved into a long peace, guaranteed by the balancing military alliances distributed roughly along the line where the victorious armed forces of the two sides met to end World War II in Europe.

Thirty years later, the Helsinki accords of 1975, which eventually contributed to the demise of the cold war, extended provisional legitimacy to this postwar European order to the national borders sanctioned by arms. The Helsinki accords have been extended in the Budapest agreements of December 1994, which strengthened the institutional structure of the Organization on Security and Cooperation in Europe (OSCE). The dissolution of the Soviet Union and the Warsaw Pact pose the problem of what new distribution of power in the post-cold war world will assure the peoples of the European continent as long a peace as the cold war. The devastating breakup of Yugoslavia—more than 100,000 reported dead, mostly civilians—urges this question on Europe now that the restraints on local conflicts exercised formerly by the cold war warriors have all but been dissolved. Exposed, too, is the impotence of NATO, the European Community, and the OSCE in stopping the bloodshed and the reluctance of their member-states to be mired in the Yugoslav morass.

The cold war also addressed the German problem.[9] In dividing Germany into two states, the threat that Germany's power had previously posed to its neighbors was provisionally solved. Moreover, each German segment was incorporated into an alliance structure that multilateralized its security policy. NATO in the West and the Warsaw Pact in the East monitored and controlled the military rearmament of the two Germanys. The Berlin accords of 1971 regularized this division and excised Berlin as an issue from cold war dispute. The entry of the two Germanys into the United Nations then seemingly legitimated Germany's division. The symbolic fall of the Berlin Wall in November 1989 and Germany's subsequent reunification once again raises the question of its role within Europe and the institutional arrangements that will harness German power to a lasting security regime for Europe. Washington and Moscow still have a converging interest in ensuring Germany's continued peaceful participation in Europe's newly emerging security system.

The cold war contained national rivalries in Europe and induced institutional solutions to transcend these conflicts. French-German hostility was muted within the Atlantic Alliance and subsequently transformed within the European Community that melded the economic and welfare interests of both peoples. These multilateral settings generated incentives for mutual cooperation within both nations in defining their national economic and security needs, whereas before, for almost a century, these calculations assumed the form of a zero-sum game. Meanwhile in Eastern Europe, Moscow imposed a not always welcome peace on ethnic and national rivalries among its Warsaw Pact allies. Central to these monitoring and regulating roles was the pervasive rule of the Soviet Communist party at home and its control of satellite parties in Eastern Europe. As an empire itself, it suppressed warring nationalities and peacefully regulated the ethnic, racial, and religious groupings composing the Soviet republics. When the Soviet Union abandoned the cold war system and launched the reforms of glasnost, perestroika, and democratization, it is not surprising—at least in retrospect—that it would be quickly beset by ethnic and national splits that it had hitherto stilled or restrained.

Finally, both the West and the East made their peace with Tito's brand of nationalist Communist rule in Yugoslavia. The cold war struggle imposed an uneasy and fragile peace on that country's bitterly divided national and religious communities. The passing of the cold war (and the erosion of the Yugoslav Communist party after Tito's death) created the conditions for civil war. There is the clear and present danger, moreover, that these national rivalries may extend to Eastern Europe and to the peoples of the former Soviet Union unless new mechanisms to restrain national rivalries can be devised to replace those that have been discarded with the passing of the cold war.

The peace that the cold war imposed on Europe and the states of the Northern Hemisphere in building a stable balance of power, in containing and multilateralizing German power, and in suppressing and dissipating national rivalries anchored U.S.-Soviet cooperation in the developing world. If the cold war spread to other regions once an impasse was reached in Europe, the experience of cooperation painfully learned in Europe was gradually and selectively extended to other regional struggles. As the discussion below argues, a new security framework that assumes the functions previously performed by the cold war in Europe is a necessary if not sufficient condition for enlarging and deepening regional cooperation in the Southern Hemisphere.

Cooperation in the Middle East. The Middle East offers an instructive example of U.S.-Soviet cooperation amid bitter and devastating regional wars, spurred if not sparked by the cold war. Although the stakes in Europe were of primary importance for Washington and Moscow, the Middle East assumed progressively greater saliency during the cold war. The strategic interests of both capitals in the region were long-standing. Those of Russia dated from at least the nineteenth century. The deployment of the Sixth Fleet after World War II underwrote the Truman Doctrine in the Mediterranean, and signaled a vital U.S. interest in access to the region's oil reserves. As the cold war spread beyond Europe, the region was upgraded again by both sides in the search for bases, allies, and outlets for the sale of arms and military technology.[10]

Washington and Moscow, however, had different but converging interests to contain Middle East conflicts, particularly the Arab-Israeli confrontation. The game was delicate and tricky. On the one hand, both sought to lever their strategic assets in the region and to support their allies and clients for maximum bargaining advantage; on the other hand, both worked (alone and together) to contain armed clashes and to prevent their eruption. The Soviet position was particularly tenuous. The United States was able to extend its protectorate over Israel and the moderate Arab states, eventually encompassing Sadat's Egypt. The Soviet Union was instead confined to the radical Arabs states, which, except for Iraq, were not among the region's major oil producers. Moreover, Washington was never convinced that the Soviet Union should be treated as a equal in addressing regional conflicts. It was perceived rather as the principal global antagonist of the United States or dismissed as unable to deliver its clients, or both. The Rogers Plan of the late 1960s and the efforts at U.S.-Soviet accord a decade later foundered on these strategic obstacles to joint and confident U.S.-Soviet peace efforts. The Reagan presidency's attack on Soviet regional penetration and Soviet support for Syria in the Lebanese civil war and for anti-Israeli elements froze Middle East cooperation between the two capitals in the 1980s.

Below the surface of this two-layered conflict between Moscow and Washington—for global ascendancy and regional hegemony—there crystallized a chain of cooperative ventures and largely tacit understandings about the rules of engagement in the region. For divergent reasons, both supported Israel in its early fight for independence. Only after Stalin's death did Soviet ideological and political constraints relax sufficiently to support so-called progressive bourgeois regimes among the Arab states as a way station to socialism's expected triumph. The U.S.-Soviet convergence over Suez, if dictated by the extension of the cold war to the developing world, also revealed that both sides could agree on how their struggle would be conducted. Both sides could be expected to assume some control over the strategic policies of their principal allies in the region. If both sides mishandled the crisis leading to the Six-Day War, both closed ranks quickly enough in support of UN Resolution 242, which still represents the basis for a long-term solution to the Arab-Israeli struggle.

The defeats suffered by the Arab states (dependent on Moscow for arms) in successive Arab-Israeli wars also created an incentive for Moscow to prevent such debacles from occurring in the future. The Soviet Union continued to send arms to its Arab clients and to support their diplomatic maneuvering, but it was always careful to intervene in a crisis at a point where its entry would not have a decisive impact, in order to preclude a serious escalation of the conflict to a global level with the United States. As Galia Golan observes, the 1967 war introduced a conciliatory pattern into U.S.-Soviet relations in the region. Among its features were "immediate direct communication between the two superpowers, mutual notification in connection with (most) acts by one power which might be misinterpreted as intervention by the other, and joint action to bring about cease-fires through the restraint on respective clients."[11] Despite some minor accidents and close calls, the fleets of the two powers learned to avoid incidents in the Mediterranean. Each also reached out to better relations with the allies of its rival, diplomatic tactics that moderated regional divisions. For example, both tilted toward Iraq in the first Gulf war, in the 1980s, and U.S. protection of Kuwaiti oil tankers was prompted by Soviet moves to provide these guarantees. Each rival-partner learned to cooperate to dampen regional conflicts by delinking their regional interests from their larger global struggle when it suited their purposes, as Zviagelskaia has already noted.

These instances of cooperation and the tissue of understandings stitched together by the United States and the Soviet Union in the Middle East should not be exaggerated. Defections from what each believed was an understanding were common, and doubt and suspicions about the intent of each rival remained the dominant features of the Cold War in the region. It could hardly be otherwise given the threat-based assumptions on which cooperation rested. The incentives for limiting conflict arose from mutual interest in avoiding escalation, the burdens of maintaining an arms race in the region, and the potentially damaging excesses of clients and allies. The security regime in the region was defined then by the U.S.-Soviet global conflict and by the divisions of the regional actors, what Barry Buzan characterizes as amity-enmity relations.[12] This security structure, as in Europe, set limits to the possibilities of cooperation. Washington, for example, interpreted Moscow's participation in the war of attrition in which Soviet personnel manned SAM units and flew air missions that engaged Israeli combat aircraft as violations of tacit restraints to be observed by both sides. Moscow obviously thought otherwise. Similarly, the participation of Soviet personnel in Syrian-Israeli clashes during the Lebanon crisis blocked U.S.-Soviet efforts to find joint solutions to the conflicts of the region.

Cooperation in Asia. The vast Asia continent offers an even more complex and varied pattern of U.S.-Soviet conflict and cooperation than the Middle East. The peoples of this gigantic land mass resisted American and Soviet efforts to determine the course of their strivings for national independence. They also successfully insisted on their right to play critical roles in defining the structure and processes of their region's security regimes. The incentives for U.S. and Soviet cooperation to limit and regulate regional conflict in Asia were shaped by two considerations: the human and material costs that they might incur in unilaterally intervening against regional foes, and a calculation of the risks run in offsetting each other's influence and in checking the expansionist drives of its rival-partner. Until Moscow's rejection of the cold war as the solution to its foreign and domestic aims and interests, Washington and Moscow pursued fundamentally conflicting notions of Asian security. Each power had to learn the hard way that it could not impose its preferences on regional powers, nor preclude its rival-partner from assisting its regional adversaries to resist the other's drive for hegemony in the region. The Korean War sobered both Washington and Moscow about the limits of their power to shape Asian security, but not enough to dissuade either from attempting to impose regimes on Vietnam or Afghanistan. The cumulative effect of these setbacks, the rising importance of other centers of power around the globe opposed to both Washington and Moscow, and growing domestic upheaval (particularly in the Soviet Union) created new incentives for cooperation that have yet to be fully exploited by both powers.

The struggle over Korea militarized and institutionalized the cold war around the world,[13] and sharply narrowed for a generation the possibilities of U.S.-Soviet cooperation throughout Asia. Until the demise of the cold war, Moscow was the central focus of U.S. containment policy. China was reduced to surrogate status, as an arm of the Kremlin. Ignored was the break between Beijing and Moscow that had already begun to develop in the 1950s. Intermittent periods of global détente with the Soviet Union did not essentially refocus the U.S. fixation on the Soviet Union as the principal challenge to its interests in Asia. The freeze in U.S.-Soviet relations, however, was not equal throughout the region. If Asia is divided into four theaters—Northeast, Southeast, Southwest, and South—important differences emerge in the patterns of U.S.-Soviet conflict and cooperative patterns in each system. Identifying the underlying reasons for these differences, particularly the role of regional states and movements, like the Khmer Rouge, to shape regional security provides a guide for assessing the prospects of successfully enlarging U.S.-Russian cooperation in the post-cold war era throughout Asia.

The Korean War locked Northeast Asia into what might be characterized as a four-by-two state security system. Central to the United States was the U.S-Japanese treaty that was forged in response to the Korean conflict. As long as the cold war held and Soviet power was the preeminent threat, the Tokyo-Washington alliance has held firm despite repeated buffetings, particularly since the 1970s when declining American economic performance confronted rising Japanese ascendancy as the world's most efficient producer of technologically advanced commercial products. With the onset of the Korean War, Japan essentially became a protectorate of the United States. To the satisfaction of most Japanese (and Japan's neighbors), Japan was restricted to the defense of its homeland. The United States underwrote Japanese security interests and its claims to the Kurile Islands held by the Soviet Union.

Japanese public opinion identified militarism with its costly and disastrous defeat in World War II and welcomed U.S. protection and the corresponding access that Japanese products enjoyed to U.S. markets. The combination of democracy at home and steadily rising Japanese economic expansion were identified by the Japanese with the U.S.-Japanese treaty. The Japanese were relieved of the burden of heavy defense spending and could concentrate their domestic capital on developing international markets. The United States got a compliant and democratic Japan fully integrated within an international trading system that substituted the discipline of the market for the lash of empire as the answer to Japan's economic welfare.[14]

The Soviet Union and Communist China formed the other parts of the great power security structure of Northeast Asia. Until the Nixon visit to China in 1972, U.S. policymakers essentially treated these two giants as a monolith, with Moscow perceived to be playing the central orchestrating role in marshalling and directing the expansion of the Communist system throughout Asia. U.S. entry into the Chinese civil war, with the deployment of the Seventh Fleet to protect Taiwan and the signing of the U.S.-Taiwanese security accord, similarly cast the United States in an aggressive role from the perspective of Beijing and Moscow. Under these circumstances of mutual suspicion and maximal perception of external threat, cooperation was necessarily limited to tactical moves of limited scope and brief duration in which choices were confined to what means would be used—military force or diplomacy—to advance unwavering aims: balancing the power and containing the expansion of the rival-partner. Soviet restraint was viewed in Washington more as a response to growing U.S. military power, particularly an announced willingness to use nuclear weapons, than as a result of Moscow's interest in stabilizing northeast Asian security relations.

Neither antagonist attributed peaceful intentions to the restraints exhibited by the other. The expansion of the Korean War above the thirty-eighth parallel appeared to confirm Washington's expansionist aims in the eyes of Beijing and Moscow. Its pursuit of a limited war on the Korean peninsula was interpreted as a consequence of Communist countervailing power, and not as a preferred choice by U.S. policymakers, whose decision to integrate both Koreas by force was frustrated only by Chinese entry into the war. Restraint derived from the fear of a global conflagration, untold loss of human life, and capture of most of the European continent before U.S. and NATO troops could be engaged if a global war should erupt. The Soviet Union certainly could not be viewed as a reliable security partner even in limited cooperation, for it was assumed that it had approved the North Korean attack and, ipso facto, transformed both the scope and the means—henceforward military force in hand with political subversion—that it would use to extend its grip over other states.

In Washington, the American effort in Korea and the French fight to retain a colonial empire in Vietnam were portrayed simply as different battlegrounds of a unified global struggle.[15] U.S. military assistance to France, the largest received by a NATO member, was accordingly justified as a contribution to the East-West contest. Moscow's support for the Korean armistice, its moderation toward the threat of U.S. introduction of nuclear weapons in South Korea and Taiwan, and its refusal either to bolster China over Quemoy and Matsu or to fulfill its commitment to assist the Chinese nuclear program did not count as cooperative gestures.[16] The intransigence of South and North Korea to resolve their differences and persistent efforts of the North Korean government to assassinate their homologues in Seoul or to subvert their rule at home solidified the cold war freeze in northeast Asia.

I. William Zartman's notion of a "hurting stalemate"[17] can be applied to Northeast Asia to explain, at least partly, why the cold war freeze gradually thawed, commencing with the opening to China under the Nixon administration. The long and costly failure of the United States to defeat Hanoi in Southeast Asia and rising internal opposition to the war forced a reexamination of U.S. policy assumptions that equated China and the Soviet Union as different parts of a single Communist conspiracy to defeat the West. In Northeast Asia, the Nixon administration chose China as its preferred Communist partner to counter what appeared to be rising Soviet power in Asia and to check Hanoi's ascendancy in Southeast Asia. As long as the U.S.-Soviet cold war struggle continued, there was a convergence of U.S.-Chinese interests to balance the Soviet Union. Japan was a silent partner to the realignment

as a function of the U.S.-Japanese bilateral security bargain and of Japanese interest in the return of the Kurile Islands from the Soviet Union. As
compensation for the "hurting stalemate" and defeat in Vietnam, the
United States rechanneled U.S.-Chinese antagonism toward opposition
to Soviet and Vietnamese expansion.

As in the Middle East and in Northeast Asia, third-party intervention
limited the U.S.-Soviet conflict in Southeast Asia and set the stage for the
transformation of that region, as the discussion below suggests, from a
zone of violent conflict, aided and abetted by the great powers, to one of
progressively greater cooperation between the United States and the Soviet Union and other interested states. The security regime of the region
is more complex than that of Northeast Asia. It comprises four interacting tiers: a three by six by one by four system.[18] The United States,
China, and a weakened Russia form the first tier of three states; ASEAN,
the second, of six nations; Vietnam, the third, as the single dominant
local power in the Southeast Asian peninsula; and at least four rival
groups in Cambodia struggling to impose their rule on the country, the
fourth tier.

The "hurting stalemate" had the unforeseen effect of lowering tensions between the United States and China in Northeast Asia and of
introducing new forces favoring peaceful change in Southeast Asia. In a
reversal of positions, Sino-U.S. cooperation gradually weighed on Hanoi
and encouraged a compromise on Cambodia, although almost a generation of strife and the horror of the "killing fields" would be needed to
create sufficient incentives for the antagonists to turn to the United Nations to resolve the conflict. An important contribution to the opening of
the peace process, as the next section suggests, was the Soviet decision,
later adopted and pursued by the Russian federation, to seek a resolution
of the Cambodian issue as part of its strategy of imperial disengagement.
This decision, however, was not unrelated to pressures emanating not
only from Beijing and Washington but also from the ASEAN states,
which, with little prompting from Washington, also joined to limit Soviet
and Vietnamese expansion after the fall of the Saigon regime in 1975
and Vietnam's subsequent efforts to extend its control over the entire
peninsula.

In contrast, South Asia and, until the Soviet invasion of Afghanistan
in December 1979, Southwest Asia were more hospitable environments
for U.S.-Soviet cooperation. The analyses of Thomas Thorton and
Maxim Bratersky elaborate on the long-term cooperative relation between Washington and Moscow that, while marked by sharp differences
—most notably in the 1971 Indo-Pakistan war—never reached the levels

of tension in South Asia that were so marked in the armed struggles in Northeast and Southeast Asia. The special arms supply relations between India and the Soviet Union, on one hand, and Pakistan and the United States, on the other, were an important and continuing source of friction, but they did not impede Moscow and Washington from cooperating to contain regional armed clashes nor from attempting to improve relations with the clients of its rival. Both capitals sided with Delhi in the Sino-Indian border war in 1962. The United States did nothing to disrupt Soviet efforts to mediate the 1965 India-Pakistan war. Both joined in urging signature by all South Asian states of the nonproliferation treaty. They reinforced each other's promptings of restraint when Sino-Indian tensions rose in 1987. They also supported India's interventions in the Maldives and Sri Lanka to contain violent internal subversions.

Until the ill-fated Soviet invasion, Afghanistan could have been considered something of a model of U.S.-Soviet restraint in their global struggle. Both tacitly supported Afghanistan's social and economic development and contributed modestly toward that aim. If the Afghan government relied on the Soviet Union and its allies in the Warsaw Pact for military training, loans, and trade, it also cultivated U.S. and western economic assistance not only to ensure the stability and development of the country but also to preserve a balance between East and West in the region. Each superpower rival recognized the interests of its opponent. For several decades Afghanistan was essentially insulated from the cold war competition. Successive Kabul governments were sensitive to these implicit superpower understandings and adapted to the narrow limits of their maneuverability between the two giants whose countervailing power underwrote Kabul's delicately balanced neutrality.

Almost overnight the bloody coup d'état that overturned the government of Mohammed Daoud in 1979 plunged Afghanistan into the cold war and destroyed the fragile accord between Moscow and Washington about its role in the East-West struggle. Instead of a buffer between the Persian Gulf and South Asian theaters of the cold war, the Afghan crisis linked these regions into a single battlefield that threatened to inflame the entire area from Iran to the Indian Ocean. Only in retrospect does it now appear clear that the Afghan crisis and the subsequent Soviet setback were important factors that convinced Moscow's leaders to withdraw not only from the war but also from all other confrontations with the West in the developing world. It is no exaggeration to argue that the Soviet defeat in Afghanistan catalyzed Moscow's decision to abandon the cold war as the central concern of its security and foreign policy. Its failure to defeat the Mujahideen, continued support for the rebellion from the United States and Muslim states (particularly Pakistan), the Soviet Union's isolation in the international community, and the incursion of growing human and material costs of a stalemate without apparent resolution led to the departure of all Russian troops at the end of the 1980s. Not without interest for future U.S.-Russian cooperation, Washington used its leverage with the rebels to facilitate Moscow's exit while still tolerating its support of the Kabul government that it had helped to install. Conversely, the Soviet Union and later the Yeltsin regime in Russia supported U.S. policy in Desert Storm, solidifying the cautious view that Washington and Moscow can cooperate in coping with regional conflicts.

Cooperation in Africa. Africa presents a more mixed and uneven pattern of East-West rivalry than other regions. Much of the reason for these differences stems from the more varied geopolitical conditions as well as the greater racial, tribal, national, and religious diversity of the African continent than elsewhere. Both powers had to learn from bitter experience that they would not be able to master these forces, but would have to adapt to them—or simply disengage to cut their losses, a learning process still underway if the hasty withdrawal of U.S. forces from Somalia is any indication. Southern Africa appeared to offer a fertile ground for U.S.-Soviet intervention. Both powers urged Portugal to relinquish its empire. However, the chaos resulting from the rapidity of the Portuguese withdrawal once it began, the particular brutal circumstances of apartheid in South Africa, and racial strife in Rhodesia seemed to offer lucrative targets for Soviet expansion at the perceived expense of U.S. and western interests. Soviet expectations were soon dashed; Moscow bet on the wrong faction in Zimbabwe's successful fight for independence and was marginalized as an influence on the country's development.

The costs of intervention in Angola proved even higher. Despite massive Soviet military assistance and the infusion of Cuban troops, Moscow's clients in Luanda became mired in a "hurting stalemate." The United States allied with the rebel forces of Jonas Savimbi; these in turn were supported by South African forces, which attempted to insulate the civil war from Namibia and to balance the intervention of Cuban troops, defending the Angolan regime (and, incidentally, Shell oil installations whose operation were critical for the solvency of the Communist government). In these circumstances, there was little room for cooperation between Moscow and Washington until the Gorbachev reforms led to the Soviet Union's disengagement, as Vasilkov has discussed.

As one proceeds north in Africa, the cold war gradually dissipated in scope and intensity, although local rivalries persisted and appeared at times to be driven by the superpower global competition. The cold war exacerbated the Congo crisis of the early 1960s, and it was later extended selectively to Angola and the African Horn in the 1970s. Nevertheless, the U.S.-Soviet struggle did not succeed in defining local conflicts as it had in the Middle East or Southeast Asia. Zaire (the former Belgian Congo) fell under western influence. Moscow and Washington did succeed in avoiding escalation in Shaba I and II in the 1970s. Neither became involved as direct competitors in the Nigerian civil war. In the Horn, the United States and the Soviet Union exchanged clients without conflict in the late 1970s when Ethiopia swung into the Soviet camp and its rival, Somalia, switched to the West and the United States. Neither great powers contested French protectorate status for Djibouti. They also resisted Somalia's irredentist claims and signaled restraint to both sides in the Ethiopian-Somalia conflict. If the U.S.-Ethiopian relations under the Mengistu were frigid, Washington did not intervene as it had in Angola in support of rebel forces against the Moscow-backed Ethiopian regime. The rebels, as Marxist separatists, held little attraction for Washington.

The Limits of Threat-Based Cooperation: Going Beyond Cold War

Cold war cooperation between the United States and the Soviet Union in managing and resolving regional conflicts was essentially driven by calculations of loss, gain, and risk in intervening and in escalating regional conflicts. Each rival-partner can be seen to have weighed at least the costs and risks of escalating such conflicts against the advantages that might have been anticipated in pressing their divergent interests in a region against the rival-partner. This essentially rational actor paradigm appears to explain much—certainly not all—of the behavior of these two giants in their response to regional conflicts.[19] The prospects of escalation that might lead to a mutually destructive war held each hostage to the other's nuclear arsenals. This specter clearly hung over the struggle for Europe and gradually spread over the globe wherever U.S.-Soviet interests clashed. For many reasons, some interests and aims also appeared not worth defending or pursuing by stirring or polarizing regional differences. Much of Latin America—Cuba and, for a time, Nicaragua excepted—fell beyond the reach of the Soviet Union. Both Moscow and Washington were wary of widening their selective struggles in Africa. Large segments of the African continent—West and North Africa—were never fully drawn within the ambit of the cold war, nor was South Asia.

This perspective of restrained, cooperative conduct below the surface of cold war rhetoric and bombast must be qualified by recognizing many instances of lapses and excesses in expected U.S. and Soviet behavior. These cases appear to have been driven by ideological concerns or domestic political and bureaucratic cares that prompted one or the other, or both, to reach beyond their grasp. Vietnam and Afghanistan exemplified these excesses. In retrospect, the gains sought by each in intervening were from the outset murky and muddled. As the costs of these engagement mounted, neither could extricate itself from its self-created morass. Rather than limiting their involvement as the costs of their engagement mounted, both increased the stakes and the scope and intensity of the violence, almost as if to ensure that they would eventually lose their risky wagers in their failed, if costly, efforts to control the regional forces that their interventions had unleashed.

Even when the leadership of both sides appeared to be in control in the calculation of gains and losses, and were keenly aware of their mutual interests in restraining regional conflict, uncertainty and miscalculation still infused the power projections and often misguided responses of determined rival decision makers in Moscow and Washington throughout the cold war era. The Soviet Union, for example, guessed wrong about U.S. security interests in Northeast Asia. The United States committed the same error in responding to Beijing's signals about extending the Korean War above the thirty-eighth parallel. These same fumblings can be seen throughout the dismal history of the Middle East since the end of World War II. None of the great powers sought to precipitate the 1967 war, but they failed to grasp the severity of the crisis or control its consequences. Misperceptions about adversary intentions and capabilities by all engaged rivals also marked the 1973 Yom Kippur war.[20] No less did uncertainty and miscalculation about the consequences of rival moves and the depth of their commitments characterize the crises over intermediate-range nuclear missiles in Europe and Asia in the 1970s or over the deployment of Soviet missiles in Cuba.

Even when both sides understood each other well and were neither blinded by their sensitivity to adversary responses nor to the limits of their power was cold war cooperation a reliable basis for limiting conflict. Neither was a fully dependable partner even when they were cooperating, explicitly or implicitly, to limit regional conflicts. From a strictly power-politics perspective, Germany was worth fighting over in the light of a century of European wars. Access to Middle East oil was not a trivial concern for the West, nor was U.S. protection for the state of Israel. Supporting Hanoi's bid for ascendancy was also consistent with

Communist ideological commitments, and the drive toward national self-determination of peoples in the developing world, however lamentable might be the authoritarian regimes that might result from this revolutionary process. Defections were prompted—indeed urged—by the seeming intractable aims and interests dividing Moscow and Washington and by the real and perceived opportunities for advantage in what was viewed essentially as a zero-sum game.

As long as the cold war was central to the security concerns of both continental powers and was a value—as a strategy and as a aim—that overrode socioeconomic development and internal political liberalization in the Soviet Union, expectations about the prospects of U.S.-Soviet cooperation had to be sober and circumscribed, limited to the boundaries set by the global confrontation between these military giants. Throughout the long struggle, even these limited opportunities for cooperation were often overlooked and neglected, or simply squandered by both sides. There is little reason today, however, for clinging to cold war assumptions if a reformed Russia, with leadership unambiguously bent on making the nation a responsible member of the world community, fully emerges from its communist past. This fundamental reorientation was already evident in Soviet "new thinking."[21] As described throughout this volume, Soviet "new thinking" was embodied in Moscow's worldwide efforts to resolve regional conflicts or, at a minimum, to control its own behavior as a source of tensions and division. Moscow's renunciation of its imperial positions around the globe and, accordingly, its contributions to regional peace were unprecedented in the long history of European expansion. In sum, these include Afghanistan, Korea, and Cambodia in Southwest, Northeast, and Southeast Asia; Angola and Ethiopia in southern Africa and the Horn; Nicaragua in Central America; the Arab-Israeli struggle in the Middle East; and Europe, where the cold war began. Soviet Moscow's support for the UN multilateral force to end Iraqi occupation of Kuwait and its joint sponsorship of the Middle East conference in Madrid were symptomatic of a complete turnabout in Soviet thinking and behavior, which has been made more ambiguous by the nationalistic regime of Boris Yeltsin. The failure of the coup d'état in August 1991 also suggests that this revolutionary shift in Russian foreign policy enjoys domestic support, although its long-term stability depends on the success of the economic and political reforms now under way in Russia and among the other republics of the former Soviet Union.

There appears to be a need for new thinking in the West to match the break of the Soviet Union and of Russia with the past. If expectations of rational calculation may be said to explain much of U.S.-Soviet cooperative behavior during the cold war, despite their ideological divergence, insufficient attention is now given to exploiting those underlying factors that induced important segments of the Soviet leadership to abandon the cold war system, to induce internal political and economic reform, and to promote integral over threat-based cooperation with the West. The narrow rationality of the cold war that was based on authoritarian rule at home as a precondition for the expansion of Soviet power abroad proved no longer politically sustainable.[22] Tight internal political control, a centralized planned economy, and an expansionist foreign policy retarded Soviet economic and technological development. Only resolution of the cold war and reconciliation with the West could establish the conditions for internal reform and access to western economic assistance, technological know-how, and markets to ensure the reform's success.

Before Russia can assume an effective role in regional conflict reduction, its political unity and economic development must first be assured and its fledgling democratic institutions strengthened. Otherwise it may well become more a part of the problem of regional conflicts than a solution to them. These political imperatives lead, then, to the ironic conclusion that the assignment of an important role for Russia in slowing and settling regional conflicts is a critical support of its leadership role among the other former republics of the Soviet Union. Now tamed as revolutionary force, its internal political and economic cohesion depends to an important, if imprecisely calculable, degree on its treatment by the United States and the West as a power of consequence to ensure its ability to play that role. It is at once, as suggested earlier, in the unenviable position of France of 1815 and 1945—a defeated revolutionary power whose national cohesion partly depends on its reintegration within the international community as a great power.

What appears imperative if regional cooperation in the developing world is to be fostered is that Russia's position in Europe itself be first stabilized. The security functions performed by the cold war system, described above, in keeping the European peace and in fostering the economic development, at least in its western half, must be assumed by a new European regional system that has yet to be created, within a global system of cooperative security. This new European order cannot be achieved in response to a Soviet threat that no longer exists, nor can it be won in the long run at the expense of the peoples of Russia and the other Slavic and Asian republics. The new imperatives of European security argue for the transformation of the threat-based cooperation of the cold war in Europe by a new system in which Russia, the Ukraine, and Belarus are integrated within the system of western democratic states. If captured and channeled, the powerful reformist forces now abroad in the former Soviet Union can be integrated within a security and economic developmental framework aimed at creating incentives for all the states and peoples of Europe to a global cooperative security system. Achieving long-term regional security, economic growth, and democratic development will depend then on whether Russia is helped by the West to play a key role as an equal to the other European powers, including the United States, in working toward these objectives. For example, the $24 billion aid package provided by the International Monetary Fund in 1992 and brokered by Washington and Bonn is a start, but only a down payment on what promises to be a long, generational recovery program.

The system's institutional structure must obviously be rethought. NATO's great asset is its military might, but it cannot long be maintained with no clear and present danger. Nor can it long survive simply to monitor and check German power. An alliance divided against itself cannot stand. On the other hand, the European Union has no military force and includes at least one neutral state. The accession to membership of the neutral states of Sweden, Finland, and Austria can only further dilute its potential security role in the near future. The controversy over the formation of a Franco-German corps within the European Union, but under the aegis of members who are also parties to the Western European Union, has had more the effect of splitting the members of the Union than uniting them around the idea of a European army whose creation, as the British fear, might invite the departure of American forces.[23] Moreover, the Union's impotence in arresting the Yugoslav crisis makes it a doubtful candidate as substitute for NATO as Europe's guarantor.

The Organization on Security and Cooperation in Europe (OSCE) is the only organization that includes all European states as well as the United States and Canada as European powers. This institutional creation of the cold war, a product of East-West cooperation, has shown remarkable resilience. The Paris summit of European states, which led to the signing of the CFE treaty in November 1990, also established a crisis center and created a small secretariat to give greater form and continuity to the organization. With more than fifty members—a veritable mini-UN—the OSCE is obviously too weak to be little more than a framework within which the major European states can discuss joint measures aimed at creating a shared and mutually supportive security system. What is critical is that the OSCE already exists; it does not have to be invented.

Among its important assets is that it already possesses institutional form, enjoys broad regional legitimacy, identifies the United States as a European power, and extends the United Nations charter to Europe in fostering regional security.

There would appear to be no necessarily insurmountable barrier to Russia's entry into NATO as a natural consequence of NATO's strategy of a "Partnership for Peace" between the states of the former rival military blocs. An enlarged NATO could then become the enforcement arm of a renovated OSCE. This idea is not as implausible as it may first appear, when viewed alongside the substantial cuts in weapons agreed to by Washington and Moscow that, earlier, would have been thought impossible and even dangerous. Within such a framework, the major powers, representing democratic peoples from Vladivostok to Vancouver, would become the permanent members of a newly formed European Security Council, patterned on the United Nations. Responsibility for the security of the Northern Hemisphere would then devolve to this group of states, including the United States, the Russian Federation, Canada, Germany, France, Britain, and Italy. The council would be expected to play several roles filled formerly (and imperfectly) by the cold war system: (a) the creation of a stable and legitimate security regime in Europe, resting on the recognition not only of the relative power of its members but also of their special concerns and interests; (b) the monitoring and management of national and ethic rivalries by the major states; (c) the elaboration of principles and values governing conflict reduction; and (d) the bolstering of the regional security systems of developing states.

The general assembly of the OSCE would be composed of all member-states. Nonpermanent members of the European security council would be elected on a rotating basis to complete the membership of the council, which would have special responsibility for European security. The peoples of the former Warsaw Pact and NATO as well as former neutral states would be joined together in a security system of their own construction, and not pitted against one another or limited to the narrow band of coerced cooperation that competing alliances induce, but which they necessarily are unable to surmount.

Russia's reintegration within an expanded European security system is a precondition for its effective contribution to solving regional conflicts in the Southern Hemisphere. Russia has already contributed much to regional stability by withdrawing support from parties to regional conflicts. It has also utilized its its good offices to bring belligerents to the bargaining table, while cautioning former clients such as Iraq and the PLO to be more conciliatory. These cooperative initiatives and those achieved during the cold war era need to be codified, first of all, to guide future efforts toward consolidating and advancing regional cooperation among local opponents. Even if regional rivals define their security and economic and political development as a function of their conflicts—and hatreds—Moscow and Washington are not obliged to maintain a hostile relationship in assisting regional friends, nor to abandon the effort to define a common approach to a regional conflict.

Second, the imposition of security regimes on regional powers against their will is not likely to work unless, as in Desert Storm and as absent in Bosnia, they are supported by the great powers and by a preponderance of local sentiment that views outside intervention as a lesser evil than continued regional hostilities. One clear lesson of the cold war experience is that national security and economic development can be assured only within appropriate multilateral frameworks. No regional security regime today can be accurately described, much less explained, as the product of any two powers. The distribution of power—and consequently of a provisional order—within a region is the consequence of the alignments of states and peoples within and outside the region. As the bargaining over peace in the Middle East, Angola, Mozambique, Cambodia, and Korea in the post-cold war era makes clear, there can be no peace without the participation and say of all interested parties. Otherwise, the disenfranchised to the bargaining have powerful incentive to exercise their veto, as often as not by appealing to violence to make their voices heard.[24]

As the Soviet experience reveals, economic growth and the spread of democratic values and human rights depend on the assistance of other states and the cooperative workings of world markets. These latter two levels of the long-term multilateral development of a stable and prosperous international system do not operate in a vacuum. No state can progress on these fronts unless it proceeds on both at the same time and in cooperation with other states and peoples who are at more advanced levels of economic and political development. The mix of states needed to achieve regional security regimes, principally based on the availability of military force to the actors in a region, are not necessarily the same set of states required to foster economic and democratic development. Russia's reversal of alliances on the Korean peninsula and its overtures to Japan for economic assistance, setting the stage for a resolution of the Kurile Island dispute, illustrate the complex sets of actors and resources that must be grouped in the pursuit of an effective geopolitical and economic strategy if positive returns on regional realignments are to be made that foster regional order, welfare, and democratization.

.   .   .

The cold war afforded opportunities for U.S-Soviet regional cooperation. These instances and the tissue of understandings that arose from them depended on the compromises that resulted from their countervailing power and the costs and risks that they incurred in intervening abroad. Such a network of cooperation necessarily rested on the shaky ground of mistrust and misperception and was daily threatened by the temptation of each rival-partner to exploit opportunities to expand its influence and power at the expense of its principal opponent. The end of the cold war provides a historic opportunity to place U.S.-Russian regional cooperation on an entirely new and more stable basis. The growing if still fragile convergence of their economic and political interests creates the nascent conditions for the development of a shared framework of cooperative security. Although the West must condemn the inept and brutal suppression of the revolt in Chechnya, it must also be alert to the security dangers arising if the Russian state disintegrates.

Progress toward integrative over threat-based cooperation depends, however, on the preservation of Russia as a centralized political body and economic unit. Assigning an important but multilateralized security role for Russia in Europe and assigning significant peacekeeping responsibilities in dampening local conflicts would contribute to its preservation as a unified state, and would strengthen its traditional leadership role among the peoples of the former Soviet Union and of Eastern Europe. Preoccupied by arduous economic and political reforms at home, Moscow is hardly prepared, any more than a defeated France after 1815 or 1945, to assume today a big power role in coping with regional conflict. In the long run, however, Russia, possessed of an energetic and talented people and rich resources, will assuredly return as a great power, as it has before. It will then assume a role in proportion to these assets. The choice facing the western coalition is whether to await this resumption of Russia's multiple regional roles on the bases of a defunct balance of power and threat-based system or, as with a defeated France, to prepare for its reentry by integrating Russian power within a cooperative framework based on mutual interests and a shared international responsibility to keep the peace.

Notes

1. This discussion is largely drawn from Kanet and Kolodziej, eds. *The Cold War as Cooperation*, esp. 3–30, 405–14, and *Coping with Conflict after the Cold War*, ed. Edward A. Kolodziej and Roger E. Kanet (Baltimore: Johns Hopkins Univ. Press, 1995).

2. The theoretical basis for two different notions of cooperation is adapted from Kenneth Boulding's seminal work on power. See his *Three Faces of Power* (Newbury Park, Calif.: Sage, 1989).

3. See Paul Schroeder's analysis of the European concert system, in his articles "The Nineteenth Century System: Balance of Power or Political Equilibrium?" *Review of International Studies* 15, no. 2 (1989): 135–53, and "The Nineteenth Century International System: Changes in Structure," *World Politics* 39, no. 1 (Oct. 1986): 1–26.

4. The concept of an international society of states is drawn from Hedley Bull, *The Anarchical Society: A Study of Order in World Politics* (London: Macmillan, 1977).

5. This is an underlying theme of de Gaulle's war memoirs and of his later speeches and discourses as president of the Fifth Republic. See my *French International Policy under de Gaulle and Pompidou: The Politics of Grandeur* (Ithaca, N.Y.: Cornell Univ. Press, 1974), esp. chap. 1.

6. The rise of an international society of states is developed at length in Hedley Bull and Adam Watson, eds. *The Expansion of International Society* (Oxford: Clarendon, 1985), esp. 13–32, 117–26, and 217–28. Bull summarizes these lapses and contradictions in superpower behavior in his essay on the revolt of the developing world against the West, 217–28.

7. Ibid., 226.

8. John Gaddis, *The Long Peace: Inquiries into the History of the Cold War* (New York: Oxford Univ. Press, 1987).

9. This argument is persuasively advanced in Anton DePorte, *Europe Between the Superpowers* (New Haven, Conn.: Yale Univ. Press, 1979). Despite the unanticipated end of the cold war in ways not foreseen by scholars and policymakers, DePorte's analysis of the German question and European security is still useful for an understanding of the security problematic in Europe today.

10. For an extended review of U.S.-Soviet cooperation, consult Galia Golan, "Superpower Cooperation in the Middle East," in Kanet and Kolodziej, eds. *The Cold War as Cooperation*, 121–46.

11. Ibid., 138.

12. Barry Buzan, *People, States, and Fear*, 2d ed. (Boulder, Colo.: Lynne Rienner, 1991), 189–90.

13. The principal impact of the Korean War was on Europe. It led specifically to the creation of NATO, the military arm of the Atlantic Alliance, the creation of multilateral command (SHAPE) with an American at its head, German rearmament, and the permanent stationing of United States troops on the continent.

14. The Northeast and Southeast Asian security systems, and in particular the changes initiated by the Soviet Union into both systems, are outlined in my "The Multilaterization of Regional Security in Southeast and Northeast Asia: The Role of the Soviet Union," *Pacific Focus* 6, no. 1 (1991): 5–38. For a sympathetic Japanese perspective, see Masaru Tamamoto, "Japan's Search for a World Role," *World Policy Journal* 7, no. 3 (1990): 493–520.

15. John Foster Dulles, "The Evolution of Foreign Policy," *Department of State Bulletin* 30, no. 761 (25 Jan. 1954): 107ff.

16. Samuel Kim outlines these cooperative moves in "Superpower Cooperation in Northeast Asia," Kanet and Kolodziej, eds. *The Cold War as Cooperation*, 367–404.

17. Zartman, *Ripe for Resolution*, chap. 6

18. The structure of this system is discussed at greater length in my "Multilateralization of Regional Security," 30–35, n. 14.

19. The theoretical framework underlying this analysis of cooperation and its possi-

bilities derives from the debate over the limits of the rational actor model to explain the behavior of states. This analysis departs in two fundamental ways from the analysis of Robert Axelrod's seminal work and of the *World Politics* symposium on cooperation. This analysis emphasizes the role of experience—or the shadow of the past—and the role of third states in widening the scope and deepening the commitments of the United States and the Soviet Union to cooperate. See n. 1 for a rehearsal of this debate and relevant citations.

20. See the chapters by Janice Gross Stein on the 1973 war in Robert Jervis et al., *Psychology and Deterrence* (Baltimore: Johns Hopkins Univ. Press, 1985), 34–88, and Richard B. Parker, *The Politics of Miscalculation in the Middle East* (Bloomington: Indiana Univ. Press, 1993).

21. Roger E. Kanet outlines the principal elements of new thinking in *The Cold War as Cooperation*, 90–120. In the same volume, Victor Kremenyuk illustrates new thinking in practice, 31–64. For a discussion of the military dimensions of new thinking, consult Raymond L. Garthoff, *Deterrence and the Revolution in Soviet Military Doctrine* (Washington, D.C.: Brookings Institution, 1990).

22. On this score, George F. Kennan's understanding of the sources of Soviet foreign-policy behavior was proven essentially correct. See his Mr. "X" article, "The Sources of Soviet Conduct," *Foreign Affairs* 25, no. 4 (1947): 566–82.

23. *Le Monde, Sélection Hebdomadaire*, 9–16 Oct. 1991, 8.

24. These points are elaborated in my "U.S.-Soviet Cooperation: The Role of Third States," *The Annals of the American Academy of Political and Social Science* 518 (Nov. 1991): 118–31.

15

Mechanisms of Conflict Resolution

During the cold war, both the United States and the USSR demonstrated repeatedly their ability to become involved in and exacerbate many conflicts in the Third World. Indeed, superpower involvement in these conflicts, ranging from supplying arms to full-fledged military intervention, was one of the most active and dynamic elements of their competition.

During Mikhail Gorbachev's primacy, Soviet-American competition in the Third World was greatly reduced, if not completely eliminated. Under Gorbachev, the United States and the USSR achieved an unprecedented degree of mutual cooperation with regard to several regional conflicts, including those in Afghanistan, Cambodia, Central America, southern Africa, and the Persian Gulf. With the breakup of the USSR, Russian-American cooperation in many areas, including the Third World, has increased.

Yet despite the end of the cold war and increased Russian-American cooperation in conflict resolution, conflict continues in many regions of the Third World. One reason for this is that while previous Soviet-American involvement exacerbated regional conflict, the United States and the USSR did not cause it. The causes of these conflicts were local disputes and grievances, which did not disappear with the end of the cold war. Another reason for the persistence of regional conflict is that the local antagonists often have massive arsenals provided by the superpowers and others in the past, which enable them to continue fighting. Possessed with both the motive and the means to fight, the local antagonists can

315

and will continue to do battle—especially in those cases where they continue to receive arms from external sources.

Can the United States and Russia act together to successfully resolve regional conflict, as opposed to simply disengaging themselves from it? A basic prerequisite to their being able to do so is that both of them *want* to resolve regional conflict. Little progress toward superpower conflict resolution can be expected if this is not the aim of one or both superpowers. This basic prerequisite is now present and seems likely to remain so indefinitely with regard to the Third World.

However, the will to resolve regional conflict by the United States and Russia alone is not sufficient to bring it about. This chapter will examine the strengths and weaknesses of various mechanisms to resolve conflicts that the two superpowers either have employed or could employ in the future.

. . .

I. William Zartman and others have concluded that a propitious opportunity for conflict arises when a "hurting stalemate" occurs. A hurting stalemate is a situation in which the antagonists in a conflict all realize that they cannot defeat their opponents militarily, and that their own strength will increasingly diminish if the conflict is prolonged. A hurting stalemate may not necessarily result in a conflict being resolved, but it can lead to a "ripe moment" when the antagonists realize that they would be better off by agreeing to a peaceful compromise ending the conflict than by continuing the fight.

Each of the mechanisms of superpower conflict resolution discussed here will be evaluated for its utility in bringing about a hurting stalemate, a ripe moment, and hence, conflict resolution. In general, there are six mechanisms of conflict resolution the superpowers have used or could employ: (1) the withdrawal of foreign forces; (2) the mutual cessation of military assistance; (3) joint diplomatic initiatives; (4) mutual cooperation in holding elections or plebiscites; (5) the joint sanctioning of military intervention; and (6) collaboration with international organizations.

The Withdrawal of Foreign Forces

Besides the downfall of Marxism in Eastern Europe, a dramatic indication that the cold war era had ended was Soviet-American cooperation to bring about the withdrawal of foreign armed forces from three regional conflicts. In April 1988, a series of accords were signed that led to the withdrawal of Soviet forces from Afghanistan; this process was completed in February 1989. In December 1988, agreements concerning Angola and Namibia were signed that led to the withdrawal of South African forces from Angola and Namibia as well as Namibia's independence in 1990, and the complete withdrawal of Cuban forces from Angola by mid-1991. Although not the subject of a formal agreement, Vietnam withdrew its troops from Cambodia by September 1989.

The primary benefit of withdrawing foreign forces (whether they belong to a superpower or its allies) has been to lessen regional conflict as a source of tension in Moscow-Washington relations. During the cold war, America feared that Soviet, Cuban, and Vietnamese troops in Afghanistan, Angola, and Cambodia threatened to lead not only to consolidating pro-Soviet Marxist regimes in these countries but also to enabling the USSR to use these countries as bases to more easily undermine pro-western governments in important neighboring countries. Soviet intervention in Afghanistan led to a halt in progress toward Soviet-American arms control for many years.

The announcement that Communist armed forces would withdraw from Afghanistan, Angola, and Cambodia and the completion of that withdrawal was important to the renewal of Moscow-Washington détente. The United States no longer feared Moscow's expansionism in the Third World. These withdrawals also helped end the USSR's isolation from the West.

Despite these benefits, the withdrawal of foreign armed forces from regional conflicts has not been notably successful in resolving those conflicts. Conflict has continued in Afghanistan, Angola, and Cambodia. Only in Namibia was conflict resolved.

Conflict resolution did not occur in Afghanistan, Angola, and Cambodia as a result of the withdrawal of foreign forces, because this step alone did not result in a hurting stalemate. In both cases, all or part of the opposition forces against pro-Soviet-Marxist regimes concluded that their prospects for achieving military victory were enhanced by the withdrawal of Communist armed forces. This was especially true in Afghanistan: both the mujahideen and their external supporters (including the United States) expected the Najib regime to collapse shortly after Moscow's troop withdrawal was completed in February 1989. Even after it did collapse in April 1992, war has continued as factions among the former rebels have escalated the conflict among themselves. In Cambodia, the Chinese-backed Khmer Rouge saw the withdrawal of Vietnamese troops not as an opportunity for conflict resolution but for militarily defeating the Phnom Penh regime, which Hanoi had sought to maintain in power. In Angola, the opposition National Union for the Total Independence of Angola (UNITA) at first saw the gradual withdrawal of Cuban troops as an opportunity to strengthen its hand vis-à-vis the Popular Movement for the Liberation of Angola (MPLA).

The perception by antigovernment forces that the withdrawal of foreign forces had weakened the Marxist regimes in these conflicts did not contribute to a hurting stalemate. In each case, the opposition saw their own prospects for military victory as greatly enhanced by the withdrawal of foreign forces; they did not see themselves as "hurting" at all by this step.

In addition, while Communist armed forces were withdrawn from Afghanistan, Angola, and Cambodia, the local antagonists in all three conflicts at first continued to receive large-scale arms transfers from the United States, the USSR, and other countries. With these massive arms transfers, the local antagonists did not see themselves in a hurting stalemate. They either thought they could use these arms to achieve victory over their opponents or at minimum avoid being defeated by them.

There are other regional conflicts to which neither the superpowers nor their allies sent combat forces (or, at least, not very many) but were heavily involved in otherwise. One such conflict—Nicaragua—was largely resolved; many others have not been. Clearly, the withdrawal of foreign forces is not relevant to resolving these conflicts.

Despite how it has improved Moscow-Washington relations, the withdrawal of foreign armed forces from regional conflicts by itself did not bring about a hurting stalemate in those conflicts. Although the side that foreign forces had supported may seek peaceful conflict resolution to avoid being defeated, the other side is likely to see the withdrawal as an opportunity to achieve military victory. If both sides continue to receive substantial military assistance from other countries, neither may see itself in a hurting stalemate. Other measures are needed to bring this about.

The Mutual Cessation of Military Assistance

If the United States and Russia cut off the supply of arms to the local antagonists in a regional conflict, this would obviously be an important step in creating a hurting stalemate between them. If the local antagonists cannot obtain additional arms, their ability to fight effectively will decline. However, cutting off the supply of arms to the local antagonists in a regional conflict is an extraordinarily difficult task.

There are now fewer obstacles than ever before to the United States and Russia agreeing to mutually cease arms transfers to antagonists in regional conflicts. Yet even if such Russian-American agreements are reached, they will not necessarily lead to conflict resolution.

One problem is that a mutual cessation of arms transfers by the superpowers does not necessarily limit equally the local antagonists' ability to continue fighting, as seen in Somalia, Afghanistan, Angola, and Cambodia. One side may possess a much larger arsenal than the other. A mutual cessation of military assistance by the superpowers, then, might leave one of the local antagonists able to defeat its opponent (or at least think it can).

A more important problem is that even if the United States and Russia can agree upon a mutual cessation of military assistance, other countries may be willing to arm one or more of the local antagonists. This could prevent a hurting stalemate. Third-party military assistance, though, will not necessarily do this. There are not many countries that are willing and able to transfer large quantities of weapons to Third World clients for free on a long-term basis, as the United States and the USSR did in the past.

After the cutoff of American arms transfers to the Nicaraguan contras and Soviet arms transfers to the Sandinistas, Cuba continued to ship arms to the Sandinistas. Thanks in part to Soviet diplomacy, Cuba did not ship enough arms to the Sandinistas so that they felt they were strong enough to avoid holding free elections or disregard their results when they lost.[1] In this case, nonsuperpower arms shipments did not prevent a hurting stalemate or a ripe moment for conflict resolution.

In general, though, protecting a hurting stalemate in regional conflicts from the influence of third-party arms transfers will be difficult in most cases and may be impossible in some. In El Salvador, the arms flow to the leftist guerrillas was greatly reduced by the change of government in Nicaragua and the decline of Moscow's interest in Central America. Cuba, however, continued to ship some arms to the guerrillas through the Sandinista army over which the new Nicaraguan government exercised only limited control.[2] It must be emphasized, though, that external arms supplies to the Farabundo Martí National Liberation Front (FMLN) guerrillas were substantially reduced while large-scale American arms transfers to the Salvadoran government continued.

As a result, the Salvadoran government (especially the Salvadoran army) did not see itself in a hurting stalemate after the electoral defeat of the Sandinistas in 1990. Initially, the Salvadoran military saw itself in a better position than ever to defeat the guerrillas by force of arms. After months of fruitless counterinsurgency efforts, however, the Salvadoran government apparently decided that it could not defeat the rebels militarily. At the end of 1991, the government and the FMLN agreed to peacefully resolve their conflict.

America was largely uninvolved in Ethiopia's civil war while Moscow had disengaged itself from it by the beginning of 1991. The conflict there, however, continued. The Eritreans, Tigrayans, and other regionally based forces fighting the Mengistu regime did not see themselves in a hurting stalemate. Instead, they saw the end of Soviet military support to Addis Ababa as providing them with an opportunity to completely overthrow the Mengistu regime—which is what they did. Although the then-rebel forces were receiving some arms from Arab sources, their main source of weapons were those that they captured from the demoralized Ethiopian army. The new government which came to power in Addis Ababa allowed Eritrea to peacefully secede from Ethiopia. Ethnic tensions, however, persist between the Tigrayan-dominated government and other ethnic groups in Ethiopia.

Yet while the superpowers could not peacefully resolve the conflict between the Mengistu regime and the forces opposed to it, Washington was able to arrange for the peaceful surrender of Addis Ababa to the rebel forces, thus avoiding a bloody battle, which the Mengistu regime could not have won and which would have resulted in many civilian casualties.[3]

A Moscow-Washington agreement to halt arms transfers to their respective allies in Afghanistan by the beginning of 1992 was reached shortly after the failed August 1991 Soviet coup attempt. The mujahideen, however, continued to receive arms from Saudi Arabia, Pakistan, and Iran, and so did not see themselves in a hurting stalemate. Hence, they pressed their attack against the Najib regime until it succumbed in April 1992, and then, turning against each other, continued the fratricidal combat.

In Cambodia, a mutual cessation of military assistance by the superpowers to the local antagonists not only failed to bring about a hurting stalemate but could also facilitate military victory by the genocidal Khmer Rouge. The Khmer Rouge has shown little interest in a peaceful settlement on terms that would not allow it to regain full power. China continued to supply the Khmer Rouge with large quantities of weapons after Vietnamese forces withdrew from Cambodia in September 1989, and after the Chinese government claimed it had stopped arms shipments to the Khmer Rouge in September 1990.[4] The Khmer Rouge is far from seeing itself in a hurting stalemate; this continued Chinese aid has resulted in its anticipating that it can achieve military victory. Unless the superpowers can persuade China to halt its military assistance to the

Khmer Rouge, or persuade Thailand to stop allowing the Khmer Rouge to operate from Thai territory, a hurting stalemate is unlikely to arise. Because of China's hatred of Vietnam and Thailand's fear of offending China, these events are highly unlikely. Thus the superpowers could attempt to create a hurting stalemate through arming the pro-Vietnamese regime in Phnom Penh. Because of the many changes that have occurred in the former USSR, Moscow may be less willing to do this. The United States has been unwilling to take any actions that might help Vietnam or annoy China even though the larger context in which Washington has pursued its Indochina policy has changed dramatically.

Domestic politics within the superpowers may also present an obstacle to a mutual cessation of military assistance by the United States and the USSR to the local antagonists in a regional conflict. A prime example is the Arab-Israeli conflict. Large-scale American arms transfers to Israel and Soviet arms transfers to Syria allowed these two countries to avoid the hurt in the stalemate between them, and between the Israelis and the Palestinians. Moscow has drastically cut back its arms transfers to Syria, but Damascus already possesses an enormous arsenal. Although American public support for Israel has declined in recent years, it is highly doubtful that American domestic politics would ever allow the United States to reduce its military assistance to Israel to the point where Tel Aviv saw itself in a hurting stalemate necessitating a peaceful settlement. Ironically, domestic politics within Russia may force Moscow to continue its support for the Arab cause. Russia's large Muslim population may insist on continuing Russian military aid to the Arabs. A democratic Russian government might continue aiding the Arab cause at its insistence for the sake of domestic peace inside Russia, if the current promising Arab-Israeli peace effort breaks down.

Another obstacle to the effectiveness of a mutual cessation of superpower military assistance is that some countries are largely independent of the superpowers and other countries for their weapons. India, for example, produces much of its own weaponry. An attempt to isolate India from foreign sources of arms in an Indo-Pakistani conflict would probably have little effect on New Delhi's war-making ability, especially if the conflict was short. Other Third World countries are also becoming relatively self-sufficient in arms production, which could result in their becoming increasingly immune to any effort to isolate them from foreign sources of weapons.

Superpower cooperation to isolate local antagonists from external sources of arms may be an essential element in creating a hurting stalemate, but will obviously be difficult to achieve in most cases. Something more is needed to persuade third countries and the local antagonists to stop fighting. To do this, some Russian-American diplomatic initiative is also necessary.

Joint Diplomatic Initiatives

In a conversation I once had with Chester A. Crocker, the assistant secretary of state for African Affairs during the Reagan administration, he explained how he convinced all the relevant parties to agree to the December 1988 Angola/Namibia accords. He indicated that the parties involved did not finally agree out of any sense of idealism or devotion to peace. They agreed because they eventually became convinced that a peaceful resolution to the conflict would better serve their interests than would continued warfare. Such a realization occurred in other cases where progress toward conflict resolution has been achieved. Conflict resolution in the future is also likely to occur only when all the parties involved see it as serving their interests.

The realization by the two superpowers that they each have an interest in resolving a conflict is clearly a prerequisite to their working cooperatively toward conflict resolution. A joint diplomatic initiative to resolve regional conflict can take several different forms: Washington and Moscow working actively together, one taking the initiative while the other plays a supporting role, or one or both encouraging their allies to lead the resolution process. Whatever form it takes, the basic function that a Russian-American initiative performs is to demonstrate to all other parties concerned that none of them can take advantage of superpower rivalry to gain their support for continuing the conflict.

For even without active superpower military involvement, third countries can continue to arm the local antagonists in regional conflicts. Without more positive inducements, an effort by the superpowers to isolate the local antagonists from external sources of weaponry will not necessarily succeed. It is also the task of a joint superpower diplomatic initiative to provide those inducements, or in other words, to help transform a hurting stalemate into a ripe moment for conflict resolution.

There are two elements to this task: persuading third parties to reduce their involvement and persuading the local antagonists to resolve their dispute. Neither of these aims is easy to achieve, though the first one may be less difficult. Although the United States and Russia may not be able to prevent third countries from supplying arms to their allies in a regional conflict, the superpowers can take action to limit their effectiveness. If, for example, a third country persists in arming one side, the superpowers can arm others until the third country realizes that increased arms shipments to its ally will not lead to military victory but only prolonged conflict. The superpowers can also raise the diplomatic and other costs that third countries must pay for their continued intervention. On the positive side, the superpowers may be able to convince third countries that their legitimate security concerns will be respected through cooperation in the conflict settlement and that this is the only way they will be secured. If the conflict continues, they will continue to experience its costs without meeting their goals.

Whether or not third countries can be persuaded to work for regional conflict resolution, it can occur if the dispute between the local antagonists is resolved. On the other hand, the dispute between the local antagonists will not necessarily be resolved even if all outside powers end their involvement. A hurting stalemate may come about, but not a ripe moment if the local antagonists still refuse to resolve their conflict because of complete mistrust among them. Even if a settlement among the local antagonists is reached, it can easily break down because of this mistrust.

An example of this may be the 1991 agreement between the Cambodian government and the tripartite opposition coalition. Each faction has agreed to disband 70 percent of its armed forces and put the rest under UN supervision. China and Vietnam, the primary backers of the contending factions in Cambodia, were the main external powers who arranged for this agreement. Washington and Moscow played only minimal roles.[5] The agreement probably does not reflect a genuine compromise among the local antagonists, but a compromise between Beijing and Hanoi, which have become increasingly fearful about what the downfall of communism in the Soviet Union means for their Communist regimes. It may also reflect Hanoi's willingness to sacrifice its allies in Cambodia in exchange for détente with China, for Vietnam is now unlikely to receive much assistance from Moscow or any other major power. Instead of peace, then, this agreement will probably lead only to further fighting or renewed Khmer Rouge domination in Cambodia.

Special attention, then, must be given to the method of resolving the conflict between the local antagonists.

Mutual Cooperation in Holding Elections or Plebiscites

Before Gorbachev, the Soviet Union did not promote free elections anywhere. Free elections now take place in many countries of the former Soviet bloc, including Russia itself. This has expanded the possibility of relying on elections to resolve conflict. Indeed, Washington and Moscow were able to promote the holding of elections as part of the process leading to the peaceful resolution of conflicts in Nicaragua and Namibia.

However, merely because resolving conflict through elections appears desirable to outside parties (including scholars) does not mean that the local antagonists will agree to hold them. For even if they recognize themselves to be in a hurting stalemate, several conditions need to be met before the contending parties agree to abide by the results of elections. These conditions are besides those necessary for a hurting stalemate and are really the prerequisites to creating the "ripe moment" for the resolution of civil wars.

The conditions necessary for holding elections to resolve conflict include: (1) confidence by all parties that the elections will be fair; (2) confidence by all parties that whoever emerges as the electoral victor will not seek to eliminate the losers politically or physically; (3) confidence by all parties (especially those likely to lose the election) that regularly scheduled elections will be held in the future that they have a reasonable chance of winning; and (4) a commitment by all parties to continue the political struggle by peaceful, democratic means, and to eschew violence. These conditions do not appear present in many civil wars.

Even if the United States and Russia can help bring about a hurting stalemate, they cannot necessarily create a ripe moment to resolve a conflict through elections. The United States and Russia cannot create trust among the local antagonists in a civil war. It is clearly difficult for trust to grow naturally among groups that have been fighting each other. The problem is compounded by the fact that none of these countries wracked by civil war has any experience with democracy. Convincing people, especially leaders, that they can benefit from democracy even if they lose the election is extraordinarily difficult when they have no experience with democracy and have no faith that it can work in their country.

Yet merely because a country has had no or limited experience with democracy does not mean that it cannot acquire it even after a civil war. After all, neither Nicaragua nor Namibia had any experience with democracy and yet free elections were held in both countries in 1990. It is possible that democracy may not survive in either country, but it is encouraging that two formerly authoritarian parties (the Sandinistas and the South West African People's Organization [SWAPO]) have come to accept it when they did not have to.

Successfully holding elections, however, does not guarantee the settlement of a conflict if the loser does not accept the results. This proved to be the case in both Angola and Cambodia. The UNITA leader, Jonas Savimbi, refused to accept his loss in the 1992 Angolan presidential elections, and resumed the civil war. In Cambodia, the Khmer Rouge resumed its war against the new coalition government shortly after the elaborate UN mechanism which oversaw the elections in 1993 was dismantled.

Despite these setbacks, there is a trend toward increasing democratization throughout the world which may also encourage the local antagonists fighting civil wars to see elections and democracy as viable for resolving their conflicts. Democratization spread throughout most of Latin America during the 1970s and 1980s. Its being accepted throughout the region may have encouraged the Sandinistas to accept it—or fear the loss of legitimacy resulting from refusing it—in Nicaragua.

Democratization has also made progress in the Far East (South Korea, the Philippines), South Asia (Nepal, Bangladesh—though retrogression may be occurring in Pakistan), Africa (Benin, Cape Verde), and most spectacularly, Eastern Europe and much of the former Soviet Union itself. The example of democratization occurring in Communist states has led many Third World Marxists to lose faith that authoritarian socialism can work in their countries and to become more tolerant of political and economic pluralism. The very fact that democratization is spreading and that many governments that previously spurned it are now embracing it may also increase the willingness of local antagonists in civil wars to accept democracy too.

Yet, although there may be some hope that contending parties in civil wars may accept elections to resolve conflict, it may be less likely that all the local antagonists in interstate conflicts or wars of secession will accept plebiscites. Unlike an electoral process, which is supposed to take place periodically, a plebiscite is designed to decide an issue once and for all. Thus, although the losing party can at least hope to do better in subsequent elections, the losing party in a plebiscite will lose completely.

There is often less uncertainty about the anticipated results of a plebiscite than an election. For example, if plebiscites were held in Arab territory occupied by Israel or in Indian-occupied Kashmir, the inhabitants would unquestionably vote to oust the occupying power. The Israeli and Indian governments fear that giving up these occupied territories would greatly increase the security problems they face. Despite progress toward Palestinian autonomy, many Israelis fear that relinquishing the occupied Arab territories will bring into question the survival of the Jewish state, and many Indians fear that allowing Kashmir to secede will lead to increasing demands by other regions for secession and to the breakup of India. As a result, the occupying powers in both cases have so far refused to hold plebiscites in these areas.

It is highly doubtful that the general trend toward democratization will positively affect these situations. Indeed, both Israel and India are democracies in which most of the voting population favors retaining these occupied territories despite the will of the territories' inhabitants. The United States and Russia may be unable to help resolve these conflicts until the occupying states see themselves in a fatally hurting stalemate—one in which continued occupation threatens their security even more than giving up the occupied territory would.

Although some governments are unlikely to allow plebiscites that will lead to part of the territory they control becoming independent, other governments may do so. The new government in Ethiopia agreed that a plebiscite on independence could be held in Eritrea. Moscow acquiesced to the independence of the non-Russian republics. Czechoslovakia split up peacefully, though a plebiscite was not held.

As a result of the precedent established by the peaceful secession of the non-Russian republics from the USSR, the appeal of secession will probably increase among those groups seeking it in other multinational states. Further, the example of the breakup of the USSR may enhance the legitimacy of secession efforts elsewhere as well as the illegitimacy of attempts to prevent secession by force.

Joint Sanctioning of Military Intervention

Washington and Moscow cooperated to an unprecedented degree in response to the Iraqi invasion of Kuwait and refusal to withdraw from it. Soviet-American cooperation in the United Nations Security Council contributed to the passage of twelve resolutions against Iraq, including one authorizing the use of force if Iraq did not withdraw voluntarily. Although the Soviet Union did not participate in combat against Iraq, this could not have been undertaken under UN Security Council auspices without Moscow's cooperation.

Could the United States and Russia cooperate again to jointly sanction military intervention against aggression? Because they cooperated in doing this once, they could do so again. The circumstances that led them to jointly sanction military intervention against Iraq, however, were exceptional and are unlikely to arise again frequently. First, Saddam Hussein was a particularly blatant aggressor. He used the pretext of the border dispute with Kuwait to invade and annex the entire country. Nor was it clear that he would stop there. An attack by one Third World country against another for more limited goals (such as to gain a region) would probably not elicit military intervention by the superpowers.

Even more exceptional than Saddam Hussein's aggressiveness and cruelty is the extraordinary economic and strategic importance of the Persian Gulf region, including Kuwait, to America and the West. There may be no other region in the Third World where the annexation of one nation by another would threaten western security interests as strongly as the Iraqi annexation of Kuwait.

Another problem is whether the United States and Russia would cooperate again to militarily reverse the annexation of one Third World state by another. If conservative forces in Russia succeed in gaining power, the two superpowers might be unwilling to cooperate in the UN Security Council, as was usually the case during the cold war. But even though Russian-American relations have cooled since 1991–92, Moscow and Washington do not seem likely to resume the competition for influence in the Third World that was a predominant theme in the cold war.

Instead, a more likely problem is that the United States, Russia, and the other permanent members of the Security Council can indeed agree on identifying and condemning aggression, but that none of them will be willing to send troops to reverse it. In other words, aggression by some Third World states against others in regions besides the Persian Gulf will not affect the interests of the great powers sufficiently so that they would undertake a massive effort to expel an invader as they did from Kuwait. Public opinion in the West and Russia probably would not necessarily tolerate large-scale intervention to halt aggression. Even the expectation of a relatively easy victory might not arouse public enthusiasm for intervention by any of the major powers, and there can be no guarantee that other aggressors will be as militarily incompetent as Saddam Hussein. Smaller-scale intervention to halt aggression may be easier to arrange, but even if this seemed likely to succeed, it would not be undertaken unless at least one major power saw its vital interests being threatened by the invasion.

As reprehensible as they would be, an Indian invasion of Bhutan, an Indonesian or Malaysian invasion of Singapore, a Senegalese invasion of the Gambia, or any other case in which a relatively powerful country could quickly and easily overrun a weak neighbor is simply unlikely to arouse the great powers the way the Iraqi invasion of Kuwait did. If the target nation is able to resist, the United States and Russia may cooperate in supplying it with some degree of military assistance against the aggressor. They are unlikely, however, to be willing or able to do anything about "splendid" invasions, which succeed before military assistance to the target nation can be organized.

Collaboration with International Organizations

In an era when Russian-American cooperation has increased so dramatically, the relationship between Moscow and Washington may be becoming a de facto alliance. Even if this alliance is more apparent than real, the perception that it exists may hinder Russian-American conflict resolution efforts, because various actors in the Third World might fear that superpower efforts at conflict resolution are an attempt to impose a joint condominium over them.

Although many in the West may dismiss such notions, there is a real possibility of their gaining currency in the Third World—where intellectual and public discussion of international relations often amounts to no more than a debate over rival conspiracy theories. If such theories about Moscow's and Washington's intentions gain credence among one or more of the antagonists in a regional conflict, the United States and Russia may be unable to help resolve that conflict.

Acting in close collaboration with the United Nations and regional organizations may help allay fears that superpower conflict resolution efforts are intended only to advance Russian and American interests at the expense of the Third World's.

The UN played a key role in bringing about the 1988 Angola/Namibia accords. An important reason SWAPO agreed to participate in national elections even though South African troops and administration remained in Namibia was the presence of the UN peacekeeping force. Condemning Iraq in twelve UN Security Council resolutions provided a much greater degree of legitimacy for military intervention against Iraq than it would have received otherwise.

Working with regional organizations is also important, because these can help raise the legitimacy of conflict resolution efforts among the states most immediately affected. In extreme cases, involving regional organizations can be crucial. It is questionable whether Saudi Arabia would have permitted even UN-sanctioned intervention against Iraq from its territory if Iraq had not been condemned by most of the members of the Arab League.

Working with regional organizations may contribute to successful conflict resolution efforts in other ways. Russian-American efforts to restrict arms transfers to the local antagonists from third parties may be greatly enhanced if such measures are backed by the relevant regional organization. Similarly, Russian-American diplomatic initiatives may have greater prospects for success if they are supported by it. In those cases where an attack occurs but the United States and Russia are unwilling to intervene, Russian-American support for intervention sponsored by a regional organization may be sufficient to contain or reverse aggression.

.   .   .

Russian-American efforts to resolve regional conflicts will encounter serious obstacles even if there is full cooperation between the superpowers. In the aftermath of the failed coup of August 1991, it may be tempting to assume that such full cooperation between Moscow and Washington will occur. It might not.

If another coup attempt should succeed at bringing a dictatorial regime (either Communist or non-Communist) to power in Moscow, there could be a setback in Russian-American relations. Even a dictatorship in Moscow, though, might seek good relations with America and the West and thus be willing to continue to work for conflict resolution in the Third World. Even the hard-line coup plotters of August 1991 expressed their desire for cooperative relations with the West. Third World governments and groups traditionally allied with Moscow, however, may hope that a successful coup would lead to a resumption of the cold war and a renewal of Soviet military and other assistance to them. This was clearly the hope of the governments and groups, such as Iraq, Libya, the Palestinians, Vietnam, and North Korea, that welcomed the August 1991 coup attempt. Though Russian-American relations might not return to the hostility of the cold war after a successful coup in Moscow, the relationship may become too unfriendly to allow close cooperation on Third World conflict resolution.

At this point, however, a successful coup in Moscow appears to be problematic. Despite the relatively peaceful breakup of the USSR, there are many territorial, ethnic, and other conflicts among and within the fifteen republics of the former USSR.[6]

Unless the relations among the former Soviet republics are managed very carefully, many more conflicts could break out among them. One of the results of this occurring is that Moscow will be too preoccupied with its own problems to cooperate with Washington on Third World conflict resolution. America and the West may face not only the task of resolving Third World conflict without help from Moscow but also the task of resolving conflict within the former Soviet Union. Managing both these tasks will not be easy.

Yet, even if relations among the former Soviet republics evolve peacefully and democracy takes root in Russia and elsewhere, cooperation between Moscow and Washington to resolve Third World conflicts will encounter the obstacles discussed here. It must be emphasized, though, that Washington and Moscow have already made good progress in this realm. If democratization proceeds in the former USSR, they may be able to further this progress. Where Russian-American efforts cannot resolve regional conflict, they may at least be able to either help reduce conflict or prevent it from spreading.

Notes

1. On the Soviet role in promoting peaceful conflict resolution in Nicaragua, see Kramer, "Anger, Bluff, and Cooperation," 35–45.

2. Lee Hockstader, "Sandinistas Charged in Missiles Sale," *Washington Post*, 3 Jan. 1991, and "Managua Says Salvador Rebels Will Return Arms," *New York Times*, 3 Feb. 1991.

3. Krauss, "Ethiopia's Leader Agrees to Give Up Capital."

4. Steven Erlander, "Khmer Rouge Get More China Arms," *New York Times*, 1 Jan. 1991. See also Rodney Tasker, "To Peking, for Peace," *Far Eastern Economic Review*, 18 July 1991.

5. Philip Shenon, "Cambodia Factions to Cut Forces 70%," *New York Times*, 28 Aug. 1991.

6. For an excellent map detailing the myriad border disputes among the republics and other subunits of the former USSR, see "Ethnicity and Political Boundaries in the Soviet Union," Office of the Geographer, U.S. Department of State, Mar. 1990.

16

Prospects for Cooperative Security and Conflict Reduction

VICTOR A. KREMENYUK AND I. WILLIAM ZARTMAN

This study has brought together two themes: the need to bring Russia, successor state to the Soviet Union, into a cooperative security concert of powers, and the need for that concert, in various roles, to work to reduce the conflicts that are wracking Third World regional systems in the absence of effective regional security regimes. The first argument is novel, the second is screamingly urgent.

Cooperative Security

In the last stages of the cold war, both superpowers came to the edge that was separating their rivalry in the Third World from possible partnership. There were agreements on Afghanistan, Namibia, and Angola, an active search for a formula for settlement in Cambodia and Mozambique, free elections in Nicaragua, and the downfall of dictators in Ethiopia and Somalia, not to speak of Eastern Europe. The Soviet Union and the United States were sponsoring eventually successful talks on the Middle East and, after the success of the UN coalition in the second Gulf war, were probing possibilities for arms control in the Third World.

Then the Soviet Union as an organized state and as a superpower in international relations disintegrated, before our astonished eyes. Its collapse had many unexpected consequences for the whole world, including the developing countries, not the least of which was its example as a precursor for other disintegrating states. It required the renegotiation of many of the agreements and understandings achieved between the United States and the USSR during the period of new thinking and raised legitimate questions both for the United States and for regional powers.

It was evident that in the post-cold war world, the United States was left as the only global power capable of assuming the role of an international sheriff in areas of world tension. For this purpose, the United States had the necessary material means (troops stationed in key areas, oceangoing navy, appropriate arms and military equipment), and the legal basis through alliance agreements, commitments in other international treaties, unilateral declarations, and other obligations that prescribed involvement in peace and security once they were endangered. There was ever a chance that the United States would fill the global vacuum, especially when President Bush raised the image of a new foreign-policy doctrine called the new world order.

Well-established international relations theories indicated—indeed, nearly predicted—precise outcomes to this situation. In the classical balance of power theory on which the realist school thrives, the basic mechanism is the reflex of leading states to ally against a rising hegemon.[1] While all analysis accepts that the United States is a declining hegemon, the results of the cold war, which leave it an uncontested superpower, also make it reappear with hegemonistic pretentions, especially when it dons its sheriff's role. The alliance reaction that the balance of power theory predicts need not be a firm military treaty; rather it will take the form appropriate to the challenge and, if need be, increase its response as the threat escalates. This response is exactly what has taken place in the increasingly integrating Europe as it grew restive in the early 1990s against American leadership in world events. The fact that the European Community, or even its Single Europe Act of 1986 which took effect in 1992 to make that Community a Union, predated the reemergence of the American hegemon does not invalidate the prediction; to the contrary. Abetted by the geographic separation of North America from Europe, it merely provides a convenient framework for a gradually increasing separatism of continental from American policies. Continental autonomy within the UN coalition during the second Gulf war, American-European friction in handling the Yugoslav crisis, and deadlock in handling major bilateral issues, such as the agricultural issue within the Uruguay Round of the GATT negotiations, all show a European response to the possibility of American hegemony.

Other responses follow, as the theory predicts. Because the balance is so delicate and debatable, those excluded by the move to alliance make their own counteralliance, for they see the alliance as the rising power. On the other hand, both the presumed hegemon and the alliance move to enlist outliers, including defeated powers, in an effect that has been called bandwagoning.[2] These two responses describe the policies of the United States and European states toward Russia upon the disintegration of the USSR. The United States has moved to tighten bilateral relations with the Russia of Boris Yeltsin, turning the cold war bipolar rivalry into partnership and pointedly overflying intervening Europe. Members of the EC, in reply, compete with the United States to recuperate Russia into a "Europe from the Atlantic to the Urals" through such means as the Franco-Russian Treaty of February 1990 and the European insistence on a high bailout contribution for the Russian economy and a high-cost Soviet reactor-safety plan. Such competing efforts to enlist Russia on one side or the other of the western partners are not close to fiercely antagonistic alliance rivalries, to be sure, but they are nonetheless policy thrusts of the 1990s clearly indicated by theory as well. The limited inclusion of Russia (and Eastern Europe) in a "partnership for peace" in NATO marks a momentary coordination of United States and European policies.

The outcomes of such policies are clearly visible too. Building on small perceptions, images, and responses, a balance-of-power-driven rivalry can split the global powers, destroy cooperation, nourish Third World conflict, and weaken global institutions such as the UN and GATT. Even if it does not arrive at a deep conflict between two military alliances, enlisting all the global powers into one camp or the other, it would certainly slow down constructive cooperation and let lesser conflicts grow large.

In the more recent cooperative theory on which the integrative school of international relations is based, the underlying dynamic is provided by the self-interested efforts of states to cooperate.[3] Cooperation initiated under the aegis of a hegemonic power will continue as long as it is in the interest of the subscribing parties, and will be perpetuated by both formal and informal institutional arrangements known as regimes.[4] Under this theory, there is a likelihood that the western alliance will perpetuate itself as its opponent falls away and western cooperation continues to serve its members' interests within a network of economic and even security regimes. Uncertain and unrewarding economic performance join defeated security interests to make Russia and Eastern Europe uninteresting under this approach.

Many events conform to this indication—less clear than a prediction

—in the middle 1990s. Although Russia and other former Communist states have joined multilateral economic institutions, Russia was initially refused entry into the G7 economic summit and has been unable to play a significant role in other economic cooperation schemes—other than as a receiver for debt relief.

The outcome of the scenario based on cooperation among the free-world leaders can be found in one of two directions. The optimistic option would see a gradual expansion of the cooperating group as new states join when they are fully competitive and able to contribute to the regime. The pessimistic scenario would see a victorious groups of states that closed ranks about its own cooperation, excluding former Second and Third World states and exacerbating the great North-South confrontation of the twenty-first century.[5] As usually happens, reality would be most likely a mixture of the two, with enough of the second to bring back the reality of the conflict over the new international economic order of the mid-1970s.

There is a fourth option for American foreign policy, one whose emphasis is both on renewed cooperation with Russia as heir apparent to the USSR in strategic matters and in the UN Security Council, and on multilateral efforts to cope with the North-South disparity and regional conflicts. This requires the United States to lead a cooperative security system that works closely with both the European countries and with Russia, avoiding a domineering position and overcoming the fissiparous frictions that arise so naturally. No theory indicates such a comprehensive policy as a natural occurrence, a fact that emphasizes the importance of will and wisdom as its source. Though this perspective has raised some doubts and skepticism in the United States and other countries over the evident signs of Russian weakness connected with its difficult economic position and growing political chaos, it is supported by the experience of 1815 in regard to France, as Kolodziej recalls, and of 1945 in regard to Germany.

Cooperative security means dampening Russian dissatisfaction and harnessing its potential for disruption by incorporating it in the concert of global states, in an enlarged G7 standing behind the UN Security Council or in a steering committee of an OSCE with extended functions. It means a collective response and responsibility for conflict reduction, as for economic cooperation, admitting various roles but under a joint coordination, in which an individual state's interest is seen served not by seeking out sides but by restoring a political framework for handling conflict. Its idea is based not only on a promise of constructive outcomes but also on an understanding that, as Kremenyuk's, Udalov's, and Vassiliev's chapters show, with its potential in economic development and political activism, Russia could soon—in three to five years—restore its capabilities in foreign policy and create problems for the United States if Washington does not work out in advance a formula for cooperation with Moscow within a global concert.

This fourth scenario is made even more compelling by the reappearance of yet another possible attitude for U.S. foreign policy in the mid-1990s, that of a widespread withdrawal role, of isolationism, of domestic-America-first mirroring the introversion also rising within the states of the former Soviet Union and the members of the European Union. The American public and business community showed greater concern over the state of the domestic economy and the outcome of domestic social issues, concerns that the Bush administration ignored and on which the Clinton administration developed an absolute fixation, abdicating any American leadership role. Such concerns raise difficult, even if not impossible, perspectives for direct U.S. involvement abroad, especially in situations not of vital importance to the United States, and impose additional leadership requirements on an American administration conscious of its global responsibilities. It is too easy to emulate the EU and Russia as they go the ways of their separate domestic preoccupations and foreign interests. Cooperative security requires leadership instead of hegemony and consensus on long-term common interests rather than short-term individual advantage.

Conflict Reduction

Even with the will established, the way is not always obvious. Bloody grass-roots conflict in the Third World hangs over the cold war's conclusion as the Kuwaiti oil smoke hung over the second Gulf war's victory. From Yugoslavia to Yemen from Somalia to Colombia, Third World fratricide evokes revulsion and incredulity, and a sense of helplessness. Where conflict managers formerly developed skills in dealing with interstate disputes, they now find themselves confronted with state disintegration and a congeries of gangs and warlords where there once was a Liberia or Lebanon, with Zaire and Nigeria awaiting their turn. Perhaps the most striking case was Yugoslavia, which reentered the Third World as it disintegrated amid severe political crisis and bloody civil war. In many places in the Middle East, Africa, the Far East, and the former Soviet area, states collapsed within a strikingly short time.[6] It has been possible to speak of a new map of conflicts, many reemerging in areas previously contained under the cold war system of world order.

Regional conflict is not only a humanitarian crisis but also a serious threat to world stability. The problem is not merely that hopes for a new harmony have proven false, but that without some sort of management by the global powers the international system could as easily disintegrate as did the USSR and Yugoslavia themselves. This could lead to a global catastrophe that would eventually damage the American and European economies, which have become highly interdependent with the outside world. The specter of a new world war through the "Sarajevo scenario" of escalating foreign involvement sucked into a disintegrating state is no longer dismissed as irrelevant or fantastic.

In this sense, reduction of regional conflicts can only continue to be an important political goal for the global community. Whoever assumes the task of reducing such conflicts, whatever mechanisms can be suggested to implement the policy, it is understood that without the United States, Russia, Britain, France, and others, as the permanent members of the UN Security Council, as the largest suppliers of arms, and as the most reliable centers responsible for world security, the goal of reducing conflicts, isolating participation, avoiding escalation, working for reconciliation, and preventing further outbreaks could not be achieved.

The general analyses and specific area studies in this collection have emphasized a number of ways in which a global cooperative security system can contribute to regional conflict reduction, referring particularly to values and roles. The realm of *values, standards, and principles* is particularly important, in two directions—for the intervenors and for the outcomes. As in any security regimes, standards are needed for the intervenors, to regulate the expectations both of the other global states and of the targets, so that both will know the limits of the intervention and not react prematurely against unknown excesses. Making explicit tacit limitations, such as governed cold war relations, as identified in Kolodziej's chapter,[7] or extending UN peacekeeping forces' self-imposed limitations,[8] or providing clear signals to inform and coordinate actions, as noted in the Lyons, Vasilkov, and Thornton and Bratersky chapters,[9] are also ways—among others—of dealing with the need for standards for intervenors, lest their efforts to reduce conflict contribute instead to its escalation.

Similarly, values, standards, and principles are needed to guide the efforts of parties and intervenors toward outcomes that contribute to more stable and desirable situations. The most important are the principles of democracy listed in Katz's chapter and discussed in application by Vasilkov and Lyons, the ground rules for intrastate conflicts of replacement. As these principles clearly indicate, democracy is more than just the mechanics of free and fair elections; it is a broader condition and even a state of mind that considers a loyal opposition a permanent part of the political system, not outside of it.

Equally important but far less clearly stated as yet is the principle governing the other side of the exercise of self-determination, the limits on intrastate conflicts of secession. In Woodrow Wilson's Fourteen Points after World War I, self-determination was limited to the empires of Europe; after World War II, it applied only to colonial units. In the post-cold war world, self-determination is now extended to any substate unit that wishes to claim independence, without any limits on its exercise. Bratersky and Thornton discuss the problem in regard to Kashmir, Lyons in regard to Eritrea and the Oromos (and others), and Zviagelskaia in regard to Palestine. What are the criteria of size, viability, history, distinctiveness, or geography that determine the units eligible for self-determination? At present, the only test is pragmatic—a body of people who can cause enough conflict to warrant their own state (including suppressing restive minorities within it)—but that test is a recipe for conflict, not for its reduction. It is also a recipe for the horrors of "ethnic purification" seen in the Yugoslav, Rwandan, and Sri Lankan civil wars.

Thus a third principle is the defensibility of the existing units. In the 1990s, the rise of intrastate conflicts of secession has increasingly been considered prima facie evidence that the old units "didn't work," despite the countertrend to largest state units marking economies of scale and integrative political systems. Without examining the viability of smaller units or their national coherence, policymakers in global powers and regional organizations have tended to question and even dismiss the sanctity of such established states as Sudan, Ethiopia, South Africa, Nigeria, Iraq, China, and others, in the wake of the Soviet Union, Yugoslavia, and Czechoslovakia. Yet a lack of support for existing units as the assumed standard only opens the field for conflict, without any competing principles of limitation.

In the realm of *roles*, a number of possibilities are open for members of a global system of cooperative security. An initial role of importance is the dampener, focusing on ending arms supplies to Third World belligerents and the restraints on easily accessible legitimization of conflict, as discussed by Katz and also in Vassiliev's and Doran's chapters on the Oil Gulf and in Zviagelskaia's chapter on the Middle East. The easy availability of "cold war surplus" arms and the continuing willingness of third parties to find commercial and political outlets for their arms industries makes arms control difficult but all the more necessary. Arms control and reluctant legitimization can be used as adjuncts to a policy by global powers to urge conflicting parties to "work it out" and try to seek political mechanisms as an alternative to violent conflict.

On other occasions, the most active role available to superpowers may be only that of a midwife, easing the performance of an already inevitable process. This was the maximum role that the United States was able to play in the Horn of Africa both before and after the end of the cold war, in Lyons's analysis, and it may be the only role left in southern Africa, as Vasilkov depicts the increasing limits on external intervention. Midwife in these cases was the only role left by the victory of one side (notably the insurgents in an intrastate conflict), but it is the mediator's dream to have only to serve as a midwife in a compromise resolution where both sides see reconciliation as preferable and attainable over the urge for victory. This is the optimal situation in the Middle East, analyzed by Zviagelskaia as she notes that outside mediators cannot force the parties to a reconciliation that they do not want or accept.

If reconciliation does not come naturally, with only minimal attention from an external party, the role of mender may be required. Menders come in several grades, ranging from the least involvement as a communicator (who merely carries messages and overcomes communications barriers), to a formulator (who thinks up solutions and overcomes imagination barriers), to the greatest involvement as a manipulator (who sweetens the pot and overcomes payoff barriers).[10] An impressive mediation exercise was carried out in Namibia and Angola by the United States acting as a formulator with Soviet assistance, as Vasilkov recounts, and then by Portugal acting as a communicator with U.S. and Soviet support, but all the mediators' forces and men were long unable to bring the conflict to an end, no matter what the U.S. and Russian involvement.

The United States has worked hard, with symbolic Russian backing, as Zviagelskaia and Katz show, to provide a setting for communication among the Mideast parties and to formulate acceptable outcomes; as has often happened, it was the parties' concerns about their relations with the mender rather than any clear, mutually hurting stalemate that brought them to the table and even influenced the Israeli electorate to choose a government in 1992 that would continue the process. The experience of all the regions (except the Andes, where mending is not an available role) supports the clear lessons of the Mideast:

1. Relations with the mender are often the strongest source of leverage.

2. The end of the Cold War leaves the United States alone in this position but does not disarm it.

3. Hurting stalemates are long abuilding and elusive.

4. Mutual recognition of the parties as legitimate is the most important key to turning the parties to the conflict into parties to its solution.[11]

Ripe moments have been the key to conflict management in Angola-Namibia in 1988 and Angola in 1991, as in Zimbabwe in 1979, and in a more limited way at Tashkent in 1965 and Simla in 1972 as well, as Vasilkov and Bratersky and Thornton show; their absence has been the key to the failure of conflict management elsewhere, and seeking a positive surrogate in a mutually enticing opportunity poses a real challenge to potential menders.[12] Much has been made of the mutual hurting stalemate as the key element in a ripe moment but the paradox in the concept is evident: It often takes more conflict to make conflict reduction possible. Cooperative security needs to seek more positive ways.

Umpires and even sheriffs may be needed too, although if conflict is to be reduced, an umpire is far preferable to a sheriff, as Vassiliev and Doran show in analyzing the Gulf wars. As noted at the beginning of this work, if the Gulf experience did not already make it plain, sheriffs do not solve problems; they only restore or reverse situations of conflict, from which a new train of events takes its course. The experience of the Gulf shows how resistant extreme cases can be to creative restructuring, often leaving the sheriff helpless between the curse of the crusader and the curse of ineffectiveness. The lesson—of the Gulf experience and of the analysis alike—is that extreme cases are better prevented, with good intelligence and creative diplomacy, than combated. This means that conflict reduction must be not just a reactive policy but a preventive—even intrusive—policy, with all the problems of judgment and coordination that policy requires. Two further lessons are clear: The coordinative aspects of cooperative security are crucial, and the need for explicit principles and guidelines is salient, as already discussed.

One final aspect of the umpire's role needs underscoring, for it bears on the characteristics of cooperative security itself. Umpires often work most effectively through security structures of the conflict region, rather than directly on the parties. All the case studies have emphasized the regional structure of relations, which turns intrastate conflicts into transnational conflicts and which provides inchoate mechanisms for contributing to conflict reduction, as Mitchell shows, even if full-fledged regional security organizations and regimes are yet absent. The Andean Group, the Contadora Group, the South Asian Association for Regional Cooperation (SAARC), Inter-Governmental Authority on Drought and Development (IGADD), and the mooted Conference on Cooperation and Security in Southern Africa (CCSSA) and Conference on Security,

Stability, Development, and Cooperation in Africa (CSSDCA) are fragile and imperfect attempts to build regional structures and to emulate the very limited security accomplishments of other regions, such as the Economic Community of West African States (ECOWAS), the Arab Maghrib Union (UMA), or the Association of South East Asian Nations (ASEAN).

The appropriate role of the global cooperative security system toward such inchoate regional structures is delicate and not always clear. Outside powers encouraged IGADD to take a timid step toward reconciling its members in 1986–88, urged ECOWAS to take on the Liberian conflict in 1991 and thereafter (and partly paid for its efforts), wrestled with the Contadora Group in El Salvador, and related in various ways to ASEAN in Cambodia. Essentially the global role has been one of encouragement and withdrawal. That role is sound but sometimes hardly distinguishable from a simple bystander's role when more attention and resources are needed. Two contributions are often possible and necessary: financial support for impoverished Third World regional organizations, and—again—enunciation of legitimizing principles to guide a solution.

So this returns the discussion and analysis to the problem of Russian-American cooperation in reducing regional conflicts. It is understood that presently Russia cannot be regarded as an equal to the United States in dealing with regional conflicts, yet it has its own interests. It has no resources for that and no message that would justify intensive efforts even if it had agreed to keep up its role. Russia can, however, at least cease to play the role of supporter for the political parties, states, and movements that were a direct source of violence and subversion of others and can provide support from a progressive leader for regional reconciliation. Even this lesser measure, together with ideological overtures among former Soviet friends and clients, could bring a helpful response. More generally, it could build on the end of the superpower rivalry in conflict regions and the denial of the possibility of local antagonists to play global powers against one another as manipulation and escalation in regional conflict.

The American role is much more directly engaged if the United States is indeed to contribute its leadership to creating a new international order. It needs to play that strong and delicate role of conducting and coordinating a cooperative effort—not just a response to crises but a preemptive and preventive program that includes encouraging and supporting regional security regimes and enunciating norms and principles for conflict situations. Such leadership will face criticism, as all policy does, and it will need to navigate among its detractors and turn their attention to the problem rather than to the problem solver. It will also need to encourage and accommodate role diversity under coordination and enlist the efforts of other states in other positions in their power cycles to keep power and role in equilibrium, as Doran points out.

Such steps by Russia and by the United States can make the reduction of regional conflicts practical and subject to further analysis. Conflict reduction strategies, as discussed and analyzed in this work, are universal tools not tied only to superpower settings (as was the case in the cold war) and are well attuned to serving the two states' goals under conditions of diminished or even absent international rivalry. These strategies, operating within a system of cooperative security, are particularly important for their focus on preemptive and preventive action to reduce conflict rather than simply responding to it. Conflict is a permanent and even constructive part of life, but by helping the parties turn it into political channels and away from violence, outside powers can reduce its deleterious effects and create precedents and conditions for their own cooperative security.

Notes

1. Waltz, *Man, State, and War;* Morgenthau, *Politics among Nations.*
2. Stephen Walt, *The Origins of Alliances* (Ithaca: Cornell Univ. Press, 1987).
3. Michael Taylor, *The Possibility of Cooperation* (Cambridge: Cambridge Univ. Press, 1987); Kenneth Oye, *Cooperation under Anarchy* (Princeton, N.J.: Princeton Univ. Press, 1986); Mancur Olson, *The Logic of Collective Action* (Cambridge, Mass.: Harvard Univ. Press, 1965); Oran Young, *International Cooperation* (Ithaca, N.Y.: Cornell Univ. Press, 1989).
4. Stephen Krasner, ed. *International Regimes* (Ithaca, N.Y.: Cornell Univ. Press, 1983).
5. Geir Lundestad and Odd Arne Westad, eds. *Beyond the Cold War* (New York: Oxford Univ. Press, 1993).
6. Zartman, ed. *Collapsed States.*
7. See also Kanet and Kolodziej, eds. *The Cold War as Cooperation.*
8. See Indar Rikhye, *The Theory and Practice of Peace Keeping* (London: C. Hurst, 1984); Paul Diehl, *International Peacekeeping* (Baltimore: Johns Hopkins Univ. Press, 1993).
9. See also Richard Parker, ed. *Stumbling into War in June 1967* (Gainesville: Univ. of Florida Press, 1995).
10. Toual and Zartman, eds. *International Mediation in Theory and Practice.*
11. See Zartman, ed. *Elusive Peace.*
12. See Zartman, "Beyond the Hurting Stalemate."

Bibliography
Index

Bibliography

XXIV s"ezd KPSS. Moscow: Politizdat, 1971.

XXVII s"ezd KPSS: Stenograficheskii otchet. Moscow: Politizdat, 1986.

1000 Dnei Revoliutsii: Rukokvoditile KPCh ob Yrokakh Sobytii v Chili. Prague, 1978.

African-American Institute. *Eritrea: A Report on the Referendum on Independence.* Washington, D.C.: African-American Institute, 1994.

Albright, David E. "The New Trends in Soviet Policy Toward Africa." *CSIS Africa Notes,* 29 Apr. 1984.

Albright, Madeleine Korbe. *Poland: The Role of the Press in Political Change.* New York: Praeger, 1983.

Alier, Abel. *The Southern Sudan: Too Many Agreements Dishonored.* Exeter, U.K.: Ithaca, 1990.

Ambartsumov, E. A. "Analiz V. I. Leninym prichin Krizis 1921 g. i putei vykhoda iz nego." *Voprosy istorii,* 1984, no. 4

Anderson, Richard D., Jr. "Soviet Decision-Making and Poland." *Problems of Communism* (Mar.–Apr. 1982).

Andreas, Peter, Eva C. Bertram, Morris Blachman, and Kenneth Sharpe. "Dead End Drug Wars." *Foreign Policy* 85 (Winter 1991/2).

Andreeva, Nina. Letter to *Sovetskaia Rossiia,* 13 Mar. 1988. Translated in Foreign Broadcast Information Service, *Daily Report, Soviet Union* (hereafter *FBIS:SOV*), 16 Mar. 1988.

Andropov, Iu. V. *Iabrannye rechi i stat'i.* 2d ed. Moscow: Politizdat, 1983.

Aron, Raymond. *Peace and War: A Theory of International Relations.* New York: Doubleday, 1966.

Assefa, Hizkias. *Mediation of Civil Wars: Approaches and Strategies—The Sudan Conflict.* Boulder, Colo.: Westview, 1987.

Assefa, Hizkias, and Gilbert Khadiagala. *Conflict and Conflict Resolution in The Horn of Africa: A Regional Approach.* Washington, D.C.: Brookings Institution, forthcoming.

Barnds, William J. *India, Pakistan, and the Great Powers*. New York: Praeger, 1972.

Beard, Charles A. *The Idea of the National Interest: An Analytical Study in American Foreign Policy*. New York: Macmillan, 1934.

Beattie, R., and L. Bloomfield. *CASCON: Computer-Aided System for Handling Information on Local Conflicts*. ACDA/WEC—141, December 1969.

Bell, Cora. *Conventions of Crisis*. Oxford: Oxford Univ. Press, 1971.

Binyon, Michael. "West Acts as Midwife at Birth of a New Leadership." *London Times*, 29 May 1991.

Blasier, Cole. *The Hovering Giant*. Pittsburgh: Univ. of Pittsburgh Press, 1980.

Blechman, Barry, and Janne Nolan. *The U.S.-Soviet Conventional Arms Transfer Negotiations*. Foreign Policy Institute Case Study no. 3. Washington, D.C.: School of Advanced International Studies, 1987.

Bloomfield, L., and A. Leiss. *Controlling Small Wars: A Strategy for the 1970s*. New York: Alfred A. Knopf, 1969.

Bogomolov, Oleg. "Memorandum." *Literaturnaia gazeta*, 16 Mar. 1988.

Bokhari, Imtiaz H., and Thomas Perry Thornton. *The 1972 Simla Agreement: An Asymmetrical Negotiation*. Washington, D.C.: School of Advanced International Studies, 1988.

Boulding, Kenneth. *Stable Peace*. Austin: Univ. of Texas Press, 1978.

———. *Three Faces of Power*. Newbury Park, Calif.: Sage, 1989

Brada, Joseph. "Soviet-Western Trade and Technology Transfer: An Economic Overview." *In Trade, Technology, and Soviet-American Relations*, edited by Bruce Parrott. Bloomington: Indiana Univ. Press, 1984.

Breslauer, George W. "All Gorbachev's Men." *The National Interest* (Summer 1986).

———. "Soviet Policy in the Middle East, 1967–1972: Unalterable Antagonism or Collaborative Competition?" In *Managing Soviet Rivalry*, edited by Alexander L. George. Boulder, Colo.: Westview, 1983.

Brezhnev, Leonid I. *The CPSU in the Struggle for Unity of All Revolutionary and Peace Forces*. Moscow: Progress, 1975.

———. *Na strazhe mira i sotsializma*. Moscow: Politizdat, 1979.

Brown, Archie. "Political Change in the Soviet Union." *World Policy Review* (Summer 1989).

Brzezinski, Zbigniew. *Game Plan: Geostrategic Framework for the Context of the U.S.-Soviet Contest*. New York: Atlantic Monthly Press, 1986.

———. *Power and Principle*. New York: Farrar, Straus, Giroux, 1983.

———. "The Premature Partnership." *Foreign Affairs* 73, no. 2 (1994).

Bull, Hedley. *The Anarchical Society: A Study of Order in World Politics*. London: Macmillan, 1977.

Bull, Hedley, and Adam Watson, eds. *The Expansion of International Society*. Oxford: Clarendon, 1985.

Bulloch, John, and Harvey Morris. *Saddam's War: The Origins of the Kuwait Conflict and the International Response*. Winchester, Mass: Faber and Faber, 1991.

Burton, John. *Conflict: Resolution and Prevention.* New York: St. Martin's, 1990.

Burton, John, and Frank Dukes, eds. *Conflict: Human Needs Theory.* New York: St. Martin's, 1990.

Bushnell, David. "Politics and Violence in Nineteenth-Century Colombia." In *Violence in Colombia: the Contemporary Crisis in Historical Perspective,* edited by Charles Bergquist, Ricardo Penaranda, and Gonzalo Sanchez. Wilmington, Del.: Scholarly Resources Books, 1992.

Buzan, Barry. *People, States, and Fear: The National Security Problem in International Relations.* Chapel Hill: Univ. of North Carolina Press, 1983.

———. *People, States, and Fear.* 2d ed. Boulder, Colo.: Lynne Rienner, 1991.

Bykov, O. "Novoe myshlenie v mezhdunarodnykh delakh." *Kommunist,* 1989, no. 8.

"Carter Center Statement on Ethiopia Negotiations." *News from the Carter Center,* 23 Mar. 1994.

Cashman, Greg. *What Causes War?* New York: Lexington, 1993.

Castaneda, Jorge. "Latin America and the End of the Cold War." *World Policy Journal* (Fall 1991).

Chubin, Shahzem, and Charles Tripp. *Iran and Iraq at War.* Boulder, Colo.: Westview, 1988.

———. *Iran and Iraq at War: Military Conflict.* New York: Routledge, 1991.

Clapham, Christopher. "The Political Economy of Conflict in the Horn of Africa." *Survival* 32, no. 5 (1990).

———. *Transformation and Continuity in Revolutionary Ethiopia.* Cambridge: Cambridge Univ. Press, 1988.

Clark, Jeffrey. *The U.S. Government, Humanitarian Assistance, and the New World Order: A Call for a New Approach.* Issue Brief (Sept. 1991). Washington, D.C.: U.S. Committee for Refugees, 1991.

Claude, Inis. *Power and International Relations.* New York: Random House, 1962.

Cohen, Stephen P. "Superpower Cooperation in South Asia." In *The Cold War as Cooperation: Superpower Cooperation in Regional Conflict Management,* edited by Roger E. Kanet and Edward A. Kolodziej. Baltimore: Johns Hopkins Univ. Press, 1991.

Colby, William, and P. Forbath. *Honorable Men: My Life in the CIA.* New York: Simon and Schuster, 1978.

Collison, William F. *Conflict Reduction: Turning Conflict to Cooperation.* Dubuque, Ia.: Kendall/Hunt, 1988.

Commersant, 1991, no. 49.

"Conflicting Peace Plans Offered in Ethiopia Strife." *New York Times,* 24 Feb. 1991.

Controlling Conflicts in the 1970s: A Report of a National Policy Panel Established by the U.N. Association of the U.S.A. New York: UNS/USA, 1969.

Croan, Melvin. "An Afrika Corps?" *Washington Quarterly* (Winter 1980).

Crocker, Chester A. "Southern Africa: Eight Years Later." *Foreign Affairs* 68, no. 4 (1989).

———. "Southern African Peace-making." *Survival* 32, no. 3 (1990).

Curtiss, Richard H. "Airlift Culminates Seventeen Years of Secret Israel Links to Mengestu Government." *The Washington Report on Middle East Affairs* (July 1991).

Dashichev, V. Article in *Literaturnaia gazeta,* 1988, no. 18.

Davidow, Jeffrey. *A Peace in Southern Africa.* Boulder, Colo.: Westview, 1984.

Davidson, Basil, Cliffe Lionell, and Bereket Habte Selassie, eds. *Behind the War in Eritrea.* Nottingham: Spokesman, 1980.

Davis, Nathaniel. "The Angola Decision of 1975: A Personal Memoir." *Foreign Affairs* 57, no. 1 (1978).

Dawisha, Karen. "Perestroika, Glasnost, and Soviet Foreign Policy." *Harriman Institute Forum* (Jan. 1990).

"Defense Minister Cites Causes for Suppression in Eritrea." *Ethiopian Herald,* 29 Aug. 1974.

Deng, Francis M., and Larry Minear. *The Challenge of Famine Relief: Emergency Operations in the Sudan.* Washington, D.C.: Brookings Institution, 1992.

DePorte, Anton. *Europe Between the Superpowers.* New Haven, Conn.: Yale Univ. Press, 1976.

Deutsch, Morton. *The Resolution of Conflict: Constructive and Destructive Process.* New Haven, Conn.: Yale Univ. Press, 1973.

Diehl, Paul. *International Peacekeeping.* Baltimore: Johns Hopkins Univ. Press, 1993.

Dolnykova, R. N. *Metodologiya i metodika prognozirovaniy vneshney politik nesotsialisticheskikh qosudarstv: opyt sistemnoy organizatsii ponyatiy* (Methodology and methods of predicting the foreign policy of non-socialist states: An attempt at a systematic organization of notions). Moscow: Nauka, 1986.

Doran, Charles F. *Systems in Crisis: New Imperatives of High Politics at Century's End.* Cambrige: Cambridge Univ. Press, 1991.

Dowden, Richard. "Addis Ababa Tricked into a 'Soft Landing.' " *Independent* (UK), 31 May 1991.

Dulles, John Foster. "The Evolution of Foreign Policy." *Department of State Bulletin* 30, no. 761 (25 Jan. 1954).

Dullforce, William. "Poor Marks for EC External Trade Practices." *Financial Times,* 17 Apr. 1991.

Economist (27 Apr.–3 May 1991).

"EPLF Withdraws from Peace Talks; Carter, Nyerere Call for Unilateral Ceasefire." *News from the Carter Center,* 14 June 1990.

Eritrean People's Liberation Front. Report on the Deliberations of the Exploratory Talks for Peace Negotiations in Washington, D.C., February 1991.

Erlander, Steven. "Khmer Rouge Get More China Arms." *New York Times,* 1 Jan. 1991.

Erlich, Haggai. *The Struggle Over Eritrea, 1962–1978: War and Revolution in the Horn of Africa*. Stanford, Calif.: Hoover Institute, 1983.

"Ethiopia: An Elusive Victory." *Africa Confidential* 31, no. 14 (1990).

"Ethiopia: Dark Days for Mengistu." *Africa Confidential* 30, no. 4 (1989).

"Ethiopia: Talks Start at Last." *Africa Confidential* 30, no. 17 (1989).

"Ethiopia Said Willing to Seek Peace." *Washington Post*, 15 Nov. 1990.

"Ethiopia Talks Build Trust." *Washington Post*, 10 Sept. 1989.

Fadin, Andrei. "Prokliat'e sily: Magii oboronnogo soznaniia." *Vek XX i Mir*, 1988, no. 11.

Federal Institute for Soviet and International Studies. *The Soviet Union, 1988–89: Perestroika in Crisis?* Boulder, Colo.: Westview, 1990.

Fidler, Stephen. "Latin American Poverty 'Deepened' by Reforms." *Financial Times*, 8 Apr. 1991.

Fisher, Roger, and William Ury. *Getting to Yes: Negotiating an Agreement Without Giving In*. New York: Penguin, 1981.

Frankel, Joseph. *National Interest*. London: Pall Mall, 1970.

Freedman, Robert O. "Moscow and Middle East Peace Settlement: From Breznev to Gorbachev." Unpublished paper, n.d.

"From One Dictator to Another?" *Washington Post*, 12 June 1991.

Fukuyama, Francis. *Soviet Civil-Military Relations and the Power Projection Mission*. Santa Monica, Calif.: Rand Corporation, 1987.

Fuller, Graham E. "The Middle East in U.S.-Soviet Relations." *Middle East Journal* 44, no. 3 (Summer 1990).

Furniss, Edgar S., and Richard C. Snyder. *An Introduction to American Foreign Policy*. New York: Rinehart, 1955.

Gaddis, John. *The Long Peace: Inquiries into the History of the Cold War*. Oxford: Oxford Univ. Press, 1987.

Gantman, V., ed. *Mezdunarodnye Konflikty Souremennosti* (Contemporary international conflicts). Moscow: Nauka, 1983

Garthoff, Raymond. *Détente and Confrontation: American-Soviet Relations from Nixon to Reagan*. Washington, D.C.: Brookings Institution, 1985.

———. *Deterrence and the Revolution in Soviet Military Doctrine*. Washington, D.C.: Brookings Institution, 1990.

"General Aman Is Informed That People of Eritrea Seek Peace, Security." *Ethiopian Herald*, 31 Aug. 1974.

"General Aman Visits Eritrea for Second Time." *Ethiopian Herald*, 11 Oct. 1974.

George, Alexander L. *Bridging the Gap: Theory and Practice in Foreign Policy*. Washington, D.C.: United States Institute of Peace, 1993.

———, ed. *Managing U.S.-Soviet Rivalry: Problems in Crisis Prevention*. Boulder, Colo.: Westview, 1983.

George, Alexander L., and Robert O. Keohane. "The Concept of National Interests: Uses and Limitations." In Alexander L. George, *Presidential Decision Making in Foreign Policy: The Effective Use of Information and Advice*. Boulder, Colo.: Westview, 1980.

Gersony, R. *Summary of Mozambican Refugee Accounts of Principally Conflict-Related Experience in Mozambique.* Washington, D.C.: Department of State, 1988.

Ghebali, Victor-Yves. *La diplomatie de la détente: la CSCE 1973–1989.* Brussels: Bruylant, 1989.

Gilkes, Patrick S. "Conflicts in Ethiopia: Roots, Status, and Prospects." Paper presented at the Woodrow Wilson International Center for Scholars Conference on Crisis in the Horn of Africa: Causes and Prospects, Washington, D.C., June 1987.

Giorgis, Dawit Wolde. *Red Tears: War, Famine, and Revolution in Ethiopia.* Trenton, N.J.: Red Sea, 1989.

Golan, Galia. *Gorbachev's "New Thinking" on Terrorism.* Washington Papers, no. 141. New York: Praeger, 1990.

———."Superpower Cooperation in the Middle East." In *The Cold War as Cooperation: Superpower Cooperation in Regional Conflict Management,* edited by Roger E. Kanet and Edward Kolodziej. Baltimore: Johns Hopkins Univ. Press, 1991

Goodman, Melvin A. *Gorbachev's Retreat: The Third World.* New York: Praeger, 1991.

Gorbachev, Mikhail. Address to Mideast Peace Conference, Madrid, 30 Oct. 1991. Transcribed in *Federal News SVC.*

———. Address to the U.N. (undelivered), transcribed in *Pravda,* Sept. 1987.

———. Address to the U.N. General Assembly, 7 Dec. 1988.

———. *Izbrannye rechi i stat'i* (Selected speeches and articles). Moscow: Politizdat, 1987.

Goshko, John M. "U.S. Plea for Ethiopian Jews Led to Mediator Role." *Washington Post,* 30 May 1991.

Gottemoeller, Rose. "Intramilitary conflict in the Soviet Armed Forces." In *The Dynamics of Soviet Defense Policy,* edited by Bruce Parrott. Washington, D.C.: The Woodrow Wilson Center Press, 1990.

Gowa, J., and Nils H. Wessel. *Ground Rules: Soviet and American Involvement in Regional Conflicts.* Philadelphia: Foreign Policy Research Institute, 1982.

Gromyko, Andrei. "Lenin's Peace Policy." *Moscow News,* 22 Apr. 1984. Translated in *FBIS: SOV,* 27 Apr. 1984.

Gross, Feliks, ed. *World Politics and Tension Areas.* New York: New York Univ. Press, 1990.

Guber, A. *Filippinskaya respublika 1898 goda i amerikanskiy imperialism.* (The Philippines Republic of 1898 and American imperialism). Moscow: Nauka, 1961.

Gupta, Sisir. *Kashmir: A Study in Indo-Pakistan Relations.* New York: Asia, 1966.

Gurr, Ted. "Tensions in the Horn of Africa." In *World Politics and Tension Areas,* edited by Feliks Gross. New York: New York Univ. Press, 1966.

Halperin, Morton H. *Bureaucratic Politics and Foreign Policy.* Washington, D.C.: Brookings Institution, 1974.

Harbeson, John W. *The Ethiopian Transformation: The Quest for the Post-Imperial State.* Boulder, Colo: Westview, 1988.

Harden, Blaine. "Eritrean Rebels to Form Own Rule, Separate from Ethiopian Government." *Washington Post,* 30 May 1991.

———. "Yugoslav Crisis Raises Questions about Nature of National Security." *Washington Post,* 20 June 1991.

Hazleton, William A., and Sandra Woy-Hazleton. "Terrorism and the Marxist Left: Peru's Struggle Against Sendero Luminoso." *Terrorism* 11, no. 6 (1988).

Henze, Paul B. *Ethiopia: Crisis of a Marxist Economy: Analysis and Text of a Soviet Report.* Santa Monica, Calif.: RAND Corporation (R–3677–USDP), 1989.

———. *Glasnost about Building Socialism in Ethiopia: Analysis of a Critical Soviet Article.* Santa Monica, Calif.: RAND Corporation (N–3022–USDP), 1990.

———. "Off the Sidelines and Discreetly into the Fray." *Los Angeles Times,* 29 May 1991.

Hicks, Irvin. Address given as part of the Forum Series of the African American Institute, Washington, D. C., 18 Nov. 1990.

Hiro, Dilip. *The Longest War: The Iran-Iraq Military Conflict.* New York: Routledge, 1991.

Hockstader, L. "Sandinistas Charged in Missiles Sale." *Washington Post,* 3 Jan. 1991.

Hoffman, Stanley. *Dead Ends: American Foreign Policy in the New Cold War.* Cambridge, Mass.: Harvard Univ. Press, 1983.

Holsti, K. J. *International Politics: A Framework for Analysis.* 5th ed. Englewood Cliffs, N.J.: Prentice Hall, 1988.

Hosmer, Stephen T., and Thomas W. Wolfe. *Soviet Policy and Practice Toward Third World Conflicts.* Lexington, Mass.: Lexington, 1983.

Hough, Jerry. *The Struggle for the Third World: Soviet Debates and American Options.* Washington, D.C.: Brookings Institution, 1986.

Hull, Richard W. "United States Policy in Southern Africa." *Current History* 89, no. 547 (1990).

Izvestia. Issues of 26 Feb. 1986, 4 June 1989, 4 August 1990, 14 Aug. 1990, 1 Dec. 1990, 15 Jan. 1991, 30 Oct. 1991, 10 Jan. 1992.

Jackson, Bruce D. *Castro, Kremlin, and Communism in Latin America.* Baltimore: Johns Hopkins Univ. Press, 1969.

Jervis, Robert. "Perception and Misperception: The Spiral of International Insecurity." In *Theory and Practice of International Relations,* 6th ed., edited by William Olson, David McLellan, and Fred Sondermann. Englewood Cliffs, N.J.: Prentice-Hall, 1983.

Jervis, Robert, et al. *Psychology and Deterrence.* Baltimore: Johns Hopkins Univ. Press, 1985.

Johansen, Robert C. *The National Interests and the Human Interest: An Analysis of U.S. Foreign Policy.* Princeton, N.J.: Princeton Univ. Press, 1980.

Jones, Ellen. "Social Change and Civil-Military Relations." In *Soldiers and the Soviet State*, edited by Timothy Colton and Thane Gustafson. Princeton, N.J.: Princeton Univ. Press, 1990.

Kanet, Roger E. "Military Relations Between Eastern Europe and Africa." In *Arms for Africa: Military Assistance and Foreign Policy in the Developing World*. Lexington, Mass.: Lexington, 1983.

Kanet, Roger E., and Edward A. Kolodziej, eds. *The Cold War as Cooperation: Superpower Cooperation in Regional Conflict Management*. Baltimore: Johns Hopkins Univ. Press, 1991.

Kaplan, Morton. *System and Process in International Politics*. New York: Wiley, 1957.

Kaplan, Stephen S. *Diplomacy of Power: Soviet Armed Forces as a Political Instrument*. Washington, D.C.: Brookings Institution, 1981.

Kasnaya Zvezda, 17 August 1990.

Kayani, Amer. *The Kashmir Conflict: Soviet Mediation at Tashkent, 1966*. Pittsburgh: Pittsburgh Univ. Press, 1987.

Keeney, Ralph L., and Howard Raiffa. *Decisions with Mulitiple Objectives: Preferences and Tradeoffs*. New York: John Wiley and Sons, 1976.

Keller, Edmond J. "Constitutionalism and the National Question in Africa: The Case of Eritrea." In *The Political Economy of Ethiopia*, edited by Marina Ottoway. New York: Praeger, 1990.

Kennan, George F. ("Mr. X"). "The Sources of Soviet Conduct." *Foreign Affairs* 25, no. 4 (1947).

Khrustalev, M. A. *Sistemnoye modelirovaniye mezduhnarodnykh otnosheniy: uchebnoye posobiye* (Systemic modeling of international relations: An educational textbook). Moscow: MGIMO MID SSSR, 1987.

Kim, Samuel. "Superpower Cooperation in North East Asia." In *The Cold War as Cooperation: Superpower Cooperation in Regional Conflict Management*, edited by Roger E. Kanet and Edward Kolodziej. Baltimore: Johns Hopkins Univ. Press, 1991.

Kintner, William. *Soviet Global Strategy*. Fairfax, Va.: New Books, 1987.

Kissinger, Henry. "Foreign Policy and National Security." *Department of State Bulletin* 74 (12 Apr. 1976).

———. *The White House Years*. Boston: Little, Brown, 1979.

———. *Years of Upheaval*. Boston: Little, Brown, 1982.

Kitrinos, Robert W. "International Department of the CPSU." *Problems of Communism* (Sept.–Oct. 1984).

Kober, Stanley. "Changing Soviet Perceptions of the Threat: From Foreign to Domestic." Unpublished paper, Wasington, D.C., 1988.

Kolodziej, Edward A. *French International Policy under de Gaulle and Pompidou: The Politics of Grandeur*. Ithaca, N.Y.: Cornell Univ. Press, 1974.

———. "The Multilateralization of Regional Security in Southeast Asia and Northeast Asia: The Role of the Soviet Union." *Pacific Focus* 6, no. 1 (1991).

———. "U.S.-Soviet Cooperation: The Role of Third States." *Annals of the American Academy of Political and Social Science* 518 (Nov. 1991).

Kolodziej, Edward A., and Roger E. Kanet, eds. *Coping with Conflict after the Cold War.* Baltimore: Johns Hopkins Univ. Press, 1995.

Kommunist, 1982, no. 12; 1986, no. 16.

Komosomomolskaya Pravda, 1 Feb. 1991.

Korbel, Josef. *Danger in Kashmir.* Princeton, N.J.: Princeton Univ. Press, 1954.

Korn, David A. *Ethiopia, the United States, and the Soviet Union.* Carbondale: Southern Illinois Univ. Press, 1986.

Kozlov, A. "Peroesmyslenie politi v trek em mire." *Mezhdunarodnaia Zhizn',* 1990, no. 4.

Kramer, Mark M. "Soviet Arms Transfers and Military Aid to the Third World." In *Gorbachev's Third World Dilemmas,* edited by Kurt M. Campbell and S. Neil MacFarlane. London: Routledge, 1989.

Kramer, Michael. "Anger, Bluff, and Cooperation." *Time,* 4 June 1990.

Krapels, Edward N. "U.S. Energy Interests in the Gulf in the 1990s." In *The Gulf, Energy, and Global Security: Political and Economic Issues,* edited by Charles F. Doran and Stephen W. Buck. Boulder: Lynne Rienner, 1991.

Krasner, Stephen, ed. *International Regimes.* Ithaca, N.Y.: Cornell Univ. Press, 1983.

Krauss, Clifford. "Conflicting Peace Plans Offered in Ethiopian Strife." *New York Times,* 24 Feb. 1991.

———. "Ethiopia's Dictator Flees; Officials Seeking U.S. Help." *New York Times,* 22 May 1991.

———. "Ethiopia's Leader Agrees to Give Up Capital." *New York Times,* 28 May 1991.

———. "U.S. Aides Meeting Foes in Ethiopia." *New York Times,* 24 Oct. 1990.

Kremenyuk, Victor A. *The Crisis Strategy of Imperialism.* Kiev: Politizdat, 1979.

———. "Gorky opyt—seryeznye vyvody" (Bitter experience—serious conclusions). *SSHA: Ekonomika, Politika, Ideologiya,* 1989, no. 7.

———. *Politika SSHA v razvivayushchikhsia stranakh. Problemy Konfliktnykh situatsiy 1945–1976* (U.S. policy in the developing countries. Problems of conflict situations 1945–1976). Moscow: Mezhdunarodniye Otnosheniya, 1977.

———. "Po staromu scenariyu interventsionisma" (By the standards of the old interventionist scenario). *SSHA: Ekonomika, politika, ideologiya,* 1981, no. 5.

———. *U.S.A.: Struggle Against National Liberation Movements.* Moscow: Mysl, 1983.

———. *U.S.A. and Conflicts in Asia.* Moscow: Nauka, 1979.

———. *Washington Against Revolution in Iran.* Moscow: Mezhdunarodnye Otnoshenia, 1984.

———. "The World War as Cooperation." In *The Cold War as Cooperation: Superpower Cooperation in Regional Conflict Management,* edited by Roger E. Kanet and Edward Kolodziej. Baltimore: Johns Hopkins Univ. Press, 1991.

"Kruglyi Stol." *Vek XX i mir,* 1988, no. 3.

Krylova, G. A. "Socialist Orientation: Reality and Theory: The National-Democratic Revolution in Light of the New Political Thinking. (With Ethiopia as an Example)." *Narody Azii i Afriki,* 1989, no. 1. Translated and annotated in Paul B. Henze, *Glasnost about Building Socialism in Ethiopia: Analysis of a Critical Soviet Article.* Santa Monica, Calif.: RAND Corporation (N–3022–USDP), 1990.

Kupez, Leo. *Genocide: Its Political Use in the Twentieth Century.* New Haven, Conn.: Yale Univ. Press, 1982.

Laipson, Ellen B. "Ethiopian Jews." *Congressional Research Service Issue Brief,* 26 June 1990.

Lake, Anthony, ed. *The Vietnam Legacy: The War, American Society, and the Future of American Foreign Policy.* New York: New York Univ. Press, 1976.

Latin America Report, 24 Jan. 1991.

Lax, David A., and James K. Sebenius. *The Manager as Negotiator: Bargaining for Cooperation and Competitive Gain.* New York: Free Press, 1986.

Layne, Christofer. "Why the Gulf War Was Not in the National Interest." *Atlantic Monthly* 268, no. 1 (1991).

Lefebvre, Jeffrey A. *Arms for the Horn: U.S. Security Policy in Ethiopia and Somalia 1953–1991.* Pittsburgh: Univ. of Pittsburgh Press, 1991.

Lefort, Réné. *Ethiopia: An Heretical Revolution?* London: Zed, 1983.

Legum, Colin. "Communal Conflict and International Intervention in Africa." In Colin Legum, I. William Zartman, Steven Langdon, and Lynn K. Mytelka, *Africa in the 1980s: A Continent in Crisis.* New York: McGraw Hill, 1979.

———. "Ethiopia: Test for American Foreign Policy." *Third World Reports,* 5 June 1991.

Lemarchand, Rene, ed. *American Policy in Southern Africa: The Stakes and the Stance.* Washington, D.C.: Univ. Press of America, 1978.

Lenin, V. I. *Imperialism: The Highest Stage of Capitalism.* Rev. ed. New York: International Publishers, 1939.

Lewis, Neil A. "His Vineyard in Shade, Africa Hand Stays Cool." *New York Times,* 23 Mar. 1992.

———. "U.S. Plans to be 'Midwife' to a New Rule in Ethiopia." *New York Times,* 26 May 1991.

Lewis, Paul. "Disaster Relief Proposal Worries Third World." *New York Times,* 13 Nov. 1991.

Llosa, Mario Vargas. *Historia de Mayta.* Barcelona: Seix Barral/Ediciones Norte, 1984.

Long, David E. *The Anatomy of Terrorism.* New York: Free Press, 1990.

Lund, Michael. *Preventive Diplomacy and American Foreign Policy.* Washington, D.C.: U.S. Institute of Peace, 1994.

Lundestad, Geir and Odd Arne Westad, eds. *Beyond the Cold War.* New York: Oxford Univ. Press, 1993.

Lyons, Terrence. "The Horn of Africa Regional Politics: A Hobbesian World."

In *The Dynamics of Regional Politics,* edited by Howard Wriggins. New York: Columbia Univ. Press, 1992.

———. "Internal Vulnerability and Interstate Conflict: Ethiopia's Regional Foreign Policy." In *The Political Economy of Ethiopia,* edited by Marina Ottaway. New York: Praeger, 1990.

———. "Reaction to Revolution: United States–Ethiopian Relations, 1974–1977." Ph.D. Diss., Johns Hopkins Univ., 1991.

———. "The Transition in Ethiopia." *CSIS Africa Notes* no. 127 (Aug. 1991).

———. "The Transition to Democracy in Ethiopia: Observations on the Elections in Welega, June 1992." Testimony before the House of Representatives Subcommittee on Africa, 17 Sept. 1992.

———. "The United States and Ethiopia: The Politics of a Patron-Client Relationship," *Northeast African Studies* 8, nos. 2/3 (1986).

Lyons, Terrence, and Ahmed I. Samatar. *State Collapse and Multilateral Intervention in Somalia: The Lessons for Political Reconciliation.* Washington, D.C.: Brookings Institution, forthcoming.

MccGwire, Michael. *Military Objectives in Soviet Foreign Policy.* Washington, D.C.: Brookings Institution, 1987.

———. "Soviet Naval Doctrine and Strategy." In *Soviet Military Thinking,* edited by Derek Leebaert. Cambridge: MIT Press, 1981.

McClintock, Cynthia. "The War on Drugs: The Peruvian Case." *Journal of Interamerican Studies and World Affairs* 30, nos. 2/3 (Summer/Fall 1988).

McCormick, Shawn. "Angola: The Road to Peace." *CSIS Africa Notes* 125 (6 June 1991).

MacFarlane, S. Neil "Intervention and Security in Africa." *International Affairs* 60, no. 1 (Winter 1983/84).

Malashenko, Igor. "Printsip svobody vyborsr mezhdunarodnyi aspekt." *Kommunist,* 1990, no. 7.

Marcum, John A. "Africa: A Continent Adrift." *Foreign Affairs* 68, no. 1 (1988/89).

———. "Lessons of Angola." *Foreign Affairs* 54, no. 3 (1976).

Marcum, John, Helen Kitchen, and Michail Spicer. "The United States and the World." In *A Future South Africa: Visions, Strategies, and Realities,* edited by Peter L. Berger and Bobby Godsell. Boulder, Colo.: Westview, 1988.

Marr, Phebe. "The United States, Europe and the Middle East: An Uneasy Triangle." *The Middle East Journal* 48, no. 2 (Spring 1994).

Materialy XXV s'ezda KPSS (Materials of the 25th CPSU Congress). Moscow: Politizdat, 1977.

Medani, Khalid. "Sudan's Human and Political Crisis." *Current History* (May 1993).

Menkhaus, Ken. "Getting Out Vs. Getting Through: U.S. and U.N. Policies in Somalia." *Middle East Policy* 3, no. 1 (1994).

Menkhaus, Ken, and Terrence Lyons. "What Are the Lessons to be Learned From Somalia?" *CSIS Africa Notes* no. 144 (Jan. 1993).

Middle East. London: Zed, 1990.

Mirsky, G. I. *Trety Mir: Obshchestvo, Vlast, Armiya (The Third World: society, power, army)*. Moscow, 1976.

Mitchell, C. R. *"Classifying Conflicts: Asymmetry and Resolution."* Annals of the American Association of Political and Social Science 518 (Nov. 1991).

———. "Motives for Mediation." In *New Approaches to International Mediation*, edited by C. R. Mitchell and K. Webb. Westport, Conn.: Greenwood, 1989.

Montville, Joseph, ed. *Conflict and Peacekeeping in Multiethnic Societies*. Lexington, Mass.: Heath, 1990.

Morgenthau, Hans J. *In Defense of the National Interest*. Lanham, Md.: Univ. Press of America, 1983.

———. *Politics among Nations*. New York: Alfred A. Knopf, 1957.

Morris, Darrell. "Marchers Protest U.S. Policy in Ethiopian Civil War." *Washington Post*, 15 June 1991.

Morris, Roger. "The Proxy War in Angola: Pathology of a Blunder." *The New Republic* (Jan. 1976).

Morrison, Stephen J. "Ethiopia Charts a New Course." *Journal of Democracy* 3, no. 3 (1992).

Msabaha, Ibrahim. "Stalled Negotiations in Mozambique." In *Elusive Peace: Negotiating an End to Civil Wars*, edited by I. William Zartman. Washington, D.C.: Brookings Institution, 1995.

Napper, Larry. "The Ogaden War: Some Implications for Crisis Prevention." In *Managing U.S.-Soviet Rivalry: Problems of Crisis Prevention*, edited by Alexander L. George. Boulder, Colo.: Westview, 1983.

Nation, R. Craig. *Conflict Reduction in Regional Conflicts: Restructuring Soviet-American Relations in the Third World*. Bologna: The Johns Hopkins University School of Advanced International Studies, Bologna Center, 1990.

Nation, Craig, and Mark V. Kauppi, eds. *The Soviet Impact in Africa*. Lexington, Mass.: Lexington, 1984.

National Democratic Institute. *An Evaluation of the June 21, 1992 Elections in Ethiopia*. Washington, D.C.: National Democratic Institute, 1992.

National Security Strategy of the United States. Washington, D.C.: The White House, 1990.

NATO's Fifteen Nations 23, no. 3 (1978).

Neumann, Robert. "United States Policy in the Middle East." *Current History* 83, no. 489 (Jan. 1984).

Neustadt, Richard. *Presidential Power: The Politics of Leadership from FDR to Carter*. New York: Macmillan, 1980.

"New Deal for Ethiopia." *London Times*, 29 May 1991.

Newsweek (1 Feb. 1971).

Nimitz, C. W. *Danger in Kashmir*. Princeton, N.J.: Princeton Univ. Press, 1954.

Northrup, Terrel A. "The Dynamic of Identity in Personal and Social Conflict." In *Intractable Conflicts and Their Transformation*, edited by Louis Kriesberg, Terrel A. Northrup, and Stuart J. Thorson. Syracuse, N.Y.: Syracuse Univ. Press, 1989.

Nye, Joseph S., Jr. "Why the Gulf War Served the National Interest." *Atlantic Monthly* 268, no. 1 (1991).

Obasanjo, Olusegun, ed. *The Kampala Document: Towards a Conference on Security, Stability, Development and Cooperation in Africa.* New York: African Leadership Forum, 1991.

Olson, Mancur. *The Logic of Collective Action.* Cambridge, Mass.: Harvard Univ. Press, 1965.

O'Mara, Richard. "Eritreans' Intent for Sovereignty Mars Agreement." *Baltimore Sun,* 2 June 1991.

Organski, A. F. K. *World Politics.* New York: Alfred Knopf, 1958.

Ottaway, David B. "Carter Opens Peace Talks Between Ethiopia and Eritrean Rebels." *Washington Post,* 8 Sept. 1989.

Ottaway, Marina. "Eritrea and Ethiopia: Negotiations in a Transitional Conflict." In *Elusive Peace: Negotiating an End to Civil Wars,* edited by I. William Zartman. Washington, D.C.: Brookings Institution, 1995.

———. "Foreign Economic Assistance in the Horn: Does it Influence Horn Government Policies?" Paper presented at the Woodrow Wilson International Center for Scholars Conference on Crisis in the Horn of Africa: Causes and Prospects, Washington, D.C., June 1987.

———. "Superpower Competition and Regional Conflicts in the Horn of Africa." In *The Soviet Impact in Africa,* edited by Craig Nation and Mark V. Kauppi. Lexington, Mass.: Lexington, 1984.

———, ed. *The Political Economy of Ethiopia.* New York: Praeger, 1990.

Oye, Kenneth. *Cooperation Under Anarchy.* Princeton, N.J.: Princeton Univ. Press, 1986.

Palmer, David Scott. "Peru's Persistent Problems." *Current History* (Jan. 1990).

———. "Terrorism as a Revolutionary Strategy: Peru's Sendero Luminoso." In *Politics of Terrorism,* edited by Barry Rubin. Washington, D.C.: Johns Hopkins Foreign Policy Institute, 1988.

Parker, John. *The Kremlin in Transition: From Brezhnev to Gorbachev, 1978–1989.* London: Unwin Hyman, 1990.

Parmelee, Jennifer. "Ethiopia and Eritrean Rebels to Open Peace Talks Today." *Washington Post,* 19 Feb. 1991.

———. "Ethiopian Regime, Residents Await Attack on Capital." *Washington Post,* 24 May 1991.

———. "Rebels Launch Attacks in Ethiopian Provinces." *Washington Post,* 27 Feb. 1991.

Parrott, Bruce. "Political Change and Civil-Military Relations." In *Soldiers and the Soviet State,* edited by Timothy Colton and Thane Gustafson. Princeton, N.J.: Princeton Univ. Press, 1990.

———. *Politics and Technology in the Soviet Union.* Cambridge, Mass.: MIT Press, 1983.

———. "Soviet Foreign Policy, Internal Politics, and Trade with the West." In *Trade, Technology, and Soviet-American Relations,* edited by Bruce Parrott. Bloomington: Indiana Univ. Press, 1985.

———. "Soviet National Security under Gorbachev." *Problems of Communism* (Nov.–Dec. 1988).

———. "The Soviet System, Military Power, and Diplomacy: From Brezhnev to Gorbachev." In *The Dynamics of Soviet Defense Policy,* edited by Bruce Parrott. Washington, D.C.: The Woodrow Wilson Center Press, 1990.

Patchen, Martin. *Resolving Disputes Between Nations: Coercion or Conciliation.* Durham, N.C.: Duke Univ. Press, 1988.

Patman, Robert G. *The Soviet Union in the Horn of Africa: The Diplomacy of Intervention and Disengagement.* Cambridge: Cambridge Univ. Press, 1990.

Perlez, Jane. "As Rebels Surge in Ethiopia, Government Seems Near End." *New York Times,* 23 Mar. 1991.

———. "Ethiopia Starts to Come Unglued After String of Military Setbacks." *New York Times,* 22 Mar. 1989.

"The Pike Papers." *Village Voice,* 20 Feb. 1976.

Pillar, Paul. *Negotiating Peace.* Princeton, N.J.: Princeton Univ. Press, 1983.

Pizzaro, Eduardo. "Revolutionary Guerrilla Groups in Colombia." In *Violence in Colombia: The Contemporary Crisis,* edited by Charles Bergquist, Ricardo Penaranda, and Gonzalo Sanchez. Wilmington, Del.: Scholarly Resource Books, 1992.

Ponomarev, Boris. "The World Situation and Revolutionary Process." *World Marxist Review* 6 (1974).

Pozdnyakov, E. A. *Sistemnyy podkhod i mezdunarodniye otnosheniya* (The systemic approach and international relations). Moscow: Nauka, 1976.

Pravda. Issues of 31 Mar. 1977, 2 Oct. 1977, 30 July 1984, 8 Aug. 1988, 8 Dec. 1988, 4 Dec. 1990, 18 Jan. 1991, 8 Mar 1991.

Preibish, Raul. "Commercial Policy in the Underdeveloped Countries." *American Economic Review* (May 1959).

Press, Robert M. "Ethiopia Edges Toward Peace Talks." *Christian Science Monitor,* 10 Aug. 1989.

Primakov, Y. M. *Anatomy of the Middle East Conflict.* Translated by H. Vladimirsky. Moscow: Nauka, 1979.

Prizel, Ilya. *Latin America Through Soviet Eyes.* New York: Cambridge Univ. Press, 1990.

Pruitt, Dean G., and Jeffrey Z. Rubin. *Social Conflict: Escalation, Stalemate, and Settlement.* 2nd ed. New York: Random House, 1994.

Quandt, William B. *Camp David: Peacemaking and Politics.* Washington, D.C.: Brookings Institution, 1986.

———. "U.S.-Soviet Rivalry in the Middle East." In *East-West Tensions in the Third World,* edited by Marshall D. Shulman. New York: W. W. Norton, 1986.

"Reagan on the Middle East Peace Process at the American Embassy." *Moscow,* 1982, no. 152.

Remnek, Richard B. "The Soviet Union and the Conference on Peace in the Horn of Africa." Paper presented at the Conference on Peace and Security in the Horn of Africa, Michigan State Univ., 29 Apr. 1988.

———. "Translating 'New Soviet Thinking' into Practice: The Ethiopian Case." Unpublished manuscript, n.d.

"Resolutions" of the Conference on Peace and Security in Southern Africa, held at the Center for Foreign Relations, Dar-es-Salaam, 28 Feb. 1991.

Richburg, Keith B. "Somalia Slips Back to Bloodshed." *Washington Post*, 4 Sept. 1994.

Ridgeway, James, ed. *The March to War*. New York: Four Walls Eight Windows, 1991.

Rikhye, Indar. *The Theory and Practice of Peacekeeping*. London: C. Hurst, 1984.

Rivlin, Alice, David Jones, and Edward Meyer. *Beyond Alliances: Global Security Through Focused Partnerships*. Washington, D.C.: Brookings Institution, 1990.

Rosecrance, Richard. "A New Concert of Powers." *Foreign Affairs* 71, no. 2 (1992).

Rosenau, James N. "National Interest." In *International Encyclopedia of the Social Sciences*. New York: Macmillan/Free Press, 1968.

Rostow, W. W. *The Stages of Economic Growth*. New York: Cambridge Univ. Press, 1990.

Rothchild, Donald, and Caroline Hartzell. "The Road from Gbadolite to Lusaka." In *Elusive Peace: Negotiating an End to Civil Wars*, edited by I. William Zartman. Washington, D.C.: Brookings Institution, 1995.

Rothchild, Donald, and John Ravenhill. "Retreat from Globalism: U.S. Policy Toward Africa in the 1990s." In *Eagle in a New World: American Grand Strategy in the Post-Cold War Era*, edited by Kenneth A. Oye, Robert J. Lieber, and Donald Rothchild. New York: Harper Collins, 1992.

Rubanov, V. "Demokratiia i bezopasnost' strany." *Kommunist*, 1989, no. 11.

Rumor, Eugene. "Soviet Professional Military Thinking." In *Gorbachev's Third World Dilemmas*, edited by Kurt M. Campbell and S. Neil MacFarlane. London: Routledge, 1989.

Samatar, Ahmed I., ed. *The Somali Challenge: From Catastrophe to Renewal?* Boulder, Colo.: Lynne Rienner, 1994.

Schelling, Thomas C. *The Strategy of Conflict*. Cambridge, Mass.: Harvard Univ. Press, 1960.

Schmid, Alex P. *Soviet Military Interventions since 1945*. New Brunswick, N.J.: Transaction, 1985.

Schroeder, Paul. "The Nineteenth Century System: Balance of Power or Political Equilibrium?" *Review of International Studies* 15, no. 2 (1989).

———. "The Nineteenth Century International System: Changes in Structure." *World Politics* 31, no. 1 (1986).

"September Preliminary Peace Talks Between the Government of Ethiopia and the EPLF Resume in Nairobi on November 18." *International Negotiation Network News* 1, no. 3 (1989).

Seton-Watson, Hugh. *The Russian Empire, 1801–1971*. Oxford: Oxford Univ. Press, 1967.

Shakhnazarov, G. "Vostok-zapad: voprosu o deideologizatsi mezhgosudarstven-nykh otnoshenii." *Kommunist,* 1989, no. 9.

Shenon, Philip. "Cambodia Factions to Cut Forces 70%." *New York Times,* 28 Aug. 1991.

Shields, Todd. "Rebels Said to Take Port in Ethiopia," *Washington Post,* 11 Feb. 1990.

Sisson, Richard, and Leo E. Rose. *War and Secession: Pakistan, India, and the Creation of Bangladesh.* Berkeley: Univ. of California Press, 1990.

Slater, Jerome. *Intervention and Negotiation: The U.S. and Dominican Revolution.* New York: Harper, 1970.

Smoke, Richard, and Andrei Kortunov, eds. *Mutual Security: A New Approach to Soviet-American Relations.* New York: St. Martin's, 1991.

Smith, Wayne S. "A Trap in Angola." *Foreign Policy* no. 62 (Spring 1986).

Snyder, Glenn H., and Paul Diesing. *Conflict among Nations: Bargaining, Decision Making, and System Structure in International Crisis.* Princeton, N.J.: Princeton Univ. Press, 1977.

Sondermann, Fred A. "The Concept of the National Interest." *Orbis* 21, no. 1 (1977).

South Africa at the End of the Eighties: Policy Perspectives. Johannesburg: Center of Policy Studies, Univ. of Witwatersrand, 1989.

"Soviet National Security under Gorbachev." *Problems of Communism* (Nov.–Dec. 1988).

"Soviet Union Holds Discussions with Rebels." *Indian Ocean Newsletter,* 22 July 1989.

Spaulding, Wallace. "Shifts in CPSU ID." *Problems of Communism* (July–Aug. 1986).

Starr, Frederick. "Tsarist Government: The Imperial Dimension." In *Soviet Nationality Problems and Practices,* edited by Jeremy Azrael. New York: Praeger, 1978.

Stockwell, John. *In Search of Enemies: A CIA Story.* New York: W. W. Norton, 1978.

Talbot, Phillips, and S. L. Poplai. *India and America.* New York: Harper, 1958.

Tamamoto, Masaru. "Japan's Search for a World Role." *World Policy Journal* 7, no. 3 (1990).

Taylor, Michael. *The Possibility of Cooperation.* Cambridge: Cambridge Univ. Press, 1987.

Thornton, Thomas Perry. *The Gandhi Visit: Expectations and Realities of the U.S.-Indian Relationship.* Baltimore: Johns Hopkins Univ. Press, 1985.

———. "The Indo-Pakistani Conflict: Soviet Mediation at Tashkent, 1966." In *International Mediation in Theory and Practice,* edited by Saadia Touval and I. William Zartman. Boulder, Colo.: Westview, 1985.

Tonelson, Alan. "What Is the National Interest?" *Atlantic Monthly* 268, no. 1 (1991).

Touval, Saadia. *The Boundary Politics of Independent Africa.* Cambridge, Mass.: Harvard Univ. Press, 1972.

Touval, Saadia, and I. William Zartman, eds. *International Mediation in Theory and Practice.* Boulder, Colo.: Westview, 1985.

Towards Peace in the Middle East. Washington, D.C.: Brookings Institution, 1975.

"Two Ethiopian Protesters Are Killed as Rebels Fire on Anti-U.S. Rally." *New York Times,* 20 June 1991.

Udalov, Vadim. "Balans sil i interesov" (Balance of power and the balance of interests). *Mezhdunarodnaya zhizn',* 1990, no. 5.

———. "The Concept of Balance of Interests and U.S.-Soviet Interaction." *Annals of the American Academy of Political and Social Science* 518 (November 1991).

Ulianovski, R. A., ed. *Revulytsionny protsess na Vostoke. Istoria i sovremennost* (Revolutionary process in the East: history and the present time). Moscow: Politizdat, 1982.

"The United States and Angola: A Chronology." *Department of State Bulletin* 89, no. 2143 (1989).

Ury, William L., Jeanne M. Brett, and Stephen B. Golberg. *Getting Disputes Resolved: Designing Systems to Cut the Costs of Conflict.* San Francisco: Jossey-Bass, 1988.

"USA/The Horn: All Federalists Now." *Africa Confidential* 31, no. 25 (1990).

Usachev, I. "Obshchechelovecheskoe i Klassovoe v mirovoi politike." *Kommunist,* 1988, no. 11.

U.S. Department of State. "Ethiopia: Exploratory Talks." Statement (press release) of 22 Feb. 1991.

"USSR Government Issues Statement on Ethiopia." *Pravda,* 14 June 1989. Translated in *FBIS:SOV* 41 June 1989.

Ustinov, Dmitri. *Izbrannye rechi i stat'i.* Moscow: Politizdat, 1979.

Vance, Cyrus. *Hard Choices.* New York: Simon and Schuster, 1983.

Varennikov, V. I. "Afghanistan: podvodia itogi." *Ogonek,* 18 Mar. 1989.

Vasquez, John A. *The War Puzzle.* Cambridge: Cambridge Univ. Press, 1993.

Vestnik MID SSSR (Bulletin of the USSR Foreign Ministry), 1988, no. 8.

Voas, Jeanette. *Preventing Future Afghanistans: Reform in Soviet Policymaking on Military Intervention Abroad.* Occasional Paper. Alexandria, Va.: Center for Naval Analysis, 1990.

"Voennyi protiv voenschcheny." *Vek XX i mir,* 1988, no. 11.

Wagaw, Teshome E. "The International Political Ramifications of Falasha Emigration." *Journal of Modern African Studies* 29, no. 4 (1991).

Wallander, Celeste. "Third-World Conflict in Soviet Military Thought: Does the 'New Thinking' Grow Prematurely Grey?" *World Politics* 42, no. 1 (1989).

Walt, Stephen. *The Origins of Alliances.* Ithaca: Cornell Univ. Press, 1987.

Waltz, Kenneth. *Man, State, War.* New York: Columbia Univ. Press, 1954.

Webber, Mark. "Soviet Policy in Sub-Saharan Africa: The Final Phase." *Journal of Modern African Studies* 30, no. 1 (1992).

Wriggins, Howard, ed. *The Dynamics of Regional Politics.* New York: Columbia Univ. Press, 1992.

Young, Oran. *International Cooperation*. Ithaca, N.Y.: Cornell Univ. Press, 1989.

Zartman, I. William. *African Insurgencies: Negotiations and Mediation*. Intelligence Research Report no. 206. Washington, D.C.: U.S. Department of State, Bureau of Intelligence and Research, 1989.

———. "Beyond the Hurting Stalemate." Paper presented to the 1992 annual meeting of the International Studies Association, Atlanta, Georgia.

———. "Explaining Disengagement." In *Dynamics of Third Party Intervention: Kissinger in the Middle East,* edited by Jeffery Rubin. New York: Praeger, 1981.

———. "Negotiating the South African Transition." In *Elusive Peace: Negotiating an End to Civil Wars,* edited by I. William Zartman. Washington, D.C.: Brookings Institution, 1995.

———. *Ripe for Resolution: Conflict and Intervention in Africa*. 2d ed. New York: Oxford Univ. Press, 1989.

———. "Strategies of De-escalation." In *Timing and De-escalation,* edited by Louis Kriesberg and Stuart J. Thorson. Syracuse, N.Y.: Syracuse Univ. Press, 1991.

———. "Superpower Cooperation in North Africa." In *The Cold War as Cooperation: Superpower Cooperation in Regional Conflict Management,* edited by Roger E. Kanet and Edward A. Kolodziej. Baltimore: Johns Hopkins Univ. Press, 1991.

———, ed. *Collapsed States: The Disintegration and Restoration of Legitimate Authority*. Boulder: Lynne Rienner, 1994.

———, ed. *Elusive Peace: Negotiating an End to Civil Wars*. Washington, D.C.: Brookings Institution, 1995.

Zelniker, Shimshon. *The Superpowers and the Horn of Africa*. Center for Strategic Studies Paper no. 18. Tel Aviv: Tel Aviv Univ., 1982.

Zhurkin, Vitaly, Sergei Karaganov, and Andrei Kortunov. "Vyzovy bezopasnosti —starye i novye." *Kommunist,* 1988, No. 1.

Zhurkin, Vitaly, and Ye. Primakov, eds. *Mezdunarodnye Konflikty* (International conflicts). Moscow: Mezduunaroye Otnoshenya, 1972.

Zubok, L. *Ekspannsionnistskaya politica SSHA v nachale XX evka* (U.S. expansionist policy at the beginning of the twentieth century). Moscow: Nauka, 1969.

Index

Abu Rudays, 49
ACDA. *See* Arms Control and
    Disarmament Agency
Adamishin, Anatoly, 231, 238
Addis Ababa Agreement, 245
Afewerki, Isaias, 253
Afghanistan, 7, 11, 20, 48, 49, 87, 168,
    194, 197, 202, 228, 307, 315, 318,
    331; arms transfers to, 319, 320; and
    Soviet Union, 47, 86, 94, 107–8, 109,
    110, 119n. 14, 165, 279, 280, 282,
    293, 299, 303–4, 306, 316–17
Africa, 13, 20, 54, 131, 134, 142, 206,
    224, 307, 315, 325; cold war and,
    304–5; East-West competition in,
    225–30; negotiations over, 231–34;
    Soviet Union in, 79, 99, 101, 103. *See
    also various countries; regions*
African Group, 14
Africanization, 207
African National Congress (ANC), 236–
    38
Akmedov, S., 156
Åland Islanders, 32
Algeria, 55
All-Africa Council of Churches, 55, 245
Allende, Salvador, 218, 223n. 22
Alvor Agreement, 226
Amharic service, 254–55
Amin, Idi, 12, 138
ANAPO, 212
ANC. *See* African National Congress

Andean Group, 221, 339
Andes, 21, 208; conflicts in, 216–21;
    international system and, 204–5. *See
    also various countries*
Andom, Aman Michael, 248
Andropov, Iuryi, 108, 109
Anglo-Argentine war. *See* Falklands War
Angola, 8, 11, 13, 16, 127, 134, 135,
    239, 304, 305, 307, 319, 325; East-
    West competition in, 225–26, 228–
    30; and negotiations over, 231, 233–
    34, 322, 331, 339; peace accords in,
    234, 317–18; Soviet Union and, 103,
    104, 226–27
Antiforeignism, 179–80
Antonov, A., 156
Apartheid, 230, 237
Arab countries, 200; Gulf crisis and,
    131–32; nationalism in, 127, 274,
    275; Soviet Union and, 169, 279, 282,
    297, 298
Arab-Israeli conflict, 8, 21, 133, 159–60,
    167, 272, 276, 297, 307; impacts of,
    280–81, 297–98; Soviet Union and,
    79, 104
Arab League, 9, 18, 21, 22, 31, 55, 328
Arab Maghrib Union (UMA), 340
Arafat, Yasir, 281
Argentina, 25, 205
Arias Plan, 18
Armenia, 116, 133, 290
Armies, 213. *See also* Military

363

Arms, 145, 173, 298; access to, 321–22; asymmetry and, 29–30; exports of, 94, 106; transfers of, 88, 93, 318–19, 320
Arms control, 107, 337–38
Arms Control and Disarmament Agency (ACDA), 84, 85
Arms races, 30, 194, 199–200, 202–3, 293, 303
ASEAN. *See* Association of South East Asian Nations
Asia, 54, 126, 131, 134, 142, 306; cold war and, 298–304; Soviet Union and, 99, 101, 103. *See also various countries; regions*
Association of Political Science, 86
Association of South East Asian Nations (ASEAN), 55, 260, 340
Asymmetries, 44, 50, 91; conflict resolution and, 32–40; of conflict systems, 57n. 3, 199; strategies and, 29–32; types of, 26–27, 28–29
Atlantic Alliance, 295
Austria, 309
Ayub Khan, 182–83, 185
Azerbaijan, 116, 133, 271, 290

Baghdad Pact, 78
Bahamas, 215
Baker, James, 144–45, 154, 233
Balance of power, 8, 12, 15, 199–200
Balkans, 4. *See also* Yugoslavia
Bangladesh, 12, 31, 325
Barco, Virgilio, 212, 215
Barre, Siad, 12, 241, 257
Basic Principles Agreement, 93
Basques, 49–50
Beagle Channel, 22
Begin, Menachim, 280
Belarus, 309
Belousov, I. S., 155
Bengali national movement, 186–87
Benin, 325
Berlin accords, 295
Berlin Wall, 295
Bernard, Daniel, 154
Bessmertnykh, A., 152, 154

Betancur, Belisario, 213
Bhutto, Zulfiqar Ali, 183, 186, 188–89
Bicesse agreements, 235
Big Five, 86
Bilateralism, 192
Bloomfield, Lincoln, 84, 85
Bokassa, Jean Bedel, 12
Bolivia, 204, 215, 218, 221
Boschwitz, Rudy, 253
Botha, Pik, 234, 238
Boutros Ghali, Boutros, 214
BPA. *See* U.S.-Soviet Basic Principles Agreement
Brazil, 205, 215
Brezhnev, Leonid, 99, 102–3, 104, 106, 108, 165, 183, 227
Brezhnev Doctrine, 231
Brzezinski, Zbigniew, 83, 86
Bull, Hedley, 292
Bush, George, 5, 62, 137, 141, 233, 236, 257, 332, 335; and Gulf crisis, 146, 152–53, 155, 174
Businesses, 55, 81
Buzan, Barry, 298
Bystander, 6, 7

Cali cartel, 215
Cambodia, 10, 11, 13, 87, 127, 209, 302, 315, 317, 318, 319, 323, 325, 331, 340; military assistance to, 320–21
Campbell, A., 79–80
Camp David Accords, 167, 279
Canada, 220, 310
CAP. *See* Common Agricultural Policy
Cape Verde, 325
Capitalism, 104–5
Caribbean, 79, 80, 206. *See also various countries*
Caribbean Basin Initiative, 220
Carter, Jimmy, 85–86, 227–28, 247, 250–51, 260, 279
Castañeda, Jorge, 207
Castlereagh, Robert, Lord, 174
Castro, Fidel, 231, 244
CAT. *See* Conventional Arms Transfer (CAT) talks

Catholic church, 209, 211, 212
Caucasus, 101, 116
Caucus for Ethiopian Jews, 253
CCSSA. *See* Conference on Cooperation
   and Security in Southern Africa
Central America, 80, 208, 218–19, 307,
   315. *See also various countries*
Central Asia, 4, 101, 116, 117, 197
CFE treaty, 309
C5-I, 17, 202–3
Chaco War, 204
Chad, 7, 8, 9, 11, 14, 148
Chamorro, Violeta Barrios de, 219
Chechen-Ingushetia, 269–70
Chernenko, Konstantin, 108, 109
Chile, 204, 218, 221, 222n. 17, 223n. 22
China, 10, 16, 145, 175, 197, 337; and
   Cambodia, 320–21, 323; and India,
   182, 187, 203n. 9, 303; and South
   Asia, 182–83, 200, 201; and Soviet
   Union, 102, 119n. 2; and United
   States, 300, 301, 306; and Vietnam,
   129, 135
Chufrin, Gyorgy, 80
Churchill, Winston, 291
CIA, 2, 225, 226
CIS. *See* Commonwealth of Independent
   States
Civil wars, 187–88, 297, 300, 305, 320,
   335, 337
Class. *See* Social class
Class struggle, 112, 121n. 36, 229
Clients, 10, 242, 276
Clinton, Bill, 62, 92, 335
CNGSB. *See* Coordinadora Nacional
   Guerrillas Simon Bolívar
Coalitions: Gulf wars, 5–6, 9–10, 19–
   20
"Code of conduct," 87–88, 93
Cohen, Herman: and Ethiopia, 247,
   251–52, 253–57
Cohen, Stephen, 199
Cohesion, 47–48
Cold war, 3, 5–6, 7, 11, 280; client-
   patron relationships and, 242, 243–
   47, 261; cooperation in, 291–305,
   306–8, 312, 331; impacts of, 207, 315
Coleman, James, 80

Collaboration, 17, 93, 202, 328–29
Colombia, 8, 11, 204, 222n. 17; drug
   trade in, 214–15; economy of, 205,
   207, 221; violence in, 211–14
Colonialism, 5, 32, 101, 119n. 1, 211,
   224
Common Agricultural Policy (CAP),
   205–6
Commonwealth of Independent States
   (CIS), 115–16, 117; conflicts in, 269–
   70; formation of, 267–69; Islam and,
   270–71; and South Asia, 197, 202.
   See also states by name
Communication, 17, 202
Communism, 11, 82, 88, 183, 307
Communist party, 118, 296
Communities, 69, 179–80
Concert, 17, 202
Condominium, 17, 202
Conference on Cooperation and Security
   in Southern Africa (CCSSA), 20–21,
   339
Conference on Security and Cooperation
   in Europe (CSCE), 20. *See also*
   Organization on Security and
   Cooperation in Europe
Conference on Security and Cooperation
   in the Middle East (CSCME), 21
Conference on Security, Stability,
   Development, and Cooperation in
   Africa (CSSDCA), 260, 339–40
Conflict(s): controlling, 84–85;
   intraparty, 47–48; regional, 8, 10, 11–
   14; types of, 25, 135–36
Conflict avoidance, 166, 173, 175–76
Conflict management, 245, 265n. 73;
   advocates of, 84–85; external states
   and, 14–15; in Gulf region, 137–38;
   intervention and, 139–40; Soviet
   Union and, 100–101, 102–3
Conflict reduction, 125; and
   asymmetries, 38–40; cooperation in,
   89, 278; external dependency and, 48–
   49; future of, 335–341; in Horn of
   Africa, 259–60; and interests, 71–75;
   as policy, 87–88; in South Asia, 200–
   201; and third parties, 40, 43–44, 45,
   46–47, 53–54

Conflict resolution, 72–73, 166, 176, 238; and asymmetries, 32–40; conditions for, 46, 55; as policy, 86–87; Soviet-U.S., 170–73

Conflict settlement, 72, 73–74

Conflict systems, 25–26, 57n. 3

Congo, 79, 96n. 19, 305

Consultation, 17, 202

Contact Group, 14, 18

Contadora Group, 18, 55, 339, 340

Contras, 18, 219

Conventional Arms Transfer (CAT) talks, 22

Cooperation, 10, 278, 313–14n. 19; cold war, 291–305, 306–8; East-West, 114, 160; guidelines for, 93–94; security, 22, 224, 289–90, 331–35, 337–38, 339; U.S.-Russian, 90–92, 307–11, 312

Cooperation North, 55

Coordinadora Nacional Guerrillas Simon Bolívar (CNGSB), 212, 213, 214

Coordination, 17, 18–19, 22

Correlation of forces, 104

Counterrevolution, 105–6

Coups, 242, 245, 247, 282, 290, 303, 329

Crocker, Chester A., 231, 232, 234, 322

Crusaders, 6

CSCE. See Conference on Security and Cooperation in Europe

CSCME. See Conference on Security and Cooperation in the Middle East

CSSDCA. See Conference on Security, Stability, Development, and Cooperation in Africa

Cuba, 117, 215, 246, 305, 317, 319; and Angola, 134, 226, 231–32, 304, 318; and Soviet Union, 68, 104, 306

Cuban missile crisis, 64–65, 66, 67, 72–73, 102

Culture of violence, 207–8

Cyprus, 11, 13, 31, 55, 96n. 19

Czechoslovakia, 221, 337

Dampener, 6, 7

Daoud, Mohammad, 303

Death squads, 213, 214

Defense: collective, 8, 9, 10

Deideologization, 19, 191

De Klerk, Frederick W., 236, 237, 238

Demilitarization, 19, 191–92

Democracy, democratization, 19, 117, 131, 255, 311, 336–37; as goal, 140–41, 255; in Latin America, 325; in South Asia, 191, 194; in Soviet Union, 110, 115

Dependency, 48–49

Derg, 247, 248

Détente, 102, 108, 172, 229, 276, 278, 279

Developing countries, 140, 142–43

Development, 19, 141, 192

Dhlakama, Afonso, 235

Dictatorships, 140

Dinka, Tesfaye, 251, 253, 254

Djibouti, 241, 305

Dobrynin, Anatoly, 227

Dominican Republic, 82

Dos Santos, José Eduardo, 231, 234

Draft Resolution N338 (Security Council), 278

Drug trade, 210, 213, 214–16, 222n. 17

Dudaev, Jofar, 269–70

East Asia, 99

Eastern Europe, 101, 102, 174, 296, 316, 325, 331. See also various countries

East Germany. See German Democratic Republic

East Pakistan, 183, 186–87

EC. See European Community

ECOMOG. See Economic Community of West African States' Military Observation Group

Economic Community of West African States (ECOWAS), 21, 55, 139, 260, 340

Economic Community of West African States' Military Observation Group (ECOMOG), 18

Economies, 81, 116, 311; of developing countries, 140, 141; Latin American, 205–7, 210, 213–15, 222n. 17; Middle Eastern, 282–83; Russian,

161, 221, 334; South Asian, 192,
198–99; Soviet Union and, 104–5,
108–9, 111, 175
ECOWAS. *See* Economic Community of
West African States
Ecuador, 204, 207, 218
Egal, Ibrahim, 246
Egypt, 13, 14, 79, 131, 274, 280, 297
Ejército de Liberacíon Nacional (ELN),
212
Ejército Popular de Liberacíon (EPL),
212
Elections: free, 323–26, 337
ELN. *See* Ejército de Liberacíon
Nacional
El Salvador, 8, 11, 55, 214, 219, 319–
20, 340
Emigration: Jewish, 169–70, 253, 282
EPL. *See* Ejército Popular de Liberacíon
EPLF. *See* Eritrean Peoples' Liberation
Front
EPRDF. *See* Ethiopian People's
Revolutionary Democratic Front
Eritrea, 7, 11, 12, 49, 244, 261, 320,
326, 337; insurgency in, 30–31, 241,
247–50; and United States, 251–53,
256, 258–59
Eritrean Peoples' Liberation Front
(EPLF), 247, 248–49, 250–51, 252,
259; negotiations with, 253, 254, 255,
256
Estoril agreement, 234
Ethiopia, 8, 11, 13, 16, 26, 130, 135,
241, 246, 307, 320, 326, 331, 337;
Carter's talks on, 250–51; during cold
war, 242, 243, 245, 305; and Eritrea,
30–31, 49, 247–50; and Soviet Union,
134, 244, 249–50; and United States,
251–57, 258–61
Ethiopian People's Revolutionary
Democratic Front (EPRDF), 248, 251,
253, 254, 255, 256
Ethnic groups, 116; in Commonwealth
of Independent States, 269–71; and
regional conflicts, 134, 138–39, 248,
337
EU. *See* European Union
Europe, 5, 10, 16, 61, 78, 215, 291, 307;
cold war in, 294–96; and Latin

America, 205–6; and Russia, 308–9,
333; and Soviet Union, 99, 107
European Community (EC), 9, 10, 18,
205, 295, 332. *See also* European
Union
European Security Council, 310
European Union (EU), 3, 11, 93, 211,
221, 332; and Andes, 216, 217, 218,
335

Fahd Plan, 281
Falklands War, 18, 25
Famines, 252, 255, 257
FARC. *See* Fuerzas Armada
Revoluccionarias de Colombia
Farabundo Martí National Liberation
Front (FMLN), 214, 219, 319, 320
Fashoda, 4, 5
Finland, 26, 309
Flexible response doctrine, 79, 82
FMLN. *See* Farabundo Martí National
Liberation Front
FNLA. *See* National Liberation Front of
Angola
"40 Committee," 226
4 Ds, 19
Fourteen Points, 337
France, 14, 94, 290–91, 295, 301, 308,
310, 336; and Gulf crisis, 9, 10, 145,
147, 154
Franco-Russian Treaty, 333
Freedman, Robert O., 277–78
FRELIMO. *See* Front for the Liberation
of Mozambique
Front for the Liberation of Mozambique
(FRELIMO), 225, 235
Front Line States, 21, 49, 55, 229, 230
FSLN, 219
Fuerzas Armada Revoluccionarias de
Colombia (FARC), 212, 213
Fujimori, Alberto, 210
Fulbright, J. William, 83
Fuller, Graham, 273

Galtieri, Leopoldo, 12
Gandhi, Indira, 187, 188–89
Gantman, V., 80

Gates, Robert, 193–94
GATT, 332, 333
Gaulle, Charles de, 291
Gaviria, Cesar, 212, 213, 215
Gaza Strip, 280
Gbadolite Declaration, 233
General Assembly (UN), 4, 8, 17
Geneva Peace Conference, 278–79
George Mason University, 86
Georgia, 116
German Democratic Republic, 101, 102, 248
Germany, 94, 135, 165, 167, 175, 295, 306, 309, 310
Gersony Report, 235
Ghana, 79
Ghebrehiwet, Hagos, 251
Glasnost, 114, 120n. 34
Goals: salience of, 49–50
Golan, Galia, 298
Golan Heights, 96n. 19, 280
"Gonzalo, President." See Guzman, Abimael
Gorbachev, Mikhail, 17, 133, 141, 165, 230, 268, 315; on Africa, 231, 242, 249; foreign policy of, 110–14, 169; and Gulf crisis, 146, 153, 168, 171; Third World policy of, 98, 99–100
Gorongosa base, 234
Gorshkov, Sergei, 106
Great Britain. See United Kingdom
Greater Somalia, 241
Grechko, Andrei, 105
Greece, 174
Grenada, 7, 26
Gromyko, Andrei, 102, 105
Group of Seven (G-7), 142, 334
GRU, 106
G-7. See Group of Seven
Gubenko, A., 156
Guber, A., 80
Guerrilla movements: in Colombia, 212–13, 214, 215; in El Salvador, 319–20; in Peru, 208–10, 218
Guevara, Che, 212
Gulf crisis, 94, 128, 174; interests and, 166–70; Soviet Union and, 148–49, 155–58; United States and, 152–54; U.S.-Soviet cooperation and, 90–92, 144–48, 149–52, 162, 326–27

Gulf region, 159, 200, 337; aggression in, 128–29; conflict management in, 137–38; interests in, 166–70; peacekeeping in, 170–73; Russia and, 160–61; United States and, 125–26
Gulf war(s), 4, 8, 25, 32, 94, 125, 131–32, 136–37, 144, 272; coalition, 9–10; Soviet Union and, 112–13, 114–15, 158–59; and United Nations, 19–20; United States and, 5–6, 7, 15, 141–42. See also Iran-Iraq War
Gumane, Paolo, 225
Guzman, Abimael, 209

Habre, Hissene, 12
Haig, Alexander, 67, 280
Haile Selassie, 242, 244, 245, 247
Halperin, Morton, 79
Harvard Law School, 86
Heikal, Mohammed Hasanein, 277
Helsinki accords, 295
Hickenlooper amendment, 218
Hindus, 179–80, 194
Hitler, Adolf, 140
Hizbollah, 210
Horn of Africa, 103, 228, 241, 305, 307, 338; client-patron relationships in, 243–47. See also Djibouti; Ethiopia; Kenya; Somalia; Sudan
"Hot line" agreement, 88
Houdek, Robert, 254
Human rights, 83, 85, 139, 311
Hungary, 221
Huntington, Samuel, 80
Hussein, King, 127, 281
Hussein, Saddam, 5, 12, 39, 125, 128, 130, 150, 155, 171, 282; aggression by, 135–36, 137, 138, 140, 144, 326–27; and Gorbachev, 153, 168; and Kuwait, 172–73; opposition to, 131, 132, 142, 152; support for, 127, 129, 156

ICRC. See International Committee of the Red Cross
Ideology, 194–95
IFP. See Inkatha Freedom Party
IGADD. See Intergovernmental

Authority on Drought and
Development
IMF. *See* International Monetary Fund
Immigration: to Israel, 169–70, 253,
257, 282, 283
Imperialism, 82–83, 89, 119nn. 1, 3,
142, 307; perceptions of, 130, 131,
142
Independence, 224, 230, 317, 269–70
India, 196, 203n. 9, 321, 337; foreign
actions in, 200–201; and Kashmir,
179, 180, 181–82, 184, 325–26; and
Pakistan, 8, 21, 129, 130, 183, 187,
188–92, 193–95, 198–200; and
Soviet Union, 79, 102, 189–90, 303;
and Sri Lanka, 16, 18, 138; Tashkent
conference and, 185–86
Indian Ocean, 88
Indochina, 79, 321. *See also* Vietnam
Indonesia, 79, 86, 96n. 19, 183
Indo-Pakistani conflict, 21, 129, 130,
133, 136, 197; arms trade and, 199–
200, 202–3; background of, 179–81;
cold war and, 302–3; domestic issues
and, 194–95, 198–99, 200–201; early
stages of, 181–84; factors in, 191–92;
interests in, 195–96, 201–2;
negotiation over, 188–89;
superpowers and, 189–90, 192–94;
and Tashkent conference, 185–86;
war in, 186–88
INF. *See* Intermediate-range nuclear
forces
INF treaty. *See* Intermediate Nuclear
Forces treaty
Inkatha Freedom Party (IFP), 237
Insurgencies, 47; asymmetry and, 30–31;
in Eritrea, 241, 247–50. *See also*
Guerrilla movements
Interest(s), 61, 255; and conflict
reduction, 71–75; and foreign policy,
62–65, 164–65; in Gulf crisis, 149,
166–70; hierarchy of, 67–71; in
Middle East, 272–73; national, 230–
31
Intergovernmental Authority on Drought
and Development (IGADD), 245, 258,
260, 339, 340
Intermediate Nuclear Forces (INF) treaty,
92

Intermediate-range nuclear forces (INF),
107, 306
International Committee of the Red
Cross (ICRC), 55
International Court of Justice (ICJ), 55,
87
International Department (USSR),
105
Internationalism, 83
International Monetary Fund (IMF),
111, 200, 309
International Negotiation Network, 55,
250
International Society for Political
Psychology, 55
Intervention, 14–15, 18, 133, 137, 174,
303; military, 326–28; United States,
79, 80, 257–58; use of, 138, 139–40
Ioannides, Dimitrios, 12
Iran, 5, 6, 8, 12, 13, 18, 21, 86, 125,
172, 177, 197, 209–10, 269; and
Afghanistan, 165, 320; and Iraq, 73,
135–36
Iran-Iraq war, 8, 20, 129, 130, 135–36,
144, 171, 194, 298
Iraq, 5, 6, 8, 11, 12, 26, 126, 137, 174,
177, 249, 276, 283, 284, 298, 337;
and Iran, 73, 135–36, 170–71; and
Kuwait, 32, 128, 135, 144, 145, 148,
154, 168, 172–73, 307, 326–27, 328;
and Soviet Union, 10, 70–71, 112,
115, 149, 150, 155, 156–57
Ireland, 55
Irredentism, 241
Islam, 270–71
Isolation, 17, 202, 210
Israel, 11, 253, 280, 282, 283, 338; and
Arab countries, 169–70, 277; and
Gulf crisis, 154–55; and Palestine, 73,
325, 326; security of, 167, 279; and
United States, 49, 153, 297, 306, 321
Italy, 94, 205, 206, 235, 310

Japan, 10, 16, 18, 93, 167, 175, 211,
221, 300; and Latin America, 207,
209, 217, 218; and Russia, 25, 311;
and United States, 78, 84, 301–2
Jaramillo Ossa, Bernardo, 213
Jardin, Jorge, 225

Jews: Ethiopian, 253, 257; Soviet, 169–70, 282
Johnson, Lyndon, 82, 86, 182–83
Joint Commission on South-West Africa, 238
Jordan, 38, 269
Journal of Conflict Resolution, 86

Kashmir, 8, 11, 13, 185, 198, 337; conflict over, 179, 181–82, 184, 186, 188, 189, 193, 195, 325–26
Kaunda, Kenneth, 245
Kazakhstan, 271
Kennedy, John F., 66, 67, 79, 82
Kenya, 235, 241, 242, 245, 246
KGB, 106–7
Khmer Rouge, 138, 299, 317, 320–21, 323, 325
Khomeini, Ayatollah Ruhollah, 130, 132
Khrushchev, Nikita, 66, 67, 68, 101, 181
Kissinger, Henry, 79, 225, 227–28, 244, 276, 278
Kommunist (journal), 108
Kondrashov, Stanislav, 272
Korea, 96n. 19, 307, 311
Korean War, 4, 5, 86, 135, 299–301, 306
Kosygin, Aleksey, 104, 201
Kurds, 26, 73, 137, 138, 168
Kurile Islands, 25, 302, 311
Kuwait, 5, 6, 11, 13, 22, 136, 307; and Iraq, 32, 128, 135, 144, 145, 154, 168, 170, 172–73, 326–27; and Soviet Union, 70, 148–49, 155; and United States, 126, 148, 298

Lahore, 185
Laos, 79, 86
LaPalombara, Joseph, 80
Latin America, 13, 204, 305, 325; trade with, 205–7, 220; violence in, 207–8. *See also various countries; regions*
Lebanon, 7, 8, 11, 18, 22, 96n. 19, 210, 297, 298
Lebanonization, 207
Legal issues, 31–32, 38, 43
Legitimacy, 31, 105

Leiss, Amelia, 84
Leites, Nathan, 80
Letta, Lencho, 253
Liberation, 78–79
Liberia, 18, 21, 22, 24n. 18, 139, 252
Libya, 148, 283, 329
Liska, George, 79
Llosa, Mario Vargas, 204
Lusaka agreement, 234

Machel, Samora, 234
Maghrib, 13, 21
Malawi, 235
Maldive Islands, 303
Manchuria, 101
Mandela, Nelson, 236
Manuel Rodriguez Front, 218
Marginalization: in Latin America, 204–5, 207
Marxism-Leninism, 103, 108, 117, 212, 213, 248, 325
Mediation, 43, 55, 125, 131, 184; in Horn of Africa, 245, 258, 259–60; in southern Africa, 233, 235, 338
Medellin cartel, 215
Mediterranean, 206, 296–97
Mender, 6–7, 331
Mengesha, Merid, 245
Mengistu Haile Mariam, 12, 241, 242, 249, 251, 252, 256, 305, 320; opposition to, 247, 248, 250, 253
Mexico, 220
Middle class, 206–7
Middle East, 13, 20, 49, 94, 106, 267, 306, 307, 337, 338; cold war and, 296–98; conflict reduction in, 54, 88; 1973 war in, 37, 47; and Russia, 117, 160–61, 271–73; security of, 159–60; Soviet Union and, 79, 99, 101, 103, 104, 112–13, 148, 159; Soviet-U.S. rivalry in, 273–84; United States and, 78, 126–27. *See also various countries; regions*
Midwife, 6, 258–59, 338
Military, 10, 117, 174, 216; assistance, 318–22; in Horn of Africa, 243, 249, 251; in Indo-Pakistani conflict, 187, 191–92; intervention by, 326–28; in

Mediterranean, 296–97, 298; NATO, 107, 309; Soviet, 110, 112–13, 146, 196, 229–30; Soviet assistance, 79, 105–6, 218–19, 242; United Nations, 159–60, 214; United States, 83, 125, 148, 169, 296–97; use of, 93–94
Military Committee (UN), 92
Ministry of Foreign Affairs (USSR), 105
Minorities, 38. *See also* Ethnic groups; Religion
Mirsky, Georgi, 80, 275
M-19, 212, 213
MNR. *See* Mozambican National Resistance
Mobutu Sese Seko, 12, 233
Mongolia, 101
Morgenthau, Hans, 67, 81
Morocco, 9, 19, 32
Mozambican National Resistance (MNR), 234, 235
Mozambique, 11, 13, 38, 44, 49, 127, 227, 233, 239, 331; East-West competition in, 225, 228–30; and regional politics, 234–35
MPLA. *See* Popular Movement for the Liberation of Angola
MRTA. *See* Túpac Amaru Revolutionary Movement
Mujahidin (Mujahideen), 47, 303–4, 320
Mukti Bahini, 186–87
Muslims, 304; and Commonwealth of Independent States, 269–71; and Hindus, 179–80; in Soviet Union, 149, 156

NAFTA. *See* North American Free Trade Agreement
Nagorno (Nagorny)-Karabakh region, 116, 133
Najib region, 317
Namibia, 7, 14, 18, 20, 96n. 19, 229, 239, 304, 339; conflict resolution in, 87, 324; independence of, 224, 230, 317; negotiations over, 231, 232, 233, 238, 322, 331
Napoleonic wars, 290
Nationalism, 111, 118, 129–30, 168,

180, 194; Arab, 127, 274, 275; in Pakistan, 186–87
National Liberation Front of Angola (FNLA), 226, 227
National Party (South Africa), 237
National Peace Accord (South Africa), 236
National Union for the Total Liberation of Angola (UNITA), 226, 227, 229, 232, 233, 317–18
NATO. *See* North Atlantic Treaty Organization
Naumkin, Vitaly, 80
Navarro Wolf, Antonio, 212
Navies. *See* Military
Negotiation, 57n. 2; Carter's, 250–51; with Ethiopia, 253–57; with guerrilla groups, 212–13, 214; Indo-Pakistani conflict, 188–89; with Iraq, 153–54; in southern Africa, 231–35, 237–38; third party roles in, 322–23
Nehru, Jawaharlal, 79
Nepal, 325
Newmann, Robert G., 280
New world order, 56, 173, 332
Nicaragua, 11, 18, 86, 87, 219, 305, 307, 318, 319, 324, 331
Nigeria, 18, 305, 337
Nimieri, Jaafar, 248
Nine Point Peace Plan (Ethiopia-Eritrea), 248
Nixon, Richard, 83, 301
Nixon Doctrine, 85
Nkomati Accord, 234
Nkrumah, Kwame, 79
Non-Aligned Movement, 190, 199, 200
Nonalignment, 181
North Africa, 216
North American Free Trade Agreement (NAFTA), 220
North Atlantic Treaty Organization (NATO), 78, 107, 110, 147, 158, 270, 295, 309, 310
Northeast Asia, 300–301, 306, 307
Northern Ireland, 55
North Korea, 101, 135, 301, 329
North-South conflicts, 142–43
North Vietnam, 103
Nuclear power, 283, 284

OAS. *See* Organization of American States
OAU. *See* Organization of African Unity
Objectives, 63, 67
October War (1973), 37, 47
OECD. *See* Organization of Economic Cooperation and Development
Ogaden, 11, 32, 241, 242; war in, 243, 244, 246
Oil, 174, 304; Gulf, 148, 149, 167, 168, 169, 171; Middle East, 49, 84, 172–73, 283
OLF. *See* Oromo Liberation Front
Oman, 272
Ombudsman, 20, 219
Organization of African Unity (OAU), 18, 21, 22, 24n. 18, 55, 260; mediation by, 245, 258; and Somalia, 19, 243
Organization of American States (OAS), 22, 214
Organization for Economic Cooperation and Development (OECD), 207
Organization on Security and Cooperation in Europe (OSCE), 8, 18, 55, 295, 309–10, 334
Oromo Liberation Front (OLF), 26, 248, 253, 254, 256, 259–60
Osgood, Robert, 79
Ottoman Empire, 32, 174
Oxfam, 55

Pacific, 80, 206
Pakistan, 7, 197, 270, 321, 325; and Afghanistan, 165, 304, 320; civil war in, 186–88; foreign actions in, 200–201; and India, 8, 21, 129, 130, 188–92, 193–95, 198–200; and Kashmir, 179, 180, 181–82, 184; and Soviet Union, 102, 196; and Tashkent conference, 185–86; and United States, 182–83, 303
Palestine, 6, 11, 38, 73, 134, 329, 337
Palestine Liberation Organization (PLO), 31, 281
Pan-Africanist Congress (PAC), 237
Panama, 7, 215
Paraguay, 204

Patriotic Front, 49, 57n. 2
Patrons, patronage, 49, 242, 276; during cold war, 243–47
Paul Nitze School of Advanced International Studies, 86
Pax Americana, 126, 142
Pax Sovietica, 244, 246
Peasants, 209
Peasants' March, 248
Perestroika, 242
Persian Gulf, 87, 315. *See also* Gulf region
Peru, 8, 11, 204, 207, 215, 216, 218, 221; violence in, 208–11
Philippines, 8, 325
Pizzaro, Carlos, 212
Plebiscites, 323–26
PLO. *See* Palestine Liberation Organization
Podgorny, Nikolay, 228, 244
Poland, 107, 110, 207, 221
Policy-making: interests and, 65–66, 68
Political change, 140–41
Political parties: in Colombia, 211–12, 213
Pol Pot, 12, 141, 209
Ponomarev, Boris, 105
Popular Movement for the Liberation of Angola (MPLA), 226, 227, 233, 318
Portugal, 16, 225, 233, 235
Powell, Colin, 233
Power: and conflict avoidance, 175–76; and foreign policy, 66–67; imbalance of, 26, 57n. 1; and South Asia, 195–96
Power-role gaps, 176
Pozdyankov, E. A., 63
Primakov, Evgeny, 80, 152, 284
Progress, 83–84
Public opinion, 155–56, 161–62
Punjab, 192, 193

Qaddafi, Moammar, 282
Qatar, 272

Race, 69, 207, 208, 209. *See also* Ethnic groups

Raj, 180
Rann of Kutch crisis, 183
Reagan, Ronald, 86, 88, 107, 233, 236;
    and Nicaragua, 18, 219; and Soviet
    Union, 279–80, 297
Reagan Doctrine, 229
Red Sea oil fields, 49
Regional structures, 13, 56
Religion, 69, 134, 138–39, 180–81
Renamo, 38, 235
Resolution 242 (UN), 297
Resolution 678 (Security Council), 150
Revolutions, 86, 106–7
Rhodesia, 57n. 2, 227, 228, 234
Rights, 27, 31–32
Rodrigo Franco Front, 208
Rogers Plan, 297
Rojas Pinillia, 212
Roosevelt, Franklin D., 94
Rosenau, James, 64
Rostow, W. W., 206
Russia, 3, 10, 25, 61, 63, 89, 94, 100,
    101, 119n. 1, 121n. 50, 130, 329–30,
    336; and Andes, 218, 219, 220–21;
    arms transfers, 318–19, 328–29;
    cooperation with, 307–11; domestic
    politics of, 116–18; elections in, 323–
    24; foreign policy of, 115–18; Gulf
    policy of, 160–61; and Indo-Pakistani
    conflict, 21, 195; and Middle East,
    271–73; military assistance by, 319–
    22; public opinion in, 161–62; roles
    of, 11, 15, 16, 18, 142, 176, 326,
    333–34, 340, 341; and South Asia,
    196–99, 200, 201, 202–3; and United
    States, 90–92, 93, 95, 158–59, 162,
    224, 289–91, 312, 316. *See also* Soviet
    Union
Russo-Japanese conflict, 25
Rwanda, 11, 127, 130, 133, 138, 337

SAARC. *See* South Asian Association for
    Regional Cooperation
SADC. *See* Southern African
    Development Community
SADF. *See* South African Defense Forces
Saint Egidio community, 235
SALT II treaty, 107

Sandinistas, 219, 319, 324
Saudi Arabia, 6, 13, 127, 130, 131, 170,
    249, 270, 272, 281, 320; and Gulf
    crisis, 147, 328
Savimbi, Jonas, 226, 233, 234, 235, 304,
    325
Schelling, Thomas: *Strategy of Conflict,*
    79
SEATO. *See* South East Asia Treaty
    Organization
Security: Asian, 45, 62, 111, 126, 167,
    246, 292, 299, 300–301, 302, 306;
    collective, 8–9; cooperative, 10, 17–
    18, 22, 91–92, 145–46, 224, 289–90,
    331–35, 337–38, 339; European, 291,
    308–11; Gulf, 127, 159–60, 171,
    327; Middle East, 274, 277, 279;
    Soviet, 99, 156, 169, 277
Security Council (UN), 4, 8, 9–10, 17,
    18, 94, 278, 334, 372; and Gulf crisis,
    146–47, 150, 153; and Indo-Pakistani
    conflict, 181, 184, 200; roles of, 22,
    24n. 18, 336
Self-determination, 11–12, 19, 32, 115,
    254, 292, 307, 337
Sendero Luminoso, 208–9, 216
Senegal, 9
Separatism, 11, 192, 193, 194
Sevostianov, G., 80
Shaba, 9, 228, 305
Shakhnazarov, G., 86
Shastri, Lala Bahadur, 183, 185
Sheriffs, 6, 7, 8, 18, 243
Shevardnadze, Eduard, 114–15, 144–45,
    151–52, 233
Shiites, 137
Shultz, George, 232, 236
Shumikhin, Andrei, 80
Sikhs, 192
Sinai, 7, 96n. 19
Single Europe Act, 332
Six-Day War, 277, 297
Slater, Jerome, 79
Smith, Wayne S., 226
Social class, 69, 70, 206–7, 208
Socialism, 104, 105
Solidarity, 110
Somalia, 11, 32, 130, 133, 135, 241,
    245, 246, 252, 304, 319; and Soviet

Somalia (*continued*)
   Union, 134, 242, 243; and United
   Nations, 19, 20, 127; and United
   States, 257–58
South Africa, 14, 229, 230–31, 232,
   337; and Mozambique, 234–35;
   politics of, 235–38
South African Defense Forces (SADF),
   234
South Asia, 199, 325; antiforeignism in,
   179–80; C5-I actions, 202–3; cold
   war and, 302–3, 305; ideology and,
   194–95; power relationships and,
   195–96, 201–2; and Russia, 196–98
South Asian Association for Regional
   Cooperation (SAARC), 18, 198, 202,
   339
Southeast Asia, 78, 301, 302, 307
South East Asia Treaty Organization
   (SEATO), 78
Southern African Development
   Community (SADC), 55
South Korea, 78, 84, 101, 135, 301, 325
South Tyrol, 38
South Vietnam, 103
South-West Africa, 232. *See also*
   Namibia
South West African People's
   Organization (SWAPO), 324, 328
South Yemen, 275
Sovereignty, 269–70
Soviet-Iraqi Treaty of Friendship and
   Cooperation, 145
Soviet Union, 13, 26, 61, 108, 134, 175,
   183; and Afghanistan, 47, 119n. 14,
   316–17; and Africa, 225–30, 231–33,
   235, 236, 237–38, 242, 243–47, 249–
   50, 252–53, 256, 261, 304–5, 320;
   and Asia, 298–304; and Central
   America, 218–19; cold war and, 7,
   291–94, 315; conflict management by,
   14, 100–101, 102–3; Cuban missile
   crisis and, 64–65, 66, 67; dissolution
   of, 115–16, 195, 267–69, 331–32,
   337; domestic change in, 113–14; and
   Europe, 294–96; foreign policy of,
   69–70, 73, 88–89, 109–10, 119n. 2,
   165–66; global role of, 104–5; under
   Gorbachev, 110–13; and Gulf crisis,

10, 70–71, 114–15, 141–42, 144–46,
   147–52, 153, 154, 155–58, 272, 326–
   27; and Gulf region, 5, 166–70, 171–
   73; and India, 187, 189–90; and Indo-
   Pakistani conflict, 181, 184, 186, 188–
   89, 192–94; interests of, 68, 69–70;
   international role of, 103–4; Jewish
   emigration from, 169–70; and Middle
   East, 273–84, 296–98; military
   assistance by, 105–6; and territorial
   aggression, 173–74; and Third World,
   98–100; and United States, 78–79,
   80, 83, 85, 86, 87–88, 306–8, 312.
   See also Russia
Spain, 49–50
Spoiler, 6, 7
Sri Lanka, 8, 11, 337; and India, 16, 18,
   138, 303
Stalin, Josef, 101
Starostin, I., 156
State system, 173–74
Stockwell, John, 226
Strategy of Conflict (Schelling), 79
Subversion, 88, 89
Sudan, 8, 11, 38, 130, 241, 242, 245,
   249, 337; and United States, 243, 257,
   258
Sukarno (Soekarno), 79, 183
Suslov, Mikhail, 105
SWAPO. *See* South West African
   People's Organization
Sweden, 309
Symmetries, 45; and conflict reduction,
   40–44; and third parties, 50–51
Syria, 18, 127, 131, 321; and Chechen
   republic, 269, 270; and regional
   structure, 13, 159; and Soviet Union,
   14, 109, 297

Tadjikistan, 271
Taiwan, 84, 300, 301
Tambo, Oliver, 236
Tamils, 11, 138
Tanzania, 49
Tashkent conference, 185–86
Taylor, M., 79
Territory: conflicts over, 11, 12, 173–74,
   204; legal imbalances over, 31–32

Terrorism, 106–7, 209–10, 258
Thailand, 84, 321
Third parties: conflict reduction and, 40, 43–44, 45, 46–47, 53–54; dependency and, 48–49; goal salience and, 49–50; roles of, 57n. 8, 322–23; symmetries and, 50–51
Third World, 15, 21, 106, 143, 319; competition over, 101–2, 104, 315; political change in, 140–41; and Russia, 116, 117, 118; and Soviet Union, 98–100, 102–3, 105, 107, 109–10, 292; and United Nations, 20, 137; United States in, 7, 80, 82, 83
Tigray People's Liberation Front (TPLF), 248, 251, 320
Tito, Josip, 296
Togo, 9, 55
TPLF. See Tigray People's Liberation Front
Trade, 55, 106, 217, 221; Andes region, 219–20; with Latin America, 205–7, 218. See also Drug trade
Truman Doctrine, 82, 296–97
Tucker, Robert, 79
Túpac Amaru Revolutionary Movement (MRTA), 208, 218
Turkestan, 269
Turkey, 21, 197, 269, 270
Turkic Commonwealth, 270
Turkish Federal Republic, 31
Turkmenistan, 101
Tutwiler, Margaret, 155

Ukraine, 309
UMA. See Arab Maghrib Union
Umpire, 6, 20, 260–61
UN High Commission for Refugees, 261
Union Patriotica (UP), 213
UNITA. See National Union for the Total Liberation of Angola
United Arab Emirates, 272
United Kingdom, 25, 32, 94, 147, 154, 165, 180, 205, 224, 310
United Nations, 4, 9, 87, 117, 118, 159, 214, 295, 310, 332, 336; conflict management by, 84–85, 96n. 19; Eritrea and, 30–31; Gulf crisis and,

141–42, 146–47, 150, 174; Gulf region and, 127, 128; and Horn of Africa, 257, 258, 260–61; and Indo-Pakistani conflict, 181–82, 184, 187, 189, 199; relations with, 19–20, 130; roles of, 19–20, 22, 55, 92, 137, 139, 162, 229, 328; and southern Africa, 234, 238
United Nations Association of the U.S.A., 84
United States, 3, 16, 26, 31, 49, 89, 211, 223n. 24, 242; and Afghanistan, 107–8; and Africa, 224, 225–30, 231–35, 236, 237, 242, 243–47, 251–61, 304–5; and Andes region, 216, 217–18, 219–21; and arms transfers, 94, 199, 200, 318–19, 328–29; and Asia, 298–304; on China and India, 182–83; and cold war, 291–94, 315; conflict management by, 14, 84–85; conflict resolution by, 86–87; Cuban missile crisis and, 64–65, 66, 67; and drug trade, 215–16; and Europe, 294–96; foreign policy linkage in, 85–86; and Gulf crisis, 5–6, 7, 9–10, 125–26, 128, 144–48, 149–54, 326–27; and Gulf region, 166–73; and Indo-Pakistani conflict, 21, 184, 187, 188–90, 192–94; and Iraq, 112, 113; Liberia and, 22, 24n. 18; and Middle East, 47, 126–27, 159, 267, 272–84, 296–98; military assistance by, 319–22; power of, 175, 176; and progress, 83–84; and regional conflicts, 13, 78–82, 130; roles played by, 7, 10–11, 15, 17, 324, 326, 338–41; and Russia, 90–92, 93, 95, 158–59, 160, 162, 224, 289–91, 307–11, 316, 333; and South Asia, 195–96, 198–99, 201–3; and Soviet Union, 87–88, 102, 157–58, 306–8, 312; and territorial aggression, 173–74; and United Nations, 181–82, 336
UNO, 219
UP. See Union Patriotica
Uruguay, 55, 222n. 17
Uruguay Round, 332
U.S.-Soviet Basic Principles Agreement (BPA), 88

Ustinov, Dmitri, 104
Uzbekistan, 197, 271

Values, 63–64
Vance, Cyrus, 67, 86, 228, 279
Van Dunen, P., 233
Vasev, Vladillen, 232
Vaz diary, 234
Venezuela, 221
Vietnam, 301, 317, 320; and China, 129, 135, 321, 323; Soviet Union and, 104, 329; United States and, 79, 82, 83, 84, 85, 93, 293, 299, 302, 306–7
Vietnam War, 103, 146
Viljoen, Constand, 234
Violence: and asymmetry, 29–30; in Latin America, 207–14
Violencia, La, 211–12
Voice of America, 254–55

Wars, 3, 16, 135, 204, 241, 303. See also Civil wars; by country or name
Warsaw Pact, 106, 295, 296, 310
Warsaw Treaty Organization, 158
Weapons. See Arms
Weddei, Goukouni, 12
Weiner, Myron, 79
West Bank, 280
West Berlin, 68
Western Sahara, 7, 13, 19, 20, 21, 32
West Pakistan, 186

WHO. See World Health Organization
Wilson, Woodrow, 337
Wolf, C., 80
World Bank, 111, 200
World civilization, 111
World Council of Churches, 55
World Health Organization (WHO), 31
World order systems, 5, 8–9, 15–16
World War I, 135
World War II, 11, 103, 135

Yahya Khan, 186
Yeltsin, Boris, 92, 115, 117, 165, 304, 327, 333
Yemen, 275
Yom Kippur War, 84, 306. See also October War
Young, Andrew, 86
Yugoslavia, 18, 19, 295, 296, 309, 332, 335, 336, 337
Yukalov, Yuri, 237–38, 251

Zaire, 228, 233, 305
Zambia, 49, 57n. 2, 235
Zenawi, Meles, 253
Zhurkin, V., 80
Zimbabwe, 7, 229, 339
Zones of influence, 5
Zubok, L., 80
Zulus, 237

Syracuse Studies on Peace and Conflict Resolution
Harriet Hyman Alonso, Charles Chatfield, and Louis Kriesberg, *Series Editors*

A series devoted to readable books on the history of peace movements, the lives of peace advocates, and the search for ways to mitigate conflict, both domestic and international. At a time when profound and exciting political and social developments are happening around the world, this series seeks to stimulate a wider awareness and appreciation of the search for peaceful resolution to strife in all its forms and to promote linkages among theorists, practitioners, social scientists, and humanists engaged in this work throughout the world.

Other titles in the series include:

An American Ordeal: The Antiwar Movement of the Vietnam Era. Charles DeBenedetti; Charles Chatfield, assisting author

Building a Global Civic Culture: Education for an Interdependent World. Elise Boulding

The Eagle and the Dove: The American Peace Movement and United States Foreign Policy, 1900–1922. John Whiteclay Chambers II

From Warfare to Party Politics: The Critical Transition to Civilian Control. Ralph M. Goldman

Gender and the Israeli-Palestinian Conflict: The Politics of Women's Resistance. Simona Sharoni

The Genoa Conference: European Diplomacy, 1921–1922. Carole Fink

Give Peace a Chance: Exploring the Vietnam Antiwar Movement. Melvin Small and William D. Hoover, eds.

Intractable Conflicts and Their Transformation. Louis Kriesberg, Terrell A. Northrup, and Stuart J. Thorson, eds.

Israeli Pacifist: The Life of Joseph Abileah. Anthony Bing

Mark Twain's Weapons of Satire: Anti-imperialist Writings on the Philippine-American War. Mark Twain; Jim Zwick, ed.

One Woman's Passion for Peace and Freedom: The Life of Mildred Scott Olmsted. Margaret Hope Bacon

Organizing for Peace: Neutrality, the Test Ban, and the Freeze. Robert Kleidman

Peace as a Women's Issue: A History of the U.S. Movement for World Peace and Women's Rights. Harriet Hyman Alonso

Peace/Mir: An Anthology of Historic Alternatives to War. Charles Chatfield and Ruzanna Ilukhina, volume editors

Plowing My Own Furrow. Howard M. Moore

Police Protesters: The American Peace Movement of the 1980s. John Lofland

Preparing for Peace: Conflict Transformation Across Cultures. John Paul Lederach

The Road to Greenham Common: Feminism and Anti-Militarism in Britain since 1820. Jill Liddington

Timing the De-escalation of International Conflicts. Louis Kriesberg and Stuart Thorson, eds.

Virginia Woolf and War: Fiction, Reality, and Myth. Mark Hussey, ed.

The Women and the Warriors: The United States Section of the Women's International League for Peace and Freedom, 1915–1946. Carrie Foster